the BIG BOOK of GARDENING S·K·I·L·L·S

BY THE EDITORS OF GARDEN WAY PUBLISHING

A Garden Way Publishing Book

Storey Communications, Inc.
Schoolhouse Road
Pownal, Vermont 05261

Cover design by Carol Jessop
Cover artwork by Charles Joslin
Text design and production by Carol Jessop
Edited by Andrea Chesman and Louise Lloyd
Indexed by Little Chicago Editorial Services

Line drawings by (alphabetical listing) Polly Alexander, Nancy Anisfield, Mary Azarian, Cathy Baker, Barbara Carter, Judy Eliason, Brigita Fuhrmann, Charles Joslin, Alison Kolesar, Mallory Lake, Cynthia Locklin, Carol MacDonald, Cindy McFarland, Ann Poole, Ralph Scott, Hyla M. Skudder, Elayne Sears, Sue Storey, and David Sylvester.

Garden Way Publishing was founded in 1973 as part of the Garden Way Incorporated Group of Companies, dedicated to bringing gardening information and equipment to as many people as possible. Today the name "Garden Way Publishing" is licensed to Storey Communications, Inc., in Pownal, Vermont. For a complete list of Garden Way Publishing titles call 1-800-359-7436. Garden Way Incorporated manufactures products in Troy, New York, under the Troy-Bilt® brand including garden tillers, chipper/shredders, mulching mowers, sicklebar mowers, and tractors. For information on any Garden Way Incorporated product, please call 1-800-828-5500.

Printed in the United States by Book Press
Sixth Printing, January 1995

Library of Congress Cataloging-in-Publication Data

The Big book of gardening skills / by the editors of Garden Way Publishing.
        p.   cm.
    "A Garden Way Publishing book."
    Includes index.
    ISBN 0-88266-796-3 — ISBN 0-88266-795-5 (pbk.)
    1. Gardening.   I. Garden Way Publishing.
SB453.B493   1993
635—dc20   92-53949
                CIP

CONTENTS

FOREWORD

I consider it my great good fortune to have been thrown, unpredictably, into the gardening publishing business.

When I was a very green trainee at Time-Life Books in the early 1970s, James Underwood Crockett brought us a manuscript that no one knew quite what to do with. It was wonderful, loaded with the insights on gardening techniques and skills that only a lifetime of practical gardening experience and deep curiosity about the nature of growing things could have produced. But gardening was literally "small potatoes" to a giant publishing corporation that was not yet aware of the depth of gardening interest in America.

So, I got to work on the project. Forget the fact that I was among the least experienced there and that I didn't even garden. Crockett, understandably, was somewhat dismayed to meet me. But with the great sensitivity and patience that he brought to everything he did, he accepted my involvement and stimulated in me a lifelong love affair with gardening.

Crockett suggested that I start small and learn from each thing I did. I hastily planted three tomato plants in the unencouraging soil of my split-level "homestead" in northern New Jersey and each day watched, childlike, with apprehension and excitement as the tomato plants grew. One shot forward, creating lots and lots of buds; the second did modestly; and the third withered and faded within a very short period of time. I was surprised. The growing conditions were identical. The soil was the same. I had paid the same attention to them all. And yet one had shot forward and the others had not.

I began, unconsciously, to dig deeper into the nature of tomato growth. What was going on here? Having checked all possible reference sources, I went to the best gardener I knew, my father-in-law, Aulton Mullendore, who lived a few houses up the street. Now, you should understand that Aulton comes from a Texas farm upbringing and has answers for just about everything. I showed him my struggling tomato patch, and he looked at it soberly and pronounced, "Well, here you have blossom-end rot," pointing to some brown and black spots on the bottom of my tomato. "You can probably save it if you throw a little calcium on it. Over here you've got some cutworms. They hide during the day but come out at night and like to chop your plants right off at the surface. And this third one looks fine, growing good healthy buds, good plants. You'll be in good shape with this one but I'd remove the other two."

On Aulton's advice, out they came, and the one plant left managed to produce enough for all of the pasta sauce that our young family needed for the summer and beyond. But I didn't soon forget that incident. Why do certain conditions lead to quality growth, and others to decay? Why do some plants grow quickly and some slowly? I was fascinated.

I read everything I could get my hands on relating to plant growth. I learned from *The Guin-*

ness Book of World Records that "the slowest flowering of all plants is the rare *Puya raimondii*, the largest of all herbs, discovered in Bolivia in 1870. The panicle emerges after about 150 years of the plant's life. It then dies." The text goes on to share the news that "the fastest growing probably of all plant species is bamboo, which has been known to reach growth rates of as much as a yard a day, or .00002 miles per hour, and can reach a height of 100 feet in less than three months."

Better versed, I was eventually able to sell lots of Jim Crockett's books, not because of my publishing (or gardening) skill, but rather because of the inherent practicality, the experience, and the pure fun that he introduced to the whole gardening process.

Inherently modest, he suggested that he was just an average gardener and that if I wanted to publish gardening books I would want to meet and talk with many others. Bob Thomson, who succeeded Jim on *The Victory Garden* after Jim's death, was one of those. A wonderful gardener, he talked with us about creating a basic landscape plan; renovating your lawn; choosing and planting the right plants, trees, and shrubs for your own situation; using flowers in the landscape; and incorporating walls, walks, pathways, and patios in your design.

On the other hand, no gardener I know is more "down to earth," and at the same time creative and imaginative, than Dick Raymond. Dick starts with the absolute basics of great soil — how to test it and how to achieve it — but then goes on to share the results of his lifetime of experimentation, including organic pest and disease control, companion planting tips, succession planting techniques, container planting, and wide-row and raised-bed gardening. He turns gardening problems into easy challenges, as he shows you how to control weeds, how to compost and mulch for low-maintenance gardens, and how to increase your vegetable and herb yields.

We now have literally hundreds of gardening friends and authors who have added insights on every aspect of the gardening spectrum — Louise Riotte on companion planting, Peter Chan on raised-bed gardening, Kate Gessert on mixing edibles and ornamentals, Linda Tilgner with dozens of "tips for the lazy gardener," Lewis and Nancy Hill on planting dates in relation to frosts and secrets of plant propagation, Henry Art on wildflowers, Phyllis Shaudys on the world of herbs.

In our new *Big Book of Gardening Skills*, you'll discover techniques from all of these great gardeners and many more. You'll find out the basics of planning and planting, soil preparation, the care of your gardens, pest and disease control, vegetables and herbs, fruits and berries, flowers, lawns and landscapes. You'll be tempted, and with good reason, to try specialty gardens, including wildflower, butterfly, flower arrangers', water and rock, shady gardens, gardens for birds, and numerous herb gardens. And, you'll take on building projects that will make for a very satisfying weekend of accomplishment.

More than all of this, you will get to know a wonderful circle of new gardening friends through the techniques they have developed and mastered. As one of our readers put it — "It's like having a master gardener at your elbow."

All of us here at Storey hope you enjoy our *Big Book of Gardening Skills*. And if ever you have a question, please don't hesitate to call. We're here most of the time and will try to help.

So here's to good health and good gardening!

John Storey

President
Garden Way Publishing
Storey Communications, Inc.

GARDEN STYLE PLANNING

How does your garden grow? In wide rows or single rows, in raised beds or trellises. Before you start digging, you have a number of decisions to make. You need to think about what kinds of plants you want to grow, where you want to grow them, and how much work you're willing to invest. Your garden can be a wonderful collage of various techniques that will ensure the greatest use of space and time, as well as a bountiful harvest.

The space you have available, the appearance you want, and the crops you choose will go a long way in determining the best design for your garden. Wide-row planting is an efficient method of planting lettuce, radishes, and many cut flowers. However, corn needs more space per plant to yield those big, tasty ears; and squashes do better in mounds where they have room to sprawl (see chapter 3 for more on planting single rows and mounds).

If your space is very limited, or if you're only interested in a few herbs, a container garden may be the best option for you (see chapter 11). Trellising peas and some flowers can also give you more growth per square foot of ground. Raised beds are often easier to tend and more attractive. Cold frames and hotbeds can help extend your outdoor growing season. You may even want to invest in a greenhouse (see chapter 12).

Companion planting allows you to take advantage of natural relationships between plants and their surroundings. You might even consider combining flower and vegetable garden concepts and plant yourself an edible landscape.

SINGLE- AND WIDE-ROW PLANTING

Traditionally, there have been two ways to plant vegetables — in single rows or in wide rows. Single-row planting means that you make an indentation in the soil — a furrow or a small trench — and plant your seeds in a single line. If you plant in wide rows, you create a row 16 to 36 inches wide and then you broadcast the seed over the area between the strings much as you would seed a lawn.

Once the seeds have germinated in a wide row, they must be thinned. Vegetable plants that grow too close together will be stunted and sickly. It is hard to pull up little plants that are growing well, but it needs to be done. For the first thinning you can slowly drag an iron rake with stiff teeth across the wide row, taking out a good share of the plants. This is done when the plants are anywhere from half an inch to an inch high.

You don't have to thin peas or beans; the seeds are larger, so it is fairly easy to control how closely you plant them. Smaller, finer seeds are harder to space because they roll off your hand as fast as you plant them.

The second thinning takes place when you start harvesting. Thin by pulling the biggest, most edible plants. The smaller ones will grow to replace the ones you remove. Keep doing this until the spacing is about right.

Ten Reasons to Try Wide-Row Gardening

Wide-row planting has several advantages over single row planting.

1. Increases Yields. In a wide-row garden, more square feet of garden space is actually producing food and less is wasted on cultivated areas between rows. There will usually be a slight decrease in production *per seed* — perhaps about 25 percent. But since a wide row contains so many more plants than a regular row, there is a big increase in production per *square foot*.

2. Saves Time. If you try wide-row planting, you will spend much less time weeding and harvesting. Also, seeds planted in wide rows, do not have to be exactly spaced. This means that at planting time, you don't have to be quite as careful about distributing the seeds evenly. You can thin them easily after they come up with an ordinary garden rake.

Plants in a wide row will have to be watered far less, in many cases not at all. Once the plants have grown tall enough to shade the ground, moisture will be held there. Any weeds that germinate after the plants are well established will not have much of a chance to grow. The only place they will appear is on the sides of the row.

3. Saves Space. Say, for example, that you would plant a row of onions 30 feet long to have enough to feed your family. To get the same number of

GETTING A JUMP ON SPRING

- A late planting of lettuce can be wintered over. Just cover with a foot or so of loose hay. Do the same with parsley for an early spring supply. It will have a stronger flavor then, but will keep you in fresh parsley until a new planting is ready.

- In northern climates, where the ground stays frozen all winter, try a planting of peas in fall, after the ground has frozen. Get a big jump on the next growing season.

- To warm up soil more quickly for heat loving crops, spread clear plastic over the ground until planting time. (It lets in more heat than black plastic.)

- Get early spring lettuce with little effort. In the fall, punch holes in two plastic containers, dishpan size if you can find them. Put 6 inches of a rich mixture of topsoil and compost in them, and store them in the cellar or garage. In late winter, moisten the soil well, then sow leaf lettuce to get plants two inches apart. Cover with clear plastic and keep under fluorescent lights 12 to 18 hours a day. Remove the plastic when the seedlings appear. As soon as possible, move them outdoors or, better yet, into a cold frame, at least during the daylight hours. You'll be eating this lettuce in less than two months. At first, harvest to thin the plants to 6 inches apart, then cut off individual plants one inch above the surface of the soil, so they can grow again. Two containers should keep a small family in lettuce until the garden crop is ready. Buttercrunch, Grand Rapids, and Salad Bowl are good varieties to try.

HOW TO PLANT A WIDE ROW

Use two lengths of string to mark off a row which is at least 16 inches wide, or about the width of a steel rake. (A) You can make the bed wider if you choose. Rake the seed bed smooth. (B) Then broadcast the seeds over the area, aiming for good coverage over the entire bed. (C) Depending on the type of seed being planted, you may need to cover seeds by sprinkling compost over them, or rake soil over them from outside the row. (D) If you are setting out transplants, stagger their positions. A pattern of 2-1-2-1 is effective.

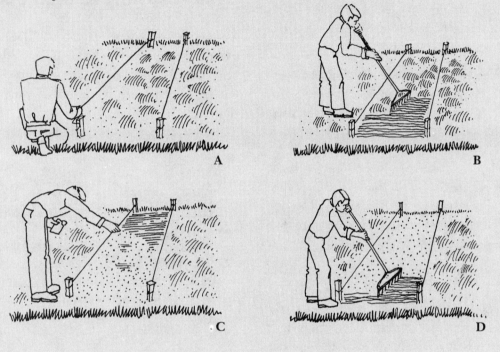

A   B   C   D

onions, you would only have to plant a row 10 feet long if the row were 1 foot wide. If you planted a row that was 2 feet wide, it would need to be only 5 feet long. By planting shorter rows you leave yourself space to plant more varieties of vegetables than you could before.

4. Saves Mulching. Many people mulch their gardens, covering the soil with a layer of material, either organic matter such as hay or straw, or a sheet of plastic material. What they are doing is keeping the sun from reaching the soil so that weed seeds do not germinate and water does not evaporate.

A band of growing foliage creates "shade mulch." It's even better because you cut out all the expense and labor of hauling in enormous amounts of mulching material. You may still want to mulch between the rows, so that you have to do no weeding, but in most cases you should never have to mulch between the plants themselves.

Wind has a strong drying effect on plants. A staked tomato plant that sticks up in the air may take twice as much moisture out of the soil as one which is allowed to run along the ground. The staked plant transpires, or releases more moisture to the atmosphere, because it is more exposed to the winds. Only those plants on the edge of a wide row feel the drying effects of the wind.

5. Makes Harvesting Easier. Since wide row crops produce so much more per foot of row, you can pick a lot more from a single location.

6. Permits Cool-Weather Crops in Heat. Shading the ground keeps it cooler. Crops such as spinach will bolt, or go to seed, quite quickly once the weather gets warmer in early summer. A wide row will continue to produce tender green leaves much longer than will a single row.

7. Improves Quality of Crops. A crop that grows in an even environment — without being overly moist after a rain or too dry during a sunny spell — will be far superior to one that has been growing under varied conditions. Vegetables will also be less prone to diseases because they will have less dirt splashed on them by raindrops.

8. Reduces Insect Damage. Healthy plants are less frequently attacked by insects. It is also true that by keeping the soil temperature constant, there is less likelihood of nematodes invading your plants. Wide rows are a lot closer to growing conditions that you find in nature. Somehow non-isolated plants are less attractive to a horde of chewing insects and pesky worms. And even if a small section of a row does get infested, there will be more than enough left over for you and your family.

9. Makes Companion Planting Easier. If you decide to adopt wide-row planting, you will see that precise seeding arrangements for companion planting are not necessary. You can spread more than one type of seed in a wide row. It is not complicated at all to plant radishes with just about anything else, or to sow beet or carrot seeds among onions. Carrots and beets will help each other in a wide row. When you pull a small beet or carrot you are automatically cultivating and aerating the soil, as well as leaving a small cavity for the other bulbs or roots to expand into.

10. Keeps Plants Cleaner. In wide-row planting, little mud splashes up on lettuce, chard, spinach, or anything else during a heavy rain.

Cleaner produce is healthier produce. One of the reasons peas are often grown on brush or wire fences is to keep the plants off the soil. Peas grown in 3-foot-wide to 4-foot-wide rows will support themselves, saving the extra time and expense needed to make any kind of supporting trellises. The

whole row may sway to one side or the other, with the wind and rain, but only a small portion of the crop, those plants on the edges, will lean over enough to touch the ground.

Head lettuce can be damaged by splashing soil. In a wide row, the only splashing it will receive will be at the edge of the row.

RAISED-BED GARDENING: THE SOLUTION TO HEAVY SOILS

A raised bed is a mound of loose, well-prepared soil, 6 to 8 inches high. The beds can be made permanent with edgings of stone, blocks, timbers, or railway ties, or they can be re-formed each time the garden is planted.

Raised beds in cross section.

Raised beds are particularly helpful if you are working with heavy soils that drain poorly. In the long run, easy maintenance and the use of hand tools make this method extremely appropriate for the home garden.

What are the benefits of raised-bed gardens? First, no one actually steps into the raised beds, and so the soil always stays porous and loose and never compacts. This loose soil provides good drainage, allowing water, air, and fertilizer to penetrate easily to the roots of your plants.

If you make permanent raised beds, the garden path just next to the raised bed is never used for growing vegetables. Because it is constantly being walked on and packed down, weeds will not grow on it. It stays dry and clean and neat, and so gardening is easy and convenient. Even after rain, you can still walk through your garden without collecting a lot of mud on your shoes. Also, when you are working in your garden, you can kneel or stoop down very comfortably without worrying about accidentally stepping on your cucumbers or squash or breaking leaves or branches and damaging your plants. All the maintenance jobs are easy to carry out, whether pulling or hoeing weeds, cultivating, or harvesting. You can pull a plastic or rubber hose along the path for hand watering without dragging it through the vegetables and crushing them.

Third, since the beds are isolated by the paths between them, you can rotate the varieties of vegetables you plant in each bed each year. This rotational planting allows you to keep one particular family of vegetables from consuming all the same kind of soil nutrients. It also discourages insect pests and pathogens associated with certain vegetables from remaining in the soil over the winter and infecting the next season's crop.

Finally, the raised-bed gardening system makes a beautiful garden that is always orderly and organized because it is so easy to maintain. You can easily reach into every corner to cultivate the beds, and to pull young weeds as they appear. Succession-planting, which keeps the garden constantly filled with vegetables, will be pleasing to the eye and enjoy a place in your garden landscape all season long.

Building a Permanent Raised-Bed Garden

The best time to begin building a raised-bed garden is in the fall or even winter, if the ground in your area doesn't freeze, so that it is fully prepared and ready for planting the following spring. First of all, lay out your raised beds by measuring the plots and establishing a pattern. This pattern should allow you, if possible, to place all your raised beds running from east to west. This way, when the sun is lower in the early morning and late afternoon, your taller plants, such as corn, tomatoes, and pole beans, will not shadow lower-growing plants.

To establish such a garden from scratch, you may have to remove a piece of your lawn or some bushes to provide a piece of flat, open ground. If your garden is on a slope, you may have to terrace to create flat places for your raised beds. Each of the raised beds should be from 10 to 25 feet long and 40 to 48 inches wide, depending on the site of the garden. When the pattern is decided, hammer four stakes into the soil to mark the corners of each bed. Use a string to connect the stakes and line out the bed. The paths on both sides of the raised beds should be from 16 to 24 inches wide, depending on your body and foot size and how much room you'll need.

Once the garden is laid out with one or more beds, dig them one by one. The soil in the bed should be dug about 10 inches deep (approximately one shovel depth) by the time you have finished. To prevent uneven digging, divide the beds into three lineal parts, digging the center part first and making sure you dig one shovel-length deep. Work backward all the time so that your own feet do not pack down the loose, freshly dug soil. After the center part is dug, move to the sides. Stand on the path and start to dig the rest of the bed from there, shoveling the soil inward as you dig. This will make the raised bed look like a long, narrow pile of loose soil when you have finished.

Let the sun dry out the soil for a couple of days to make it easier to work with. As it dries, pick out all the visible debris and lightly rake the top until it is flat and level. Then, using a long-handled spade, cut a straight line along the string guidelines of the bed between the path and the bed; push the soil up to separate the path from the bed completely. The ditch that is thus formed between the path and the bed will provide a run-off for excess water and liquid fertilizers. Also, it will keep the path dry at all times. In order to keep the shape of the raised beds and prevent the sides from collapsing after heavy rain or watering, the sides of the beds should be sloped inward slightly. Use a hand trowel to shape and gently pat the edge to the desired angle.

That's all it takes to create raised beds. You'll find that all of the benefits of raised beds — good drainage, ample pathways, rotation planting, ease of maintenance, and nice appearance — make it a great system for the home garden.

Wooden Frames for Raised Beds

Some people like to build a wooden frame around their raised beds, because they feel it makes a tidier-looking garden. A wooden frame is especially nice if built of something like cedar or redwood, both of which are resistant to rot. Rot is always a potential problem because there is so much water associated with gardening. Railroad ties will last even longer than cedar, but they are treated with chemicals that may make them less desirable.

If you frame your raised beds with wood, whether cedar planks or railroad ties, there is one thing that will happen to you if you live in an area where there is lots of moisture, like the Pacific Northwest — you will have a slug problem. The slugs like to hide between the soil and the wood, and the planter actually becomes a slug haven. A solution to this problem is to build a frame that can be disassembled easily so that it can be aired and dried out occasionally.

Build the frame of 2" x 6" lumber and fasten the corners with nuts and bolts, rather then nails or screws. This allows it to be put up and taken apart quite easily. About once a month, on a sunny day, loosen the nuts and flip open the sides. You will find both slugs and slug eggs, which can be removed quite easily, and enormously decrease the problem. It will also help dry out the wood, and the frame will last longer.

Raised Beds: An Easy Way

Start with a well-prepared seedbed. Enrich it with compost, manure, other organic matter or fertilizer. The raised beds can be formed with either hand tools or a tiller with a hilling attachment.

1. Mark the bed with stakes and strings. The width can be whatever you find most convenient, from 16 inches up to 4 feet. Walkways can be up to 20 inches wide. (One gardener makes them the width of a bale of hay for efficient mulching of walks.)

2. Use a rake to pull soil from walkway to the top of the bed. Stand in one walkway and draw soil toward you from the opposite walkway. When you have completed one side, repeat the process from the other side.

3. Level the top of the bed with the back of the rake. Sides should slope at a 45° angle. A lip of soil around the top edge of a new bed will help reduce erosion.

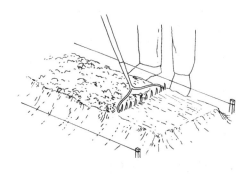

CENTURIES-OLD COMPANION PLANTING

It has been known for centuries that some plants grow better when certain other plants are growing nearby. Science has gradually unearthed reasons why some combinations of plants are successful, but many other combinations that can be observed to be beneficial have as yet received no explanation.

In general, herbs and other aromatic plants like tomatoes, marigolds, and onions are helpful in warding off insects. Usually, the more powerful the smell of the plant, the more effect it has. Certain colors, like the orange of nasturtium and marigold flowers, are thought to repel some harmful flying insects.

VEGETABLE COMPANION GUIDE

	Beans, bush	Beans, pole	Beets	Cabbage	Carrots	Celery	Corn	Cucumbers	Eggplant	Lettuce	Melon	Onion	Pea	Pepper	Radish	Spinach	Squash	Strawberry	Tomato	Special
Basil	-	-	-	-	-	-	-	-	-	-	-	-	-	X	-	-	-	-	X	-
Beans, bush	-	-	X	X	X	X	X	X	X	X	-	O	X	-	X	-	-	X	-	1
Beans, pole	-	-	O	-	X	-	X	X	X	X	-	O	X	-	X	-	-	-	-	2
Beets	X	-	-	X	-	-	-	-	-	-	-	X	-	-	-	-	-	-	-	-
Cabbage family	X	-	X	-	-	X	-	-	-	-	-	X	-	-	-	-	-	O	X	3
Carrots	X	X	-	-	-	-	-	-	-	X	-	X	X	-	X	-	-	-	X	4
Celery	X	-	-	X	-	-	-	-	-	-	-	X	-	-	-	-	-	-	X	-
Corn	X	X	-	-	-	-	-	X	-	-	X	-	X	-	-	-	X	-	O	-
Cucumbers	X	X	-	-	-	-	X	-	-	X	-	-	X	-	X	-	-	-	-	5
Eggplant	X	X	-	-	-	-	-	-	-	-	-	-	-	X	-	-	-	-	-	-
Lettuce	X	X	-	-	X	-	-	X	-	-	-	X	-	-	X	-	-	X	-	-
Marigold	X	X	-	X	-	-	-	X	-	-	-	-	-	-	-	-	-	X	X	-
Melon	-	-	-	-	-	-	X	-	-	-	-	-	-	-	X	-	-	-	-	-
Nasturtium	-	-	-	X	-	-	-	X	-	-	X	-	-	-	X	-	X	-	X	-
Onion	O	O	X	X	X	X	-	X	-	X	-	-	O	X	-	-	X	X	X	6
Parsley	-	-	-	-	-	-	-	-	-	-	-	-	-	-	-	-	-	-	X	-
Peas	X	X	-	-	X	-	X	X	-	-	-	O	-	-	X	-	-	-	-	7
Pepper	-	-	-	-	-	-	-	-	-	-	-	-	X	-	-	-	-	-	-	-
Radish	X	X	-	-	X	-	-	X	-	X	X	-	X	-	-	-	-	X	-	8
Sage	-	-	X	X	X	-	-	O	-	-	-	-	-	-	-	-	-	-	-	-
Spinach	-	-	-	-	-	X	-	X	-	-	-	-	-	-	-	-	-	X	-	9
Squash	-	-	-	-	-	X	-	-	-	-	-	X	-	-	X	-	-	-	-	-
Strawberry	X	-	-	O	-	-	-	-	-	X	-	X	-	-	-	X	-	-	-	-
Tomato	-	-	-	X	X	X	O	-	-	-	-	X	-	-	-	-	-	-	-	10

X Good Companions   **O** Bad Companions

SPECIAL COMPANIONS

1. Savory, tansy
2. Savory, tansy
3. All strong herbs
4. Sage, no dill
5. No strong herbs
6. Savory
7. Turnips
8. No hyssop
9. Cauliflower
10. Mint, no fennel

HERB COMPANIONS

Herbs are easy to grow and a boon to the gardener who doesn't want to work at pest control. They may discourage insects by their specific effects or by breaking up a large planting of one crop, which is an open invitation to pests. Onions, garlic, and marigolds are often effective companions.

Herb	Companions
Basil	Companion to tomatoes, *dislikes* rue. Repels flies and mosquitoes.
Borage	Companion to tomatoes, squash, and strawberries; deters tomato worm.
Caraway	Plant here and there; loosens soil.
Catnip	Plant in borders; deters flea beetle.
Camomile	Companion to cabbages and onions.
Chervil	Companion to radishes.
Chives	Companion to carrots.
Dead Nettle	Companion to potatoes; deters potato bug.
Dill	Companion to cabbage; *dislikes* carrots.
Fennel	*Most plants dislike it;* plant away from gardens.
Flax	Companion to carrots, potatoes; deters potato bug.
Garlic	Plant near roses and raspberries; deters Japanese beetle.
Horseradish	Plant at corners of potato patch; deters potato bug.
Henbit	General insect repellent.
Hyssop	Companion to cabbage and grapes; deters cabbage moth. *Dislikes* radishes.
Marigolds	Plant throughout garden; it discourages Mexican bean beetles, nematodes, and other insects. The workhorse of companion plants.
Mint	Companion to cabbage and tomatoes; deters white cabbage moth.
Mole plant	Deters moles and mice if planted around garden.
Nasturtium	Companion to radishes, cabbage, and cucurbits; plant under fruit trees. Deters aphids, squash bugs, striped pumpkin beetles.
Petunia	Companion to beans.
Pot Marigold	Companion to tomatoes, but plant elsewhere, too. Deters tomato worm, asparagus beetles, and other pests.
Rosemary	Companion to cabbage, bean, carrots, and sage; deters cabbage moth, bean beetles, and carrot fly.
Rue	Companion to roses and raspberries; deters Japanese beetles. *Dislikes* sweet basil.
Sage	Plant with rosemary, cabbage, and carrots; *dislikes* cucumbers. Deters cabbage moth, carrot fly.
Southernwood	Companion to cabbage; deters cabbage moth.
Sowthistle	In moderate amounts, this weed can help tomatoes, onions, and corn.
Summer Savory	Companion to beans and onions; deters bean beetles.
Tansy	Plant under fruit trees; companion to roses and raspberries. Deters flying insects, Japanese beetles, striped cucumber beetles, squash bugs, and ants.
Thyme	Companion to cabbage; deters cabbage worm.
Wormwood	As a border, it keeps animals from the garden.
Yarrow	Plant along borders, paths, and near aromatic herbs; enhances production of essential oils.

Sometimes, one plant's physical structure benefits that of another. Melons or cucumbers will provide dense shade for the roots of corn, while the corn provides a windbreak and some shade for the vines below. Many plants produce root exudates that discourage burrowing insects, or that are hostile to other plants. Sunflowers tend to inhibit the growth of nearby plants. And some plants seem to lower the resistance to disease of others grown nearby. Potatoes are vulnerable in this respect because their resistance is lowered by many other plants.

Some plants are used as "trap" crops so that when grown near more valuable plants, they will attract harmful insects away. But as a general rule, plants that attract the same harmful insects should not be grown close together or they will invite a proliferation of the pest.

Even fairly large animals can be discouraged by companion planting. Rabbits dislike onions, so garlic and chives are usually grown with the leafy greens rabbits like so well. Rue, a hardy blue-green herb, is said to repel cats, and pot marigolds keep dogs away.

Some of the plants that are commonly believed to benefit each other are in the chart on page 7. Those that do well when grown together are shown by an X. Those that should *not* be grown near each other are marked by an O.

EXTENDING THE SEASON

Imagine your Thanksgiving table graced with a beautiful salad of crisp baby lettuce, tangy onions, crunchy radishes, and your very own tomatoes. Imagine homegrown lettuce by mid-April.

While this may sound like the northern gardener's fondest fantasy, you can make it come true through the use of simple, inexpensive cold frames, hot caps, and plastic tents.

Starting Seeds Indoors

One way to extend the gardening season is to start plants indoors and have them ready for transplanting outside as soon as the soil can be worked or as soon as the danger of frost has passed.

When it comes to growing indoors under lights, some vegetables resemble weeds and need little fussing over. Cabbage, cauliflower, broccoli, Brussels sprouts, and lettuce are all in this category and start easily, even in cool temperatures and poor light. Peppers, eggplants, tomatoes, celery, petunias, begonias, and many other plants need more care and attention, however. They like heat, lots of light, and exactly the right amount of moisture. For more about starting seeds indoors, see chapter 3.

Cold Frames

Every gardener is familiar with the terms "hotbed" and "cold frame." Both are simple to build and operate, and can be valuable for home growers.

Cold frames are simply frames or shallow boxes built of wood with no top or bottom, often sunk partially into the earth. The top is covered with a glass window, a sheet of clear, flat fiberglass, plastic film, or a similar transparent material. Usually the unit is constructed so the top slopes toward the east or southeast in order to collect the maximum amount of early spring sunlight.

With a cold frame you can start seedlings outside earlier than is possible without such protection. Since they provide no heat other than that of the sun, however, they can be used only in late spring and only for crops that don't object to cool

Cold Frame

temperatures, such as the cabbage family, lettuce, and many perennials.

A cold frame is a very useful season extender, especially if your home has no good place for starting seeds inside. There are drawbacks to it, however. It needs frequent attention, since the limited air space in it can warm up or cool off quickly. The cover must be opened slightly on warm days, more on warmer days, and taken off entirely on hot days. Since the weather may change frequently in the spring, you may have to adjust the frame several times each day. (See chapter 15 for cold frame building plans.)

Hotbeds

A hotbed is merely a cold frame with some type of bottom heat provided to warm up the soil, enabling growers to start plants a few weeks earlier than with a cold frame. Even when the snow is deep, you can start plants that feel comfortable in warm surroundings, such as tomatoes, peppers, eggplants, celery, and annual flowers.

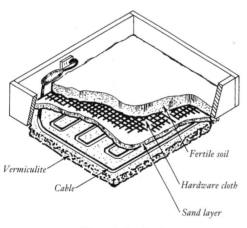

Vermiculite

Cable

Fertile soil

Hardware cloth

Sand layer

Electric hotbed

Soil cables are commonly used now for heating hotbeds, but some gardeners still use the old-time method of fermenting manure to provide heat. Fresh horse manure is the best choice, but fresh poultry manure can be used too. Both heat up quickly when they're piled in a heap, dispensing quanti-

ties of heat and strong fragrance.

To build a hotbed, dig a hole about 2 feet deep in a sunny spot sheltered from the wind. Dump in about one-and-one-half feet of manure, and cover that with about four inches of good, sifted, sandy soil. Then allow the manure to heat up for a few days before planting your seeds in late March. Manure is tricky to use because it isn't easy to get the right amount. There must be enough to supply sufficient heat to keep the soil warm until the seedlings no longer need it, yet there should not be so much heat that the seedlings are baked to a crisp.

Soil cables provide an easy solution to the heat problem and eliminate the guesswork. Lay out the cables in a series of loops on the bottom of the hotbed and cover it with a wire screen so that digging out the seedlings wouldn't disturb the cable. Then cover the screen with three to four inches of sifted soil.

Soil cables need a thermostat, just as heating pads do, to prevent overheating. Sometimes the thermostat is built into the cable and preset at a temperature of about 75°F., which is about right for most plants. Others must be bought separately and can be adjusted to suit your requirements. If you must buy a thermostat, obtain one that works on soil temperature rather than air temperature.

The plants in hotbeds and cold frames must be as carefully watered as if they were grown indoors. Water them well in the morning and check the plants often throughout the day to see that they are not drying out. Always warm the water slightly. Use a bulb-type sprinkler or fine mist sprayer on the seeds so that you don't uncover them, and water the new seedlings gently to avoid breaking their fragile stems.

After the seedlings have developed their first set of true leaves, the heat can be shut off whenever the days are warm enough. Eventually the heat should be shut off entirely, and the hotbed should be treated as a cold frame. Like a cold frame, on cool, sunny days the glass must be opened slightly for ventilation, and on warm days it can be removed entirely.

On cold nights and some early spring days, the glass or whatever transparent material is used may not be protection enough. It may be necessary to cover the whole bed with old rugs, insulation bats, blankets, or quilts. During prolonged cold spells you can save the plants by putting in a small light bulb and keeping it lit all night.

Hot Caps

Individual covers, usually called hot caps, make good miniature greenhouses for delicate transplants. You can buy the kind produced commercially, such as Hotkaps, which are made of translucent waxed paper or plastic; or you can make your own by cutting the bottom out of a plastic gallon milk or cider jug. Anchor them solidly to the ground with a stake and leave the caps off. These make good heat collectors for warm-weather plants, yet they don't get too hot because they are not clear plastic and they have top ventilation.

Hot caps

Commercial fiberglass cones also serve as excellent heat gatherers and are useful in both spring and fall for frost protection. Their cost may limit their wide use, but if they are stored inside when not in use, they should last for years.

By putting out hot caps a few days before the plants are set out, the soil will be warmed beneath them and the plants will be happier when they are moved in. It is not necessary to "harden off" transplants if you are protecting them with hot caps, but you must water them.

Plastic Tents

You can build a plastic tent over a bed or row of tender seedlings or transplants to protect them on raw, windy days and collect heat from the sun, even if days are cloudy.

Some growers stretch clotheslines, ropes, or wires supported by poles over their plantings and throw plastic tents of polyethylene (usually of 4 mm thickness) over them, much as you would throw clothes over a clothesline. These may be used as heat collectors in the spring and for frost protection in the early fall. On windy days, however, the plastic must be carefully weighted or pegged down.

Since strings and ropes often stretch and sag, and occasionally break, some gardeners prefer to make shelters rather like greenhouses out of cheap lumber and posts or frames out of plastic or aluminum pipe. These are often constructed in the shape of a Quonset hut or like a row of large croquet wickets. The plastic is stretched over them in such a way that it can be open at both ends for ventilation during the day and closed when necessary on cold nights. Only a few minutes of direct sunlight on a tight, clear plastic house will quickly bake the plants inside beyond recovery. If you tighten up this kind of structure for a cold night, be sure to rise early and open it the next morning. In the heat of the summer, the plastic is removed entirely.

Fall Frost Protection

When frost threatens, get out the large cartons, sheets, and blankets and cover vulnerable plants. In the fall the soil is usually much warmer than in the spring, so protect the plants in a way that takes advantage of ground heat by covering them in late afternoon before the earth chills, including plenty of soil surface under the insulation.

Corn and beans are difficult to cover, so turn the sprinklers on them if you can. Even if you save only part of the crop, it is usually worth the extra trouble.

If you were too lazy to get your plants covered before that early fall frost, don't write off your crops. Spray with a fine mist early in the morning, before sun hits the leaves, and you may earn a reprieve for your plants. Most damage after frost occurs when leaves warm up too fast in the sunshine. If you can thaw them with cool water first, they may survive.

Greens Into Winter

The cold frame can be used for growing salad crops when the weather turns cooler in the fall.

The hardy standards — spinach, lettuce, and radishes — will thrive inside the cold frame when outside conditions make gardening impossible.

Seeds sown several weeks before the first frost should yield radishes and salad greens late in the fall or early winter. Bank the cold frame with bags of leaves and straw, and use the blanket covering. Daytime temperatures can still become extremely high inside the cold frame, even though the days are growing shorter and the sunlight is becoming less intense.

Successive sowings of radish seed can be made at least a month after the first frost with expectations of a good yield. Judicious pruning of the spinach and lettuce plants will keep them productive up to Thanksgiving.

How late in the year the cold frame will continue to bear is up to Mother Nature, but in an average year in northern climates any harvests taken after December 1 should be considered a blessing.

PLANTING VEGETABLES ACCORDING TO GROWING TIME

Group 1	Group 2	Group 3	Group 4
Crops that will occupy the ground for a year or more.	*Crops planted early that occupy the ground only first part of the season.*	*Crops that occupy the ground the major portion of the season.*	*Crops to be planted in July and later for fall and winter gardens.*
Asparagus			
Rhubarb	Early beets	Bush and Pole beans	Bush beans
Chives	Early cabbage	Lima beans	Beets
Horseradish	Lettuce	Cabbage	Broccoli
Winter onions	Onion sets	Celery	Chinese cabbage
	Peas	Sweet corn	Carrots
	Radishes	Cucumbers	Cauliflower
	Early spinach	Eggplants	Endive
	Mustard	Muskmelons	Kale
	Turnips	Okra	Kohlrabi
		Peppers	Radishes
		Potatoes	Spinach
		Pumpkins	Turnips
		Squash	Collards
		Tomatoes	Lettuce
		Watermelons	
		Swiss chard	

Regardless of the shape of your garden, decide in what section you will want to plant each group. Then, as the planting dates arrive, plant each in its respective area. Group 2 will all be planted before it is time to plant crops in Group 3. Group 1 should always be planted so that it will not interfere too much with normal cultivation — preferably at one side of the garden. Group 4 will be planted in the area formerly occupied by Group 2 as the early crops are harvested.

Cooperative Extension Service of the University of West Virginia

Successful Succession Planting

Some vegetables take up garden space all summer because it takes them so long to ripen. Others mature much faster, and once these have been harvested or have passed their peak, the space they occupied will stand idle unless you make use of it. Plant succession crops — crops that can be planted after a previous fast-maturing crop has been harvested.

Crops that mature early include radishes, beans, peas, beets, cauliflower, cabbage, kohlrabi, onions (from sets), mustard, spinach, turnips, and early corn. As soon as these have been harvested, either pull them up and put the plant residues in the compost pile, or till them directly back into the garden soil. Have a succession crop ready to go in. It is not a good idea to plant the same crop that was there before. If there were beans in an area, replace them with carrots or beets. Some crops can be planted more than once in the same season, but others don't do well during really hot weather — peas, for example, and lettuce, spinach, and turnips. Wait at least until late July before replanting these vegetables so that they will mature during the cool days of fall.

As you plan the second generation of your succession crops, use early-maturing varieties. The later varieties take too long to mature, and there is likely to be frost before the last plantings have a chance to make it.

TRELLISES FOR VERTICAL GROWING

Don't have room for sprawling pumpkin vines? Settling for bush beans instead of the variety of colors, textures, and tastes offered by pole beans? Don't savor the idea of tangled masses of space-hogging vines of cucumbers, melons, or rambling squash? Free yourself to grow whatever your heart desires, for no matter how little square footage you have in your garden, chances are you have been totally overlooking most of your available growing area — that often neglected vertical space.

ADVANTAGES OF VERTICAL GROWING

- Fruit is cleaner and less susceptible to damage from rotting, insects, or slugs.
- More air and sunlight reach the plants, reducing likelihood of fungus or mildew infection.
- Cultivating and harvesting are easier.
- Less space is used.
- Yields are generally higher (unless you prune).
- Creates a shady garden spot.
- Provides a frame work for plant coverings.
- Allows more efficient watering.
- Makes monitoring and managing pests easier.
- Earliest, cleanest, and longest lasting harvests.

Stakes

The simplest of all plant supports are stakes or poles. They are driven into the soil near the base of the plant and the vines instinctively latch onto them.

Tie the plant to the stake to support the vine as it grows to the full length of the stake. Then prune the excess growth at the top.

Garden centers usually offer a range of wooden, bamboo, or manufactured stakes. Scrap lumber in 1x2 or 2x2 sizes, pieces of metal or PVC pipe, or other thin, rigid material sometimes can be commandeered for service.

Even an old Christmas tree with the branches removed can be used to support growing plants.

Tepees

Tepees make excellent supports for beans, peas, or tomatoes; honeysuckle, trumpet vines, and climbing roses; as well as heavily fruited crops, such as melons and squash. Many vines may be supported on sapling poles or bamboo, but those that bear heavy fruit demand a sturdier structure.

Tepee trellis

To build a tepee, you will need three to six poles — thin ones for flowers, peas, or beans and stouter ones for squash, melons, or heavy sweet potato vines. Cut the poles 10 to 12 feet long to have at least 1 or 2 feet to sink into the ground to solidly anchor the finished tepee. Use twine, raffia, or strips of rawhide or cloth to lash the poles together near the top. Pull the poles into a tight bundle, wrapping the twine around the bundle a few times and tying it snugly. Prop the bundle of poles over the planting area and position the bottom ends so that each pole will support one or two vines.

If you are using large poles, 2 to 3 inches across, they are heavy enough to be freestanding. There is usually no need to drive them into the soil. Their extra weight makes it nearly impossible to erect the tepee all at once; instead, tie the poles together in twos. You will need a helper to hold up the first set of two while you straddle it with the second set, arrange the legs, then wrap the tops together. A four-legged tepee (two sets of two poles) works wonderfully for squash, melons, and sweet potatoes.

Running tepee trellis

Additional support for heavy vines can be worked into a tepee design by wrapping heavy twine or rope around one leg of the structure near the bottom and continuing up and around toward the top.

A variation on the tepee method is a running tepee, for long wide rows of crops such as beans or peas. To build, start with either a pole tepee at either end of the row or a post (a height of 6 feet will accommodate most crops). Tie a long thin pole to

PLANTS FOR TRELLISING

A surprising variety of crops are suitable for trellising:

Vegetables

- **Cucumbers** — Fence trellises with wire mesh for plant supports works well. A-frames, pipe, wooden lattice designs, and the zig-zag series of A-frame trellises work well also.

- **Basellas Malabar Red Stem summer spinach** — use twine, wire, poles, or bean towers.

- **Pole beans** — Use bean poles, tepees, fences, bean towers.

- **Peas** — Branches pushed into the soil will support dwarf varieties; for the taller growing varieties, use vertical fences of wire mesh, fitted A-frames, or tepees.

- **Squash and Gourds** — Use tepees, fences, and A-frames. Slings supports for large fruits may be required.

- **Sweet potatoes** — Use a fence-type trellis with heavy wire mesh, or an A-frame or tepee with extra rope supports. Train the vines onto the supports by weaving them in and out of the mesh or ropes.

- **Tomatoes** — Use stakes, cages, wire mesh arches, fences, zig-zag fences.

Fruits

- **Blackberries** — Erect varieties do best with a clothesline trellis; train trailing varieties to any type trellis. Fence trellises work well.

- **Grapes** — Use arbors, wire-fence trellises.

- **Hardy kiwis** — Use well-supported clothesline-type trellises.

- **Melons** — A sloping support with a mesh at least 6 inches square is ideal. Use cloth slings to support all but the smallest individual fruits.

- **Raspberries** — Use fence-type trellises or V trellises where the top wires are spaced farther apart than the bottom wires.

Ornamental Vines

- **Clematis** — Use any type trellis, fence, or arbor.

- **Honeysuckle** — Use any type trellis.

- **Ivy** — Will climb on nearly any surface; can do damage to wood, stone, concrete, or stucco.

- **Morning Glory** — Use any fence, trellis, arbor, or lamp post.

- **Roses** — Must be trained and tied to grow on a trellis.

- **Trumpet vine** — Train along sturdy wooden or wire trellises; can damage wooden, stone, or brick walls.

- **Wisteria** — Easily trained up porch pillars and along horizontal beams. Stone or brick walls make appropriate backdrop. Wooden supports must be sturdy.

the top of the end tepees or posts so that it connects the two, or string a heavy wire or rope between the tops of the posts and tighten. The last step is to lean poles (saplings, scrap 1x2s, or bamboo are perfect) along the length of the connecting pole in pairs, tying each pair together at the top. Seed directly or transplant along the length of each row created by the feet of the tepee poles.

Fences

Drive a post at each end of a row and place other posts in between where needed. String with twine, wire, netting, or wire mesh and you have a fence-type trellis. These are among the easiest, most versatile, and most used trellises found in gardens everywhere. The standards, or end posts, can be anything from wood or steel fence posts to pipe or, in a pinch, existing trees. Tie, wire, staple, or nail a plant support to the standards so that it is taut enough to hold the vines without sagging.

Many trellises, from stake and netting dwarf pea fences to freestanding post and wire espalier trellises, follow this very basic design. Some need bracing at the end posts or additional posts in between. Fences over 20 feet long should have an extra post installed every 10 to 12 feet.

Double Fence or Clothesline Trellis

By attaching cross arms to the end posts and running wires between them, the simple fence trellis is converted into a double fence or clothesline trellis

Clothesline trellis

that can support two or four lines instead of just one. This type of trellis allows you to plant double rows and is useful for many annual crops and berry brambles. Since the posts in double fences must bear twice the weight of those in a simple fence, it is a good idea to brace them at each end.

Cages

Another simple and efficient method of containing errant sprawlers is with a cage. Cages can be nailed together from scrap 1x2 lumber or made with wire mesh. Choose a wire mesh sturdy enough to retain its shape under the weight of vines and fruit. Bend the mesh into shape and arrange it over transplants, such as tomatoes or cucumbers.

Round or square cages, 2 to 3 feet in diameter and 3 to 4 feet high will both contain and support a variety of vines. Connect snaps to the ends of the mesh and snap the cylinders together, or add a few inches to the final measurement and bend the wire back over the opposite end of the mesh to hold it in place. Drive a stake into the ground through the wire mesh to anchor the support against the wind.

A simplified version of a cage is popular for cucumbers and squash. Cut stiff, self-supporting wire in 6-foot to 8-foot lengths and using a straight edge, such as a board or pipe, bend the panels in the middle to form a V. Flip the panels over and place several V-bends along the row so that the ends are a few inches apart. This creates an uninterrupted zig-zag trellis. Set transplants in the spaces between the individual cages and train the vines up the sides of the cage on either side.

A-Frames

Construct the A-frame of lightweight lumber — 1x2s or 2x4s. Wire mesh fencing, garden netting, or vertically or horizontally strung wire or twine will all serve well as the plant support. While you may design an A-frame in any dimensions to suit your site, bear in mind that if it is to be portable, it must be of manageable size. Better to build and move four 6-foot components than one 24-foot monster.

A-frame trellis

Another advantage to the A-frame design is that both sides of the trellis are used and the shaded corridor created between the sides is a perfect spot to plant some greens, making the row even more productive.

Depending on the type of materials used, this is a wonderful all-purpose trellis. It can be made sturdy enough to support even heavy crops, such as gourds or pumpkins. By changing its position in the garden every year, the same structure can be used to support cucumbers one year, squash the next, then tomatoes, and later beans or peas. It can pull double duty as the framework for shade cloth and bug-proof or bird-proof crop covers, or can be made into an instant greenhouse by tacking clear plastic sheeting to the frame. If versatility were not blessing enough from this useful design, consider that the structure can be built of scraps which adds economy to the list of advantages.

Arches & Arbors

Garden books and magazines are fairly bursting with patterns of beautiful, permanent landscape trellises. Often these indulgent structures serve as the focal point of the garden, setting either a formal, informal, or even rustic tone.

Choosing deciduous plants to climb the trellises will create shade in the summer while still allowing the sun to shine through in the winter. Permanent vines can dominate the trellis or annual vines can be trained each year or worked in among longtime residents. So even though the structure is permanent, it can still be varied and versatile.

Architectural designs range from the rustic to prim Victorian or sleek contemporary. Lash peeled wooden branches together for a rustic look or create swooping scrolls and archways for a formal approach. Attach a trellis to a bare wall to convert it instantly into an elegant backdrop. Consider, however, attaching this elegant trellis with hinges or pivot bolts so that it can swing down, just in case you ever need to get to that wall.

Arched arbor

The horizontal beams of an arbor provide not only support for vines, but also a secluded shady spot for the gardener. Doorways, paths, patios, gazebos, or any other special outdoor area can be transformed with a vine-covered archway. Consider including a planter box in your designs. Create a private corner with an arch or arbor or use it as camouflage for whatever you may wish to hide. Living screens are also an excellent means of providing a windbreak, or to the often overwhelmed city dweller, a much needed noise and/or pollution barrier.

Despite the nearly limitless possibilities for arbor design and construction, the gardener must always consider the cost of construction and the plants that will climb it. Posts should be driven or dug 24 to 30 inches deep, or set in at least 18 inches of concrete. Vertical supports should be well anchored to the horizontal beams that define the frame of the trellis with galvanized nails or screws. Overhead horizontal supports must be strong enough to bear the weight of the vines. A double layer of crisscross lattice is sturdy and attractive.

Overhead arbor

EDIBLE LANDSCAPING: THE BEAUTIFUL FOOD GARDEN

You may want a garden that is entirely edible, where every plant is both attractive and productive, or a garden that combines food plants and standard ornamentals. Many "edible landscapes" are better described as partly-edible landscapes; they have plenty of food plants, some inedible flowers to provide extra color, and inedible woody perennials to help give the garden strong year-round structure.

Some purely ornamental plants provide effects few food plants can equal. Broadleaf evergreen shrubs, for example, are inedible, and some are even poisonous, but they are important if a garden is to look good in winter. Most spring-flowering bulbs are inedible. Certain inedible ornamentals have important food-related uses: They are used as companion plants or as a food source for wildlife. We all have plants we especially like; we feel our gardens would be incomplete without them. Some of them are plants that seem very beautiful or interesting to us, and some are full of personal associations. Probably not all of them are food plants.

When you choose plants for your garden, think about what type of plant is needed for a specific environmental niche and purpose in the garden, and see if there is a food plant that will fit in that situation. In some cases, there is no food plant that will work, and an inedible ornamental fits perfectly. But in many other cases, a food plant is just as satisfactory as the purely ornamental alternatives, and you will have the added pleasure of being able to use it for food.

When you choose an attractive food plant for your garden, consider whether you like the food plant enough to get around to eating it. What will happen if you don't eat it? If you ignore a plum tree, there will be a sour-smelling mess of rotten fruit, but if you do not pick the currants on a currant bush, or the leaves on kale, the plant will still be an attractive part of the garden.

When considering a particular kind of attractive food plant, you must decide how many plants you want. If growing space is ample, you may deliberately plant more of something than you are going to eat, because you like the way it looks. For example, you may decide to plant thyme, the plant you feel is best both for the visual purpose you have in mind and for the environmental conditions available in that place. It is unlikely that you will eat all the thyme growing on the bank, but you will certainly enjoy some of it!

Plants for Edible Landscaping

Amaranthus. Bold, vigorous plants with large, ovate leaves that may be green, red-brown, scarlet, or variegated. Eat tender, young leaves for greens.

Artichoke, globe. Plant in rows for summer hedge or garden space divider. Plants are striking in front of a dark wall or evergreen hedge.

Asparagus. Makes a light beautiful hedge or airy backdrop for a border.

Basil. Looks good massed in beds and borders, edging paths or growing in containers. 'Dark Opal' contrasts well with yellow flowers or

Basil

with bright green parsley.

Beans, bush snap. Good edging plants. Plant densely.

Bean, runner and pole. Trellis beans alongside patio for privacy and shade, grow along fences, or for a jungle effect, grow vertically with cucumbers, wax gourds, morning glories, and other flowering vines.

Burnet. Useful ground cover for partially shaded areas; also thrives on land that is sunny and hard to water. Grow in a bed, or as an edging plant. Leaves taste like cucumbers.

Cabbage. Looks great in beds or formal rows. Good companion to chrysanthemums.

Calendula. Blooms quickly from seed in cool weather and provides cheerful color to go with the foliage of spring and fall food plants. Use as inexpensive saffron substitute.

Carnations. Neat bush carnations are great edging plants. Make an attractive combination with blue-green or purple cabbage. Petals lend a clovelike flavor to foods; leaves may be poisonous.

Calendula

Carrot. Plant in a feathery mass or grow as an edging.

Celery. Bright green foliage and erect growth of good celery varieties have many uses. Looks good with other green leaves, such as parsley, and blue-green leaves such as kale.

Chives. Best grown in beds where leaning leaves are less noticeable. Most attractive in spring.

Chrysanthemum greens (shungiku). Good background plant. Leaves good in stir fries.

Cilantro. Best grown in closely planted bed near the foreground of a border.

Corn. Good backdrop for a mixed border. Make

sure nearby plants are at least 3 feet high.

Cucumbers. Grow bush cucumbers in containers, vines on trellises. Good camouflage for chain link fences and stumps.

Day lilies. Good ground cover under trees. Flower buds and open flowers are used fresh in stir fries. Buds are dried for Oriental golden needles.

Dill. Plant thickly to eliminate need for staking. Flowers look sickly next to intensely yellow flowers or bright green foliage.

Eggplant. Looks best massed in groups.

Endive and Escarole. Make good, neat edging plants and look good in beds, especially near other plants with bright green leaves and yellow flowers.

Dill

Fennel. Combines nicely with other feathery-leaved plants, such as asparagus or cosmos. Makes excellent background plant or hedge; grow in rows, beds, or masses.

Ornamental Kale and Cabbage. Looks striking against a somber background of evergreen bushes or gray walls.

Geranium, scented. Plant where people are likely to sit or brush against as they pass. Use in teas and jellies.

Scented Geranium

Gourd, fuzzy and winter melon. Grow on trellis, along fences, or on a string frame. Harvest fruits when young.

Husk Tomatoes. Large, sprawling plant. Grow near other large, bold plants, such as eggplant, okra, sunflower, cleome.

Kale. Plant as edging, in masses, or in containers.

Combines nicely with almost any shade of green.

Leeks. Best planted where they are fairly inconspicuous in summer, and striking during fall, winter, and spring.

Lettuce. Sow thickly in containers or group in the foreground of mixed borders. Different varieties can be combined to create geometric designs.

Nasturtiums. Grow in raised planters or on terraces. Eat flowers in salads, buds can be pickled and used as capers.

Nasturtium

Okra. Effective background plant used alone or with other big plants, such as corn, hollyhock, or roses.

Oregano. Excellent ground cover that is especially useful on banks or eroded slopes. Use alone or with creeping thyme.

Parsley. Good in borders, edgings, masses, planters, and window boxes.

Parsnip. Foliage combines well with many colors; grow in rows or masses.

Pea. Tall, vining varieties most useful in landscape; train onto string or trellises for early-season screens and backdrops.

Swiss Chard. 'Rhubarb' Swiss chard can be planted in rows, small groups, and masses, in beds, borders, and containers.

Thyme. Upright varieties can be lined up as edging plants, massed in beds and borders, or planted in pots and window boxes. Creeping thyme makes a strong-growing ground cover.

Garden thyme

Tomato. Plant small bush tomatoes singly or in groups and rows. Small vining varieties can cascade from hanging baskets. Surround tomato cages with flowers. Trellises can be shared with vigorous flowering vines, such as morning glory.

GETTING STARTED: PREPARING THE SOIL

Growing strong, healthy plants is easy. All you must do is see that the plants get (1) light, (2) mechanical support to keep them from falling over, (3) warmth, (4) air, (5) water, and (6) nutrients. Except for light, the soil plays a major role in providing *all* of these things. So having a healthy garden depends on providing good soil.

BASIC SOIL INFORMATION

Learning about your soil can help to make you a more successful gardener. When you evaluate your soil, you have to consider both its texture and its structure. A soil's texture simply refers to the size of the particles that make up the soil; fine textures characterize clay soils, coarse textures mean sandy soil. A soil's structure describes the way these particles are arranged in groups — sometimes called crumbs or aggregates. Good structure is far more important than good texture. Aggregates are formed as decayed organic matter binds or glues soil particles together, giving the soil much more favorable qualities.

Organic Matter and Humus

About 95 percent of soil consists of minerals, while only three to five percent of its total weight is organic matter. But never underestimate the importance of once-living material in the soil. It is something that must be renewed constantly if the soil is to stay in good condition. Organic matter is a ma-jor source of phosphorus and sulfur (major nutrients that plants require), the main source of energy for soil microorganisms, and essentially the soil's only source of nitrogen.

Humus is more than just rotting organic matter. True humus has decomposed to the point where the original organic material can't be recognized any longer. Basically it is slimy stuff, gelatinous in texture, and it is humus which surrounds soil particles and sticks them together into aggregates.

To build up your soil, you will want to add organic matter — in the form of manure, rotted leaves, compost, and so on — to your soil at regular intervals.

Soil Organisms

Fertile soil is rich with organisms living within the

soil. One of the largest and most beneficial life forms in the soil is the common earthworm. Worms consume large quantities of organic matter and soil particles, modifying them through digestion into forms readily available to growing plants.

Microorganisms also help with the reduction of organic matter and soil particles, liberating plant foods in the process.

EARTHWORMS AT WORK IN THE GARDEN

Earthworms will do a great job of making compost in a small pile that is only 1½ or 2 feet high. The succulent organic matter you put there will invite them from the ground below. You can even *buy* earthworms through the mail, if you like, and add them to your modest collection of grass clippings, leaves, and vegetable wastes.

Mail-order worms should not be confused with the kind of worms you might dig up or buy on the roadside for use as fishing bait. They are usually "compost worms," and they sport impressive names like Red Wiggler, Red Hybrid, or California Red. These worms have been so pampered and well fed that they will thrive *only* in your compost pile and will probably do poorly in common everyday garden soil. To buy "reds" or "blue-gray thins," look for advertisements for earthworm companies in gardening magazines. Once you have introduced a few earthworms into your pile, they will double their numbers in about a month's time.

You can also use earthworms to make compost out of your food scraps during the winter. All it takes is building a home for them and feeding them your leftovers. Mary Appelhof, worm-composting expert and author of *Worms Eat My Garbage*, recommends a wooden box 1 foot by 2 feet by 3 feet for food waste from a family of four. Fill it with a bedding of shredded newspapers, manure, or leaf mold. Locate the box where temperatures stay above freezing and below 84°F. Add some redworms or others sold expressly for indoor composting. You'll need twice as many worms as the average daily amount of garbage you'll be asking them to process (i.e., if you generate ½ pound of garbage per day, you'll need 1 pound of worms). Then simply feed them your food garbage daily, preferably after if has been ground up in a blender. In this size box, worms can process about 6 to 7 pounds of kitchen scraps per week.

Worm castings, which look very much like coffee grounds, are five times richer than the most fertile soil and loaded with microorganisms. The simplest method of removing the castings from the worm composter is to move the bedding and worms to one side of the box every two or three months and fill the other side with new bedding. Bury your garbage in the new bedding, and when worms have migrated to the new side, remove the castings from the other side. Use this precious compost as a top-dressing on potted plants and flower beds or as a potting and seed-starting medium, and add some to planting holes for flower and vegetable transplants. Brew up some castings tea by soaking a handful of castings in water and use it on your potted plants and young transplants.

Not all soil life is beneficial. Moles ruin lawns, white grubs gnaw off roots, and nematodes burrow into roots to strangle the necessary flow of nutrients and water to garden plants. Other microbes are responsible for wilt diseases, root maladies, and outright destruction of plants.

Supplying your soil with plenty of organic matter will ensure a good population of beneficial soil organisms.

Air

Under ideal conditions, about 25 percent of the volume of a soil will be filled with air. This circulates through passages between the soil granules, aiding in the decomposition of organic matter and sustaining soil life. Earthworms rise to the surface after a rainstorm because their breathing passages have become waterlogged. Many microbes are dependent on the air supply as well, causing the poor growth of some crops on soggy soil.

Water

Another quarter of the soil is water. Its value is obvious to anyone who has ever witnessed a drought.

Water occupies part of the pore space between the soil granules, mostly as a thin surrounding film. It also becomes absorbed into organic matter, which is generally capable of holding several times its own weight in water.

Water furnishes plant food, especially hydrogen, and facilitates the liberation of plant food from rock particles and decaying organic matter.

Water also transports nutrients to the roots of growing plants and disperses the nutrients through the plants.

Soil Types

Soils are classified by the size of their particles. Generally, they range from coarse to fine or from light to heavy.

The coarser the soil, the earlier it warms in the spring and the earlier it can be worked. Also, coarse

SOIL TYPES

Type	Characteristics
Sandy	Easily tilled
Sandy loam	Well drained
Loam	Warms quickly; Poor nutrient retention
Silty loam	Hard to work
Clay loam	Slow drainage — great moisture retention
Clay	Warms slowly; Excellent nutrient retention

particles of sand retain less moisture than fine particles of clay. Coarse soils require less spring sunshine to reach a temperature suitable for seed germination.

Delay working the soil until it is dry enough so that a compressed ball of soil will break apart when dropped from the height of your hip. Soil that is worked when too moist forms compact clods and makes root growth difficult.

ANALYZING YOUR SOIL

The ideal garden soil is rich in organic matter, well drained, slightly acid, and replenished with plant nutrients. How good is your soil? The amount of nutrients and the level of acidity can be determined by soil tests.

These tests are performed by the Extension Service at little or no charge. Or, you can do your own test, using a kit purchased through the mail or at a garden supply store.

If you use the Extension Service, contact the nearest office and request specific instructions.

Usually this is how you will be asked to collect your soil samples:

- Use a trowel to dig up small amounts of soil at a depth of about six inches.

- Take several samples from across the garden. Mix these in a bucket to get an accurate indication of average soil conditions.

- Avoid soil where peas, beans, or other nitrogen-fixing crops have been grown in previous years.

- Dry two or three handfuls of the soil from the bucket at room temperature. Drying in an oven can lead to a false indication of the need for lime. Send a small plastic bag of the dry soil to the nearest Extension Service office.

Soil pH

The acidity or alkalinity of the soil (the pH level) is an important factor. While some plants are adapted to extreme conditions, most vegetables and flowers thrive in soil with a pH between 6.0 and 7.0. A pH level of 7 represents neutrality, when the soil is neither acid nor alkaline. Levels higher than 7 indicate alkalinity, while numbers below 7 indicate an acid state.

PRIMARY PLANT FOOD ELEMENTS

Element Symbol	Function in Plant	Deficiency	Excess Symptoms	Sources
Nitrogen **N**	Gives dark green color to plant. Increases growth of leaf and stem. Influences crispness of leaf crops. Stimulates rapid early growth.	Light green to yellow leaves. Stunted growth.	Dark green. Excessive growth. Retarded maturity. Loss of buds or fruit.	Urea Ammonia Nitrates
Phosphorus **P**	Stimulates early formation and growth of roots. Gives plants a rapid and vigorous start. Is important in formation of seed. Gives hardiness to fall-seeded grasses and grains.	Red or purple leaves. Cell division retardation.	Possible tie up of other essential elements.	Superphosphate Rock phosphate
Potassium **K**	Increases vigor of plants and resistance to disease. Stimulates production of strong, stiff stalks. Promotes production of sugar, starches, oils. Increases plumpness of grains and seed. Improves quality of crop yield.	Reduced vigor. Susceptibility to diseases. Thin skin and small fruit.	Coarse, poor colored fruit. Reduced absorption of magnesium and calcium.	Muriate or Sulfate of Potash

SECONDARY PLANT FOOD ELEMENTS

Element	Symptoms of Deficiency	Symptoms of Excess	Sources
Magnesium	Loss of yield. Chlorosis of old leaves.	Reduced absorption of calcium and potassium.	Magnesium sulfate (Epsom Salts) Dolomite is ⅓ magnesium.
Manganese	Mottled chlorosis of the leaves. Stunted growth.	Small dead areas in the leaves with yellow borders around them.	Manganese sulfate
Copper	Multiple budding. Gum pockets.	Prevents the uptake of iron. Causes stunting of roots.	Copper sulfate Neutral copper
Zinc	Small, thin, yellow leaves. Low yields.	None known.	Zinc sulfate
Iron	Yellowing of leaves, the veins remaining green.	None known.	Iron sulfate (Copperas) Chelated iron
Sulfur	Looks like nitrogen deficiency.	Sulfur burn from too low pH.	Sulfur Superphosphate
Calcium	Stops growing point of plants.	Reduces the intake of potassium and magnesium.	Lime Basic slag Gypsum
Molybdenum	Symptoms in plants vary greatly.	Poisonous to livestock.	Sodium Molybdate
Boron	Small leaves. Heart rot and corkiness. Multiple buds.	Leaves turn yellowish red.	Borax

MANIPULATING THE SOIL

Even if your soil analysis tells you your soil is in poor condition, don't despair. There are plenty of easy-to-apply remedies.

A garden of heavy clay can be lightened by working in quantities of sand. Likewise, mixing clay into coarse soil will improve its body.

If soil life is deficient, you can purchase microbial treatments or mail-order earthworms, though you will have to supply them with organic matter to live on.

Excessive water can be removed by drainage; a deficiency can be made up by irrigation.

Frequent cultivation helps improve the aeration of the soil.

The key to managing the soil for fertility is adding lots of organic matter. The organic material will benefit the soil drainage, its capacity to hold water, its microbial life, and its aeration.

No matter what type of rock particles predominate in the soil, the addition of organic matter will help improve its texture. In coarse sand, decaying organic matter will act as a sponge for water, reducing the tendency of the soil to dry quickly. A clay soil will be lightened and made less soggy as organic matter helps open up and maintain a more porous structure.

Adjusting Soil pH

Excessive soil acidity is usually corrected by adding ground limestone (calcium carbonate) or hydrated lime. (See the box below for quantities.) Spread the lime as evenly as possible and work it into the top three or four inches of soil uniformly.

(If you should need to substitute one form of lime for another: 100 pounds of ground limestone equals 74 pounds of hydrated lime.)

Adding Fertilizers

Most fertilizers contain varying amounts of the three essential plant foods: nitrogen, phosphorus, and potassium. On the label of commercial fertilizer bags, the elements are listed in the order given above. A bag of fertilizer listed as 10-15-20, for example would contain 10 percent nitrogen, 15 percent phosphorus, and 20 percent potassium.

TO RAISE SOIL ONE UNIT OF PH

	Hydrated Lime	Dolomite	Ground Limestone
Light Soil 100 square feet	1½ pounds	2 pounds	2½ pounds
Heavy Soil 100 square feet	3½ pounds	5½ pounds	6 pounds

TO LOWER SOIL ONE UNIT OF PH

	Sulfur	Aluminum Sulfate	Iron Sulfate
Light Soil 100 square feet	½ pound	2½ pounds	3 pounds
Heavy Soil 100 square feet	2 pounds	3½ pounds	7½ pounds

Note: The amount of lime you use doesn't have to be as precisely measured as this chart suggests.

Fertilizers are also available in organic forms, that is, derived from animal, or vegetable, or mineral sources. Commercially prepared organic fertilizers tend to be more expensive than chemicals and slower acting, but they provide a more sustained feeding of the plants and generally improve the soil condition.

IMPROVING YOUR SOIL

The use of organic amendments in the garden soil is an investment in the future. In the first few years after the soil-building is undertaken, you may not perceive dramatic results, but as the initial applications of compost, mulch, cover crops, and other materials break down, you will begin to see results.

The soil should become darker in color, easier to work, and faster to warm in the spring. You should begin to see more earthworms, and the soil will need fewer waterings. The texture of the soil should improve to a crumbly condition. Your soil tests should start to return with advice to add lime only, and that only every third year.

Building a garden soil is a long-term investment, but one that needn't involve any great cost. Keep out a sharp eye for materials to add to the garden, use green manure crops whenever the opportunity arises, and try to cut the waste of organic materials around your home to a minimum.

COVER CROP GARDENING

One of the best ways to improve the organic content of garden soils with minimum effort is by growing green manure crops. These are crops grown specifically to be plowed under at an immature stage of growth for the express purpose of boosting the organic content of the soil.

Benefits of Green Manures

Green manures are an economical way in which to boost the fertility of garden soils. Seed sufficient to plant a garden of 1,500 square feet should cost no more than a few dollars.

Green manuring is easy. Sowing the seed takes very little time and the immature crop can be rototilled into the soil in short order.

Green manures help to fight weeds in the garden. If seeded at a relatively thick rate, the chosen crop will create a dense stand that will grow vigorously enough to deny light, moisture, and nutrients to competitive weeds. Even such tough perennials as quack grass will succumb to successive plantings of green manures.

Another plus for green manures is the amount of time and effort that they save. Unlike lawn debris, they needn't be raked into piles, carried to the garden, and then spread about. The organic matter from green manure is already in place exactly where you want it. While animal manure might land in thick clumps in some spots and not at all on other areas of the garden, a good stand of green manure, when turned under, will provide an even blanket of benefits to the soil.

The organic matter from green manures — particularly the legumes — is more rapidly available to the plants than that from many other types of soil amendments. Turned under when the growth is succulent and well filled with water, the plants decompose rapidly. The nitrogen added by leguminous varieties hastens this process even further.

The rapid breakdown of the organic matter means that succeeding crops will benefit quickly from the plant foods being thus liberated.

Growing Green Manures

Under ideal conditions, you should have two plots. While one is in use for vegetable production, the other can be used for the growth of soil-improving cover crops. Alternation of the cropping pattern allows for steady improvement in both areas.

If you have space enough to expand your current garden, consider this approach. Even if you can't double your current space, creating room enough for the growth of cover crops every year over a third of the space would prove of definite benefit.

Even if you are unable to expand your garden area, you can grow valuable cover crops. They can be grown in between rows during the regular gardening season. Also, they can occupy the ground at any time the soil isn't filled with crops. One of the easiest ways to do this is to plant the early produce in a different location within the garden each year. For example, peas, radishes, and lettuce are all out of the ground relatively early in the gardening season as they can be planted as soon as the ground is workable. When harvest of these spring crops is completed, turn under their residue, level a good seedbed with a rototiller or rake, and plant a green manure crop.

Green manures can also be planted in among certain vegetable plants. It takes a long time for cucumbers to go from seed to sprawling vines. Take advantage of that period to sow a short-season green manure crop that can be turned under before the vines run.

Getting a Good Stand

If your choice of green manure is a legume, note that different types of legumes need different types of rhizobia to fix atmospheric nitrogen.

Many legume seeds come inoculated with the appropriate rhizobium from the seed company. These will need no treatment, and should be labeled as such. If the seed has not been inoculated, you will need to purchase a packet of the correct inoculant, which your seed supplier should have in stock.

Some legume seeds, usually those of plants grown for food such as beans, peas, and soybeans, are treated with a fungicide to prevent rotting of the seed in the ground. The fungicide will also kill rhizobia, so don't waste money buying inoculant for seed treated with captan or a similar fungicide.

Make sure that the seed you purchase is fresh, labeled for the year in which it is to be grown. The seedbed for cover crops needn't be prepared as finely as you might for vegetable seeds. Since covering each individual seed is impractical for broadcast seeds, some roughness of the soil surface is desirable so that tamping or rolling the seeded soil will produce adequate coverage.

When the seedbed is prepared, you may want to spread some commercial fertilizer to aid the growth of your cover crop. A 12-quart pail of 10-10-10 is enough for 1,000 square feet. You won't use this if you're strictly organic — you won't need to use it if your soil is good. This is an excellent time, too, to add lime if your soil needs it.

Rake the fertilizer into the top few inches of the soil.

Before sowing the seed, practice the motion of sowing with the fertilizer or some substance like flour. Try to swing your arm and wrist to get good coverage and spread.

Sowing cover crops on a prepared seedbed.

Divide the quantity of seed into halves. Sow half the seed in one direction, east and west, for example, then sow the other half north and south. This will help provide even coverage.

If the seed is very large, such as peas or beans, you may want to rake it into the soil. For fine seeds,

Cover larger seeds with soil.

such as clover or alfalfa, tamping with the teeth of a rake or with a lawn roller will suffice.

Unless the soil is quite damp, hose down the seeded area with a fine mist from an adjustable garden hose nozzle. Germination of most green manure crops should occur in less than two weeks if soil conditions are good.

Water newly planted seedbeds.

The crop should need no care, unless you have planted legume seed treated with fungicide. In that case, apply the inoculant through a watering can or sprayer after the seedlings have developed a pair of true leaves.

Returning Green Manures to the Soil

Some green manure crops, such as alfalfa, will give the greatest benefit if left growing for more than one year. Others are short-season crops that can be returned to the soil in six weeks.

Except for legumes, which contain their own supply of nitrogen, the decomposition of green manure crops can be hastened by spreading a high nitrogen fertilizer, such as blood meal, about two weeks before the crop is to be turned under.

Never allow the green manure crop to go to seed. A weed has been defined as a plant out of place, and it holds true for alfalfa as well as for crabgrass.

Decomposition of the organic matter will be greatly retarded if the plants are allowed to reach a woody state. Turn under a green manure crop when it is actively growing, tender, and succulent. When the water supply is within the plant, the process of decay will proceed much faster than if the dead organic matter must draw its water from the soil.

Commonly Used Green Manures

The following list contains information on some of the more commonly used green manure crops.

Alfalfa. The king of soil building crops, alfalfa will grow roots as deep as 20 feet if left in place for two years. A perennial legume, it will not tolerate wet growing conditions or the absence of calcium in the soil. This can be supplied with ground limestone. Alfalfa is excellent to harvest for a mulch.

Alfalfa

Alsike Clover. This biennial legume is best adapted to the northern states, faring better on poorly drained or unlimed soils than most other clovers. Sow in the spring, turn under in the fall.

Allyce Clover. Adapted to the deep South, this annual legume demands good drainage.

Clover

Barley. A non-legume, this cereal crop is a good grower in the North where it should be sown in the spring.

Buckwheat. For rebuilding a neglected, poor soil, this non-legume is unsurpassed. Sown as soon as the ground is warm, buckwheat will be ready to plow down in six weeks. Its vigorous top growth, coupled with a massive root system, allows for the addition of as much as 40 tons of green matter per acre per summer. Buckwheat is able to use nutrients locked up in the rock particles of the soil far better than most crops.

Buckwheat

Bur Clover. Seed for this legume are sown about September 15 to overwinter south of the Mason-Dixon Line. Will do well on heavier soils.

Bur clover

Cowpea. An annual, this legume makes fast growth on a wide range of soils throughout the United States. Like other deep-rooted crops, it improves aeration and brings sub-soil minerals up to become available for succeeding crops.

Fenugreek. This legume can be sown in the fall on alkaline soils in the Southwest and turned under in the spring.

Field Brome Grass. This non-legume is among the hardiest of the soil-building crops. It can be sown in early spring or late summer throughout the northern half of the United States. Planted in the fall, it's a good winter cover.

Brome grass

Field Peas. Leguminous annuals, field peas have a wide climatic range and are tolerant of many types of soils. It can be seeded in the spring in northern states and in the fall in the South.

Hairy Indigo. A tall, thick stand of this annual legume can be expected even on poor, sandy soils. Adapted to the South, it should be sown in spring.

Lespedeza. This legume is adapted to all but the coldest northern states. The Korean and sericea varieties will handle the most rugged climates. Sericea will grow well on depleted, unlimed soils.

Oats. Seeds of this non-legume will germinate in cool soils and thus are among the earliest crops that can be sown by the northern gardener. Fall sowing is possible in mild climates.

Lespedeza

Rape. This biennial is not a legume but is widely adapted to varying climates. It grows best in cool, moist weather.

Red Clover. As this legume does poorly in high temperatures, its best growth will occur only in northern states. Sow in early spring. This crop is exceptionally fast to decay and thus of more immediate benefit to following crops.

Rye. Another cereal grain, rye is not a legume. It can be purchased as an annual, which will die as the first freezes come in the autumn, or as a perennial (winter rye), which will put up new growth in the spring.

Soybeans. New varieties have allowed northern gardeners success with this excellent legume. Since you are after organic materials rather than the beans themselves, select a variety of long-season soybeans as these will make the largest plants.

Bean

Sweet Clover. Varieties of this biennial legume suitable for any United States climate can be found. Sow in the spring and turn under the following spring to secure maximum growth of the nitrogen fixing roots.

Velvet Bean. This annual legume is best suited to the South, where it should be sown when the soil is warm. It will produce good growth in poor, sandy soils.

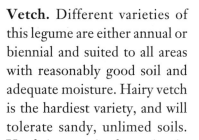

Sweet clover

Vetch. Different varieties of this legume are either annual or biennial and suited to all areas with reasonably good soil and adequate moisture. Hairy vetch is the hardiest variety, and will tolerate sandy, unlimed soils. Vetch is sown in the spring in northern climates and in the fall elsewhere.

Vetch

MULCHES: LOW-COST SOIL IMPROVEMENT

Another excellent method for improving the soil at low cost is to mulch the garden.

MULCH MATERIALS

The following list of mulching materials should be found available free, close to home, or at minimal cost nearby.

Leaves
Leaf mold
Pine needles
Sawdust
Seaweed
Wood chips or shavings
Spoiled hay
Straw
Rotten wood
Hulls or shells
Corn cobs or stalks
Newspaper
Scrap material

A mulch is a layer of material spread on the surface of the soil to retain moisture and retard weed growth. Although you can use black plastic as mulch to check weeds and conserve soil moisture, it obviously adds nothing to the soil. Organic mulches are good soil builders, although they will not increase fertility quickly.

Mulch helps protect the soil from temperature extremes, keeping the ground warmer in the winter and cooler in the summer. Mulches greatly cut down on the need to weed and water the garden. Mulch also prevents sprawling plants like cucumbers and tomatoes from coming in contact with bare ground, preventing many rot and fungus problems. Soil erosion from wind or water is minimized in a mulched garden.

Most gardeners who use mulch turn it into the soil at the end of the gardening season, where the action of water and microbes can start the process of making the organic material available as plant food.

Others leave the mulch in place year after year, replenishing the protective covering as it starts to decay on the soil surface. This is the closest imitation of natural fertilization that the home gardener can undertake, and after a period of a few years, it will yield noticeable benefits. A single disadvantage is that mulched soils are very slow to warm up in the spring. The mulch, of course, can be pulled away, then put back in place when the crops begin to grow.

When green manure crops or mulch materials are returned to the soil, their benefits will be most quickly realized if the materials are reduced in size by chopping or shredding to allow more exposure of the organic matter to decay organisms and water. You can do this with a rototiller in the process of tilling your garden soil. If you lack power equipment, use your lawn mower to chop them, then compost the organic materials before adding them to the garden.

MANURE AND OTHER FERTILIZERS

Manure is a time-tested soil enricher. Farm manures — cow, sheep, pig, horse, or poultry — are all good. Well-rotted manures are better than fresh ones for fertilization, provided they have been kept covered and haven't lost their fertility because they overheated or were leached out by rains. Old manures also give vegetables and berries a better flavor than fresh manure. Poultry manure has more nitrogen than others, so less is needed. In fact, it must be used sparingly, or it may burn young, tender seedlings or strawberry plants.

Both poultry and horse manure are considered "hot," and are valuable additions to a compost pile to help speed decomposition. Don't pile up big masses of either horse or poultry manures, however, without mixing in bedding or other green material, because much of their value can be lost by burning.

You may find it more convenient to use commercially dried manures. Although they are more expensive, they are easier to use, less smelly, and contain no weed seeds.

To get the speediest growth possible, a great amount of fertilizer is essential. It must be in a form that is readily available for plant growth, however. New organic gardeners are sometimes surprised if, after using hundreds of pounds of expensive bonemeal, rock phosphate, kelp, green sand, and partly rotted compost, their gardens do not resemble those shown in the seed catalogs. All of the excellent materials they applied, unfortunately, were not able to help the plants because they take several months to decompose into a form that can be used. It is best to put them on in the fall and till them in so that they will be available to the plants a season later.

Although great amounts of fertilizer are good, too much can be applied, especially when it is chemical fertilizer. Gardeners have been known to reason that if a few pounds of 5-10-10 work well, twice as much of 15-15-15 would do an even better job. They are likely to be disappointed, because even a tiny bit too much will "burn" the plants, and may kill them.

A soil full of organic humus is full of earthworms that bring trace elements up from the subsoil in adequate amounts, so additional applications of these minerals are not necessary.

Soil that is well supplied with manures and rich compost should be adequately fertile, but sometimes it doesn't supply quite enough push to give plants a quick start and the necessary speedy growth in early summer. Some gardeners use liquid chemical fertilizers for this purpose: Rapid-Gro, Peter's Soluble Fertilizer, Miracle-Gro, and others. Organic gardeners prefer liquid fish oil, liquid seaweed solution, or a manure tea made of dried or farm manure mixed with water. Water the plant with any of these every week or two during the first four to six weeks of the growing season.

THE BENEFITS OF COMPOSTING

A good compost pile recycles wastes from the garden and yard, as well as kitchen scraps, creating *free*

COMPOST WITHOUT A PILE

Do you plan to purchase a new shrub or tree? The summer or fall prior to planting, dig the hole bigger than you think it needs to be. Layer it with composting materials and soil, building a small compost pile. Mulch lightly. In spring, the rich friable soil in the hole will come out easily and be ready to feed your new tree or shrub.

Make compost for fruit trees right under the trees. Leave a space three feet from the trunk, then layer materials for composting from there out to one foot beyond the drip line, about two feet high. The "doughnut" will feed the tree as it decomposes and do double duty as a mulch.

Sheet composting eliminates carting. Spread leaves, manure, grass clippings, weeds, spent plants, and kitchen wastes directly on the soil and till them in. In cold climates, this is a good way to dispose of autumn leaves that bury lawns. Run a mower over the leaves first, and they'll decompose more quickly.

Try strip composting. Heap organic matter and manure on top of vegetable rows from which early crops have been harvested. The next season simply leave the composted material where it is, and at intervals scoop out a small hole for a shovelful of soil. Plant squash or cucumbers, or other heavy feeders, such as cabbage.

fertilizer for the garden, saving money, and lessening the need for outside fertilizers. Composting also helps the community because it reduces the amount of garbage other people have to deal with.

Good compost makes excellent fertilizer because in addition to some important nitrogen, phosphorus, and potassium, it often contains trace elements you don't ordinarily find in commercial fertilizer. With a wide variety of materials (coffee grounds, wastes from fruits and vegetables, wood ashes, etc.) in your compost pile, you're apt to get a good sampling of the secondary and minor nutrients needed for plant growth. You shouldn't have any worries about deficiencies of trace minerals in your soil.

The best compost pile will heat up and start to decompose the material in it *fast*. Research shows that the longer a compost pile sits, the less useful it will be for your garden. What happens is that the nutrients leach steadily through the pile into the ground. Later, when you put the compost in the garden, it hasn't got much fertilizer zing to it.

In the decomposition process, a compost pile gets pretty hot. On a cool fall morning, you may see the steam rising from the center of the pile. A pile that is decomposing well will produce temperatures of 140 to 160°F. At these temperatures weed seeds and many plant disease organisms are killed. But high heat is not crucial; a good compost pile will break down material at much lower temperatures.

Compost piles rarely have a bad smell and shouldn't attract pests if you never put meat scraps or bones in the pile. Odors can occur when a pile is too big or packed too tightly and air can't circulate. Provide a good flow of air into and through the pile. (See chapter 15 for building plans for a three-bin compost system.)

All Compost Piles Need an Activator

To get a compost pile working, it's essential to have several layers of an activator throughout the pile. An activator is a source of both nitrogen and protein — ingredients that help all the various microorganisms and bacteria break down compost material.

Alfalfa meal is one of the cheapest, quickest-acting activators. If you can't find any at your garden or feed store, look in the supermarket for Litter Green, a kitty litter product that's 100 percent alfalfa meal.

Every time you add new material to the compost pile, dust it thoroughly with alfalfa meal and moisten the pile a little. Alfalfa meal is an excellent source of nitrogen and protein. It is made from alfalfa hay and is usually 14 to 16 percent protein. Besides alfalfa meal, good activators include barnyard manure, natural products such as bonemeal, cottonseed meal, blood meal, and good, rich garden soil. Anytime you add to your compost pile, dust the works with a little activator.

RECIPE FOR COMPOST

To get organic material to compost properly, you should mix materials so that the mixture is about thirty parts of carbon to one part of nitrogen. There is nothing precise about this, but gardeners should be aware that a mixture with too much carbon, such as a pile of leaves, will not heat up, while a mixture with too much nitrogen will manufacture ammonia — and the nitrogen will be wasted.

In the following list, the figure given is the amount of carbon per one part of nitrogen:

Straw	150–500
Ground corn cobs	50–100
Sawdust	150–500
Pine needles	60–110
Oak leaves	50
Young weeds	30
Grass clippings	25
Manure with bedding	25
Vegetable trimmings	25
Animal droppings	15
Leguminous plants	15

COMPOSTING SYSTEMS AT A GLANCE

Type	Advantages	Disadvantages
Slow outdoor pile	Easy to start and add to. Low maintenance.	Can take a year or more to decompose. Nutrients are lost to leaching. Can be odorous and attract animals and flies.
Hot outdoor pile	Fast decomposition. Weed seeds and pathogens are killed. More nutrient-rich because less leaching of nutrients. Less likely to attract animals and flies.	Requires lots of effort to turn and aerate and manage the process. Works best when you have lots of material to add right away, as opposed to a little bit at a time.
Bins and boxes	Neat appearance. Holds heat more easily than a pile. Deters animals. Lid keeps rain off compost. If turned, decomposition can be quite rapid.	Costs you time to build the bins or money to buy them.
Tumblers	Self-contained and not messy. Can produce quick compost. Relatively easy to aerate by turning the tumbler. Odor not usually a problem. No nutrient leaching into ground.	Tumblers are costly. Volume is relatively small. Works best if material is added all at once.
Pit composting	Quick and easy. No maintenance. No investment in materials.	Only takes care of small amounts of organic matter.
Sheet composting	Can handle large amounts of organic matter. No containers required. Good way to improve soil in large areas.	Requires effort to till material into the soil. Takes several months to decompose.
Plastic bag or garbage can	Easy to do year-round. Can be done in a small space. Can be done indoors. Requires no back labor.	Is mostly anaerobic, so smell can be a problem. Can attract fruit flies. Need to pay attention to carbon/nitrogen ratio to avoid a slimy mess.
Worm composter	Easy. No odor. Can be done indoors. Can be added to continuously. So nutrient-rich it can be used as a fertilizer. Good way to compost food waste.	Requires some care when adding materials and removing castings. Need to protect worms from temperature extremes. Can attract fruit flies.

EASY COMPOSTING SYSTEM

1. Set up a wire collector. Choose a well-drained spot, preferably a shady one that's not too far from the house or garden. It's nice to be near a water source, too. Set up a wire collector for your pile. A good choice is strong turkey wire with a 2-inch or 4-inch mesh and a height of 3 feet. Cut off a 9-foot section of mesh and shape it into a circle, fastening the ends together. If you want, you can loosen the soil up a little where the collector sits. This will help drainage.

2. Make the first layer. Loosely place leaves, hay, straw, or other good compost materials in the bottom of the collector in a layer about 2 inches thick.

3. Add protein material. Sprinkle a large handful of alfalfa meal or other protein-rich meal over the first layer. Dust the entire surface.

4. Do it again. Repeat steps 2 and 3 by adding the same amounts of organic matter and meal as before.

5. Sprinkle with water. Moisten the pile thoroughly. Compost piles that don't work are usually too dry or too wet. The material should be moist but not soaked. In warm, dry weather you may have to water the pile every three or four days to keep it in good working condition.

6. Keep the center loose. Never compact the center of the pile — keep it loose. The composting process depends on the ability of the air, water, and activator to contact all the material as completely as possible. Good circulation is a must. A good compost pile is a balance of thirds; one third air, one third material, and one third moisture.

7. Fill the collector. Whenever material becomes available, repeat steps 2 through 6, until the collec-

tor is full. Keep everything loose and never tightly packed down.

8. Turn the pile in a week. If the pile is made correctly, the temperature should reach 140 to 150°F. within two or three days. After a week or so of heating and decomposing, it's time to turn the pile.

Lift off the wire collector, set it up beside the pile, and then fork all the material back into it. Put the outside, drier material in the center of the new pile. If the material seems *too* dry, moisten it. The heating process will start up again. It should be ready to use — but still coarse — in 15 days.

LOW-COST SOIL BUILDERS

While green manure crops and composted materials from around the house will help a good deal in building a soil of lasting fertility, many gardeners find the need to go further afield to secure quan-

LEAF MOLD

In a hurry-up world, the making of leaf mold is largely forgotten. Because leaves have little nitrogen, they decompose slowly and do not heat up as they would do if high-nitrogen material is added to them.

The two-year process of decomposition can be hastened by running the leaves through a shredder before piling them. Fence in the pile with wire netting to keep the leaves from spreading back across your lawn. Stamp the pile down. Expect to see it half its original size when the leaves have turned to leaf mold and are ready for use.

After a year, turn the pile, cutting and mixing it as much as possible. In this stage it can be used as a mulch, and will be welcomed by the earthworms in your garden.

tities of soil-building organic matter.

The next most immediate source of materials is in your neighborhood. People are often glad to give away raked **leaves** for the favor of not having to haul them to the local landfill. The same is often true of **lawn clippings. Ashes** from your fireplace and woodstove are high in phosphorus and potassium.

If you live near the sea, **seaweed** is free for the gathering and is a very valuable source of trace minerals as well as readily available organic matter.

Folks in the country can sometimes obtain **manure** at a low cost by offering to clean out a neighbor's horse stable, chicken coop, or pig pen.

WOOD ASHES

Don't forget the final, valuable product from your wood stove — the wood ashes.

They're a valuable source of potash. If you bought them as you might buy commercial fertilizers, bagged and ready for use, the bag would be marked 0-1.5-8, with that latter figure, indicating the percentage of potash, varying from 1 to 10.

Remember that ashes are very alkaline, and so have the same effect as if you spread lime on your soil. For this reason don't spread them heavily in one spot, or where you will raise acid-loving plants, such as potatoes and blueberries.

About 10 pounds per 100 square feet is a good quantity. Before planting, work them into the top two or three inches of soil.

To get the most from your ashes, store them where the rain won't leach away the potash. A metal trash can is fine. Don't use flammable containers. House and barn fires have started from "dead" ashes stored in flammable containers.

GRASS CLIPPINGS: IDEAL FOR IMPROVING GARDEN SOIL

Grass clippings can be a great soil amendment if handled properly. Don't leave fresh clippings in a pile, or they will quickly turn to a smelly, brown mess. And, don't pile them too high, either, if you're using them as mulch, or the same thing will happen.

Here are several ways to use them:

- Add them to the compost pile. They'll give you the nitrogen you need to make the pile "cook." Mix them well with other materials, such as weeds, leaves, or hay.

- Spread them around the garden area, then till them in. They're an excellent green manure.

- Spread them in thin layers when green, or let them dry before spreading them in the garden, and they'll provide one of the best mulches you can find.

Even the local barber shop can be a source of fertility for the garden. **Human hair** contains about 12 percent nitrogen and will help speed the decomposition of other organic materials in the garden. If you provide a separate container and make regular collections, the barber just might be willing to save his refuse and give you a free supply of clean, light, rich organic matter.

Consider also the manufacturing activities in your area. A shoe factory will have quantities of **leather scraps,** a potent source of nitrogen that will decompose quickly in compost. **Apple pomace** from cider pressing is high in potassium and phosphorus, which are basic plant foods. **Brewer's waste** from beer making is also rich in potassium.

Feathers from poultry processing contain about 15 percent nitrogen, while egg shells contain roughly 1 percent. Scraps and lint from wool and cotton cloth manufacture also contain fertilizing elements.

Cannery wastes are another good source of organic matter. **Pea** and **bean pods, potato skins, corn cobs, peanut shells, fish scraps** and the like will all boost soil fertility.

The **waste from the local supermarket** can be a fortune in free organic materials for you. To please the eye of the shopping public, produce managers trim away unsightly parts of vegetables and discard all but the best produce. The culls are generally free for the asking. It is best to provide your own container and collect the refuse regularly. What can't be sold can be recycled through the soil into vegetables far better than you could find in any market.

Saw mills can also supply you with organic materials for free or at a minimal cost. Keep in mind that **tree wastes** are largely deficient in nitrogen and some fertilizing elements will have to be added to hasten decay of wood materials. In order to keep saw blades sharp longer, most mills use debarking machines to peel off the outer layers of the logs and the dirt and stones stuck in the bark. This bark will be coarse and should probably be composted first, using a liberal dosage of nitrogen. Screen the finished product well to remove inorganic debris.

Sawdust will cost a few cents per cubic foot as it has other uses, such as for animal bedding. Unless your garden soil is already in a high state of fertility, avoid incorporating sawdust into the soil as nitrogen necessary for good plant growth will become tied up in the decay of the sawdust. When the sawdust is used as a mulch material, this fixation will be less likely to occur. Sawdust is an easy mulch to apply to give uniform coverage around plants and makes for a very attractive garden. If the plants begin to slow in their growth and exhibit a yellowing of the foliage, a nitrogen deficit probably exists and can be corrected with a side dressing of high-nitrogen fertilizer.

FERTILIZER POSSIBILITIES

If your garden soil tests show shortages of nutrients, you can eliminate those shortages through the application of organic fertilizers.

Manures, while they vary greatly in the percentages of nutrients, have one thing in common — application of them will overcome those shortages — and improve the texture of your soil as well. Manures range from the "hot" 2.5-1.4-0.6 of rabbit manure to the "cold" 0.5-0.3-0.5 of pig manure.

Manure should be applied much more heavily than is the practice of most gardeners. One hundred pounds of cow manure per 100 square feet of garden space is about right; use half this amount if spreading the "hot" chicken manure and litter.

If you are trying to overcome specific shortages, select from this list. (The substances set in italic type are those with the greatest percentages of the nutrients.)

Nitrogen

Cottonseed meal	Brewery wastes
Dried blood	Peanut shells
Hair and feathers	Animal urines
Bone tankage	

Phosphoric Acid

Rock phosphate	Dried blood
Bonemeal	Wood ashes
Apple and citrus wastes	Fish

Potash

Granite dust	Garbage
Greensand	Hay and leaves
Wood ashes	Melon rinds

PREPARING A NEW GARDEN SITE

Choosing the right tool to prepare a new garden site will lighten the chore and help you finish the job sooner. The best tool for working the soil is a round-pointed shovel. It's easy to drive into the soil and chop clumps of earth, and it's usually lighter than other digging tools. Choose a shovel with a long handle so you won't have to bend much to dig up and turn the sod.

The spading shovel is a good tool for cutting and digging a straight border around your garden because it has a sharp flat edge. That's about all it's good for. The spading fork has four strong tines. It's good for preparing soil in an established garden. It will break up clumps of soil easily. The spading fork is also good for loosening any layers of hard-packed soil or hardpan below your topsoil.

You don't need all three tools, of course. The long-handled round-pointed shovel will do most jobs very well.

Turn over new sections of the garden *in the fall* to expose weed seeds and to give roots and grass sod a chance to decompose over the winter.

If you can't work the soil in the fall, don't fret. You can turn over new ground in the spring and still plant a garden. There will probably be more weeds to contend with during the first season, though.

Preparing a New Garden Bed

1. Stake out the dimensions of your new garden.

2. Starting at the outside edge (with your back to the garden site), turn up a chunk of sod and earth. Continue digging across the width of the garden.

THE IDEAL SITE FOR A VEGETABLE GARDEN

A vegetable garden needs:

■ day-long sun (at least eight hours)

■ good drainage (a slight slope to the south is ideal)

■ protection from cold wind

Keep it away from trees (their roots will steal nutrients from the garden) and as near to the kitchen as practicable. You'll take better care of a garden that is close to the house. You won't have to walk as far to and from the garden, so you'll spend more time there, gather crops more conveniently, and be on the lookout for garden problems and pests.

Try a salad garden — perhaps a small raised bed — just outside the kitchen door. Plant ruby and green looseleaf lettuce, romaine, two pepper plants, two Pixie tomato plants, herbs such as basil (sweet and opal), chives, parsley (curly and Italian), and a few marigolds. Put a couple of stepping stones in the center. Often-used herbs are just a snip away, and the palette of greens and varied textures makes a garden as eye-pleasing as any purely ornamental planting.

3. Place all soil from this first row in a garden cart. When you finish you'll have an open furrow down one edge of your garden.

4. To start the next row, face the open furrow with your back to the garden site and again dig into the sod. Turn this chunk upside down into the open furrow.

By flipping every chunk into the open furrow

ahead, you make sure that all the roots and pieces of sod end up below the soil where they will decompose.

5. Dig up the rest of the garden, always turning the sod upside down into the open furrow in front of you.

6. After you've dug the soil out of the last furrow, take the garden cart with the sod chunks to the last row and turn the sod pieces upside down into the open furrow.

7. After a couple of days, chop up the clumps as well as you can with a strong hoe. It pays to do this several times.

Some gardeners handle sod in a new garden differently. They dig up the sod pieces, shake out the soil over the garden and toss the grass and roots into the compost pile. The green matter increases the nitrogen content of the pile, and the soil clinging to the grass roots helps activate the heap.

If you remove sod from the garden site, you'll find the soil a little easier to dig and smooth out for planting and you'll probably have fewer weeds, too.

8. In subsequent years, it's a good policy to spade the garden at least twice before planting. The first time, dig in 6 or 8 inches, turn the soil over into the holes, and break up any big clumps of soil.

After a week or so, spade the area again, but only to *half the depth* of your first spading. This makes for easier spading, but also gets rid of many weeds in the top two or three inches of soil and helps keep it loose and aerated for planting day.

If you have enough time to do this half-depth spading two or three times before planting day, go ahead. It will pay off in reduced weeding and it will keep the soil loose and crumbly.

ALL ABOUT PLANTING

Bird song fills the air, and the yearning to plant consumes you. Here's where restraint is needed, before the elixir of damp earth intoxicates you. Chant "Wait, wait," and check to see if the soil is dry enough to be worked. Scoop up a handful and squeeze. Open your hand. If the soil sticks together, it is still too wet. If it crumbles when poked, it is ready.

Never work wet soil, especially clay. You may ruin its structure for the entire season and end up tripping over solid, sun-baked clods instead of early lettuce.

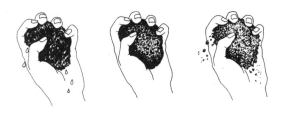

The "fist test" is the simplest way to tell if your garden is dry enough to be tilled.

If you pick up a handful of soil and can squeeze water from it, it is obviously too wet. If the soil compresses into a ball and stays that way, it needs more drying time. If it is dry enough to crumble in your hand, it is "friable" and is ready to be worked.

Did you incorporate lots of organic matter into the soil in fall? If you do that every year, you will find increasing ease of preparation in spring, as your soil becomes more spongy and fluffy. It will also be ready to work earlier in the spring.

TIPS ON TIMING — WHEN TO PLANT

Cool weather crops — peas, spinach, lettuce, onions, garlic, and brassicas — can go in as soon as the ground can be worked. Although beets, carrots, chard, and radishes can grow in cold soil, they are likely to be decimated by tiny flea beetles. They seem to appreciate a couple of week's grace.

Don't try to plant the rest of your garden too early. If the seeds manage to sprout before rotting in cold soil, the plants will probably struggle, and you will fuss and sputter. Most crops need soil that has warmed up.

Find out the average date of the last spring frost in your area (ask your Agricultural Extension Agent). Wait until then to plant beans, sweet corn, and New Zealand spinach.

Crops that need thoroughly warm soil are cucumbers, squash, melons, tomatoes, peppers, eggplants, and lima beans. Wait at least a week after the average date of the last frost before setting them in the garden (unless you are willing to provide

AVERAGE SPRING FROST DATES

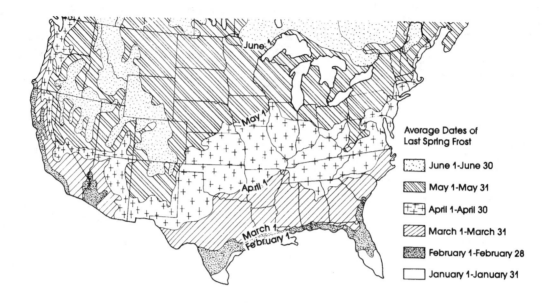

Average Dates of
Last Spring Frost

	June 1-June 30
	May 1-May 31
	April 1-April 30
	March 1-March 31
	February 1-February 28
	January 1-January 31

hotcaps or some other kind of protection; see pages 9 to 11).

SEED TESTING

Before you invest a lot of time and effort with pots, shovels, and soil, it's a good idea to know that your seed is likely to grow. Commercial growers have all kinds of complicated equipment for testing seeds, but you can accomplish a lot with a few common household items.

Start by placing a disk of white blotting paper or flat paper towel in a shallow dish. Wet the paper, scatter 25 to 100 seeds, and cover with another piece of paper and then with an inverted dish or piece of glass. Keep the project at room temperature and gently add water periodically to keep the paper moist.

After the third day, gently remove the upper paper. Count the number of seeds that have sprouted. Keep checking every day for a couple of weeks.

The number of seeds that actually sprout will indicate how viable your seed is. This will also give you a better idea of how to distribute your seeds; a vigorous batch of seeds can be spread more thinly than one with a lower sprouting rate.

Seeds from your germination test need not be wasted. You can always plant the sprouts.

SEED HANDLING TECHNIQUES

Many seeds require special handling, so there are a few tricks you should know to ensure that your seeds will sprout. If you are buying commercial seed, check the package or ask your nurseryman if your selections require any special handling.

Scarification. Seeds with especially hard outer shells often benefit from a little abuse. Scarification involves nicking the outer shell with a file, knife, or sandpaper to make it easier for the plant to start growing. It takes a little practice to make a cut that's deep enough to be effective, but not so deep that you damage the tiny plant embryo inside.

Nick hard-shelled seeds with a file.

Soaking. Many seeds sprout more readily if they are soaked before planting, because this helps to soften hard seed coats. Soaking peas, corn, and beans is a popular practice, but not always desirable. It is very important not to soak the seeds too long (overnight is usually enough). If the seed becomes waterlogged, it is likely to decay when planted in moist or cold soil.

A quick hot water treatment is often effective. Pour three or four times the seed volume worth of water at 190–212°F. over the seed and leave it to cool overnight before sowing.

Stratification. Plants often need a recreation of natural cycles for seeds to grow. Natives of cold climates often drop their seeds in the fall, but don't start growing until spring. They expect moist, warm or cold, and sometimes even freezing conditions before they'll start growing. The simplest practice is to place the seeds in a sealed container or plastic bag with four or five times their volume of moist (not dripping) peat moss or vermiculite. Place the container in a warm spot for warm stratification, or in the refrigerator for cold stratification (in the freezer if 32°F. temperature is required). After the first month or so, examine the seed every few weeks to see if germination has started. When small, white primary roots appear, the seed should be sown in soil or potting mixture immediately. On a larger scale, you can place layers of seeds between layers of sand in a plastic can and bury the can in the ground under a layer of leaves for the winter.

Germinate seeds in a container with moist vermiculite.

Cold stratification requires temperatures of 35–40°F. for various periods, depending on the species, usually a few months. Warm stratification calls for temperatures of 68–86°F., usually for a few weeks to a month or two. For warm or cold stratification, the seed must be kept moist.

SOWING SEEDS INDOORS

Why start seeds indoors? There are a number of reasons. Many annuals and vegetables have such a long growing season that they won't flower or fruit if they don't get a head start indoors, especially in the North. Others may not need to be started indoors, but will flower or be productive for a much longer time if started early. Plants with fine seeds should be started indoors to protect them from the ravages of weather. Indoor seed starting eliminates worrying about weeds, insects, diseases, and excessive heat. When intercropping, you'll make more productive use of your land if you start with plants instead of seeds.

Annuals that must be started indoors include begonia, coleus, geranium, impatiens, lobelia, African marigold, petunia, salpiglossis, salvia, browallia, ornamental pepper, vinca, gerbera, lobelia, monkey flower, cupflower, poor-man's orchid, wishbone flower, pansy, and verbena.

While many vegetables are sown directly into the garden bed, others must be started indoors since the growing season, in all but the warmest parts of the country, is not long enough for them to produce. These include broccoli, Brussels sprouts, cabbage, cauliflower, celery, eggplant, leeks, okra, peppers, and tomatoes. Lettuce, onions, and melons are often started indoors as well.

For starting plants inside, it is important to have either a good, sunny window with a southern exposure or some cool-white fluorescent bulbs. Keep heaters and heating ducts in mind as you select a place to start your plants. If there is a heater directly under your seed-starting window, your seedlings will dry out very quickly, and you will have to water them quite often.

Containers

There are all kinds of seed-starting containers for sale: peat pots, Jiffy Sevens (little cubes complete with soil), and flats. You can also use tin cans, milk cartons, and egg boxes. A lot of people use cardboard egg boxes, but they absorb a lot of water, which causes plants to dry out too quickly. The egg boxes that work best are the ones made of polysty-

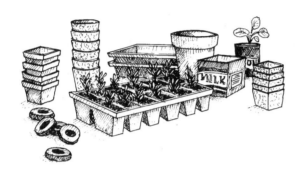

rene. Try cutting the cover off and setting the bottom part of the box inside the cover. This double reinforcement will make the box more solid.

Any container used for starting seeds must have holes in the bottom to allow excess water to escape. Most purchased pots and flats already have them. Peat pots, being very absorbent, drain readily, even without holes. Poke a dozen holes in an egg container with something sharp, like a nail. If you're using a large container, like a two-quart milk carton, make some holes in the bottom, then put in about half an inch of gravel or crushed stone before you add soil.

Start your sowing process by assembling your containers and making sure they are clean and have drainage holes.

If the container is made of fiber or peat, it must be soaked thoroughly before a growing medium is placed in it or it will act as a wick and pull moisture out of the medium later on. Fill the container with water and allow it to absorb all that it can, draining off the rest, or place the flat or pot in a larger container of water until it has absorbed all it can. When

the flat is thoroughly moistened, place a layer of stones or gravel in the bottom.

To judge how many seed flats to prepare, use this rule of thumb: A 5½" x 7½" flat will hold a hundred seedlings from large seeds, two hundred seedlings from medium seeds, and three hundred seedlings from fine seeds. Always sow about twice as many seeds as the number of plants you want since all of the seeds won't germinate, and some seedlings will be lost in the thinning and transplanting processes.

The container should be filled with premoistened sowing medium to within ¼ inch of the top. You can wet the grow mix in a plastic bag or a pot before placing it into the container (4 cups of grow mix and 1½ cups of water should be enough for one 5½" x 7½" flat). Or you can put it in the container dry and let it draw up water from the bottom. Do this slowly so the grow mix won't separate. Dry grow mix is very difficult to evenly moisten with top watering. Once the medium is moist, make sure it is leveled out and patted down firmly, especially in the corners.

At this point, it is a good idea to drench the sowing medium with a solution of benomyl fungicide (½ tablespoon per gallon of water) to prevent "damping-off" disease. The mix should be moist but not wet for sowing; if the soil is allowed to drain for approximately 2 hours after moistening and drenching, it should be perfect.

Fiber and peat containers and sowing medium should never be reused for seed sowing, for they may not be sterile. Any leftover soil mix from previous sowings can be used for transplanting or in containers. If compressed peat pellets are to be used, soak them in water until they reach full size, which will take only minutes.

Growing Media

Seeds can be started in any of several soil mixtures or in soil substitutes, such as vermiculite or sifted sphagnum. Seeds started in these sterile soil-less mediums are protected from damping off; just be sure to transplant the seedlings to a soil mixture which will provide adequate nutrients as soon as the first true leaves appear. Some good commercial soil mixes (based on the excellent Cornell Mix) are Redi-Earth, Jiffy Mix, Pro-Mix.

You can use good garden soil in your mix, but you may have to lighten it with sand or peat moss.

To make a batch of Cornell Mix at home, blend together 4 quarts of shredded peat moss or sphagnum, 2 level tablespoons of ground limestone, and 4 level tablespoons of 5-10-10 fertilizer.

For a large batch of soil, you might mix two bales of peat moss, three 4-cubic-foot bags of vermiculite, 6 pounds of 5-10-10 fertilizer, 2 pounds superphosphate, and 5 pounds agricultural lime. To mix large batches, shovel roughly mixed ingredients from one cone-shaped pile to another, adding each shovelful to the top of the pile and allowing soil to tumble down the sides of the cone.

Here's a simple mix: 1 part loam, 1 part clean sand or perlite, and 1 part leaf mold or moist peat.

Sterilizing Soil

Sterilizing soil kills off weed seeds and potentially harmful disease organisms, but it is a messy job. Pasteurizing is a partial sterilization, generally intended to kill off disease organisms, but retain some of the beneficial organisms. Large quantities of soil can be fumigated with chemicals. Be sure to follow manufacturer's instructions exactly.

Smaller amounts of soil can be sterilized in the oven. Put soil in a shallow tray and bake at 350°F. for 1½ hours. Shallow containers take less time. To test, place a potato in the soil; when it is done, soil is ready. It's a good idea to keep a thermometer on hand. Soil is pasteurized when it reaches 140–145°F. Complete sterilization occurs at 180–185°F. If the soil is overcooked, compost or other organic fertilizer can restore many beneficial microorganisms.

Alternate methods: Thoroughly soak the soil and bake at 275°F. until the surface begins to cake (about one hour). Or place the soil in a flat, pour in boiling water, cover, and let it sit for about 30 minutes. You may need to drain it through a fine mesh sieve, if it's too wet. It is important to let the soil cool before use.

Sowing Seeds

Fill a flat to within ¼ inch of the top with potting mixture and level the surface with a flat board (A). If you are going to plant the seeds in rows, use the edge of the board to make ¼-inch troughs in the soil. Otherwise, spread the seed over the soil, evenly and not too thickly (B), then press them in with the flat side of the board. Cover them, remembering that they should be buried to a depth of about four times their own diameter (C). Obviously, very fine seeds will require very shallow covering. Try to make sure that you spread an equal amount of soil over the

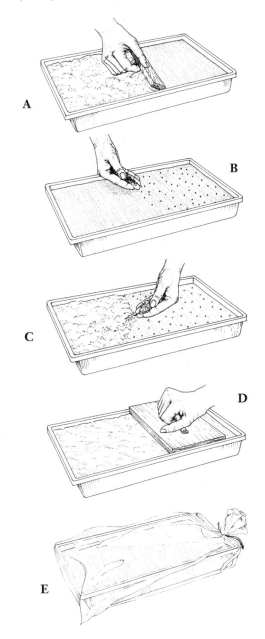

whole area. Use a flat board to firm the soil a second time (D).

Newly planted seeds should be watered liberally but gently — preferably with a fine spray that will not disturb them. Next, the flats or pots should be put in plastic bags (E) or covered with plastic to seal in moisture. You should not have to do any more watering until the seedlings come up. Put them in a place where the temperature remains in the neighborhood of 70–75°F.

You can put heating cables and trays under the germinating containers, whether that be on a windowsill or countertop or under fluorescent lights. The cables will heat the flats to 70–75°F. When the flat gets warm enough (add a thermometer to your equipment list), simply pull the plug. Some have a built-in thermostat which automatically turns the system on and off. Waterproof soil heating cables can also be used in outdoor beds and cold frames.

If seeds are germinated indoors during the heat of summer, room temperatures will probably go high enough so that heating cables and heating trays will not be necessary (unless the house is air conditioned).

When cool temperatures are required, germinate the seeds indoors in an unheated garage, attic, basement, or porch which must, of course, have a source of natural or artificial light. Outdoors, this temperature is achieved in early spring or fall. Sow directly into seed beds, or set the flats outside in a spot protected from sun and wind, or in a cold frame.

Moisture and Humidity

Moisture and humidity are critical for seed germination. The germinating medium must be kept evenly moist, but never soaking wet. If there is too little moisture, germination will not occur; too much and the seeds will rot. If a good medium is used, watered thoroughly and allowed to drain for several hours before sowing, the moisture level should be perfect.

It is best to slip your seed flats into plastic bags or cover them with glass until the seeds germinate.

This will keep the level of moisture and humidity just right, so the seed flats will not have to be watered often, if at all, before germination. This will eliminate the problems caused by overwatering, forgetfulness, or accidentally dislodging tiny seeds before they germinate.

Light

The final environmental factor, but one equally as important as the others, is light. Some seeds require light to germinate, while others need a complete absence of it to sprout. If light is needed for germination, the solution is not to cover the seeds. If darkness is necessary, cover the seeds completely with medium, unless they are too fine to be covered. In that instance, place the seed flats in total

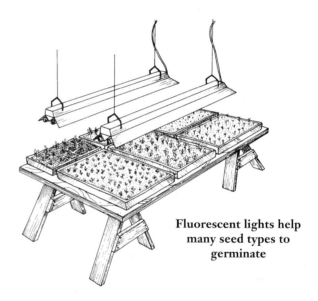

Fluorescent lights help many seed types to germinate

darkness or cover them with a material like newspaper or black plastic to block out the light until germination occurs.

Once germinated, all seedlings need ample light to develop into strong, healthy plants. In fact, seedlings have the highest light intensity requirements of all plants. Using fluorescent lights or growing seedlings in a greenhouse is best, but if you do not have these available, an unshaded south window will do well.

Light is necessary to enable the plants to convert water and carbon dioxide into sugar (its food)

PLANTING HINTS

- Soak seeds of beets, Swiss chard, and peas for 15 to 20 minutes before planting. Soak parsley, New Zealand spinach, and celery seed overnight to hasten germination.

- Make multiple plantings of lettuce. Looseleaf lettuces are quicker and easier to grow than heading types. Plant Romaine for a crunchy, meatier leaf that does quite well in hot weather.

- Start seeds of buttercrunch lettuce in beds. Transplant seedlings 8 inches apart in all the empty spaces in the garden — between rows of onions, or between young brassicas.

- Plant early lettuce between asparagus rows.

- Does spinach bolt too soon in your garden? Try New Zealand spinach, which does better in warm weather, or grow Malabar spinach on a fence or trellis.

- Leaf crops like lettuce, spinach, chard, and parsley do well in partially shaded locations.

- Always treat your legume seed with an inoculant before planting. It adds a fresh culture of nitrogen-fixing bacteria to the seed, which will increase yield and quality of peas and beans. Moisten seeds and shake with the powder just before planting.

- For earliest peas, prepare the planting trench in fall. In spring, just push seed into the soil.

- For no-work peas, early in the season, till up a 10-foot square of your garden. Scatter 1 pound of a shorter-bushed pea, such as Little Marvel. Till or rake in the peas, then walk over the soil. No need for fences or other support — the peas will support each other. You should harvest 50 pounds of pods from that tiny space.

- For the vegetable that requires the least effort to grow, plant a few tubers of Jerusalem-artichoke in a bed in one corner of your garden. Dig them up in the fall or early spring. You'll miss a few — and they'll grow to provide your crop for the next season.

- Lima beans need warm soil. Pre-sprout seeds before planting to reduce chances of their rotting in the garden.

- To start brassicas in the garden, put sticks in the ground 18 inches apart. Plant a few seeds by each stick. Gradually thin to one plant per stick. Plant the empty spots between the sticks with lettuce or spinach, which will be harvested by the time the brassicas need more space.

- Learn to recognize "volunteers." Once you plant dill, you'll never have to plant it again. Let seeds from a few flower heads scatter each year.

- For potatoes without digging, place seed potatoes 1 foot apart on top of last year's mulch, or on a few inches of leaves, preferably shredded. Cover with a foot of loose hay. When the tops die down, just rake off the hay.

- Stick seeds of winter squash in a partly finished compost pile. The squash plants camouflage the pile, which gives the squashes nourishment and the room they need to sprawl.

VEGETABLES SUITABLE FOR TRANSPLANTING AND METHODS OF SOWING SEED

Easy to transplant. Can be sown in flat in rows and transplanted bare root.

Vegetable	Weeks from sowing to transplanting
Broccoli	(5–7)
Brussels sprouts	(5–7)
Cabbage	(5–7)
Cauliflower	(5–7)
Celeriac	(7–12)
Celery	(7–12)
Chinese Cabbage	(5–7)
Collards	(5–7)
*Eggplant	(6–8)
Lettuce	(5–7)
Onion	(8–10)
Parsley	(8–10)
*Peppers	(6–8)
Sweet Potato	(3–4)
(Start from tuber and not seed)	
*Tomato	(6–8)

Must be started in individual containers and transplanted without disturbing roots.

Cantaloupe	(3–4)
(all muskmelons) (3–4)	
Cucumbers	(3–4)
Squash	(3–4)
(summer & winter)	
Watermelon	(5–7)

* Sometimes sown in flats and then transplanted into individual containers before transplanting to garden.

( ) Number in parentheses is approximate time (weeks) from sowing seed to transplanting to garden.

---

in a process known as photosynthesis. If the light intensity is too low, which often happens during the short days of winter or prolonged cloudy periods, the plants will be unhealthy, tall, and spindly.

Germinating

Once your seed flat is ready, place it in a location where it will receive the proper light and temperature for seed germination. If you have an area in the house, such as a spare room, attic, or basement, where your seed garden would be out of sight and where a water spill or other accident wouldn't cause a problem, so much the better. If you will be using a windowsill, it's wise to protect it from moisture and watch for extreme changes in temperature.

With very few exceptions, seed flats should be placed in good light but not in direct sun while germination is taking place, or under fluorescent lights.

The use of a soil thermometer will ensure that the medium is the right temperature for germinating.

The germination times given in the table on the left are average ones and may vary by 25 percent in either direction, depending on environmental factors. Don't give up too early if your seeds don't germinate. If, however, too much time has gone by, try to figure out what went wrong and start again.

Even though the glass or plastic covering on the seed flat should minimize the need for watering, check the medium once in a while to make sure it isn't drying out.

Condensation on the plastic or glass does not necessarily mean the flat has been overwatered; a change in temperature may cause moisture to form. Feel the medium to be sure. If it is too wet, leave the glass or plastic off for several hours to dry it a little, and then cover it again. Don't, however, let the growing medium dry out completely at any time.

Once the seeds have started to germinate, remove the plastic or glass from the seed flats. Gradually move the seedlings into full sun or strong light; sudden changes in light may injure tender seedlings.

Germinating Under Lights

If you have the space, germinating seeds under lights is the more productive method. You won't have to worry about short and cloudy days or limited space on windowsills. Light gardens can be situated anywhere as long as electricity is nearby and the temperature is right.

You can purchase one of the many fluorescent lights available for indoor gardens, bur since seedlings need light in the blue and green area of the spectrum to grow properly (yellow, orange, and red wavelengths promote flowering), you can also use common household cool white lights. (See chapter 15 for building plans for a lighted indoor potting stand.)

Except for those seeds requiring darkness to germinate, place seedling flats under lights for 24 hours per day until germination occurs. After that, the light duration should be cut down to 12 to 14 hours per day. Once the plants start to grow, the light source should be 3 to 6 inches above the top of the seedlings. To accomplish this, you'll need a system to either raise the lights or lower the shelves as the plants grow.

If the leaves turn downward or look burned during growth, the lights are too close. If the seedlings are starting to grow tall and spindly, the lights are too far away.

Seedling Care

In the following weeks, how you care for your seedlings is critical. Water, of course, is most important. The root systems of the new seedlings are not yet well developed, so the medium must always be kept moist, but never completely wet, or the seedlings will suffer from poor aeration. If the medium starts to lighten in color, that is a sign that it is drying out. Check every day to see if water is needed. Watering from the bottom is best until the seedlings reach a fairly good size, since watering from above can dislodge young plants or knock them over. If you do water from above, water the medium between the seedling rows.

Most plants will grow successfully at normal

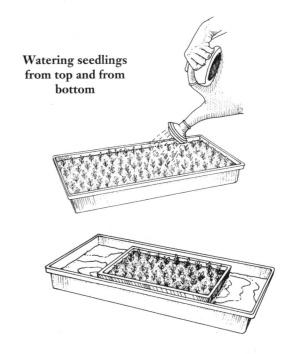

Watering seedlings from top and from bottom

room temperatures of 60 to 70°F. Those that require cooler germination temperatures will usually like cooler growing temperatures as well.

If seedlings are grown on the windowsill or at the edge of the lighted area, they should be turned regularly so they will grow straight and evenly.

Once the first true leaves have developed (the first growth you will see are the seed leaves (cotyledons), which are food storage cells), it is time to start fertilizing. No food is needed prior to this point, since the seedling is using food that was stored in the seed. Use a soluble plant food such as Hyponex, Miracle-Gro, or Peters at one-quarter the label strength when seedlings are small, increasing to one-half the label strength as the plant matures. It is better to fertilize with this weak solution once a week instead of feeding with full-strength solution once a month; growth will be more even and burning of the seedlings will be avoided. When bottom-watering young seedlings, mix the fertilizer into the water; later on, the seedlings can be fertilized from above.

Transplanting

It is possible to plant seedlings directly from the seed flat into the garden, but this is generally not advised. The seedlings should be transplanted to a larger container first or at least thinned so they will not be crowded, leggy, weak, or susceptible to damage. One transplanting is usually enough, and it will guarantee good, strong root development and easier adjustment of the plant to the garden. Seedlings started in individual pots do not need to be transplanted.

After the seedlings have developed four true leaves, it is time to transplant or thin. If thinning, leave at least 1 inch between seedlings in the flat. Larger seedlings will need more space. These seedlings may now be left to grow until it is time to transplant them into the garden, although they will benefit from transplanting at this point into their own pots.

There's one interesting fact to be aware of when thinning or transplanting seedlings: The weakest seedlings in annual mixtures such as snapdragons and phlox often produce the most unusual colors and types. For a good balance, transplant all seedlings, large and small.

When transplanting, first water the seedlings thoroughly. Peat pots, pellets, or small plastic pots are best for transplanting. If the seedlings are being transplanted into peat pots or flats, wet the containers as well, and don't forget to premoisten the medium to be used for transplanting. Seedlings can also be transplanted into flats; those with dividers or compartments lead to more compact root development and easier transplanting, without shock to the roots.

You may use the same medium you used for germinating for transplanting, or use leftover medium from previous seed sowings. It is not critical that medium for transplants be sterile.

Fill the container with pre-moistened medium to just below the top of the container. With a label stick or pencil, open a hole in the center of the medium, deep and wide enough to fit the seedling's roots.

Using a label, spoon handle, fork, or similar tool, gently lift the seedlings from the flat (A). Separate them carefully so as not to break any more roots than necessary. A small amount of medium should cling to the seedling's roots. Always handle a seedling by its leaves and *never* by its stem; if dam-

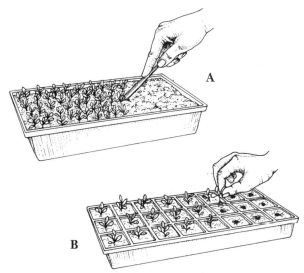

Transplanting seedlings

age is accidentally done, the seedlings will grow a new leaf, but never a new stem.

Lower the seedling into the hole you made in the medium, placing it slightly deeper than it was growing in the seed flat (B), and gently press the medium around the roots. Don't forget to label the container!

Peat pots and pellets should be set into an empty tray or flat to keep them intact and to catch excess water.

Transplants will often droop or wilt because they have lost some of their roots. They will recover quickly if properly cared for. Keep the transplants in good light but not full sun for several days, increasing the light intensity gradually. If you've transplanted during cloudy weather, the containers can go right onto the windowsill; if you grow under lights, the transplants can go under the fluorescents right away. If the plants become tall and spindly later on, they're not getting enough light.

Water when necessary, never allowing the transplants to wilt, and keeping the medium evenly moist but not soaking wet. Once a week, when watering, add soluble fertilizer at one-half the recommended label strength.

Several plants benefit from pinching while in the transplant stage. Single-stemmed plants such as snapdragons, dahlias, and chrysanthemums will be more bushy and colorful if pinched. Those that are getting too tall before the weather is right for outdoor planting should also be pinched. Simply reach into the center of the plant and nip out the growing tip.

Pinching back seedlings

Once roots start to show through the container walls, the plants are ready to be moved to the garden. If it's too early for outdoor planting, they may be held in the container for up to four weeks until the weather is right.

plants, which have been protected from wind, cool temperatures, and strong sun, and gradually gets them used to their new environment.

Move the trays or flats of potted plants outside into a sheltered, shady area such as a porch, cold frame, or under a tree or shrub. If it gets cold at night, move them back inside. After two or three days, give them half a day of sun, increasing the exposure gradually to a full day. Make sure the transplants are well watered during this hardening off period. If at all possible, don't place transplants on the ground if slugs are a problem in your area.

Hardening Off

One week before indoor-grown seedlings — raised at home or in a commercial greenhouse — are shifted outdoors to the garden, start to harden them off. This process acclimates the soft and tender

TRANSPLANTING TO THE GARDEN

Whether you're working with home-grown plants or nursery stock, most seedlings are handled the same way. Double-check planting dates before you start moving plants outside. Most annuals and vege-

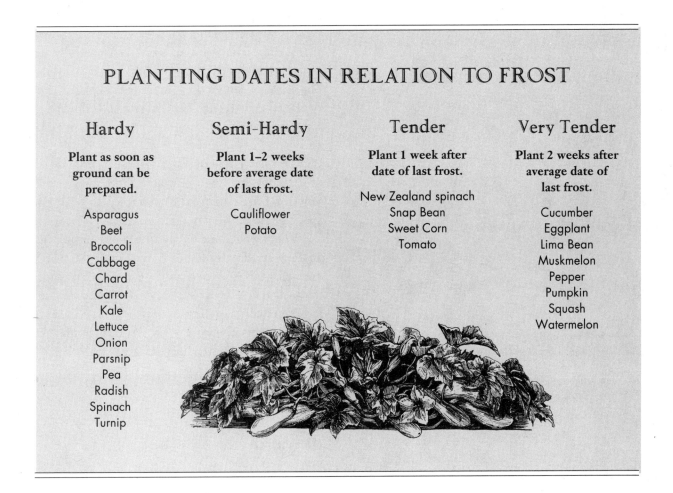

PLANTING DATES IN RELATION TO FROST

Hardy	Semi-Hardy	Tender	Very Tender
Plant as soon as ground can be prepared.	**Plant 1–2 weeks before average date of last frost.**	**Plant 1 week after date of last frost.**	**Plant 2 weeks after average date of last frost.**
Asparagus	Cauliflower	New Zealand spinach	Cucumber
Beet	Potato	Snap Bean	Eggplant
Broccoli		Sweet Corn	Lima Bean
Cabbage		Tomato	Muskmelon
Chard			Pepper
Carrot			Pumpkin
Kale			Squash
Lettuce			Watermelon
Onion			
Parsnip			
Pea			
Radish			
Spinach			
Turnip			

tables must wait until danger of frost is past to be placed outside; some can go out earlier. Tomatoes, eggplant, and peppers should wait until the ground has completely warmed up.

Plan the garden in advance. Select plants for sun and shade, and check planting distances. It's also a good idea to consider companion plants (see chapter 1) to take advantage of natural plant relationships.

The soil must be well prepared in advance to get the most from your flowers, vegetables, or herbs. (See chapter 2 for tips on soil preparation.)

Before moving your plants into the garden, water both the ground outside and the transplants. This will cut down on transplanting shock. It's preferable to do your transplanting on a cloudy day or late in the afternoon so the heat of the sun won't cause excess wilting. If you've used individual peat pots or peat pellets, transplant shock and wilting will be held to a minimum.

Dig a hole about twice the size of the root ball (A). Set the transplant into the hole so the root ball will be covered by ¼ inch of soil, and press soil firmly about its roots so there is good contact between the soil and the roots. A small depression around the plant stem helps the plant to trap moisture (B).

Planting a peat pot

Seedlings in peat pellets can be planted as they are. When planting a peat pot, cut back or peel whatever you can off the pot before planting so the walls of the pot will not confine the roots. Be sure the peat pot is completely covered with soil so it will not dry out and act as a wick, allowing moisture to escape from around the roots.

If your transplants have been growing in flats that are not compartmentalized, very carefully cut out a root ball with a knife or a trowel. If the transplants have been growing in individual plastic pots or flat compartments, turn them upside down and tap them on the bottom, and they will come out easily.

The newly set-out plants may look a little sparse at first, but they will grow and fill in quickly, and you won't want them to be overcrowded. Adequate spacing also cuts down on disease.

Water well immediately after transplanting and again every day for about a week until the plants are well established and growing. Some transplants may wilt at first, but misting them every day or shading them will help them to revive quickly.

From this point on, a few simple maintenance practices will ensure a successful garden and a lot of enjoyment.

Frost Protection

If an unexpected late frost occurs after transplanting, you will need to protect your tender seedlings

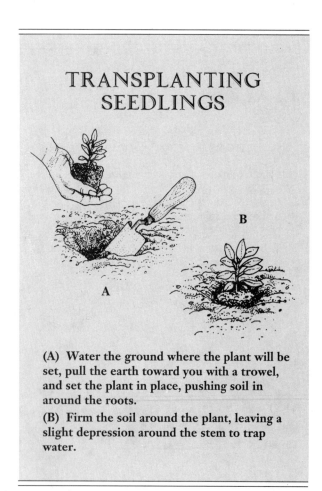

TRANSPLANTING SEEDLINGS

(A) Water the ground where the plant will be set, pull the earth toward you with a trowel, and set the plant in place, pushing soil in around the roots.

(B) Firm the soil around the plant, leaving a slight depression around the stem to trap water.

from frost damage. This can be done by placing Styrofoam cups or hot caps over the plant when frost threatens and removing them when the temperature warms up (see page 11).

STARTING SEEDS OUTDOORS

An outdoor seedbed starts out much like wide-row planting. Create a loose seedbed about 6 to 8 inches deep. (And don't walk on it!) You can use a rototiller for this; it makes the chore easy and fast. Excellent seedbeds can be readied with hand tools, also. (See chapter 2 for more details on soil preparation.)

To sow seeds in a seedbed, use a string to establish the edge of the row. That tells you where your first walkway will be. Then stay right there in the *walkway* to plant, as well as perform all your other gardening chores. There's no reason to set foot in the planting area.

Use a rake to mark the exact width of beds, at least 15 or 16 inches. Drag your rake down the bed, keeping the edge of the rake close to the string. This marks off a 16-inch wide row. Don't bother to rake the entire garden; rake only the areas within the rows where you're going to broadcast seeds.

Smooth the soil with the back of the rake, moving the soil gently until the seedbed is as smooth and level as possible. In smoothing the row, remove large stones, clumps of soil, and large pieces of organic matter.

The easiest way to sow seeds is by sprinkling or broadcasting them over the bed like grass seed. Firm in the seeds for good germination, using the back of a regular hoe. To germinate well, a seed should come in good contact with warm, moist soil on all of its sides. Tamping down gives them this necessary contact.

Now comes an important step — covering the seeds with just the right amount of soil.

Small seeds like carrots and most annuals usually need about ¼ to ½ inch of soil to cover them. Larger seeds such as peas and beans need about 1 inch of soil. The rule of thumb for all seeds is to cover them with enough moist soil to equal four

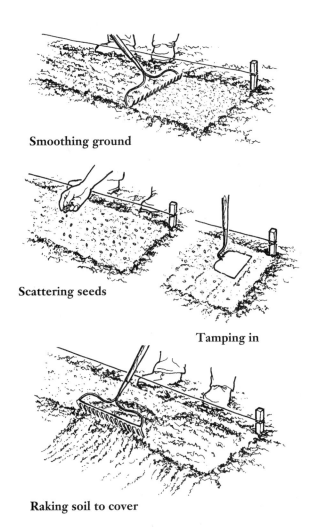

Smoothing ground

Scattering seeds

Tamping in

Raking soil to cover

times their own diameter.

The easy way to cover seeds is to use a rake and pull soil from 1 or 2 feet beyond the row up onto the seedbed. This may sound tricky, but it isn't. Simply pile the soil in the center of the seedbed. The important thing is to lift the soil up onto the bed and not to rake *into* the seedbed. Once you have little mounds of soil sitting on the entire seedbed, smooth them out with the back of the rake, pushing the soil around until it spreads evenly over all the seeds. Each seed should be covered by the same amount of soil. Since they've already been tamped down, the seeds won't move as you push and pull soil above them. Once the seeds are covered evenly, tamp the whole seedbed down gently with a hoe. This packs soil and moisture around each seed and protects it from air which could dry out the seed as it's germinating.

Outdoor Seedling Care

Keep the seedbed moist. If the soil is dry on planting day and there's no rain in the forecast, you can use a sprinkler on your rows *after* you've planted. It's important to keep the soil slightly moist until the seedlings come up. Once the seeds begin germination, you can't let them dry out.

Early in the spring, most garden soils have quite a bit of moisture, and watering is usually unnecessary. Later in the season when the days are longer, sunnier, and hotter, the soil surface will dry out faster, and keeping the seedbed moist will be more of a job.

To save on hot-weather watering, put ½ inch or so of light mulch over the row after it's planted to hold in moisture and to keep the sun from baking a hard crust on the surface. You can use a thin layer of hay, peat moss, or straw, and the plants will grow right up through it.

After a rain or watering, clay soil may occasionally develop a hard, crusty surface as it dries. Sometimes the soil gets so hard that young seedlings don't have the strength to burst through and are deprived of needed oxygen.

Here's how to beat crusty soil: Four or five days after planting, drag a garden rake over the seedbed with just enough force to break up the crust — the tines should penetrate the soil only about ¼ inch. You may have to water hard-packed seedbeds before loosening your soil ¼ inch down. This will allow plants to emerge and continue their growth.

Thinning Outdoor Seedlings

Depending on the crop, the germination rate, and the density of your planting, you may have to do some thinning when the seedlings get going. A wide-row crop like lettuce can stand a lot of crowding, but your flowers and others may want some elbow room.

The amount you thin will depend almost entirely on what you are growing, but there's one basic rule to keep in mind: the larger you expect an individual plant to grow the more space you need to give it, so it will have less competition for light,

moisture, and nutrients. You will also need to keep in mind that there's safety in numbers to a certain extent. Dense growth shades the soil and prevents moisture from evaporating. Wind and insects are frequently less trouble here as well. So, while an individual plant may not grow as large, you'll have more growing activity in a thicker stand of plants.

Transplanting Outdoor Seedlings

More often than not, you're probably going to leave outdoor seedlings to grow where they were started, but you may have good reasons to move them. It may be easier to start annuals of one kind all together and arrange them in the landscape when they're more mature. You might have one corner of the yard that doesn't dry or thaw as early in the season as another area does. Perennials and biennials might spend a whole season in a nursery bed before you move them to a more prominent place in the garden. Or, you may choose to till a small area for starters, and then spread plants out later on.

First of all, you need to know whether your plants are of the sort that cooperate in transplanting. Some plants simply don't like it. Second, keep in mind that without the constraints of flats and pots, bed-planted seedlings are likely to develop more spread-out roots.

The basic principles of transplanting container-grown seedlings also applies to bed-planted seedlings. Water plants thoroughly and give them time to drink as much as they can before you start digging, and pick a cloudy day or late afternoon for this operation.

Transplanting is most successful when root disturbance is kept to a minimum. Select a new site and dig a hole a little bit larger and deeper than the rootball *before* you dig up your seedling. You might take this opportunity to mix a little fertilizer or well-rotted manure with the soil in the bottom of the transplant hole below where the roots will be set, so they can reach down to it as they grow.

With a knife or trowel blade pointing straight down into the soil, cut all the way around the seedling so the diameter of the rootball is at least as large as the leaf spread. Gently lift the rootball out of the ground using the trowel blade (or, it may be easier to wedge it between two trowel blades), and move it to the new hole. The plant should sit just a little lower than it did in the nursery bed. Fill the hole around the plant, leaving a small depression around the stem for moisture to collect. Water thoroughly, and continue care as you would for container-grown transplants.

STARTING SEEDS IN OUTDOOR ROWS AND MOUNDS

For many annual flowers and vegetables, especially those that resent transplanting, it makes the most sense to start seeds right in the garden plot where they will mature. While wide-row planting is effective for many smaller plants, others are going to need more space. For these plants, you can make the most of your seed and row space by tailoring your planting to the needs of individual plants. Plants that grow very tall, like corn, do better in rows. Sprawling plants like pumpkins and zucchini grow better and are easier to care for in hills or mounds.

Planting in Rows

Preparing the garden for single-row planting is very much like wide-row planting, except that the rows are narrower. The row width will depend on the crop you're planting (consult the Garden Planning Chart on page 56 for recommended distances). The thing to be careful of here is to make rows the right width. If they're too narrow, the plants won't have room to grow. If they're too wide, you could be wasting space, allowing weeds room to intrude, and preventing the cross-pollination necessary for producing fruits or vegetables.

It is best to fertilize below or between the rows (see more on side-dressing in chapter 4), rather than enriching the soil immediately surrounding the seed. Very rich soil will stimulate early leaf development, but plants will do better if they start with a good root structure.

When planting tall crops, you'll want to orient the rows from north to south so that each plant gets the most sunlight possible. It is also better to plant several short rows, rather than a few long ones, to ensure cross-pollination. On a small scale, you can form single rows by raking loose soil into narrow furrows and rows with a garden rake. On a larger scale, a motorized tiller may be necessary. You may want to set out stakes and strings as guides to help keep the rows straight.

Once your rows are formed, plant seeds in a straight line at the center of the row. Spacing will depend on the crop, but it is always better to plant extra and thin later than be disappointed by a poor germination rate. Always firm the soil over the seeds to bring them in contact with moisture held in the soil. Water thoroughly after planting and regularly until the plants are established. Mulch applied between the rows will help cut down on weeds and hold moisture in the soil.

Planting in Mounds

First, loosen the soil with a tiller, as you would for any planting effort (see chapter 2 for information on garden site preparation). You may add fertilizer to the whole area, but mound planting offers an opportunity to target your efforts a little. After the soil is tilled for planting, mark the area for each mound. The distances will vary depending on the plant, but mounds 1 to 2 feet in diameter spaced 3 feet apart is a common average for squash and related plants.

Dig a hole about 8 to 12 inches deep where each mound will be located. Mix half the removed soil with well-rotted manure, compost, or fertilizer, and place it back in the bottom of the hole with the remaining fresh soil on top. Then add soil from around the spot to create a slight mound, up to 6 inches high in the middle and 1 to 2 feet across. This way, the fertilizer won't burn tender new roots, but food will be available when the plants are large enough to grow down to it.

Plant seeds at intervals around the mound (spaced appropriately according to the selected crop). It is a good idea to plant two or three seeds

GARDEN PLANNING CHART

Vegetable	Seeds or Plants for a 50' row	Distance Between Rows in Inches	Plants or Feet of Row Per Person	Spacing Between Plants in Inches
Beans, dry	4 oz.	18	20–30'	6–8
Beans, shell	4 oz.	18	30'	8–10
Beans, snap	4 oz.	18	30'	2–4
Beets	½ oz.	12	10–15'	2–4
Broccoli	25 plants	24	5 plants	12–24
Brussels sprouts	25 plants	24	5 plants	12–24
Cabbage	25 plants	24	10 plants	12–18
Cauliflower	25 plants	24	5 plants	14–24
Carrots	⅛ oz.	12	10'	1–3
Corn	1 oz.	24	25'	9–15
Cucumbers	¼ oz.	48	10–15'	12
Eggplant	25 plants	24	5 plants	18–36
Endive	⅛ oz.	18	10'	8–12
Kale	⅛ oz.	18	12'	18–24
Kohlrabi	⅛ oz.	18	10'	3–6
Lettuce, head	⅛ oz.	15	5–10'	10–15
Lettuce, leaf	⅛ oz.	12	5–10'	10–12
Muskmelons	12 plants	48	3 plants	12
Onion sets	1 lb.	12	10–20'	2–4
Parsnips	¼ oz.	18	5–10'	3–6
Peas	8 oz.	24	50–100'	1–3
Peppers	33 plants	18	5 plants	12–24
Potatoes	33 plants	30	50'	9–12
Pumpkins	¼ oz.	60	1 hill	36–60
Radishes	½ oz.	12	5'	1–2
Salsify	½ oz.	18	5'	2–4
Spinach	½ oz.	15	20'	2–6
Squash, summer	¼ oz.	60	1 hill	24–48
Squash, winter	½ oz.	60	3–5 hills	24–40
Swiss chard	¼ oz.	18	5'	3–6
Tomatoes	12–15 plants	30	5 plants	12–24
Turnips	¼ oz.	15	10'	2–6
Watermelon	30 plants	72	2–3 hills	72–96
Zucchini	¼ oz.	60	1 hill	24–48

per hole and thin later, in case some don't sprout.

When the seeds are in the ground, water thoroughly. Then add a layer of mulch around the mounds (but not on top of them) to hold in moisture, keep weeds down, and even give you a clean walkway between the mounds. Later on, this mulch will keep vine-ripened vegetables from sitting directly on the soil.

GARDEN CARE

The first thing to remember in caring for your garden is that it's easier to prevent a problem than to cure one. Maintenance chores will be minimized if you take proper care in planning and planting your garden. In this chapter, we provide tips for garden cleanup, weed control, mulching, watering, and fertilizing.

AN OUNCE OF PREVENTION

Keeping the garden cleaned up will go a long way in preventing many problems. Once established, a healthy crop will beat weeds in the contest for moisture and nutrients. And keeping the garden free of weeds and debris will help to starve out a large insect pest population.

When you have finished harvesting a crop, work it into the ground right away — the greener it is, the better it is for your soil. Leaving crop residues to wither away above ground is bad policy. They become a refuge for pests and disease organisms which could trouble you later. Green plants are the most beneficial for earthworms and other soil life, and are the easiest to digest and break down. Tough, old plants are the hardest to work into the soil.

If you have a good tiller, you can put crops back into the soil in just a few minutes. Make several passes over the area to chop up the residues and to mix them deep into the soil. This way they'll decompose faster.

Morning is the best time for tilling or spading crops. The plants have the most moisture in them early in the day and they cut a lot easier — even vining crops, which are a problem for some gardeners to put under.

Most tillers can handle all crop leftovers in the garden, including cornstalks. But if your machine can't, don't strain yourself trying to get the residues under. Sometimes you can pull heavy residues like caulliflower, broccoli, or early corn, or mow them down, or somehow chop them up before tackling them with your tiller.

If you work with hand tools, use a long-handled, round-pointed shovel for spacing. Chop up the plant remains a bit, turn them into the soil about 4 to 6 inches deep, and then drive the shovel down to chop them some more. Small pieces of green matter will break down best.

BEAT THOSE WEEDS!

You *can* have a garden that's practically weed-free, without spending a lot of time hoeing or pulling weeds by hand.

CREATING A WEED FREE ZONE

To lick weeds, concentrate your efforts for just one year. This approach works particularly well on areas that haven't been gardened before, but may be full of weed seeds. In the spring, till, then plant buckwheat at the rate of 4 pounds per 1000 square feet. This is heavy seeding. After it has blossomed, but before the dark seeds form, till the buckwheat under. A day later, plant another crop of buckwheat, again 4 pounds per 1000 square feet. Again, the buckwheat will come up, and so, too, will the weeds, but the buckwheat again will outgrow and eventually kill off the weeds by shading them out. This time, be particularly sure the seed hasn't formed before you till it, or the buckwheat will be the weed you're faced with next year.

After tilling in the second crop of buckwheat, plant another cover crop, such as annual ryegrass or winter rye. The result will be three cover crops tilled into the soil, enriching it, plus almost all the weeds eliminated from the site. This is an excellent method to use before raising strawberries.

One of the first steps to a weed-free garden is understanding the difference between *annual* and *perennial weeds*. It's important because there are different techniques for controlling each kind.

Annual weeds grow only one season. Their goal is to produce seeds before cold weather kills the plant. If you let annual weeds grow, they will create hundreds, even thousands, of seeds. These seeds then tumble down to the ground or get blown all over the garden. Many of these will germinate the following year, and then it's their turn to make a new batch of seeds.

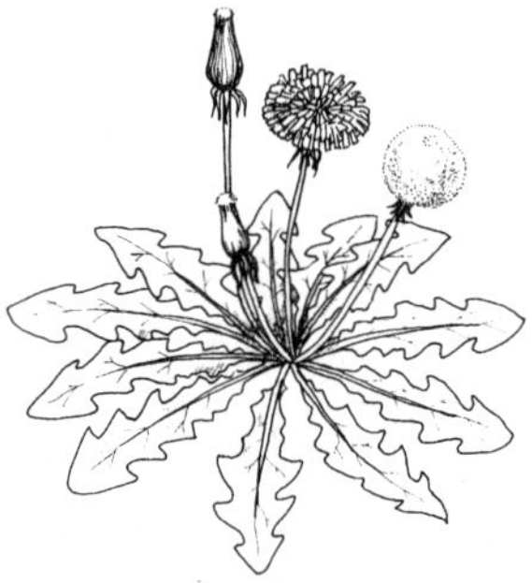

Dandelion

Perennial weeds spread by means of underground stems and root parts, but they will go to seed also. A single hoeing or tilling doesn't do much to them because pieces of their roots left in the soil have enough energy to send up new shoots right away.

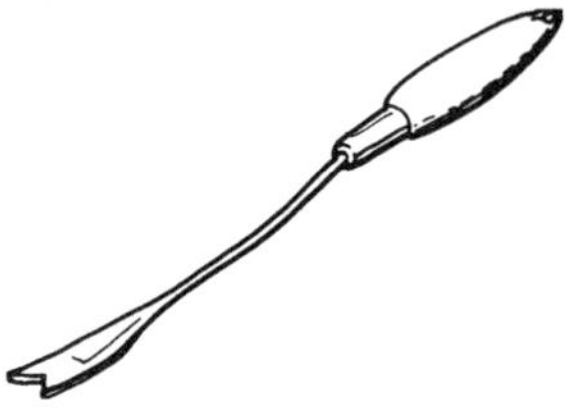

Dandelion weeder

The new green growth captures energy from the sun and begins to replenish the root system. As long as the roots have energy they will be able to send up new growth.

Getting Rid of Annual Weeds

The seeds of annual weeds are often so small that they can germinate only in the top ¼ inch of soil. If the seeds are deeper, they don't have enough strength to push up through the soil.

When you work the soil deeply in the spring, you bring up thousands of these tiny seeds to the germination zone. If you let the soil sit for two or three days and then plant your seeds, many of the tiny weeds in the zone will germinate and overwhelm your vegetables. That's getting your garden off on the wrong foot!

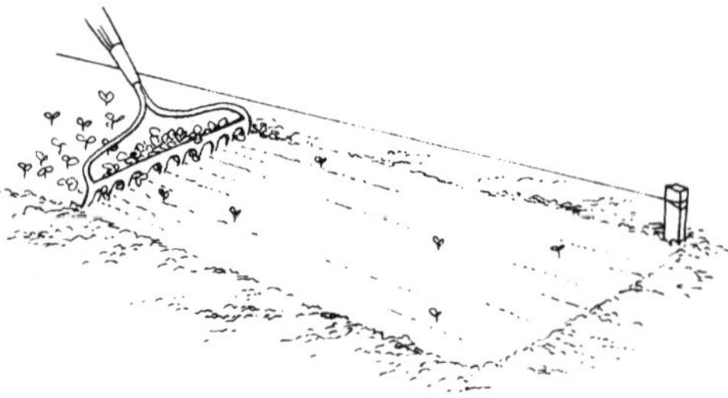

Thinning annual weeds with a rake

GARDEN PROBLEM GUIDE

Symptoms of common garden problems and their possible cures.

Symptoms	Possible Cause	Possible Cures
Dying young plants	Fertilizer burn Disease (damping-off)	Mix fertilizer throughly with soil. Treat seed; don't over-water.
Stunted plants, pale to yellow	Low soil fertility Low soil pH (too acid) Poor soil drainage Shallow or compacted soil Insects or diseases Nematodes	Soil test for fertilizer recommendations. Soil test for lime recommendations. Drain and add organic matter. Plow deeper. Identify and use control measures. Soil test for treatment recommendations.
Stunted plants, purplish color	Low temperature Lack of phosphorus	Plant at recommended time. Add phosphorus fertilizer.
Holes in leaves	Insects Hail	Identify and use control measures. Be thankful it was not worse.
Spots, molds, darkened areas on leaves and stems	Disease Chemical burn Fertilizer burn	Identify, spray, or dust, use resistant varieties. Use recommended chemical at recommended rate. Keep fertilizer off plants.
Wilting plants	Dry soil Excess water in soil Nematodes Disease	Irrigate if possible. Drain. Soil test for treatment recommendations. Use resistant varieties if possible.
Weak, spindly plants	Too much shade Too much water Plants too thick Too much nitrogen	Remove shade or move plants to sunny spot. Seed at recommended rate. Avoid excess fertlization.
Failure to set fruit	High temperature Low temperature Too much nitrogen Insects	Follow recommended planting time. Follow recommended planting time. Avoid excess fertilization. Identify and use control measures.
Tomato leaf curl	Heavy pruning in hot weather Disease	Don't. Identify and use control measures.
Dry brown to black rot on blossom end of tomato	Low soil calcium Extremely dry soil	Add liming material. Irrigate.
Misshapen tomatoes (catfacing)	Cool weather during blooming	Plant at recommended time.
Abnormal leaves and growth	2,4-D weed killer Virus disease	Don't use sprayer that has previously applied 2,4-D. Don't allow spray to drift to garden. Remove infected plants to prevent spreading. Control insects that transmit.

Never work the soil one day and plant it the next. Always rototill it *immediately* before setting up stakes and string and planting. If you don't have a tiller, stir up the soil in the seedbed with a rake or hoe.

This last-minute stirring of the soil turns up hundreds of weed seedlings. They are so tender at this point that the slightest disturbance will kill most of them.

Thinning wide rows with a rake is one of the most important weed-fighting steps of all. As soon as wide-row vegetables get ¼ to ½ inch high, drag an iron garden rake across the row with the tines going in about ¼ inch. This thins out some of the closely planted vegetables, but more importantly, the rake tines shake up hundreds of sprouting weed seeds. Don't use this rake thinning method on peas, beans, or onion sets and plants.

Tiny weed plants are not anchored into the soil, so they spill out easily and die. In most cases, one pass across the row will do the job, but if the plants appear too thick after the first pass, drag the rake over the row a second time.

The best time to get rid of annual weeds in the germination zone is shortly after a rain or watering. A rain brings moisture to hundreds of weed seeds and they start sprouting.

When the surface of the soil gets dry, stir up the top inch or two of soil between rows and near the plants. This stirring, or cultivation, wipes out hundreds of weeds before they come to the surface.

Two good things happen when you cultivate at a shallow depth. First, you don't bring any new weed seeds into the germination zone from deeper layers of soil; and second, you avoid cutting any roots of vegetables which grow out under the walkways.

After four or five shallow cultivations, most of the annual weed seeds in the top layer of soil have germinated. You won't have to do much weeding after that.

Another good thing about regular shallow cultivation is that it helps the soil absorb and hold water. Packed soil doesn't hold much moisture. Loosening the soil lets water seep down.

More Cultivating Tips

Let plants dry off before you weed. If the leaves are wet, it's possible to spread a disease by brushing your legs against them as you move down a row.

Do any hand weeding around the plants *before* tilling or hoeing the walkways. Leave the walkways with as few footprints as possible. That lets water drain into the soil easily, and keeps weeds from sprouting because they need firmed soil for that.

Work weeds into the soil or throw them on the compost pile. As long as they haven't produced seeds, they're good organic matter which you should try to get into your soil.

Weed after the harvest, too. Annual weeds will keep trying to produce seeds no matter how late in the season. Keep after them.

Perennial Weeds: How to Fight Them and Win

If you're having trouble with grass and other perennial weeds, an all-out attack on them is in order. You can't control them the way you do annual weeds.

Some perennial weeds are much more of a problem than others. Quackgrass, Bermudagrass, and nutgrass are the worst because they have extensive root systems. Their stored energy lets them send up new shoots when others are cut down. After a tilling, you may think your soil is rid of them, but in a few days they've started up again thicker than ever. It's important to realize that each time they rebound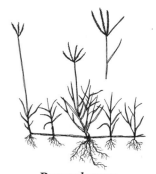

Bermudagrass

with new growth, they have used up some of their reserve. They draw on these reserves until there's enough top growth to start capturing the sun's energy and replenishing the root reserves. Usually this starts when the plants are ½ inch or so high.

But if you *prevent* perennials from putting on

SOME OF THE TOUGHEST PERENNIAL WEEDS

Bermudagrass. You might think of Bermudagrass as the South's version of quackgrass. As a lawn or pasture grass in the South, it's fine — but in a garden, it's big trouble. It spreads by both seed and creeping roots.

If the ground in your area freezes during the winter, kill Bermudagrass by a thorough tilling in late fall to expose the roots to the cold. This won't work in areas with mild winters, but smother crops will. Starting in the fall, plant a smother crop, such as rye, and follow it the next year with two or three thick crops of buckwheat. Their dense shade should destroy most of the grass.

Quackgrass. One of the worst perennial weeds for gardeners in the North. It will grow through most mulches and can produce abundant seed.

Quackgrass competes with vegetables for light, water, space, and nutrients. It may take a full season to weaken and kill a heavy infestation. During this time it's important to prevent new shoots from getting much more than 1 inch high.

Quackgrass likes cool weather so it is most aggressive during the spring and fall months.

Nutgrass. There's a northern and southern version of nutgrass. The northern variety, sometimes called "yellow nutgrass," prefers poorly drained soils. Both species can be identified by their shiny, erect blades and the hard little tubers or "nuts" that form on the roots.

Even when the roots are chopped and tilled thoroughly, the little nuts survive to send up new plants. When pulling nutgrass by hand, pull very carefully so that the tubers don't break off and remain in the soil.

Bindweed. Bindweed's extensive root system can penetrate as deep as 16 feet. It's most abundant and troublesome in the West.

This viney perennial is a member of the morning glory family, and can reproduce both by seed and by creeping roots. Don't even try to plant a garden where bindweed is a bad problem. To get rid of it, till the plot every two or three weeks to drain root reserves. After a while, plant successive smother crops of buckwheat and till them in. The next year you'll be able to plant a garden without much trouble.

this ½ inch of growth, you'll starve out their root reserves and they'll die. It is not an overnight process. One way to do this is to till the soil and then quickly cover it with black plastic sheeting or a very heavy mulch for a whole season. Another way to starve the roots is by continuous tilling at a shallow depth to kill the small blades coming up without chopping up a lot of the root system. If you till for a *whole season* whenever the grass first appears — probably every four to seven days — you can force the roots to use all their energy. When they're out of energy, you win.

THE IMPORTANCE OF MULCHING

Mulching means blanketing the soil surrounding garden plants with a layer of material. It has several beneficial effects and is a boon to gardens in dry and normal seasons.

■ **Reduces the loss of soil moisture.** Wind and sun speed the evaporation of water from the upper six to eight inches of soil. Merely shading the ground reduces evaporation by 30 percent; with a thick application of straw mulch, evaporation can be reduced by as much as 70 percent.

■ **Prevents weeds.** Keeping the weed population small means less work for you and more water and nutrients for the vegetables. In order for the mulch to reduce the weed population, it must be spread thickly. Any weeds that do grow through usually can be pulled up easily as their root systems will be poorly anchored.

A slight depression in the mulch surrounding your plants will help catch rainwater.

■ **Insulates the soil.** Mulching will keep the soil temperature even. It will keep the soil temperature cooler on hot days, which will mean less moisture loss by evaporation and transpiration. Also, it will keep the soil warmer on cool nights, and this will speed growth.

■ **Prevents a soil crust from forming.** Clay soils have a tendency to bind together and form a hard crust that prevents water absorption. A mulch allows the water to seep into the soil slowly and prevents crusting.

■ **Adds nutrients.** Organic mulches add nutrients to the soil. They can be tilled into the soil along with other garden residues each fall, adding to the organic content of the soil.

Mulching Materials

Mulch can be composed of organic or inorganic materials. Black plastic sheeting and aluminum foil are common inorganic mulches. Commonly used organic mulches include straw, hay, peat moss, leaves, pine needles, wood bark, and newspapers.

Many gardeners find that black plastic holds the heat in the soil, which speeds growth and subsequently yields better results in many warm-weather crops, such as melons, eggplants, peppers, and squash. Also, the plastic sheeting allows you to mulch close to the stem. But the plastic sheeting may cause excessive heat build-up, which can harm the plants. Likewise, aluminum foil can heat up the underside of plants, a positive effect in early spring, but detrimental in the heat of the summer.

Inorganic mulches add nothing to the soil and eventually need to be removed and recycled or thrown away. But organic mulches slowly decompose and add nitrogen, potassium, and other nutrients to the soil. At the end of the growing season, organic mulches can be tilled into the soil, adding humus and improving the water-retaining qualities of the soil. For these reasons, we recommend the use of organic mulches.

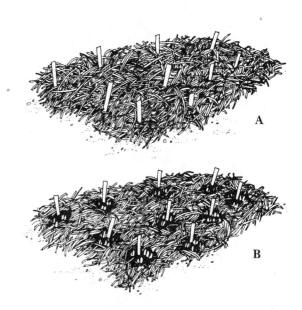

Winter mulch. Especially in cold regions, it is advisable to remove winter mulch (A) slowly. Start by uncovering only the plant crowns (B) for a time before taking all the mulch away.

MULCHING MATERIALS

Materials	Pros	Cons
Straw/Hay	Cheap; generally available; adds organic matter	Can contain weed seed, insects, and/or disease
Leaves	Readily available; generally free; rich in nutrients	Can mat down or be too acid for some plants
Grass clippings	Easy to get and apply; good source of nitrogen	Can burn plants; may contain weed seeds
Pine needles	Attractive; easy to apply	Large quantities hard to collect; may be too acid
Wood shavings	Weed and disease free; easy to apply; available	Can be acid; tends to tie up nitrogen in soil
Manure	Great source of fertility and organic matter	Should be well-rotted; expensive to buy; usually contains weeds
Newspaper	Easy to get and apply; earthworms thrive in it	Decomposes very fast; must be weighted down
Plastic	Total weed control if opaque is used; warms soil for early start; heavy plastic can be used more than one season	Expensive, unattractive; adds nothing to soil; must be weighted down and cleaned up in the fall

When to Mulch

Because mulch acts as a soil insulator, wait until the soil has warmed up in the spring before mulching. Once the soil is warm, spread the mulch right around the young, emerging plants.

Get the most water retention from mulches by spreading your mulch after a good rain. Try spreading the mulch over the entire garden surface in the spring, then clearing a space for your seeds and transplants. You will be able to mulch much closer to the plants in this way. Keep the mulch away from the tops of root crops, such as carrots, beets, and potatoes, to avoid crown rot.

As the season progresses, add new mulch as the old mulch decays and becomes compacted.

Mulching in the fall will keep the soil temperatures warm and extend your growing season. Using mulches around cold frames and plastic tents will keep plants growing beyond the first frosts.

How Much Mulch to Apply

A good rule of thumb is the smaller the individual particles of mulch, the thinner the layer of mulch should be. A half an inch of coffee grounds can be as effective a mulch as a foot of coarse straw. If mulch is spread too sparsely, weeds will thrive and soil will dry out easily. Too much mulch and the plants will not be able to breathe; they will not be healthy plants. Common sense should be your guide.

WATERING YOUR GARDEN

Water only when plants need it. A simple statement, but how can you tell when they need water? Look at your plants. Feel the leaves. How do they look the day after a deep watering, three days after, one week after? There will be a change in leaf gloss, and subtle changes in leaf color and the height the leaves are held.

Most plants are about 90 percent water. This fluid is necessary to carry on the vital functions of photosynthesis, respiration, and transpiration. (Often, more than three-quarters of the water absorbed by plants is transpired, or given off for cooling.) Water pressure (within the cells) helps to keep

All plants need adequate water.

plants, without woody stems, erect. When they do not have enough water, plants droop and wilt. Plants will often wilt in the heat of a hot afternoon because they are giving off more water than they are absorbing. With this type of wilting, the plant usually recovers by late evening or the next morning. If plants are still wilted in the morning, the soil is too dry; water immediately.

For healthy growth, plants need about 1 inch of water a week (which is about 62 gallons for 100 square feet). The best way to be sure your vegetables are getting their weekly water is to set up a rain gauge in your garden. A wide selection of gauges is available for sale in garden centers and through seed catalogs. They are easy to use and simple to monitor. Or, you can make your own rain gauge by using a tin can with the top removed. Measure the rainfall in your homemade gauge with a ruler.

DRY WEATHER GROWING TIPS

- Do not stake or heavily prune your tomatoes during a drought. Let them sprawl on the ground. The foliage will shade the soil, keeping the roots cooler and reducing evaporation of water from the soil. A determinant variety will sprawl less than an indeterminant, making harvesting easier. Mulching under the plants keeps the fruits cleaner.

- In an extreme drought, try planting tomatoes and other water-loving, fruit-bearing plants in large plastic bags. Dig a hole in the garden large enough to accommodate a large, plastic garbage bag filled with soil. Water the soil to saturate it. Insert the young tomato plant deeply inside the bag, removing all but the top leaves, and covering the rest of the stem with soil. Secure the bag around the stem. The bag will hold the moisture in, and you will not have to water more than a few times a season.

- During a drought, do not grow vines on a trellis; allow them to sprawl on the ground.

- Interplant tall and short crops so that the tall plants can provide shade for the shorter ones.

- When mulching with newspapers, do not use the funnies. The colored ink in most newsprint contains lead, which is harmful to the plants.

- Herbs are a good dry season crop because most originated from the hot, dry Mediterranean area.

DRY SEASON GROWING PROBLEMS

- Irregular water and heat may produce physiological disorders in your plants. Common symptoms are growth cracks and blossom end rot on tomatoes, sunscald on peppers and tomatoes, knobby potatoes, or tip burn on head lettuce. You can still eat these plants. Drip irrigation will prevent these problems.

- Drought-weakened plants are particularly vulnerable to disease. Powdery mildew is a real threat in dry weather. And when a dry period is followed by a wet period, downy mildew or blight is likely. Contact your extension agent for the best controls of these diseases.

- Overwatering can cause root rot and may lock up the magnesium in the soil. The symptom of magnesium deficiency is a yellowing of the lower leaves between the veins, which remain green.

Check the gauge after every rainfall and note the amount of water that fell. Mark it in a journal or on your garden calendar. Add it up each week to see if the 1-inch quota has been fulfilled. If rainfall was too low, water.

One inch of water will wet a sandy soil down about 12 inches; a loam soil about 8 inches; and a clay soil 4 to 6 inches. Sandy soils drain more quickly and often need more frequent watering. Know your soil type (see page 23) and adjust your watering accordingly.

Many people purchase moisture meters to tell them when to water. These have metal probes that go into the soil and dials that show when the soil is too wet or dry or just right. Some people take a soil sample.

Allow the soil to dry *slightly* between slow, deep waterings. This enables air to mix with the soil particles to aid in plant growth. The perfect soil is 50 percent soil particles and 50 percent spaces, optimally filled half and half with air and water.

Water Properly

If you must supplement the rainfall, be sure to follow these guidelines to use the water most effectively.

- **Apply water slowly, deeply, and uniformly.** Watering to a depth of 5 to 6 inches encourages the growth of deep roots, enabling the plant to seek out water at different levels in the soil. Plant growth is interrupted if the soil is allowed to become very dry and then soaking wet. Constant moisture supply is very important for continuous growth and maximum yields. With

WATERING TIPS

- For a plant, the most critical period of growth, when adequate water is essential, is just after blossoming when the fruit is beginning to form.

- Always cultivate before watering to ensure that the soil is loose and will absorb the most water. Otherwise, the water will cause a hard crust to form on the surface of the soil, preventing both water and air from circulating.

- Rain barrels and other containers set out to catch rainwater should be tightly capped when not collecting to prevent evaporation. Add a few drops of oil to discourage mosquitoes from breeding in the water.

SETTING UP A DRIP IRRIGATION SYSTEM

When water is in short supply one of the easiest and most efficient ways to water plants is with a drip irrigation system. The drip system applies water in the root area of the plant one drop at a time, rather than wetting the entire area as a conventional system would.

A drip system, which can be buried or left on the soil surface, consists of ½-inch PVC (polyvinylchloride) pipe, which connects to the main water valve at the house. The ½-inch PVC pipe branches off to ¼-inch PVC pipe that branches off to lateral lines that are connected to water emitters. The emitters may have bubbler or spray heads or flexible tubing to disperse the water.

Through the use of pressure valves, water is emitted in a very slow, controlled way directly to the root zone. The system is automatically controlled to apply water at the same rate that the plants absorb it. The correct mixture of moisture and air is maintained in the soil so plants do not suffer between wet and dry conditions. The controlled moisture content of the soil results in large, healthy, quick-growing plants. Run-off problems virtually disappear.

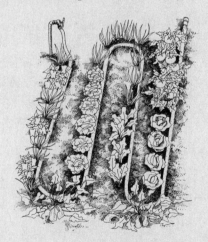

Soaker hose drip irrigation system

Weed growth is significantly diminished.

The water in a drip system moves down through the soil as gravity acts on it. The really high-quality water emitters will wet only the soil surface in an area the size of a quarter so loss of moisture to evaporation is greatly reduced. Beneath the surface the soil is moistened to a depth of 2½ to 3 feet. Water moves through sandy soil rapidly; thus with a drip system, the soil is wetted in a narrow, deep area. As water moves more slowly through clay soil, the area beneath the surface is saturated in a wide and shallow area.

A water savings of 40 to 60 percent can be realized with a drip system. Some vegetable gardeners feel that production can increase as much as 15 percent. The system can be made completely automatic. With special attachments, a drip system can apply fertilizer with the water. Self-flushing emitters can be purchased, making the system practically self-sufficient.

Drip irrigation systems can be obtained from nurseries, hardware stores, and mail-order garden catalogs; or check in the yellow pages of the telephone directory under landscape architect, sprinkler systems, or irrigation systems.

If the idea of a drip irrigation system is appealing but a bit too costly, devise one of your own. Turn a soaker hose face down and apply water *very* slowly to avoid run-off. Or make a homemade drip system from large coffee cans or milk cartons with the tops removed and holes punched around the bottom of the sides. Place the cans at regular intervals in the vegetable garden (before you set the plants in so you don't disturb the roots). When necessary, fill with water. The water will slowly stream out. The cans will need to be refilled several times to provide moisture to the correct soil depth.

CHECK SOIL MOISTURE

Take a moisture sample with an auger (which can be purchased at a nursery center or hardware store). It is a metal tube that is stuck down into the soil several inches. When pulled up, the soil sample is easily read for moisture content. Try using a finger; it does the same thing, is free, and puts you in closer contact with the plants and the soil. It is important to check the soil moisture in the plant root zone, not just on the surface.

frequent, shallow watering, a large percentage of moisture is lost in evaporation.

- **Apply water when the air is still.** This way all the moisture goes into the soil and is not carried away by wind.

- **Water in the morning when humidity is usually the highest and temperatures the lowest.** Watering during the heat of the day sacrifices a lot of water to evaporation, while watering late in the day or in the evening may encourage fungus disease.

FEEDING YOUR GARDEN

There are many approaches to providing nutrients to growing plants. Strictly speaking, anything you add to the soil to provide nutrients for growing plants might be considered a fertilizer. Other soil amendments, such as lime, are sometimes used, not as feeding elements, but to adjust soil chemistry so that nutrients are more easily absorbed.

Choosing Soil Amendments

The most successful fertilizing programs are tailored to match existing soil with the needs of particular crops. Soil testing kits are often available in seed stores. The simplest kits measure soil acidity, designed as the "pH" level. Some kits also allow home gardeners to measure the plant nutrients available in the soil. However, for the most accurate results, it is often best to send samples to a soil testing laboratory.

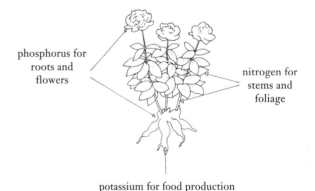

phosphorus for roots and flowers

nitrogen for stems and foliage

potassium for food production

Balanced garden fertilizers provide nitrogen (N) for foliage and stem growth, phosphorus (P) for root devolopment and flower production, and potassium (K) for plant metabolism and food production.

Organic fertilizers can include just about any animal or vegetable material, ranging from packinghouse by-products to seaweed, but well-rotted animal manure and compost are the most common. Cover crops grown during the off season and tilled into the soil provide many of the same benefits. Often the slower feeding action of organic materials breaking down in the soil have a longer and safer effect than fast-acting chemicals. In most cases, you can have an extremely productive garden every year simply by turning compost and green manure crops into the soil in the spring and fall. (See more on improving your soil in chapter 2).

Inorganic fertilizers may be derived from natural minerals or from synthetic chemicals. Most commercial fertilizers are a combination of nutrients and elements that make nutrients easier for plants to absorb. While these amendments may give you a bumper crop for one season, in the long run they may weaken your soil.

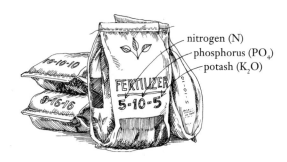

nitrogen (N)
phosphorus (PO_4)
potash (K_2O)

A "complete" fertilizer contains nitrogen (N), phosphorus (P), and potash (K), the three most common elements that are needed for good plant nutrition but lacking in the soil. Commercial fertilizers are labeled in N-P-K order according to their percentage of these elements. A common all-purpose mixture is 5-10-5, or 5 percent nitrogen, 10 percent phosphorus, and 5 percent potash. (For more on soil amendments, see chapter 2.)

Applying Fertilizers

Many vegetables don't like a big serving of fertilizer at planting time. They prefer to take their plant food from the soil a little at a time. When the plant starts to blossom, it needs extra food to develop buds and blossoms, to set fruit, and to grow seed pods.

Giving crops an extra boost of fertilizer is often called side-dressing or top-dressing. Good side-dressings help crops grow evenly and smoothly — and help deliver better harvests.

If you've mixed plenty of organic matter into your soil over the years and grow green manure crops like peas, beans, and buckwheat, chances are your soil is pretty rich in nutrients. As long as you add a little fertilizer to the soil before planting, your crops probably will do very well without side-dressing. But it's a good idea to side-dress corn and onions, two big feeders.

On the other hand, if you're just starting to improve your soil by adding organic matter, side-dressings are important. For example, in a sandy soil with little organic matter, plant foods drain down through the soil and away from the roots of your crops. To keep crops growing smoothly, you'll probably need to side-dress.

Not every crop needs side-dressing. Peas and beans, greens such as lettuce and spinach, and root crops grow fine when fertilized only at planting time. Carrots, beets, and turnips do well with a little extra bonemeal fertilizer at planting time. This assures a good supply of phosphorus, the plant food that helps root crops develop the best roots.

Three Ways to Apply Side-Dressing

Circle the Plants. With tomatoes, peppers, broccoli, and other transplanted crops, dig a shallow circular furrow around each plant. Sprinkle the fertilizer in evenly and cover it. Put this circle of plant food about 5 or 6 inches away from the plant stem.

SIDE-DRESSING AMOUNTS

If you have good natural fertilizers on hand and want to use them instead of the complete fertilizer 5-10-10, here are some equivalents:

1 tablespoon complete commercial fertilizer (such as 5-10-10) equals:

- 2 handfuls good compost or
- 2 handfuls dehydrated manure or
- 1 to 2 tablespoons alfalfa meal

But if the plant is quite large, put it right around the outer leaves or "drip line" of the plant. There are many shallow feeder roots there so the fertilizer will move down into the soil with the next rain and be taken up quickly.

Side-dressing banding method

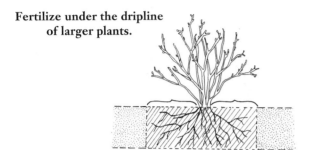

Fertilize under the dripline of larger plants.

Banding. With the corner of a hoe, open a furrow 1 or 2 inches deep in a straight line next to a row of plants. Keep the furrow about 5 or 6 inches from the line of plants. Then put the fertilizer in the furrow and cover it with soil. It's important to cover

any commercial fertilizer so the rain doesn't splash it up onto plant leaves. The nitrogen can burn the leaves and set the plants back.

Top-dressing. Sprinkle natural fertilizers, such as alfalfa meal, dehydrated manure, or compost, over wide rows. With chard, for example, cut all the plants 1 inch above the ground and fertilize right in the seedbed to encourage quick, new tender growth. Scratch the fertilizer in with a rake and then water.

SIDE-DRESSING GUIDE

Broccoli

Side-dress when the head begins to form. It may be only the size of a fifty-cent piece when you notice it, but go ahead and side-dress. Amount needed: 1 to 2 tablespoons complete fertilizer per plant.

Brussels Sprouts

Side-dress Brussels sprouts when you harvest the first small marble-size sprouts. Amount: 1 table-spoon complete fer-tilizer per plant.

Cabbage

The best time to side-dress cabbage is when it starts to form a head, when the leaves of the plants are about to completely shade the row. Amount needed: 1 tablespoon of complete fer-tilizer per plant.

Cauliflower

Because cauliflow-er heads form so fast, side-dressing when you first see the head usually won't help. Side-dress when the plant's leaves seem to be as big as they're going to get, usually five or six weeks after transplanting. Amount: 1 to 2 tablespoons complete fertilizer per plant.

Chard

Side-dress right after harvesting crew-cut style. Cut the plants 1 inch above the ground and side-dress with a natural fertilizer such as de-hydrated manure. Amount: 1 handful for each foot of wide row (16 inches wide).

Corn

Because corn takes more plant food than most other crops, side-dress it twice: when it's about knee-high, and when it starts to tassel and silk forms on the stalks. Fertilizer helps to make good ears. Amount: about 1 tablespoon complete fertilizer per plant or about 3 cups per 25 feet of row each side-dressing.

Cucumbers, Melons, and Winter Squash

These vine crops should be fertilized before they start to spread out and run. At this point they stand up straight and tall. It's easy to get the fertilizer close to the plants where the main roots are. Amount: 1 tablespoon complete fer-tilizer per plant.

Eggplant

When blossoms or first small eggplants are visible, apply side-dressing. Amount: 1 ta-blespoon complete fertilizer per plant.

Leeks

Side-dress when 8 to 12 inch-es tall. Pack several big hand-fuls of compost high around each stem. This provides a slow release of nu-trients and shades or blanches the stalks somewhat so they will get white and tender. Amount: 2 to 3 handfuls compost mounded around each plant.

Okra

Side-dress when the plant blossoms. If you have a long harvest of okra, you can side-dress again about a month after the first time. Amount per side-dressing: 1 tablespoon complete fertilizer per plant or 3 cups per 25 feet of row.

Onions

Side-dress when they are 6 to 8 inches tall and every couple of weeks after that until the bulbs start to expand. Onions can take quite a bit of fertilizer. Amount: 2 to 3 cups complete fertilizer per 10 feet of wide row 16 inches wide. Don't fertilize onions if their tops have started to fall.

Peppers

Peppers are very sensitive to fertilizer. They need it in small doses only at blossom time. Amount: no more than 1 tablespoon complete fertilizer per plant.

Pole Beans

Beans usually don't need any side-dressing. But in long-season areas down South, side-dressing will keep plants in top shape. Side-dress within a week or so after your first picking and every three or four weeks after that. Amount: 1 teaspoon complete fertilizer per plant.

Potatoes

Side-dress potatoes about six or seven weeks after planting. This is when some of the plants start to blossom and when it's time to hill the plants for the last time. Side-dress *before* hilling so you can cover the fertilizer with soil as you hill. Amount: 1 tablespoon complete fertilizer per plant or 3 cups per 25 feet of row.

Summer Squash and Zucchini

Side-dress when you see flower buds or blossoms. Amount: 1 to 2 tablespoons complete fertilizer per plant.

Tomatoes

Side-dress when you see the first blossoms, or wait until you see the first small green tomatoes to be sure the extra fertilizer goes toward nourishing the fruits. Amount: 1 to 2 tablespoons complete fertilizer per plant.

GARDEN PESTS AND DISEASES

Having a healthy garden is the best way to prevent damage from pests and diseases. General management techniques can lure or discourage pest birds or animals, and they contribute to insect and disease management. You don't want to wipe out every bug in the garden, just establish and maintain a controlled balance. A few pests must survive to maintain the populations of the beneficial insects who prey on them. Also, you must consider where your personal margins of acceptable insect presence or actual damage lie — you can lose a few plants to insects and still have a good garden. By using a combination of natural defenses, you can forget about the spray bottle of insecticide, and rely instead on careful observation, planning, and a good deal of trial and error.

Clean gardening practices are essential, as many insect species breed or overwinter in piles of garbage, weeds, and clippings. These supply the little beasties with food and shelter and are considered an open invitation to a great variety of bugs. Likewise, allowing diseased or dead vegetation to collect near growing plants promotes plant diseases.

Many practices will deter a wide range of bugs, and certain methods zero in on specific invaders.

HEALTHY PLANTS RESIST PROBLEMS

Simply put, healthy plants in healthy soil do not attract insects or disease organisms.

Ever notice that bugs seem to besiege plants that were already in a weakened state? It's true. Tests consistently confirm that healthy plants tend to stay healthy while sickly ones are in for a struggle. A plant that has been weakened by disease, transplant shock, improper hardening off, poor nutrition, or other insects is an easy target. The plant's color changes, and some bugs pick up on that. It may smell or taste different to the insects' superior sensitivity in these areas (a compound known as stress ethylene is often released by plants under stress). Sick plants are physically less sturdy, stems lose the stiffness associated with adequate water retention, cuticle (outer surface) composition changes, and wilting softens the plant tissues, making them easier for bugs to chew or suck. Any holes chewed into plant tissues cause microscopic amounts of volatile essential oils of that plant to be given off into the atmosphere, and insects can be attracted by only a few molecules of their favorite fare.

One tactic toward raising "tougher" plants is to water them less. When plants are subject to slight water shortages they react by developing a tougher outer layer to protect the plant from loss of moisture. Therefore, while plenty of water produces plants that brag about being tender and juicy, slight-

Earwig

ly underwatered plants may have tougher, less bug-appealing stems, leaves, and other parts. While it's unlikely that the human consumer of these garden goodies will detect any differences in produce quality, to the bugs such differences may be substantial enough to send them buzzing off.

PLAN AHEAD TO DISCOURAGE PESTS AND DISEASES

Sound management practices will go a long way in discouraging pests and disease in your garden. A relatively new approach called *integrated pest management* (IPM) combines preventive planning and carefully targeted controls. The idea is to maintain a healthy, balanced environment in your garden, where pests won't feel welcome and plants will thrive.

It is feasible to maintain a balance between controlling pests and growing healthy plants — just as long as certain principles are understood and followed.

■ Pest control is an important consideration in all phases from planting and pruning through harvesting.

■ Before applying organic or chemical pest controls consider what you are after. Any control is far more effective when carefully timed and targeted at a specific problem.

■ Spraying or dusting with chemicals is only one part of a thorough pest control plan and may not, in itself, be sufficient to curb insect and disease problems. Often chemicals can be avoided entirely if other methods are employed first.

■ Preventive measures are usually more effective than spraying after insects and disease have damaged plants. Healthy preventive measures include crop rotation, timing your planting and harvest around bug emergence, planting resistant varieties, companion planting, and using plant coverings.

Crop Rotation

Crop rotation has been used by farmers and gardeners for centuries. By never growing the same crop or family of crops in the same place two years in a row, many soil-borne diseases and insects can be controlled. Rotating, or moving crops to different locations at each planting, works by interrupting the life cycles of harmful organisms. Insects that lay eggs, pupate, or otherwise overwinter in the soil wake in the spring ready to devour those first tender shoots (or roots). They expect to find the same feast before them that they saw the previous season. By planting a crop from an entirely different family, you can cut them off from their food source. For instance, root maggots waiting for tasty broccoli roots can starve in a healthy pea patch.

Alternate cover crops with vegetables to allow garden soil time to replenish vital nutrients.

Certain pests are more resilient than others. This is one reason it is often necessary to plan on *not* using a patch of garden for the same crop for three to five years. This is especially true for brassicas, or cabbage family crops, such as broccoli, cauliflower, Brussels sprouts, cabbage, and kale.

PLANTS THAT DETER INSECTS

Asters	Most insects
Basil	Repels flies and mosquitoes
Borage	Deters tomato worm—improves growth and flavor of tomatoes
Calendula	Most insects
Catnip	Deters flea beetle
Celery	White cabbage butterfly
Chrysanthemum	Deters most insects
Dead Nettle	Deters potato bug—improves growth and flavor of potatoes
Eggplant	Deters Colorado potato beetle
Flax	Deters potato bug
Garlic	Deters Japanese beetle, other insects and blight
Geranium	Most insects
Horseradish	Plant at corners of potato patch to deter potato bug
Henbit	General insect repellent
Hyssop	Deters cabbage moth
Marigold	The workhorse of the pest deterrents. Plant throughout garden to discourage Mexican bean beetles, nematodes, and other insects
Mint	Deters white cabbage moth and ants
Mole Plant	Deters moles and mice if planted here and there
Nasturtium	Deters aphids, squash bugs, striped pumpkin beetles
Onion family	Deters most pests
Petunia	Protects beans
Pot Marigold	Deters asparagus beetles, tomato worms, and general garden pests
Peppermint	Planted among cabbages, it repels the white cabbage butterfly
Radish	Especially deters cucumber beetle
Rosemary	Deters cabbage moth, bean beetle, and carrot fly
Rue	Deters Japanese beetle
Sage	Deters cabbage moth, carrot fly
Salsify	Repels carrot fly
Southernwood	Deters cabbage moth
Summer Savory	Deters bean beetles
Tansy	Deters flying insects, Japanese beetles, striped cucumber beetles, squash bugs, ants
Tomato	Asparagus beetle
Thyme	Deters cabbage worm
Wormwood	Carrot fly, white cabbage butterfly, black flea beetle

Some crops, such as corn, celery, and tomatoes, are considered to be "heavy feeders" because they demand more nutrients than other crops. Your soil, and thus future plantings, will benefit greatly by alternating such crops with peas, beans, or another legume, or cover crops to replenish nitrogen and other nutrients.

Timed Planting

Every year at about the same time the same bugs make their spring debuts. Their first appearance depends on the temperature, humidity, and food supplies as well as the time of year. But barring extremes, their emergence can be predicted. By carefully checking for insects in your garden on a daily basis and keeping notes on what you find (type of insects, stage of development, and numbers present) and where (geographic location within the garden, type of plants, including differences in varieties, and whether the bugs appeared on the tops, bottoms, flowers, leaves, or fruits of plants), in a few seasons you can consider yourself a regional expert!

The benefits of knowing when certain insects will stage their yearly coming-out parties are substantial. If you know, for instance, that the striped cucumber beetle will be out and hungry in early May, you can delay setting out your transplants for a few weeks. By this time the beasties will have scoured your plot, found it sadly lacking in sustenance, and either moved on or perished.

If you plan to release predators to gobble up the gobblers, it makes a world of difference if they find their intendeds readily. Otherwise they may wander off in search of their supper. Release them when their prey is plentiful. By knowing precisely when pests will be bursting on the scene, you can plan your planting, transplanting, and release of beneficial insects much more effectively.

Companion Planting

For generations gardeners have noticed that some plants seem to do better in the presence of others. Part of this happy coexistence is attributed to the ability of certain plants to repel, ward off, or confuse insect attacks. Staggered plantings of different crops — a patchwork garden — will interrupt the spread of insects. It's easiest for them to go down a neat row of vegetables, one plant after the other.

Rather than barring insects, some plants, by attracting them, serve as a *trap crop*. The bugs actually prefer them to your main garden crop. Trap crops can be removed and destroyed when infested to eliminate the pests, or may be left in place to keep them otherwise occupied. Some trap crops, such as dill for tomato hornworms, attract the pests and thus make them more vulnerable to other means of control, such as handpicking.

Resistant Varieties

What makes some plants more resistant to bugs than others? Nature builds defenses into wild plants, and as humans have altered and invented plants to suit their own tastes, some of those natural defenses have become lost in the process. Cuticle composition, sticky hairs, tighter corn husks, even naturally occurring bug toxins within the plant cells are being rediscovered by plant breeders and crossed into garden vegetable strains. Check with your state university for any resistant varieties they may be testing, and with your nursery for commercially available resistant varieties.

Plant Coverings

There is a variety of horticultural fabrics on the market capable of excluding insects if used properly. These fabrics provide a physical barrier between the crops and the critters, discouraging bugs, bunnies, and birds. There are also fringe benefits to covering certain plants, such as season-extending heat retention, wind and hail protection, and the exclusion of airborne weed seeds.

Some coverings, such as Reemay, are made of spun-bonded polypropylene. They are porous, allowing air and water to pass through freely, and translucent, letting 70 to 80 percent of available sunlight through to growing plants. Though extremely lightweight (barely ½ ounce per square yard), these fabrics have spun-bonded fibers that

SOIL SOLARIZATION KILLS PROBLEM INSECTS AND DISEASES

If there were a sure way to destroy virtually every kind of harmful insect egg and larvae in your garden soil, would you be interested? How about if the process were easy, cheap, and carried a host of other benefits along with it? Solarization is a simple, five-step process that kills insects, plant diseases, nematodes, harmful fungi, and weed seeds. At the same time helpful microorganisms within the soil apparently benefit, possibly from the lack of competition, and thrive. Soil that has been solarized allows plants to draw on the nutrients, especially nitrogen, calcium, and magnesium, more readily. Seeds germinate more quickly. Plants grow faster and stronger, often maturing earlier with substantially higher yields than in unsolarized soil.

Solarization works in the same way as a greenhouse, where a transparent covering, in this case 3 or 6 mm plastic sheeting, traps the sun's heat. After several days of sunshine, soil temperatures rise to as high as 140°F. at the soil surface and well over 100°F. as far down as 18 inches. It takes four to six weeks of sunny weather to pasteurize the soil. For most of the country that means planning to spread plastic somewhere between the end of June and the first of September.

Any size plot, down to a 3-foot-wide bed, will retain enough heat to do the job, although the larger the area, the more heat is generated and maintained, *and* the longer lasting the effects. It's easier to lay plastic down in a narrow strip than a wide patch, so that is a major consideration. And therein lies the solitary expense in using the sun's energy to improve your soil: a strip or roll of clear (*not black*) plastic large enough to cover your area and overlap on all sides by at least a foot.

Five Steps to Purifying Your Soil through Solarization

1. **Prepare the soil.** Pull any weeds or old crops. Turn in any soil amendments and then rake the surface smooth. It's important to remove any stones or clumps that might raise the plastic and create air pockets that could cause uneven heating.

2. **Water thoroughly.** Leave a sprinkler on for several hours or overnight to soak the soil. This creates 100 percent humidity under the plastic, which acts with the heat to kill all those unwanted critters.

3. **Dig a trench** all around the bed or plot 6 to 8 inches deep.

4. **Lay a clear plastic sheet,** 3 to 6 mm thick, over the area, overlapping the trench on all sides. Fill the trench back in, weighing down the plastic while pulling it as tight as possible.

5. **Sit back, relax, and wait.** Although cloudy weather will slow things down by cooling the soil under the tarp, a few weeks of sunshine will improve your soil dramatically, easily, and inexpensively. If you live in an area with cool or cloudy summers, or if you just don't want to wait all season, you can speed up the process by adding a second sheet of plastic. Using the hoops commonly used to elevate row covers or bird netting, raise the second sheet of plastic over the ground-level sheet. The airspace in between acts as a temperature buffer zone during cloudy weather, and the combination of the two sheets of heat-absorbing plastic serves to raise the soil temperature as much as 6° F.

make them very strong and tear-resistant. They can be used for several seasons if treated with care. Avoid walking on the coverings, lift and place them out of the way when cultivating, and store them when not in use.

All plant coverings trap heat. This makes them wonderful season extenders, both by aiding early planting and by protecting crops in the fall. But in spring and summer they can raise temperatures underneath by 15 to 35°F., too much for many plants.

Lay these fabrics over the crop as soon as it goes in the ground. Weigh the edges and ends down securely with soil or boards so that nothing can creep underneath and to prevent the wind from blowing the fabric off plants. Leave extra headroom for the plants as they grow. The cover can rest on

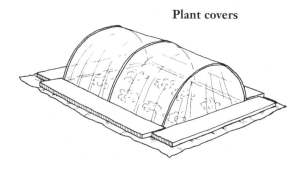

Plant covers

the plants with no ill effects or can be draped over hoops or supported by other structures, even by intercropping with taller, faster-growing plants.

SPRAYS AND DUSTS

Despite your best efforts, there will be years when insects and diseases threaten to overwhelm your garden. Of course, you will want to take action. Some insecticidal preparations have less environmental impact than others. Sometimes a powerful stream from a garden hose is enough to dislodge unwanted visitors from plants, without side effects. The dazed bugs can then be collected and disposed of.

Chemical pesticides cause enormous health and environmental problems and like (other forms of) war, seldom solve the problem. One of the major advantages of organic pesticides is that they break down quickly, posing no threat of chemical build-up in soil or plants, or groundwater contamination. This speedy decomposition may also be considered one of their main disadvantages, however, as it often makes several applications necessary, especially after rainfall.

Soap Sprays

Soap sprays are among the safest of preparations and are very effective against a variety of soft-bodied insects. Aphids, mealybugs, spider mites, spittlebugs, stinkbugs, crickets, and grasshoppers can all be washed up by a soap spray. Mix 3 tablespoons of mild soap such as Fels Naptha, Ivory Snow (laundry soap), or Safer's Insecticidal Soap to a gallon of water and apply to foliage with a hand sprayer.

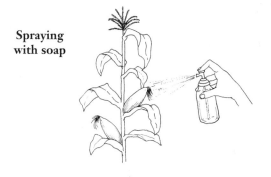

Spraying with soap

Most bugs will die within an hour, done in by the fatty acid salts of the soap. To kill requires a direct hit, as the solution degrades quickly, so spraying must be repeated often. Whether insects are killed by desiccation, suffocation, or some other means is unclear, but whatever the mechanism, many beneficial insects are apparently immune.

Some plants are more susceptible to damage from soap sprays than others, particularly Chinese cabbage, cucumbers, melons, and other large-leafed plants. A residue from repeated sprayings can cause leaves to brown on the edges and curl. Rinsing the plants with water a few hours after spraying may prevent this. If a growing tip is damaged, plant maturity can be delayed. Any soap spray may somewhat reduce crop yields.

One important note: Stronger concentrations of soap are *no more effective* at killing bugs, but *cause significant plant damage.*

Dormant Oil

Dormant oil spray is used primarily on fruit and nut trees. It must be applied early, when no leaves or buds are present (during dormancy) but after temperatures are above freezing (when insect eggs begin to hatch). Late winter is usually best. Its use should be considered as a last resort, *only* against a known insect problem, as it harms beneficial insects as well as such pests as aphids, mites, and thrips. Improper application may damage trees.

Select a product that is 97 percent petroleum oil with 3 percent inert ingredients. Avoid those that include arsenate of lead, lime sulfur, or Bordeaux mix. A lightweight (#10) motor oil can be used. Mix ⅔ cup per gallon of water and spray to coat each tree thoroughly, paying particular attention to joints. The solution cuts off air to the tree, and this suffocates insect eggs and emerging larvae. Dormant trees obtain most of their oxygen through their roots, so they are not affected, unless the oil is applied after buds have appeared. This can also cause leaves to burn, or leaves or fruit to drop.

Bug Juice

This is a remarkably effective method of insect control. After determining which pest is doing the damage, collect about ½ cup of the offending insects and put them in a blender with about 2 cups of water. Liquefy, strain (through cheesecloth), pour about ¼ cup into a 1-gallon hand sprayer, dilute by filling with water, and spray away. Cover the entire plant, hitting both sides of leaves. Some successes have been reported by drenching the soil with bug juice as new seedlings emerge to prevent bugs from getting started. This stuff can be diluted many times for repeat uses. Freeze any extra promptly to prevent bacterial contamination.

Bug juice has been reported to work against a variety of pests, including aphids, pill bugs, Mexican bean beetles, cutworms, stinkbugs, and armyworms — even slugs! *Warning: Do not try this against fleas, mosquitoes, or others that feed on blood and transmit diseases.*

Plant Juice

Plant juice is a simplification of the bug juice method. It's especially good for tiny insects such as aphids, which are too much trouble to handpick. Load the blender with infested leaves and proceed as before.

Another variation is to make an extract from the leaves of nonpoisonous plants that are not bothered by bugs. Try pine, poplar, or various herbs. Spraying such concoctions on afflicted crops repels such pests as scale, beetles, codling moths, mealybugs, and boll weevils.

Garlic and hot pepper sprays as well as several herbal brews are effective against many insects, as the bugs are very sensitive to differences in the smell or taste of their preferred foods. Naturally occurring sulfur compounds in garlic repel a great many pests, from insects to large animals. Butterflies even have taste receptors in their feet, which tell them upon alighting whether dinner is underfoot.

Bacillus Thuringiensis (Bt)

Bt is a naturally occurring bacterium that infects and destroys a multitude of insect pests, most notably leaf-chewing caterpillars, such as cabbage worms, loopers, and hornworms. It kills through a toxic protein crystal that adheres to the insect's gut and perforates it, causing the critter's vital fluids to seep out. It must be eaten to work, so application must be timed for when pests are feeding. Plants must be sprayed thoroughly, including all parts and the undersides of leaves. Stickers and wetting agents increase effectiveness.

To get the most from Bt, spray while the caterpillars are small, preferably under ½ inch long. The smaller bugs are more susceptible than large ones.

Since Bt residues break down almost immediately (fastest when exposed to sunlight), it poses no health risk and may be applied right up to harvest time. Bt is available under several brand names through nursery outlets, in either a spray or a wettable powder.

Botanical Insecticides

Rotenone, pyrethrum, ryania, nicotine, sabadilla, and neem are natural plant derivatives that are nearly harmless to people and animals. They decompose much more quickly than their chemical cousins, so they present little environmental threat. However, they are still potent bug killers that often don't discriminate among their victims.

Buy the purest form of botanical insecticides. This is not made easy by manufacturers who often combine products or include additives. One additive, a synergist called piperonyl butoxide (PBO), should be avoided.

Rotenone. A tropical plant extract, it is commercially available as a powder or wettable dust. Lethal to a vast array of insects including bees and other beneficials, it should be applied in the evening when bees are least active to minimize casualties. A powerful stomach poison to insects, it is extremely toxic to pigs and fish (it's also toxic to humans in sufficient amounts) and should never be used near waterways. Allow three to seven days before harvesting treated crops, as it takes that long for residues to disappear, despite the one-day claim of many products labels.

Nicotine. An alkaloid commonly derived from tobacco, nicotine is present in other plants. It performs best against soft-bodied insects. A strong contact poison, nicotine is (surprise) very toxic to humans. Residues break down quickly, allowing nicotine solutions to be applied to plants within 48 hours of harvest.

After using, wash your hands with milk to neutralize tobacco mosaic virus, which can be spread by homemade solutions. This even eliminates the risk of smokers spreading the disease!

Pyrethrum. Another powerful insecticide, pyre-

thrum is made from the blossoms of the pyrethrum flower, *Chrysanthemum cinerariifolium*. It is sold as a concentrate or in combination with other botanicals. It controls dozens of pests while not affecting birds, animals, or humans (except in cases of allergic reaction), but it is just as lethal to fish as rotenone.

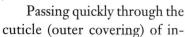
Pyrethrum

Passing quickly through the cuticle (outer covering) of insects, pyrethrum acts on the nervous system, quickly stunning their victims senseless. Confused bugs stumble out into the open where they can be finished off, either by the pyrethrum or some other method.

Apply in the late afternoon or evening as sunlight accelerates the degrading process. Don't combine with a soap spray or lime program, as they are mutually incompatible.

Ryania. From the roots and stem of the South American shrub *Ryania speciosa*, ryania is most often sold in compounds with rotenone or pyrethrum, which are toxic to bees and fish. Both a contact and stomach poison, ryania in its pure state makes bugs so violently ill that they forever avoid any plants treated with it after a brief initial encounter. It is most effective against the codling moth, corn earworm, and other caterpillar pests.

Sabadilla. Used for bug control since the sixteenth century, sabadilla's toxic alkaloids are derived from the seeds of a South American lily, *Schoenocaulon officinale*, and is made into a dust or wettable powder. Many hard-to-kill bugs succumb to its effects as a contact or stomach poison. Harlequin bugs, stink bugs, lygus bugs, striped cucumber beetles, cabbage worms, and leafhoppers are among the defeated. Wear a face mask when applying, as it can be irritating to mucous membranes.

Neem Oil. Made from the seeds of the native Indian neem tree, *Azadirachta indica*, neem oil acts upon many insects as an appetite suppressant and on some as a growth or development inhibitor. Aphids, cucumber beetles, mealybugs, mites, and more shun plants treated with this extraction.

Insect-Repelling Plants. Many other flowers and herbs have insect-repellent qualities and are valuable either as companion plants or in home bug remedies. Marigolds (not the scentless varieties), nasturtiums, tansy (not ragwort), rue, feverfew, camomile, lavender, southernwood and other artemisias, and many kinds of mints, especially pennyroyal, have long been relied upon for their abilities to repel bugs. Most cooking herbs also keep bugs at bay and at the very least are pleasant to work around. It seems the more wonderfully aromatic the herb, the more unappealing they are to insects.

Diatomaceous Earth. The skeletal remains of tiny prehistoric sea creatures called diatoms is known as diatomaceous earth. The shells of these single-celled fossils are broken down during processing into needlelike silica particles that penetrate the bodies of insects on contact. Since a bug's outsides are all that holds its insides in place, the insides gradually ooze out and the bug dies of dehydration. Dusting after a light rain or mixing the powder into a spray will help insure that it stays where you put it. Note: Although considered safe to people and animals, it does irritate some people's lungs. It is also harmful to beneficials, including earthworms. Be sure to buy the diatomaceous earth produced specifically for garden use, and not the product used for cleaning swimming pools.

KNOW THY ENEMY

Just because you have *insects* doesn't automatically mean you have an *insect problem*. Often it is better to accept a level of infestation or damage than to launch a control program. Certainly a small amount of cosmetic damage is preferable to the bother, expense, and ecological disruption of chemical intervention.

But, assuming the damage is significant enough to warrant some measure of control, the next step is to determine which insect is responsible, after eliminating the possibility that soil deficiencies, plant diseases, or pure gardener error (like planting shade-loving crops in full sun) aren't responsible for the damage you see.

Bug identification can be especially challenging. To begin with, the sheer number of species and the adaptations of each serve to fill every imaginable nook and cranny of nature. In the garden, bugs are in the air, on the ground, under the ground, and in the foliage, fruits, and flowers. Some burrow into roots, some bore into stems, some tunnel in between the surfaces of leaves.

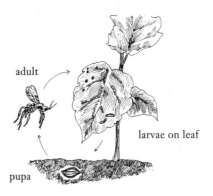

Aphid midge life cycle

As if the vast diversity of bugs weren't confusing enough, the immature insect may bear no resemblance to the mature one. Insects that undergo incomplete metamorphosis begin life as eggs. The eggs hatch into larvae, called nymphs, which grow and proceed through stages, referred to in bug lingo as *instars*. As the larvae grow, the hard outer covering, the exoskeleton, gets tighter and tighter until finally it is shed and the nymph grows into its next form. Some nymphs do resemble the adult form of their species; others look totally different.

Other insects go through a total change. They also begin as eggs, hatching into larvae. The larvae grow, and may or may not pass through various instars, but at a certain point, ordained by nature, they make a dramatic change. They pupate. Some spin cocoons, some retreat to underground cells, and while to an outside observer they appear to be dormant, they go through such drastic physical changes that they lose forever their previous forms to emerge as adults.

Typically, adult forms of insects have six legs

and three main body segments, which may not be obvious in each species. The head, with or without antennae, is followed by the thorax (middle segment), with the abdomen bringing up the rear.

So, the challenge of identifying a bug problem is not only to find out *if* the bugs are a problem, or *which* bug is a problem, but *what form* of the bug is a problem. Sometimes only larvae do damage, sometimes only the adults, and sometimes all stages cause trouble. In any case, adults are unwanted because they perpetuate the species. Use the insect pest and disease guide at the end of this chapter to identify and control your insect pests.

DISEASE CONTROL

Diseases in the garden may be caused by fungi, viruses, bacteria, or physiological disturbances. Symptoms vary widely, but most are aggravated by poor growing conditions, such as drought, excessive moisture, lack of proper nutrients or overfeeding, improper soil acidity, too low or too high temperatures, and air pollution. Diseases often enter through wounds caused by insects, careless pruning or cutting, rodents, or storm damage.

Treatment for diseases consists mainly of prevention. Keeping in mind the conditions in which pests and diseases thrive, you should recognize that maintaining vigorous plants is the greatest form of pest and disease control. Of course, you will get a head start by planting virus-free and disease resistant varieties whenever they are available.

If you can prevent plant disease with good cultural practices, then you'll never need to spend time trying to save an unhealthy garden. A few good tips to keep in mind are:

■ Immediately after a rain, when plants are still wet, rest. That way, you won't be in the garden, brushing up against plants and possibly spreading disease.

■ Locate plants where they'll have good air circulation and plenty of sunlight.

■ Mulch. It not only saves weeding and watering, but prevents soil-borne diseases from being spread to plants by mud splashed up during rainstorms.

■ Don't throw diseased plant material into the compost pile.

■ If you're pruning trees and shrubs for fire blight, take an extra minute to dip your pruning tool into bleach before each cut and burn infested twigs afterward.

■ Practice good sanitation. Under roses, for instance, rake up all old rose leaves in fall and spring. They harbor black spot and other fungus diseases. For more on cleaning up the garden, see chapter 4.

Treating Plant Diseases

More often than not, the best thing to do with a sick plant is to destroy it before the problem spreads. But there may be cases where you want to try to rescue a long-established perennial bed, fruit trees that are just mature enough to bear fruit, or a favorite berry bush.

The first step in treatment is to remove and destroy all affected parts of the plant. *(Burn it. Don't put it on the compost pile!)* Be sure to disinfect your tools between cuts, or you may end up spreading the disease. Next, identify what's causing the problem. If you're not sure, a local agricultural extension agent or nursery may be able to help you identify it.

As a general rule, diseases caused by bacteria or viruses are difficult, if not impossible, to cure. The most recognizable symptoms are sudden dying of shoots, foliage, or new growth and discolored, mottled, or rotting patches on plants without the telltale growth of fungus. If this is the cause of your problem, you'll do better to destroy the plants before the problem spreads.

Although the symptoms may be similar, physiological problems are not really diseases, but caused by improper growing conditions. Plants can be weakened by insect or weather damage, malnutrition, overfertilization, improper soil acidity, too much or too little water, unfavorable temperatures, and pollutants. Unless the damage is extreme, once you identify and correct the problem, your plants should revive.

Perhaps the most common plant diseases are caused by some form of fungus. These are actually a lower form of plant life characterized by a lack of chlorophyll, which makes higher plants green. Because plants need chlorophyll to manufacture food, fungi obtain it from other plants and animals. In addition to weakening your plants, fungi can be identified by mold and spores on leaves, stems, and fruits.

Keeping in mind that fungi tend to thrive in damp conditions and rotting plant material, your first step should be to keep the garden free of such debris. Depending on the cause, a fungicide may be useful. Fungicides come in spray or dust form and a variety of formulas. Bordeaux mixture, a bluish powder of lime and copper sulfate developed by French vinardists in the 19th century is probably the most common.

The most important thing to remember is choose products and time your applications carefully. A spray program that is targeted and timed to control a specific problem is far more effective than blanketing the garden with excessive sprays that may burn leaves and fruits.

For more on identifying and treating plant diseases, refer to the guide at the end of this chapter.

PEST PROOFING YOUR GARDEN

Nothing beats a secure fence for keeping out rabbits, woodchucks, raccoons, dogs, and cats. It even helps to control the traffic of neighborhood kids scooting through the yard.

Get your fence up early, *before* animal pests make their first forays. Once they get a taste of what's in your garden they will be determined to

get back in for extra helpings, fence or no.

An effective fence can be made of 3-foot-high chicken wire (1-inch or 1½-inch mesh), topped by a strand of electric wire 1 inch above the top. An electric fence is the best way to keep raccoons out

of the corn patch. The jolt a raccoon gets when he grabs the electric wire convinces him to try a garden somewhere else. You can save electricity by energizing the wire only just before and during the corn harvest. Run it from late afternoon until early morning.

Gates should be at least 5 feet wide to allow a big work cart and even a vehicle through.

If you use good materials and build your fence solidly, it should easily last 10 or 20 years with only a little upkeep each season.

Early spring is a good time for fence-mending. Check around the base of the fence for open spaces where animals can sneak under. Sometimes the freezing and thawing of the ground will raise a few fence posts and open gaps. Drive the posts back into the ground. As the season passes, cut the grass and weeds around the fence. If you let some get tall they can short out the wire strand on top and allow animals a free pass into your garden.

Rabbits

If you have rabbits in your neighborhood, you have *lots* of rabbits. They mate several times a year and each litter can have six or seven young ones. You don't need a calculator to figure that the possibilities are tremendous.

Rabbits like to feed at twilight, but they have no rules. They will feed at dawn and even in the middle of the day. Rabbit damage can be rough in spring. Just a few bites into your broccoli, lettuce, cabbage, or cauliflower transplants can set them back. And if they nibble the center bud, the plants won't ever produce. They can do a number on young beans, too.

There are only a few defenses if you don't have a fence. In a small garden, sprinkle black pepper on your transplants in the evening. Rabbits sniff everything and after a sneezing fit they'll move on. If you can find their path to the garden, you can scatter some *moth crystals* along it. Don't use mothballs; they are dangerous and kids often think they are candy. Some folks say if you sprinkle blood meal at the edge of the garden and on the plants, rabbits will avoid your garden. I guess if they smell blood they think someone means business. If you tie a dog near the garden, you can usually keep rabbits at bay; just be careful not to let your dog do more damage than the rabbits do.

Young fruit trees are another favorite rabbit meal. They'll nibble through the bark to get at the tender layer underneath. To protect fruit trees, wrap the bottom 24 inches of trunks with perforated plastic strips (available from garden suppliers) or build a cylindrical fence of chicken wire or hardware cloth. This protection will help to discourage mice as well. Check the fencing annually to be sure that it does not girdle a growing tree.

Woodchucks

A woodchuck will eat any green thing it can get its teeth into. Woodchucks, often called groundhogs, come out of their underground burrows at dawn for their first meal. They're lazy and like to make their home near a convenient food source — like a nice vegetable garden. You can tell if a woodchuck is eating your crops because it moves efficiently down one row at a time, eating everything in its path.

After their morning eating binge, woodchucks go back underground to sleep it off. You might spot them later in the day coming out for another meal.

They prefer not to travel very far from home to get food. If you can get them to relocate their burrows away from your garden, they may not bother you again.

Many tactics have been proposed to keep woodchucks out of the vegetable garden. Popular methods involve pouring noxious substances, like used motor oil, down their burrows. However, you may want to think twice about whether you want that stuff in your soil and ground water.

You will be most successful combatting woodchucks if you learn their habits and make them as uncomfortable as possible.

Find all the woodchuck holes around your garden. They like dry spots for a burrow and they dig two entrances. Woodchucks also like to keep their fur clean and dry. The first thing to try is flooding burrows by running a hose down the entrance. Some deterrents, anything from moth crystals to dog feces, will also discourage them.

It may help to tie the family dog near the garden, but groundhogs have been known to figure out the length of the dog's chain and calmly eat the vegetables just out of range. Woodchucks are easy to catch in "Havahart" traps. Be sure to release them at least a mile or so from your garden.

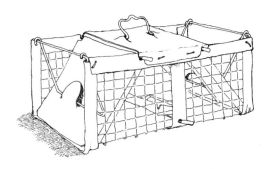

The Havahart trap allows tender-hearted gardeners to capture garden villains and release them a few miles away.

Raccoons

There are many old-time tricks to keep raccoons out of the corn patch, but only one rule: put your defense in action *before* the raccoons set foot in your garden. Don't wait until their first attack. Once raccoons get a taste of your sweet corn, it will be almost impossible to keep them out.

If you are growing extra-early sweet corn, get ready to protect it. The local raccoons will sniff it out because it will be sweet and delicious well before any of your neighbors' corn.

If you don't have an electric fence, try spreading moth crystals between corn rows at each edge of the garden. Raccoons hate the taste of moth crystals on their paws. If it rains, you'll have to put down more crystals.

If you are a careful observer, you may find paths through tall grass that raccoons take to the garden. If so, sprinkle a little creosote along the path. Raccoons don't like getting this on them either, and it may discourage them.

Mice

Field mice can be destructive. When the season is still young, they sometimes dig up big seeds before they have a chance to germinate. Unsuspecting gardeners often think that they've planted wrong or had a bad batch of seeds.

Mice are troublesome at harvest time, too.

They love beets. They can hide under the lush foliage and nibble away to their heart's content. In bad years, they'll take bites out of almost every beet in some rows. Carrots, potatoes, and strawberries are favorite targets, too.

To control mice, keep a cat. With a cat lurking around the garden, most of the rodents will stay away. Also, avoid using heavy mulches until well into the gardening season. Mice will take shelter and breed in a thick mat of hay or straw when the weather is still cool. If you can, use mulches that contain few seeds. Mice just love hay seeds. This is especially important if you plant potatoes under mulch, because after eating a lot of seeds they'll chew the potatoes.

Mice can be particularly damaging to tree bark in the orchard. They'll build a cozy nest in your winter mulch and chew on the tree bark all winter long. To discourage mice from wintering in your neighborhood, avoid placing winter mulch until after the ground has frozen and mice have found other homes.

Moles

If there are moles in your garden, you'll know it. Their zig-zagging tunnels are easy to recognize. Moles burrow close to the surface searching for earthworms, grubs, snails, and slugs, and this burrowing can really damage a garden. Moles can lift seeds and transplants out of the ground and those west of the Rockies (slightly bigger than the "eastern" moles) may eat root crops, flower bulbs, or even sprouting pea and corn seeds.

There are several good techniques for repelling moles. Cut some thorny blackberry canes into 3-inch or 4-inch sections. With a piece of wire, poke small holes into the mole tunnels at different spots. Then push a short thorny cane down through each hole into the tunnels. Moles have tender skins and they will be so annoyed that they will leave.

You also can squirt a little creosote on the runs every six or eight feet, and the moles will probably leave. Another good idea is to drop moth balls into the first run you see to discourage moles from tunneling further in the area.

Birds

Birds are usually nice to have near a garden because they eat many kinds of insect pests, but they can be a problem, too.

Crows and blackbirds are notorious for digging up corn seeds and small plants. There are commercial coatings you can put on the seeds before plant-

ing, but they don't work very well. By the time the birds discover they're getting a stomachache, they've dug up two-thirds of the row.

You can put some 12-inch-wide wire mesh over your corn rows, shaping it like a tent, until the plants get too big for the birds to pull. This works well.

Birds can be destructive at harvest time. Berries and grapes are particularly vulnerable. Netting is the top deterrent here. Birds love sweet corn and sunflower seeds, too. People often pull open an ear of sweet corn to see if it's ready. Don't do this; it just gives birds a helping hand. Put mesh bags over the sunflower heads when you see the first bird trying to peck some seed.

Squirrels and Chipmunks

No fence will prevent squirrels and chipmunks from decimating your corn and sunflowers. They jump so well and scurry into the garden so fast that an electric shock doesn't stop them.

In the sweet corn or popcorn rows, squirrels climb right up the stalks and eat the ears. Often they only work the inside rows so you won't notice them. In a row of sunflowers they can jump from one stalk to the next as if they were in a tree.

In a small garden you may be able to use old stockings or cheesecloth on the sunflower heads and corn ears to foil the squirrels at harvest time. In a big garden, an active cat or an eager dog may be your only hope.

IDENTIFYING AND CONTROLLING INSECT PESTS AND DISEASES

For additional information about pest and disease problems on specific plants, refer to the growing information in chapters 6 through 12.

INSECTS

Aphids

Physical Description

Aphids are tiny individuals, most under ¹⁄₁₀ inch long. Their soft bodies are pear shaped, with two long, whiplike antennae at the tip of the head, and a pair of tubes, called *cornicles*, jutting from the other end of the body. The cornicles fire a defensive spray when the aphid is threatened.

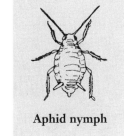

Aphid nymph

Mouthparts are specialized structures designed to pierce plant tissues and suck out the sap.

Aphids come in a variety of colors ranging from the translucent green of cabbage aphids to the pearly black of bean aphids, with pink, red, purple, and blue varieties included in the spectrum. The

Aphid adult

woolly apple aphid resembles a mealybug with his tufts of cottony fluff. Many species are winged, but even within these only intermittent generations develop wings.

Habits

Due to their rapid and constant reproduction, aphid populations can build up tremendously. Since they tend to congregate, they are often found in clumps on stems or under leaves. Aphids are drawn to the color yellow, possibly as a means of zeroing in on weak plants or the pale green, tender growing tips of plants.

Through feeding they transmit disease among their host plants. They also secrete honeydew, a sticky, sweet goo that promotes damaging mold growth on leaves and attracts ants. The ant-aphid relationship is similar to that of the farmer and his cows. In exchange for honeydew, Farmer Ant protects his herd of aphids from predators and even moves it to greener pastures when food supplies are depleted.

Range and Habitat

Found throughout North America, aphids inhabit orchards, fields, gardens, and meadows.

Garden Targets

Most vegetables and ornamentals are susceptible. Cabbage aphids infest brassicas to the point where entire plants are not worth harvesting. It's nearly impossible to dislodge the masses once they have accumulated inside the heads of Brussels sprouts, broccoli, or cauliflower. Pea aphids mob peas and beans, while bean aphids swamp not only peas and beans but spinach, chard, beets, and rhubarb as well. Apple, pear, and other orchard trees

Aphid colony

can be damaged — even stunted — by woolly apple and green peach aphids. Root aphids are taken by ants to feed on the roots of beans, carrots, corn, lettuce, and parsley, to name but a few.

Damage and Signs

Aphids feed in such numbers that leaves often turn yellow as the entire plant begins to weaken. Leaves of potato plants turn brown and curl. Tomatoes suffer from blossom end rot, dead spots on leaves, leaf roll, and stunted plants. Fruit trees with swollen twigs and branches, covered with a white fluff, have been taken over by the woolly apple aphid.

Deterrents

Cultural Practices. Remove plant remains from previous crops, especially cole crops, and till soil afterward to displace and kill eggs. Repeated tillage helps to discourage ants that nest underground. Rotating crops will help. Aphids are especially fond of plants that have been overnourished with nitrogen, so don't overfeed.

Plantings of sunflowers and milkweeds make good trap crops.

Aluminum foil mulch disorients flying aphids, keeping them from lighting on plants surrounded by it.

Repellents. Alliums such as garlic and chives, as well as anise, coriander, nasturtiums, and petunias can be interplanted as repellent plants.

Exclusion. Row covers effectively protect vegetables.

Traps. Sticky traps can be made of bright yellow tiles, boards, or banners coated with motor oil, petroleum jelly, or commercial stick-em such as Tanglefoot. Place these near target plants. Bright yellow plastic plates filled with a little soapy water will drown any aphids that fly into them. These work best positioned at the base of target plants.

Bio-control. Gardeners have long thought of ladybugs as the aphid predator of choice, but they can be fickle gals who don't think twice about crossing property lines. Lacewings devour aphids to the tune of about a hundred each per day. Spiders, assassin bugs, big-eyed bugs, and soldier bugs also dine on aphids and may be easier to keep at home.

Parasites such as the chalcid wasps and others can help reduce aphid populations once they become established. Look for "aphid mummies," the hollow remains of aphids who have already been parasitized. Do not disturb. Friendly bugs have left their legacy within and when the eggs hatch, more parasites will emerge to claim more aphids. The orange wormlike larvae of the gall, or aphid midge, will also do in gobs of aphids.

Sprays and Dusts. Soap sprays are highly effective against aphids on garden vegetables.

Dormant oil spray for fruit trees and roses will prevent larvae from emerging from eggs laid on bark or stems. Both of these methods *can* harm beneficial insects as well as aphids.

Many homemade sprays have been successful against aphids. Water sprayed with force directly at infestations can wash them away. Tea made from 1 part mint to 4 parts water, steeped and filtered, will deter them. Tea made from tobacco stems or soaked cigarette butts is effective, but toxic to people and animals. Don't plan to use it on roses, however, as it turns the blooms black. Also, tomatoes, peppers, and potatoes are susceptible to tobacco mosaic virus, which tobacco preparations can spread. Boiling rhubarb leaves distills oxalic acid, poisonous to man and beast as well as aphids if consumed. Use 2 pounds of leaves per quart of water, and after boiling, add 1 teaspoon of liquid soap. Use elder leaves instead of rhubarb to spray rose bushes. Teas made from garlic or green onions work. Strong limewater is an old-time cure. Three parts 70 percent rubbing (isopropyl) alcohol to 4 parts water with a tablespoon of liquid soap added makes a very effective desiccant. Finally, plant juice made from infested leaves will wipe aphids out.

Both rotenone and diatomaceous earth will kill aphids, but beneficial insects will suffer as well.

BEETLES

Flea Beetles

Although there are about 20 varieties of flea beetles, only a handful bother garden crops. They are beetles, not fleas, but are probably so named because of their tremendous, flea-like jumping ability.

Range and Habitat

Flea beetles are found throughout North America. Habitat is nonspecific.

Physical Description

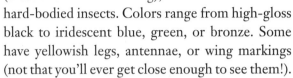

Flea beetle

Flea beetles are tiny (most under ¹⁄₁₀ inch long), hard-bodied insects. Colors range from high-gloss black to iridescent blue, green, or bronze. Some have yellowish legs, antennae, or wing markings (not that you'll ever get close enough to see them!).

Management

Prevention is better than cure. Keep garden debris (their winter home) cleaned up.

Exclusion. Crop covers will keep young, tender targets free of damage.

Traps. A shallow beer trap, similar to that used for slugs, has worked for some people.

Sprays and Dusts. Teas made from repellent plants such as wormwood, mint, or catnip can help to botch up the flea beetles' odor radar, as can sprays from garlic, onion, or hot peppers.

A sprinkling of wood ashes or ground limestone discourages flea beetles, who dislike the dustiness. Resort to rotenone for serious infestations.

Colorado Potato Beetle

For many gardeners, the Colorado potato beetle is one of the most reliable crops in the garden. This potato bug is so common it's not surprising that it is also very resistant to controls, including most pesticides.

Physical Description

Adult beetles are about ⅓ inch long, with a hard, very rounded outer shell. The wing covers alternate creamy yellow with ten black stripes. The head and thorax are decorated with irregular black marks.

The fat, reddish larvae sport two rows of black dots along either side, as well as a black head and legs. They plump up to about ½ inch long before going into the pupal stage.

Range and Habitat

The Colorado potato beetle ranges throughout North America, except in the South and Pacific Northwest. It had its origin in mountain meadows but now will settle in just about anywhere.

Habits

As chewing insects, all stages of larvae and adults eat and eat and eat, pausing only long enough to mate and lay more eggs.

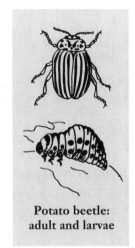

Potato beetle: adult and larvae

Garden Targets

Members of the Solanaceae family — potatoes, tomatoes, eggplant, and peppers — are particularly vulnerable. Cabbage and petunias are also susceptible.

Damage and Signs

These pests can strip plants of foliage. They do the most damage in small plots, killing plants and at the very least reducing harvests. Characteristic black excrement can be found on damaged leaves and stems.

Deterrents

Cultural Practices. Rotate solanaceous crops with other types of plants, and try resistant varieties, such as Sequoia potatoes. Potatoes can be grown above ground, making it nearly impossible for grubs, or larvae, to move up into the plants from the soil. Keep a foot-deep layer of mulch over the developing tubers to protect them from sunlight (it turns them bitter and green) and to further stymie the grub migration.

Repellent plants like snap beans, marigold, garlic, onions, flax, catnip, coriander, nasturtiums, tansy, dead nettle, and especially horseradish can be interplanted to keep the beetles away.

Because they're not very enthusiastic climbers, fat grubs can be halted by a thick mulch.

Exclusion. Crop covers tucked over vulnerable plants will protect them from incoming beetles but can't help to keep ground-level grubs from their regularly scheduled trek from the soil up into plants.

Bio-control. A strain of Bt, *Bacillus thuringiensis san diego*, sold as M-One, is reported to be about 90 percent effective against newly hatched larvae when applied early.

Predators include toads, paper wasps, and ground beetles. Normally considered stink bug predators, *Perillus bioculatus* and *Podisus maculiventris* also enjoy a fat potato beetle.

The parasite wasp *Edovum puttleri* and a fungus (*Beauveria bassiana*) can keep them in check. Tachinid flies also parasitize these beetles, but not until so late in the season that the damage has already been done.

Sprays and Dusts. One great remedy against potato beetles is to feed them to death. Sprinkle plants with water, then dust well with wheat bran. The bran, once moistened, swells to a point where the beetles' cuticle gives under the pressure. Greedy beetles down the bran as they devour plant leaves, expand, explode, and expire! Teas or sprays made from basil or boiled cedar boughs have been reported successful as repellants. Spraying a solution of 2 tablespoons epsom salts dissolved in a gallon of water also turns them away.

"Beetlejuice," the beetle version of bug juice, destroys the small percentage of beetles it doesn't deter. Triple Plus (rotenone, pyrethrum, and ryania) annihilates them.

Cucumber Beetles

Here is a pair of outlaw cousins, the striped cucumber beetle (*Acalymma vittata*), the common garden criminal, and the spotted cucumber beetle (*Diabrotica undecimpunctata howardi*), alias the notorious corn rootworm. The only difference between them is their chosen repast.

Physical Description

The adult striped cucumber beetles grow to ¼ inch long, while their white wormy larvae grow to about ⅓ inch. An adult beetle is bright yellow, with three broad, black stripes running down the length of the wing covers and a black head. His accomplice, the spotted cucumber beetle, fits a similar description except his greenish yellow wing covers are disguised with 11 large, black spots (12 in western species). Destructive larvae grow to ½ inch in length and are beige with a brown head and brown spot at the rear.

Striped cucumber beetle

Range and Habitat

Both the striped and the spotted cucumber beetles are found in the eastern United States and in parts of southern Canada. Similar species of beetles occupy the West. "Stripes" is most frequently seen in home gardens west of the Rocky Mountains, while "Spot" frequents large cornfields from Mexico to Colorado, and going northeast into Canada.

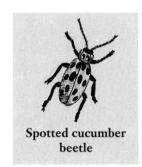

Spotted cucumber beetle

Habits

These greedy eaters will tunnel underground to go after germinating seeds before the sprouts can push through the soil. So gluttonous they can strip entire plants practically overnight, they do their worst damage early on, devouring seedlings before they can get a roothold. Although adults will take on almost any part of the plant, they can most often be found on the underside of leaves.

Garden Targets

Starting with cucumbers and other cucurbits (related plants such as melon, squash, and pumpkin), "Stripes" will proceed to vandalize beans, peas, corn, beets, eggplant, tomatoes, potatoes, and more, including flowers such as daisies, cosmos, dahlias, roses, zinnias, and sweet peas. "Spot" goes for corn, cucurbits, tomatoes, eggplant, potatoes, and even some tree fruit.

Damage and Signs

Holes chewed through foliage, flowers, even fruit may indicate cucumber beetles. They can decimate plants. Their crimes also include transmitting deadly bacterial wilt and cucumber mosaic virus.

Deterrents

Cultural Practices. "Spot" is most easily kept from corn by crop rotation.

Traditionally, heavy mulching has been used to discourage the upward mobility of "Stripes." Larvae find it tough to negotiate through it on their journey from ground level into plants. Late planting, in zones that will allow for it, helps to avoid the heaviest damage inflicted by the first wave of emerging adults. Interplanting is helpful, especially with repellants like catnip, tansy, marigolds, or radishes in and around hills. These beetles are also reported to dislike goldenrod.

Exclusion. Crop covers placed over transplants will keep adult beetles from getting to them. Be aware, however, that these will trap larvae emerging from the soil.

Traps. A trap can be made from a stiff paper milk carton using a piece of bitter melon as bait.

Sprays and Dusts. A spray made of equal parts wood ashes and dehydrated lime, mixed with water, is said to banish the beetles. Make sure to apply to all sides of foliage. Juice from geranium stalks and leaves repels "Stripes." Whiz up a batch in the blender, dilute, and strain into a sprayable consistency. While you have the blender out, a batch of cucumber beetlejuice makes a lethal preparation.

Rotenone, pyrethrum, and neem are all effective.

Japanese Beetles

Physical Description

The adult Japanese beetle is metallic green with copper-colored wing covers. Peeking out from under the wings are small tufts of short, white, bristly hairs, and downy gray hairs cover the belly. Japanese beetles are about ½ inch long and ¼ inch wide, males being somewhat smaller than females.

The maturing larva is a dingy white grub with a brown head. It grows to 1 inch long and has ten abdominal segments. The underside of the last segment has two rows of spines that form a V, an iden-

tifying mark found only in Japanese beetle larvae.

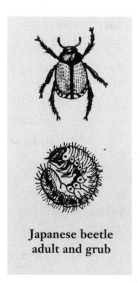

Japanese beetle adult and grub

Habits

Masses of Japanese beetles will feed on one host plant, leaving the next one untouched. They also consider mating a group activity. A moving mass of up to 30 males may engulf a single female, all with the same idea at the same time. Preferring to dine in direct sunshine, they feed heaviest in temperatures between 83 and 95°F. Temperatures of 70°F. and above keep them active and flying about, while low humidity (below 60 percent) reduces flight activity and promotes feeding. Cool weather, wind, or clouds slow both activities, and rainy days bring them to a halt.

Range and Habitat

The Japanese beetle's territory is the eastern United States and is expanding westward. Originally found in open woods and meadows, the Japanese beetle can now be found in any park, lawn, or garden.

Garden Targets

Versatile little guys, they like various fruit and nut trees, especially those bearing ripe or overripe fruit, ornamentals, raspberries, rhubarb, corn (silks), and, for the grubby kids, lawn after yummy lawn. Grassy areas such as lawns and golf courses, especially those that are frequently mown, provide their favorite fare of tender grass roots.

Damage and Signs

Leaves of victims are skeletonized, with only the lacy pattern of veins remaining. Flowers are consumed and fruits are devoured down to the pits.

Lawns may sustain extensive damage due to feeding larvae. Large patches of brown, dead grass appearing in late summer or early fall may be the work of these grubs.

Deterrents

Cultural Practices. Keep trees free from over-ripe fruit and put off planting corn until after the beetles have staged their main feast. Maintain a high pH level in lawn soils wherever grubs are a problem, as this discourages them.

Grow borage as a trap crop; white geranium, garlic, and rue are repellent plants. The beetles avoid forsythia, honeysuckle, and privet; lay out boughs or use these in sprays. Larkspur not only attracts the beetles, it is fatal to them.

Handpicking. Try placing a tarp under infested foliage and shaking the beetles onto it. If done early in the morning while it is still cool and damp, the groggy beetles can't fly off. Dunk your catch in a little kerosene and dispose of them.

Exclusion. Plant covers offer absolute protection from flying adults. But since some adults as well as larvae overwinter in the soil, crop covers may trap them in with plants.

Bio-control. Milky spore disease *(Bacillus popilliae)* is a Japanese beetle control that is catching on quickly. It is a naturally occurring infection, so named because it turns the larvae's blood from clear to milky white. Lethal to grubs but harmless to plants and animals, it is sold in the form of a dust, and may be applied to lawns or other grassy areas anytime except when the ground is frozen. Don't apply with an insecticide, as this wipes out the host for the disease and it will be useless.

It may takes years for this infection to become established, and unless near neighbors are cooperating with your efforts, it may never get a fair chance. Ask your county extension agent for help in coordinating a community effort.

Many birds eat the beetles, and there are several parasites. A parasitic nematode, *Heterohabditis heliothidis*, tested 90 percent effective against the grubs while still in its experimental stages. Begin application of this agent in mid-May. Two wasps, the fall tiphia *(Tiphia popilliavora)* and the spring tiphia *(T. vernalis)* also attack the larvae. Two tachinid flies, *Hyperectein aldrichi* and *Prosena siberita*, parasitize the adult beetles.

Traps. One of the most popular methods of dealing with the adult beetles is to put out traps. These can be homemade or commercial and baited with either food or sex attractants (pheromones). Suggested lures include geraniol (rose scent), anethole (a flavoring made from anise or fennel oil), eugenol (from clove oil), and commercially produced lures, as well as pheromones Japonilure and Integralure. Be forewarned that these lures work! Combining food and sex lures multiplies the effectiveness.

Sprays and Dusts. Teas made from branches of plants that beetles naturally avoid may deter them around garden plants. Japanese beetle-flavored bug juice will also repel them. Rotenone is effective.

Mexican Bean Beetles

The black sheep of the ladybug family, the Mexican bean beetle's resemblance to its helpful cousin is only wing-cover deep.

Physical Description

Young adult beetles are yellow, maturing to the characteristic ladybug copper color. Wing covers are sprinkled with 16 black spots, but there are no white markings between the head and body — a sure sign that this beetle is no "lady." They are rounded, about ¼ inch long and nearly as wide. Larvae are light yellow, covered with bristles, and about ⅓ inch long.

Mexican bean beetle adult

Habits

Both adults and larvae prefer to feed from the bottom side of leaves, but will occasionally nibble on stems or beans.

Range and Habitat

Different species of bean beetles occur throughout the United States; the Mexican bean beetle is found in the eastern United States as well as parts of Texas, Arizona, Colorado, and Utah. Habitat is nonspecific.

Garden Targets

Beans, cabbage, kale, collard, and mustard greens.

Damage and Signs

Feeding habits of all stages skeletonize the leaves, leaving only the lace-like skeleton of veins intact.

Mexican bean beetle larva

Deterrents

Mexican bean beetles are sensitive to high temperatures and drought; some summers nature will contribute to their control.

Cultural Practices. If possible, plant early. Clear away plant remains as soon as the harvest is finished. Keep the garden free of debris that could provide winter quarters.

Interplant beans with potatoes (each plant benefits), nasturtiums, garlic, or savory. Rosemary and petunias are somewhat repellent. Try resistant varieties of beans.

Handpicking. Search and destroy by daily handpicking and you will reduce much of the current season's problems as well as some of the potential for future generations. Turn over leaves to look for clusters of the rounded yellow eggs. Toss the collected beetles in a can of water with a little kerosene, or reserve them for Mexican beetlejuice.

Exclusion. Row covers work well on bush beans. Other plants can also be well protected, but pole beans are awkward to cover.

Bio-control. Predators include assassin bugs and soldier bugs. A wasp, *Pediobius foveolatus*, is a commercially available parasite. Some ladybugs seek out the eggs and larvae.

Sprays and Dusts. A spray made from boiling cedar chips reportedly deters these beetles. Another suggestion is a spray made from corn oil and mashed turnips. Resort to rotenone or pyrethrum only when necessary.

BORERS

Squash Vine Borers

Physical Description

The adult is an elusive, quick, red and black moth, with clear red wings. Up to 1½ inches long, it may look like an oversized hornet. Larvae are ugly, wrinkled, white caterpillars with brown heads, growing to about an inch in length. Eggs are flat brown circles, about ⅒ inch across, attached to stems at the base of the host.

Squash vine borer adult

Habits

The larvae bore into the base of stems shortly after hatching, crawl within, and feed on the soft insides. They leave the plant only at maturity to go underground and pupate. Adults visit plants only momentarily while depositing eggs and are rarely even seen. Females locate the egg site on the stem by touch and will settle for any place within a few inches of where the stem touches the ground.

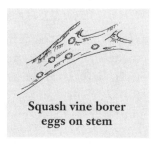

Squash vine borer eggs on stem

Range and Habitat

Found in the United States and southern Canada east of the Rocky Mountains, the squash vine borer's habitat includes any cultivated open area.

Squash vine borer larva in vine

Garden Targets

Targets include summer and winter squash, pumpkin, melons, and cucumbers.

Damage and Signs

When all seems well until vines suddenly wilt, suspect the squash vine borer. Deposits of crumbly greenish yellow residue called *frass* collect at the base of stems or near holes in vines.

Deterrents

Cultural Practices. Early plantings may resist attack, and late plantings may be timed to miss the main July onslaught. Mounding soil up over the plants to the flowers or over any leaf joints encourages rooting and decreases vulnerable surface area. Keep old vines cleaned away, and scrape and squish any eggs you find.

Radishes interplanted in hills of the garden targets help repel vine borers as do wood ashes, camphor, and black pepper sprinkled around potential egg-laying sites. Butternut varieties of squash are the most resistant.

Handpicking. Split the vines with a razor blade at the borer's entrance hole and gouge out (a small crochet hook works great) or stab the culprit to death. Several larvae per stem often must be removed or killed to prevent further damage. Heap moist soil over all plant wounds to aid healing and rooting.

Exclusion. Crop covers, foil collars molded around the base and lower stems of plants, or nylon panty hose wrapped around the stem from the ground up all serve to exclude the egg-laying moths. No eggs, no caterpillars.

Bio-control. Injections of Bt or beneficial nematodes *(Neoplectana carpocapsae* or *Heterorhabditos heliothidis)* into the stems, using a 3cc syringe (from the drugstore, doctor, or vet's office) placed 1½ inches above the soil line can control borers remarkably. Administer just after the first flowering to hit the invading larvae and prevent them from ever entering and damaging the plants. If the caterpillars are already inside the vines, inject at 5-inch intervals along the stem and repeat every few weeks.

Tiny trichogramma wasps parasitize the borers.

Sprays and Dusts. Rotenone or pyrethrum powder will control them if applied regularly as soon as the vines start to run.

Harlequin Bugs

Physical Description

Harlequin bug

Vivid orange-red and black patterns decorate the flat shield-shaped adults, which grow to about ⅜ inch long. Barrel-shaped eggs are laid in precise double rows on the flip side of leaves. White and black bands around them make them easy to identify. Nymphs are red and black. Harlequin bugs at all stages have an unpleasant odor.

Habits

Adults and nymphs feed by piercing plant tissue and sucking out fluid.

Range and Habitat

The harlequin bug can be found in fields, orchards, gardens, and meadows in southern regions of the United States.

Garden Targets

Harlequin bugs feast on cabbage and related crops, such as broccoli, cauliflower, Brussels sprouts, turnips, radishes, kohlrabi, as well as horseradish and mustard.

Damage and Signs

Harlequin bug feeding causes bleached spots on leaves and may lead to wilting, brown, and dying plants.

Deterrents

Cultural Practices. Thorough garden clean-up is essential. Trap crops of turnips or mustard may lure them from other plants. Pull up these crops when they are infested and dunk them into a bucket of water and kerosene. Resistant varieties include Grande, Atlantic, and Coastal broccoli; Copenhagen Market 86, Headstart, Savoy Perfection Drumhead, Stein's Flat Dutch, and Early Jersey Wakefield cabbage; Early Snowball X and Snowball Y cauliflower; Vates, Morris Improved Heading, and Green Glaze collards; Vale kale; and Red Devil, White Icicle, Globemaster, Cherry Belle, Champion, and Red Prince radish.

Exclusion. Crop covers will keep adults off plants.

Sprays and Dusts. Soap sprays offer good control. If faced with a heavy infestation, sabadilla or pyrethrum are recommended.

Squash Bugs

Physical Description

Mature adults are dark brown, ⅝ inch long, with flat backs, long legs and antennae, and piercing mouth-parts. Young nymphs are a pale pearly green with a reddish head and legs. Eggs are shiny gold when laid, changing to red-brown. Arranged in patterns around the center leaf vein, each is about ¹⁄₁₆ inch long.

Squash bug

Habits

Hatching from clusters of eggs, the young tend to stay in groups. Both adults and nymphs feed by piercing plant tissue and sucking out the sap, while injecting digestive juices toxic to the host.

They seek dark, damp hiding places.

Range and Habitat

Squash bugs inhabit fields and gardens throughout North America.

Garden Targets

Squash, pumpkins, melons, and cucumber are the squash bug's preys.

Damage and Signs

Young plants are easily killed by squash bugs. Older plants suffer wilting leaves that eventually blacken and die. Yields may be drastically reduced or eliminated.

Deterrents

Cultural Practices. Garden cleanup of previous vine crop residues, piles of trash, and boards removes overwintering sites. Rotate vine crops as far away from previous plantings as possible. Start plants indoors so that they are large and healthy when transplanted.

Radishes, tansy, marigolds, and nasturtiums interplanted with squash help repel the bugs. Interplanting with peas has also deterred squash bugs.

Trellising (growing plants upward on supports) gets foliage off the ground, reducing the moist, covered areas that the bugs seek. Avoid loose mulches, like hay, and opt instead for paper, plastic, compost, or sawdust.

Look for resistant varieties like Table Queen, Royal Acorn, Early Golden Bush Scallop, Early Summer Crookneck, Early Prolific Straightneck, and Improved Green Hubbard squash.

Handpicking. Crush eggs and toss any adults you can catch into a can of water with kerosene.

Exclusion. Crop covers or screening left on until flowering helps young plants get established before having to fend off any attacks.

Bio-control. Predators include wolf spiders and a red and black tachinid fly, *Trichopoda pennipes.*

Traps. Leave a board out as a trap near the squash plants for the bugs to congregate under. A quick stomp will flatten any takers. Toss any die-hards into a can of water with a little kerosene.

Sprays and Dusts. Soap sprays work well if started at the first sign of adults and kept up throughout the season. A liberal misting of imitation vanilla apparently fouls up their squash sensors. Try sprinkling plants with water that has soaked with a handful of wood ashes and a handful of lime for at least 24 hours. Sabadilla dust works, too.

CATERPILLARS

Cabbage Loopers and Imported Cabbage Worms

These two caterpillars are very similar in habits and appearance as well as in the damage they do. They may be confused with diamondback moths, garden webworms, or alfalfa loopers.

Physical Description

The cabbage looper is green with white stripes down the back and sides. He is most easily recognized by his "humpback." With no legs between his front and hind ends, he moves one end at a time, "looping" or "inching" along. The nickname inchworm comes from his way of going rather than his length, which is more likely to be about 1½ inches.

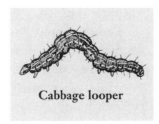
Cabbage looper

Adults are bark brown moths, with a silver marking at the center of each wing.

Imported cabbage worms are a paler green with a yellow stripe along the back. They are about 1¼ inches long and covered with velvety hairs. Adult moths have white wings, 1½ to 2 inches across, decorated with black wing tips, yellowish undersides, and black spots (two for females, one for males).

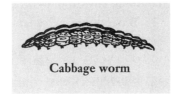
Cabbage worm

Habits

Larvae are chewers, preferring leaves to other plant parts.

Range and Habitat

Cabbage loopers and cabbage worms can be found throughout the United States and parts of southern Canada. Habitat is nonspecific. Loopers may appear in any garden where brassicas are grown.

Garden Targets

Both worms and loopers are primarily cabbage or cole crop (broccoli, cauliflower, kale, kohlrabi, radish, turnip) pests. They will also eat lettuce and some flowers. Loopers expand their diets to include peas, beans, tomatoes, spinach, celery, parsley, potatoes, and carnations.

Damage and Signs

These caterpillars chew large, irregular holes in leaves. As they mature they may bore into the center of heads to feed. Cabbage worms leave green fecal pellets to punctuate their damage.

Deterrents

Cultural Practices. Early damage can cost plant vigor and affect yields. If these pests are a chronic problem, consider planting earlier to give crops a head start. Winter pupation sites for loopers can be eliminated by keeping weeds away from the garden area.

Varieties like Mammoth Red Rock, Savoy Chieftain, and Savoy Perfection Drumhead cabbage are more resistant to damage because of the tight formation of the heads.

Cabbage worm chrysalis

Plants repellent to cabbage worms can be interplanted or used as a border for garden targets. Try onion, garlic, tomato, tansy, celery, hyssop, mint, sage, rosemary, or thyme.

Handpicking. Regular handpicking and destruction of the eggs (greenish white spheres on the tops of leaves for loopers and yellow "bullets" for worms) will prevent damage from the caterpillars. Check both sides of leaves, and do away with any stages of the pests you find.

Exclusion. Crop covers help to extend the growing season as well as to prevent the adults from depositing their eggs. Often they may be left on fall cole crops until harvest. Since the cabbage worms pupate underground, crop rotation is necessary to avoid trapping them under the covers as they emerge.

Bio-control. Bt is even more potent than chemicals against these caterpillars. Be sure to hit them while they are still small, preferably under ½ inch long.

For a homemade pathological control for loopers, make "sick juice." This takes advantage of a naturally occurring disease, nuclear polyhedrosis virus (NPV). Infected caterpillars turn chalky white and lethargic, and usually die in three or four days. They often just sit on leaves motionless. Gather a few loopers (four will successfully treat a quarter-acre garden) and proceed as for bug juice. The difference here is that rather than repelling potential offenders, you are killing present pests with past pests.

Predators and parasites include yellow jackets, trichogramma wasps, and brachonid wasps, but most birds will turn up their beaks at them.

Sprays and Dusts. Repellent sprays work better against cabbage worms than cabbage loopers. Try a mixture of some or all of the following: chopped onion, horseradish root or leaves, garlic, mint, hot peppers, black peppercorns, or powdered limestone. Many gardeners have had success shaking pulverized flour and salt, rye flour, or even plain table salt onto wet cabbage heads.

The Last Resort. If all else fails, and you end up with wormy produce, soak it in a tub of either warm salt water or a solution of vinegar and water for about 15 minutes before preparing it to eat, can, or freeze. The caterpillars shrivel up and float to the top. Some are sinkers, but either way, they die and fall out of the vegetable.

Corn Earworm
(also known as Tomato Fruitworm, Cotton Bollworm)

Physical Description

The earworm is actually an unattractive caterpillar. It grows to about 2 inches long and comes in shades of green, pale yellow, or brown, with light

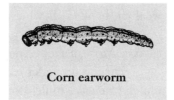

Corn earworm

or dark sidewalls. Adults are dull beige or gray moths, decorated with a few black spots and bearing 1½-inch wingspans.

Habits

Adults are night fliers, attracted to lights, and more amorous during a new moon. This accounts for the cyclic fluctuations in their numbers according to lunar phases.

Range and Habitat

Earworms are found throughout North America. Habitat is nonspecific; they may appear wherever host plants are found.

Garden Targets

Favorite targets include corn, tomatoes, cotton, peppers, eggplant, okra, potatoes, squash, beans, and peas.

Damage and Signs

In corn, earworms begin munching the tender shoots as soon as they break ground, especially on late plantings. They are most infamous for their work on the corn ears. Chewing the silky tassels interferes with the plants' pollination and kernel development. Later, earworms worm their way through the husks into the ears, where they ruin kernels and leave gobs of fecal material. The results are ears that are deformed and open to mold and diseases.

They chew a hole in tomatoes through the stem end of the green fruit, sometimes feasting on one, sometimes moving through many.

On other crops they eat chunks out of tender new leaves and buds. Peppers will show brown, pinhead-sized holes where the worms move into and out of the fruit.

Deterrents

Cultural Practices. Fall and spring tilling helps by exposing the pupae to wind, weather, and predators. Early plantings of corn may avoid damage, and cold, damp weather discourages earworms almost as much as it does the corn. (Note: The European corn borer *prefers* the earlier plants.)

Corn varieties with tight husks are physically more resistant to earworm damage. Try Country Gentleman or Silver Cross Bantam. Clipping a clothespin on the tip of each ear can help to keep husks tight.

Plant cosmos as a repellent, or smartweed or sunflowers as trap crops. Grassy strips between corn rows help to attract predators.

Handpicking. Earworms can be handpicked from corn (after silks have browned) by carefully pulling back the husk and picking them out with a crochet hook. Infested tomatoes or other crops should be culled and discarded or burned. Trim damaged ends of ears of corn and enjoy the rest.

Bio-control. Bt sprayed on at the first sightings of caterpillars will do them in. Once they have penetrated the ears (or fruit), they are harder to control.

Tachinid flies, wasps, brachonid wasps, and ichneumon flies are important egg and larvae parasites. Elcar, a commercially available virus, and nuclear polyhedrosis virus (NPV) are lethal control agents. NPV can be spread by finding a few infected earworms and turning them into sick bug juice. (See explanation under Cabbage Loopers.)

Moles and soldier beetle larvae attack on the ground. Lacewings, fire ants, damsel bugs, bats, redwing blackbirds, woodpeckers, English sparrows, and even grackles assault from the air. Birds can do more damage to the corn than the earworms, as they enthusiastically dig for the hidden caterpillars.

Even earworms eat earworms.

Traps. Blacklight traps will destroy the moths, and any elevated outdoor nightlight draws a crowd for bats to feast on.

Sprays and Dusts. Garlic and onion teas have been used successfully against young earworms. Some gardeners sprinkle ground lime on corn ears as soon as silks show to deter the pests.

A mineral oil treatment has long been recommended as a useful remedy. By squeezing an eye-dropperful of mineral oil into the tip of each ear (half is enough for smaller ears), any resident earworms are suffocated. Some gardeners give this an extra punch by mixing with pyrethrum or pureeing with African marigolds or geranium leaves.

While plain mineral oil will not affect the taste of corn, it may cause spoilage of the ears, especially in hot, dry weather. Also, don't apply until pollination is complete and silks have turned brown and withered, as the oil can hinder or even prevent this essential process. (Corn is pollinated by the breeze, not insects.)

Rotenone will control earworms.

Cutworm

Cutworm is a catchall name for the destructive larvae of hundreds of different species of moths. They may be subdivided according to their means of attack — as climbers, tunnelers, subterraneans, and armyworms, who attack on all fronts.

Physical Description

Soft, ugly, fat, bristly caterpillars, ranging in color from gray, brown, or black to greenish white and red, their average size is 1½ inches. Often their common names come from distinguishing marks or colors, such as

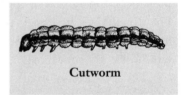

Cutworm

stripes or patches in a variety of hues including yellow, bronze, red, and black. The black cutworm, *Agrotis ipsilon*, is dirty gray to black with a lighter strip down its back, and the variegated cutworm, *Peridroma saucia*, marked by yellow side panels and blotches along its back, are among the most common examples found in home gardens.

Adults are generally small, plain-looking brown moths, about ¾ inch across.

A cutworm can be positively identified with a touch test. If it coils up into a ball, it's a cutworm.

Habits

Cutworms flourish in warm, moist spring weather, happily chewing through stems or leaves or underground parts of plants, depending on the species. Most surface feeders do their dirty work at night, curling up under cover of soil or nice, cozy mulch (they *love* mulch) during the day to rest up for the next all-nighter. The moths are also active at night, and are irresistibly drawn to light.

Range and Habitat

Cutworms are found throughout North America. Garden plots that were in grass or weeds the previous season are especially attractive to them. Unless tilled and left open all winter, or solarized, such areas provide ideal conditions for the emerging larvae.

Garden Targets

Favorites are tender seedlings or transplants. Older plants may sustain less obvious damage. Cutworms aren't particular, but will start with brassicas, beans, corn, and tomatoes, and move on to everything else.

Damage and Signs

Though some species climb into plants to feed, the classic sign of busy cutworms is seedlings gnawed at the base until they fall over. A telltale tunnel, about ¼ to ½ inch wide, may be found near the base of the victim. The damage is done during the night, so if tender plants look fine in the evening but are felled (or even missing) in the morning, suspect cutworms.

Deterrents

Cultural Practices. By tilling soil as early as it can be worked in the spring and not planting for two weeks, weed seedlings that the first wave of larvae depend on are destroyed. Reports of near total population control have been attributed to removing their earliest food source. Soil displacement also exposes larvae to predators.

Keeping a garden area free of weeds and grass removes egg-laying sites.

Interplant onion, garlic, or tansy to repel cutworms. Or plant sunflowers as a trap crop.

Handpicking. Handpicking is easiest and most productive following a rain or thorough watering, and done after dark. Spot cutworms with a flashlight and pluck them in the act. Scratching gently around the base of seedlings, especially in the early morning, will also expose their hiding places. Use a clump of clover, mullein, milkweed, or sprouts, half buried as bait to draw a crowd that can be easily collected or stomped. No need to locate the bait away from other plants, as the caterpillar won't travel away from its main food source.

Exclusion. The most effective line of defense against cutworms is to put a collar between them and the objects of their digestion. These should be about 3 inches tall and can be made from toilet paper rolls, pieces of paper towel or wrapping paper rolls, tar paper, linoleum, foil, bottomless paper cups, or any material stiff and flexible enough to fashion around the stems and push about an inch into the soil.

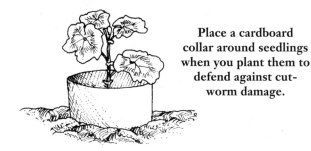

Place a cardboard collar around seedlings when you plant them to defend against cutworm damage.

Other barriers that have reported some success are rings of wood ashes, eggshell, or chicken manure, or a mulch of oak leaves.

Bio-control. Predators that relish the fat, juicy caterpillars include robins, meadowlarks, blackbirds, bluejays, moles, shrews, toads, ground beetles, and firefly larvae. Chickens or hogs released on a freshly tilled plot will pig out!

Commercially available parasites include trichogramma wasps and the caterpillar nematode, *Neoplectana carpocapsae*.

Bt can also be used.

Traps. Cutworms will devour cornmeal, which may do them in on its own, since they can't digest it, or cut it with powdered Bt for a fatal feast. They also go for molasses. An old-time trap is to mix molasses, hardwood sawdust, and wheat bran and spread it around susceptible plants. Lured to the molasses, cutworms wallow around in the stuff, which stiffens as it dries into an immobilizing cast that leaves them vulnerable to the elements and predators, including vengeful gardeners.

Adult moths can't resist their fatal attraction to light. Bug zappers will fry a fair share. Or just run a light up a pole or tree to give your friendly neighborhood bats an easy midnight snack.

Tomato Hornworms

Physical Description

A large and distinctively marked caterpillar, the hornworm is easily identified. The larvae grow to a length of 4 inches. They are stem green with seven or eight diagonal white stripes down the sides, each shadowed by a row of black dots and punctuated by a false eye spot. The telltale tail is black on the tomato hornworm and red on the tobacco hornworm.

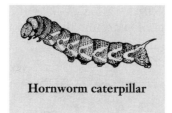

Hornworm caterpillar

Adults are huge grayish brown moths, known as sphinx, hawk, or hummingbird moths. They have wings up to 5 inches across, covered with wavy lined patterns. Orange spots mark the body.

Pupae hibernate in hard cases in the shape of a 2-inch-long spindle with a curved handle.

Habits

Expert at camouflage, larvae chew leaves in broad daylight, while the monster moths take flight at dusk. Mothers may be mistaken for hummingbirds as they hover before flowers, feeding on nectar.

Range and Habitat

Found throughout North America, hornworms prefer open, cultivated areas.

Garden Targets

Hornworms dine on tomatoes, peppers, potatoes, eggplant, dill, or tobacco, in the case of tobacco hornworms.

Damage and Signs

Sometimes nibbling at fruits, the hornworms consume a tremendous amount of leaves. Little souvenirs, very similar to rabbit pellets, are left behind.

Deterrents

Cultural Practices. Fall tilling helps to destroy underground pupae. Rotating crops and providing crop covers will keep hornworms off the plants. Borage, opal basil, and marigolds serve as repellent plants. Dill makes an excellent trap crop, as the lumbering giants are easily spied clinging to the delicate stems.

Handpicking. Handpicking is the most recommended method of control. Although hornworms are huge, there usually aren't all that many to contend with. Spraying plants with a blast of cold water sends them into a thrash dance, making them easier to spot.

Bio-control. Spray susceptible plants with Bt and you can forget about hornworms.

Braconid wasps lay eggs on the caterpillar's body. If you happen to find a parasitized hornworm, you'll know it. The body is covered with tiny cocoons of these wasps. Do not disturb this hornworm, as he is about to expire anyway, and he is carrying the next generation of a very beneficial insect. Trichogramma wasps parasitize the eggs.

EARWIGS

Physical Description

About ½ to ¾ inch long, red-brown with small, nearly useless wings, earwigs are instantly recognizable by their nasty-looking pincers at the hind end. White, globular eggs are laid in the soil.

Earwig

Habits

Earwigs like to sneak around in cool, dark, hiding places by day. They come out to feed at night, sometimes in overwhelming numbers. They can't hurt you — they use those dangerous-looking pincers to stave off rear attacks from ants.

Range and Habitat

Various species can be found throughout North America. Earwigs like dark hiding places, underneath objects.

Garden Targets

They eat the foliage and flowers of many plants — bean and beet seedlings, sweet corn, lettuce, celery, potatoes, strawberries, dahlias, zinnias, and hollyhock. However, decaying matter, and even other garden pests, make up the mainstay of their diet.

Damage and Signs

Holes in foliage or flowers and young plants or shoots nibbled down mark their presence. To be sure earwigs are at fault, you must grab a flashlight and catch them in the act.

Deterrents

Unless you actually see them doing damage, controls are not generally recommended. But if they are indeed your culprits, follow the remedies below.

Bio-control. Earwig predators include a tachinid fly, *Bigonicheta spinipennis*.

Traps. If necessary, earwigs can be trapped in hollow tubes left out in the garden overnight. Bamboo, sections of pipe, or garden hose will work. Pick up the traps each morning and dump the contents into soapy water or water and kerosene. A beer trap will do them in vast numbers. Place fresh beer in old cat food or tuna fish tins around susceptible plants or sink them flush with ground level. Empty and replace every few days.

Another trap uses bacon grease smeared in a ring around the inside of a can or jar about 2 inches from the top. Fill the container with water and a dash of soap to just below the grease line. Bury the works so that the opening is flush with the ground. Attracted to the grease, earwigs crawl in and drown.

Sprays and Dusts. Corn can be protected by dusting silks with boric acid.

FLIES

Carrot Rust Fly

Physical Description

The adult is a ¼-inch-long fly with a shiny greenish black body. It has a straw-colored head and legs and huge red eyes. Larvae are yellowish white maggots that grow up to ⅓ inch long.

Habits

As is frequently the case, it's the kids who cause the trouble. Hatching from their crown-point eggs, they tunnel ever downward through the stem and feast on the smaller fibrous roots, as well as main tap-roots.

Carrot rust fly

Range and Habitat

Carrot rust flies are most prevalent in the Pacific Northwest, and are also found in Utah, Wyoming, Colorado, and Nebraska. Sadly, these flies seem to favor soils rich in organic matter. They also prefer plots surrounded by brush or woods, or those next to buildings.

Garden Targets

Carrots, parsnips, celery, celeriac, parsley, fennel, and dill are eagerly consumed by carrot rust flies.

Damage and Signs

The visible tops of victim plants usually appear fine, while the underground portion silently suffers. Tunnels carved throughout carrots are marked with rust-colored fecal matter. The roots may be stunted or yellowed and are very susceptible to rot. The damage generally gets worse the longer the carrots are left in the ground.

Deterrents

Cultural Practices. Don't store carrots in the ground. It's far too convenient for these pests. Late plantings or early fall harvesting may sidestep damage. Keep weeds, especially stinging nettle, away from the garden to avoid supplying alternate hosts. Rotate carrot and other target patches.

Repellents. Onions and other alliums, pennyroyal, rosemary, sage, coriander, black salsify, and wormwood planted nearby repel the flies. They won't lay their eggs in carrots that have been dusted with pulverized wormwood or rock phosphate. The maggot larvae avoid carrots planted with a pinch of used tea leaf in the hole.

Exclusion. Crop covers are effective in preventing damage from carrot rust flies. Put in place at planting time and left there until harvest, they will virtually eliminate damage.

Cut It Out. When all else fails, cut away and discard affected plant parts when harvesting. The remainder is still edible.

GRASSHOPPERS & LOCUSTS

Physical Description

Full-grown grasshoppers of some species can top 4 inches in length, but those most likely to find their way into the home garden are barely knee-high to those grasshoppers, usually under 2 inches long. They may be green or various shades of brown. Large jaws and oversized hind legs have won them their two claims to fame

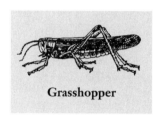

Grasshopper

— unrelenting chewing and spring-loaded jumping.

Habits

Famous for swarming in hordes during drought, the masses that appear are triggered by the optimum hatching conditions and the inability of predators to keep up with their sudden numbers. When disturbed, they combine the forces of their powerful hind legs and wings for a quick getaway. They are active during the day.

Range and Habitat

Different species can be found throughout North America. Grasshoppers thrive in areas with long, hot summers and are legendary for their outbreaks in the Midwest. They are most common in dry areas — those averaging from 10 to 30 inches of rainfall a year. Before they make it to garden

sites, they infest overgrown grassy or weedy areas such as roadsides, ditches, or fencerows. Solid, unworked ground is preferred for egg-laying.

Garden Targets

Grasshoppers prefer grasses, clovers, and some weeds to garden vegetables, but when faced with famine will gratefully digest whatever you have to offer.

Damage and Signs

Leaves and stems can be stripped if sufficient numbers are present.

Deterrents

Grasshoppers in the egg and nymph stages are highly susceptible to weather fluctuations. An early warm spell followed by cold can coax the eggs into hatching prematurely and then retard or kill the immature nymphs. Wet and cold weather hampers hatching and nymph development and fosters disease.

Cultural Practices. Fall tilling exposes eggs to weather and predators, and the turned earth discourages further egg-laying. Freeing the garden and surrounding areas of weeds and grasses further reduces available egg-laying sites.

Exclusion. Crop covers will protect plants from grasshoppers.

Bio-control. All stages of grasshoppers are vulnerable to predators and parasites. Many birds, and animals from cats to skunks to coyotes, will pounce on them. Snakes, toads, spiders, mantises, and rodents will eat 'hoppers; some will even excavate for the underground egg clusters. Red mites and nematodes parasitize the eggs, while ground beetles, blister beetles, and bee flies lay their own eggs with those of the grasshoppers as a handy food source of their hatching larvae. *Nosema locustae*, a commercially available parasitic protozoa, will kill up to 50 percent of the available grasshopper population within four weeks of application. Currently, viral control agents, such as Entomopox, are being tested. This one offers a 50 percent kill rate within as few as ten days.

Traps. Clover and ryegrass make appealing trap crops, which may be combined with a contraption called a "hopperdozer" to catch multitudes of 'hoppers. Make your own by attaching wooden strips for runners to the bottom of a large pan and adding a backboard of aluminum sheeting to one end of the pan. Fill the pan with water and a little kerosene and drag it across the infested areas. Disturbed grasshoppers spring up and either land in the pan or ricochet into it from the backboard. Repeat often and destroy your catch.

Another trap involves setting several large jars of water and molasses around the garden. Drawn to the sweet stuff, 'hoppers' that enter don't exit.

Sprays and Dusts. Add grasshoppers to the list of those repelled by hot pepper sprays.

LEAFHOPPERS

Frequently the most serious damage from these fancy-looking bugs is caused by the two diseases they spread, curly top and aster yellows.

There are many varieties of leafhoppers, the more common garden pests being the aster (six-spotted) leafhopper, the beet leafhopper (*Circulifer tenellus*), the potato leafhopper (*Empoasca fabae*), and the red-banded leafhopper (*Graphocephala coccinea*).

Physical Description

Shaped like a tiny wedge, most species don't exceed ¼ inch long. Aster leafhoppers sport six black spots over greenish yellow, beet leafhoppers lack the spots, potato leafhoppers are light green with white spots, and the flashy red-banded leafhopper displays bright red, green, and blue markings. Nymphs are usually a smaller, paler version of the adults.

Leafhopper

Habits

Leafhoppers feed by puncturing plant tissues and sucking out vital juices, usually from the underside of leaves. In the process they transmit plant diseases.

Population booms can occur quickly as adults migrate in from the South, traveling on the prevailing winds. They fly off suddenly when disturbed, while nymphs scuttle away in a sideways crab walk.

Range and Habitat

Various species of leafhoppers are found throughout North America. Most prefer dry, sunny, open areas.

Garden Targets

Beans, beets, potatoes, tomatoes, eggplant, vine crops, rhubarb, celery, and other vegetables; some flowers, including asters and dahlias; and many weeds are all favorites.

Damage and Signs

Many plants withstand a great deal of leafhopper feeding without showing any significant signs of injury. However, saliva injected while feeding is toxic to plants and, with heavy infestations, can cause stunting and discolored leaves. Hopperburn or tipburn caused by potato leafhoppers affects potatoes, beans, eggplant, and rhubarb. Edges of leaves curl up, turn yellow or brown, and die, reducing the plant's ability to photosynthesize. Serious infestations can reduce yields.

Some of the worst plant damage caused by leafhoppers is secondhand, caused by the diseases these bugs spread, aster yellows and curly top. Both can cause serious crop losses, manifesting differently in different plants. Aster yellows, *Chlorogenus callistephi*, affects many hosts, including carrots, celery, cucurbits, endive, New Zealand spinach, potatoes, onions, strawberries, and tomatoes, as well as many annual and perennial ornamentals and weeds. Affected plants commonly crack and yellow, with the veins turning clear and plants developing uncharacteristic or distorted stems, leaves, and roots. Carrots grow short, thick, hairy, and discolored. Lettuce pales. Tomato and potato leaves roll, while stunted celery stalks twist.

Curly top, *Ruga varrucosans*, also called Western yellow blight, is limited to the western United States, unlike aster yellows, which is prevalent throughout the United States and southern Canada. Among the many plants affected are beans, beets, carrots, celery, crucifers, cucurbits, New Zealand spinach, Swiss chard, and many ornamental plants. Symptoms depend on the plants affected, but thick, curling leaves and characteristic plant yellowing in tomatoes give this ailment its common names. Beet veins turn clear, then leaves curl up, yellow, wilt, and die. Abnormal root growth is common. Growing tips on cucurbits darken and turn up, while older leaves yellow. Other plants also show discoloration and curling of leaves.

Deterrents

Cultural Practices. When practical, plant in sheltered areas away from weeds. Shading and crowding plants close together reduce light and increase moisture, conditions leafhoppers avoid. Leafhoppers dislike perennial grasses, so these can be maintained near susceptible crops. Petunias and geraniums also repel them. Providing windbreaks (try interplanting with corn or sunflowers) makes it harder for the windblown hoppers to light on protected plants. Remove affected plants and keep the garden area free of weeds and debris. Experiment with resistant varieties such as Delus potatoes and Roza, Columbian, Rowpac, and Saladmaster tomatoes.

Exclusion. Crop covers are as close to a sure thing as you can get in dealing with these pests. Apply at planting or transplant time and leave on until plants flower. You may wish to re-cover plants after they are pollinated in times of heavy infestations. Remove any hoppers before putting the cover back.

Bio-control. Predators include some wasps and flies as well as big-eyed bugs and lacewing larvae.

Traps. Black light traps will draw and destroy adults.

Sprays and Dusts. Some types of leafhoppers can be repelled or killed with soap sprays. Diatomaceous earth helps cut down numbers, and either rotenone, pyrethrum, or a combination product will control them.

LEAF MINERS

Several species exist to pester the home gardener. Probably the most familiar is the spinach leaf miner, *Pegomya hyoscyami*.

Physical Description

Adults are small flies, about half as big as a housefly. They are hairy and black with yellow markings. The troublesome miner larvae are miniature plump green maggots.

Habits

The miners burrow between the surfaces of leaves almost immediately upon hatching and proceed to "mine" the middle layer. This makes them unaffected by insecticides.

Range and Habitat

Leaf miners infest target crops throughout North America.

Garden Targets

Spinach leaf miners go for spinach like Popeye, but will also ruin chard, beets, and lamb's-quarters. Other miner species violate blueberries, blackberries, potatoes, peppers, and cabbage, as well as some flowers, including columbine, roses, nasturtiums, and chrysanthemums.

Damage and Signs

The miners eat out tunnels inside the leaves. The tunnels show as random squiggly lines or blotches and may result in yellowing foliage.

Leaf miner damage

Deterrents

Cultural Practices. The most effective defense against leaf miners is to cover susceptible crops. Rotate crops to avoid the leaf miners emerging from the soil. Early plantings may avoid damage. Fall tilling will destroy pupae. Crush any eggs found on leaves. Cut and burn any infested leaves.

Sprays and Dusts. Soap and hot pepper sprays are effective against some varieties. Soak chopped rhubarb leaves in water with a touch of liquid soap for a few days, then strain. This makes an effective spray. Sabadilla dust will kill miners, but nothing affects them once they dig in. Sprays must be applied before or while the eggs begin to hatch to kill the larvae as they emerge. Timing is critical.

MITES

Spider Mites

These tiniest of garden wildlife are not insects, but are miniature cousins to spiders and scorpions. Red spider mites and two-spotted spider mites are the most likely garden pests.

Physical Description

Mites are barely noticeable specks, about the size of a grain of salt. Their color apparently varies according to their diet, from red to yellow to green. Through a magnifying glass eight pairs of legs are seen, but not wings or antennae.

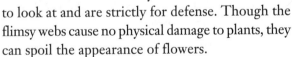

Spider mites

Habits

Like their cousins, spider mites spin fine, silky webs. These are not fancy to look at and are strictly for defense. Though the flimsy webs cause no physical damage to plants, they can spoil the appearance of flowers.

Spider mites feed by piercing leaf tissue and sucking up the plant fluids.

Range and Habitat

Found throughout North America, spider mites thrive in hot, dry areas.

Garden Targets

Strawberries, melons, beans, corn, tomatoes, eggplant, flowers, and other garden plants suit spider mites.

Damage and Signs

Leaves turn yellow, first along the veins, then throughout. Foliage wilts and the plant's health declines. To identify mites as the cause of these problems requires some detective work with a magnifying glass. Angelhair-like webs found clinging to leaves and stems mean that mites are around somewhere.

Deterrents

Cultural Practices. Mites love marigolds. *Never* plant marigolds if you have mite trouble. Keep weeds down in the garden area, especially lamb's-quarters, another mite favorite. Onions, garlic, and chives repel them. A blast of cold water from the hose may dislodge them. They dislike both wet and cold conditions, and heavy, moisture-retaining mulches may help by making the area less comfortable for them.

Bio-control. Ladybugs and lacewings both enjoy mites. One of the most promising means of mite control is a commercially available cannibal, *Amblyseius californicus*, itself a predatory mite.

Sprays and Dusts. It may seem ironic that the more pesticides used on a given plot, the worse the mite problem becomes. This is just another inescapable example of Mother Nature's pesky logic. Spraying kills off their natural enemies, and with such quick life cycles, the mite populations soon skyrocket.

Soap sprays are effective against mites, while not eliminating their natural predators. Many gardeners swear by a buttermilk spray. Mix ½ cup buttermilk with 4 cups wheat flour to 5 gallons of water. Garlic or onion sprays repel them. Alcohol spray, made from 4 parts water, 3 parts rubbing alcohol, and a squirt of dish soap, makes a lethal spray that kills by desiccation. A tea of rhubarb leaves will kill mites. Be sure to coat both sides of leaves when using any sprays.

NEMATODES

Physical Description

Without a microscope, or at least a magnifying lens, you'll probably never see a nematode, no matter how many of them you have. They are tiny threads of life, as small as 1/125 inch long, tapered at both ends. Root-knot nematodes are the most common garden pests, although lesion, lance, and stubby root nematodes are found in some areas. Occasional egg masses can be seen in the soil as small, pearly lumps.

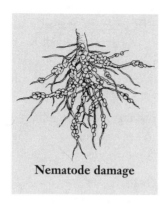

Nematode damage

Habits

Nematodes ruin crops, reproduce, and never leave the underworld.

Range and Habitat

Various species found throughout the United States. Nematodes are most abundant in coarse soils. They are widespread, thanks to contamination by farm machinery moving from place to place and infested drainage water.

Garden Targets

More than 2000 plants including strawberries, potatoes, beans, cabbage, lettuce, peas, turnips, carrots, tomatoes, cucumbers, squash, and other garden vegetables are susceptible.

Damage and Signs

Plants are deformed, sometimes chlorotic (yellowed) or dying. Root knot nematodes cause knobby, grotesque-looking roots, resulting in stunted, yellowed, and wilted plants with distorted roots and poor yields. Other varieties also affect plant development, health, and yields.

If plants are failing inexplicably, a soil test may expose the culprit. During the growing season take several soil samples from different places around the roots of affected plants, from the surface down to about 6 inches deep. Mix and put about a cupful in a plastic bag to keep it from drying out. Your local nursery or county extension agency can direct you to a testing facility.

A home soil test requires collecting enough samples to fill six planter pots. Keep half in a plastic bag and freeze the other half — and thereby any invading nematodes — for at least three days. Divide the soil. The freezer-treated soil goes into three pots and the plastic bag soil into another three pots. Plant radish seeds in all six and judge their progress. If the freezer-treated dirt samples do noticeably better than the untreated samples, suspect nematodes.

Deterrents

Cultural Practices. Never plant in infested soil if at all possible. Sterilize soil and garden tools (soak tools in bleach water and let dry in sunshine), and work in as much organic matter as possible to help build up parasitic fungi and other predators. Incorporate compost, then grow and till under cover crops. Rotate crops with, or interplant with, those that are immune or resistant, such as marigolds, brassicas, alliums, mustard, cress, rutabaga, and ground cherry for rootknot nematodes; watermelon or hot peppers for sting nematodes; or beets, rutabaga, yams, or radish for meadow nematodes. Cyst nematodes flounder in pH extremes. Two years of immune or resistant crops, or fallow ground, should starve them out.

Repellents. Plants toxic to nematodes include asparagus, hairy indigo, velvet beans, crotalaria, salvia, and calendula. Tilled-under timothy, fescue, or ryegrass release nematode toxins as they decompose. French or African marigolds also release nematode poisons through their roots, but evidence suggests that these are most effective the season after the flowers are grown.

Bio-control. Predators in the soil include other nematodes, as well as fungi and other dirt-dwelling microbes.

Sprays and Dusts. Corn oil mixed with water suffocates nematodes when sprinkled near plant roots, used as a soil drench, or used as a root dip for transplants. A fertilizer of 70 percent fish emulsion and 30 percent yucca extract (Pent-A-Vate) seems to produce plants unappealing to nematode palates.

Clandosan, a soil amendment containing urea and a natural complex of proteins and chitin (a tough, protein-based component that gives the shells of crabs and other arthropods their strength), works by stimulating microorganisms found in the soil. These fungi and other tiny predators destroy the hapless worms.

ROOT MAGGOTS

Root maggots destroy entire plants or, just as infuriating, the cultivated roots. Cabbage maggots (*Hylemya brassicae*) and onion maggots (*Hylemya antiqua*) are but two of several species.

Physical Description

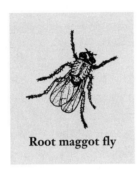

Root maggot fly

Adults of most species appear similar to houseflies. The onion maggot fly has an odd humpback. The larvae are generally fat, whitish grubs, growing to ⅓ inch long and tapering to a pointy head.

Habits

Up to 200 tiny white eggs may be laid in the crown or at the base of each host plant. Upon hatching, the larvae begin a downward trend, eating their way through the root systems.

Range and Habitat

Root maggots prosper in moist, cool soil. Various species exist throughout the United States and southern Canada.

Garden Targets

Species abound to mutilate onions, cabbage, broccoli, cauliflower, Brussels sprouts, turnips, radishes, and rutabagas.

Damage and Signs

In cabbage and related crops, all may appear well until seedlings suddenly yellow, wilt, and die. This is especially obvious during hot or dry spells. Yank up the victim and you'll find the grubby mag-

gots clinging to the mangled roots. Interfering with germination, seed corn maggots affect many vegetables, including all vine crops.

Root crops may wilt somewhat, but the worst damage is underground. Scars and tunnels, often further desecrated by rot and disease, mar the root and make it inedible.

Deterrents

Cultural Practices. Start seedlings under protection, in a cold frame or other cover. Cabbage and related plants survive better if given an early start. Onions are susceptible any time, but often sustain the worst damage early. By interplanting onions throughout the garden, the maggots are prevented from readily proceeding from one onion to the next. White onions are the most susceptible, red the least, and yellow are somewhat resistant.

Radishes make good trap crops. Pull and destroy them once infested. Likewise, cull any infested plants and remove crop residues promptly. To protect radishes for eating, try interplanting with extra-hot radish varieties, such as Black Spanish.

Exclusion. The *most* effective means of controlling maggot damage is by excluding the egg-laying flies with crop covers. An old home remedy of placing 4-inch-wide tarpaper collars around each seedling at transplant time also works. The flies don't care for the tarpaper smell and look for other places to deposit their eggs. Cut a small hole in the center of the paper, just large enough to fit the seedling stem through. Slit the collar to fit it around

Tarpaper collar

the transplant, and slide into place. These measures also mandate crop rotation, as the pests originate in the soil.

Bio-control. The beneficial nematode *Neoaplectana carpocapsae* destroys cabbage maggots and can remain active in the soil for up to two years.

Sprays and Dusts. Sprinkling wood ashes, rock phosphate, or diatomaceous earth around the base of plants discourages the maggots. Old-timers insist that improper lime content of the soil invites infestations and recommend a limewater drench. Soak 2 pounds of lime in 5 gallons of water for at least 24 hours, making sure the lime has settled to the bottom of the bucket. Pour off the clear water and use it to soak the soil at the base of target plants. A mulch of oak leaves is said to serve the same purpose.

THRIPS

Of the many varieties home gardeners face, onion thrips, flower thrips, and gladiolus thrips are among the most common.

Physical Description

Thrips

Without a magnifying glass, thrips are identifiable as throngs of tiny crawling spots before your eyes. Magnified, they are elongated, slim insects with double wings decorated with fancy fringe. No more than 1/16 inch long, they range in color from yellowish to near black. Larvae are smaller than adults, wingless, and pale yellow to white.

Habits

Thrips are gregarious, living and feeding in large groups. They are quick and constantly on the go. They feed by scraping plant tissues and slurping up the seeping fluids.

Range and Habitat

Seeking the security of close quarters, thrips seek places where plant leaves fit snugly together, such as the overlapping petals at the base of blossoms or inside cabbage heads. Various species are found throughout the United States and southern Canada.

Garden Targets

Hosts include onions, beans, peas, carrots, tomatoes, potatoes, cucumbers, squash, and other garden vegetables and many flowers, especially gladioli and roses.

Damage and Signs

Affected leaves develop silvery spots or streaks from the drained surface cells. These are often punctuated with tiny dark spots of excrement. Serious damage can lead to wilting or rot, and very young plants may die.

Flower buds either turn brown or unfold into deformed, browned blossoms. Onions may become stunted as leaves die back. The necks swell and bulbs fail to fill out. Cabbage leaves are pitted and may develop dark patches.

Deterrents

Cultural Practices. Remove weeds and grass around the garden to eliminate alternate hosts. Immediately destroy any infested blossoms.

Foil collars and mulch, extending past the plant by at least a foot on all sides, are reported to work for low-growing plants. For those over 2 feet tall try foil-covered panels, suspended by stakes between plants or from branches, to foil the thrips traveling from one plant to the next.

Spanish-variety onions are more resistant than others. Also, Blueboy, King Cole, Early Jersey Wakefield, and Danish Ballhead cabbage offer some resistance. Gladiolus thrips can be eliminated by treating corms to a hot bath (110 to 125°F.) for 20 to 30 minutes before storing for the fall. Corms should be dug and cured in the fall a few weeks before treating, then stored and replanted in early spring.

Sprays and Dusts. Try a blast of cold water to remove thrips from plants. Soap sprays are often very effective. Rotenone, pyrethrum, or diatomaceous earth dusted at the site of damage or around the crowns of onions will help, but shelter-seeking thrips are tough to discourage.

WASPS

Yellow Jackets

Physical Description

Yellow jacket

Adults are from ½ to 1 inch long with bright yellow and black, or white and black patterned bands decorating the abdomen. Wings are transparent and folded back when not in flight. The stinger is actually a modified *ovipositer* (egg-laying apparatus) of the sterile female worker. It is sheathed within the abdomen until the worst possible moment.

Queens are twice as big as workers and males (drones) are also huskier than the working-class females. Eggs and larvae remain concealed in paper-like cells in the nest until they emerge as adults.

Habits

The most famous and fearsome aspect of the yellow jacket is the furious attack it makes in defense of its nest. Unlike a honeybee, who can sting but once, this wasp does not lose its stinger once it penetrates a victim. It can, and does, sting repeatedly.

Nests are constructed underground or within cavities such as walls or hollow trees. Even when hidden out of sight, they are built the same way: cells of chewed wood pulp connected into combs and surrounded by an envelope of "paper," with just one opening.

If you approach too near, you may get a warning as a worker charges, headlong and fast. Quick motions such as panicked running and arm flailing, especially when accompanied by screams, only agitate them.

Yellow jackets become more active and many believe more aggressive on hot, sunny days, and toward the end of summer when they are hungry and facing the bitter end of their way of life.

Their one weak point is that they don't see well in the dark. Nearly all of them return to the nest for the night.

Range and Habitat

Found throughout North America, yellow jackets nest in the ground, often preferring open grassy areas or the edge of woods.

Garden Targets

Adults lap up pollen and nectar and prey on garden insects. They will chew up sweet ripe fruit such as strawberries, blueberries, tree fruit, melons, and other fruits and berries. Perhaps the most notable target is gardeners themselves. The presence of yellow jackets makes harvesting a tricky job.

Damage and Signs

Sure signs are holes in ripe fruit, and a nasty pain in your arm, or leg, or whichever limb gets in the way.

Deterrents

Live and Let Live. Even if you choose to *try* to eradicate the wasps, it is still in your best interest to understand the basis of peaceful coexistence.

Traps. Tie a slice of melon, fresh fish, or meat to a stick and suspend it over a 5-gallon bucket (a blue one is most attractive to the wasps) partially filled with water and a squirt of dish soap. Workers flock to the bait, gorge themselves, and plunk!, hit the water too full to float. The soap prevents them from treading water by breaking the surface tension. Place this trap away from people and protect meat lures with netting or by constructing a protective cage, or erect a tripod to raise the bait out of reach of any competing dogs, cats, or other animals.

Queens emerging in early spring can be caught in a shallow pan half filled with sugar water and just a drop of liquid soap. Use a blue or yellow pan if possible. The sweet lure attracts the hungry queens into the water and the soap makes it almost impossible to escape. Every queen trapped eliminates an entire future nest.

Destroying Nests. Underground nests can be eradicated by pouring in gasoline or rotenone, then covering the entrance hole. Work after dark and move swiftly.

Mother Nature will do the dirty work if you ask sweetly. Pile a mound of sweet molasses horsefeed, suet, or other tasty treat near the entrance hole. Hungry skunks, opossums, or other night marauders will excavate your problem for you.

Elimination of aerial nests calls for chemical or even professional help. *Don't try to knock it down.* They will object! Even if you succeed, they will only rebuild and be all the more fierce in their defense.

WEEVILS

Bean weevils, cabbage curculio, carrot weevils, and vegetable weevils are but a few of the many destructive pests at large.

Physical Description

Weevils are a form of beetle. Most are under ½ inch long and have hard wing covers. Garden varieties are usually dull colored, ranging from gray or brown to dark green. A distinctive snout, exaggerated and curved in the cabbage curculio, bears the mouthparts at the tip and a pair of antennae about halfway down.

Bean weevils are very tiny, 1/10 to ¼ inch long, and come in shades of brown or dark camouflage green. The larvae are fat, whitish grubs. Cabbage curculios have the typical long, curved beak and are black with downy yellow hairs covering all ⅛ inch of their bodies. Carrot weevils reach a size of ¼ inch, are dark brown to bronze colored, and have

Bean weevil

tough, hard wing covers. The larvae are dingy white with a brown head and no legs. They grow to about ⅓ inch in length. Vegetable weevils are dull grayish brown, marked with a V on the back. They grow to ½ inch long. The greenish creeping larvae resemble little slugs and will eat their way to ¼ inch long.

Eggs of most types of weevils are either gray or white and usually oval shaped. Often they are deposited in punctures or slits in plant tissue, making them difficult to find.

Habits

Bean weevils infest stored beans and may contaminate the next crop in so doing. They leave the seeds riddled with holes as the adults emerge from within the beans. Cabbage curculios enter stalks to feed and chomp on leaves as well. Carrot weevils burrow into the tops of host plants, leaving a wiggly tunnel behind them. They walk from their wintering places to their host plants, and therefore do not wander far from their place of origin. Vegetable weevils will chew their hosts down to the bare stems. The adults can be very damaging, but the larvae are by far the worst pests.

Range and Habitat

Fields, gardens, woods — you name it and weevils can be found there. Various species are found throughout North America.

Garden Targets

Many weevils attack fruit trees, cotton, rhubarb, and various vegetables. The bean weevils infest both beans and peas. Cabbage curculios feed on broccoli, cauliflower, cabbage, and turnips, but will settle for other related crops if these are not available. Carrot weevils attack carrots, dill, celery, parsley, and parsnips. Vegetable weevils are pests of lettuce, spinach, carrots, beets, radishes, turnips, tomatoes, potatoes, onions, and cabbage.

Damage and Signs

Bean weevils leave hollowed-out bean shells, with holes in them where the adults make their exits. Cabbage curculios feed within the stalks, so little damage is seen. Carrot weevils damage the roots or hearts of crops with their tunneling. Often damage is not evident until harvest. Plants may wilt and die with serious infestations. Vegetable weevils may eat away at leaves until only bare stems remain.

Deterrents

Cultural Practices. Crop rotation is effective against carrot weevils because they don't travel far from their place of origin. Cultivation may help eliminate hibernating adults.

To eliminate bean weevil infestations in harvested beans, dry the seeds thoroughly, then freeze for at least 48 hours. This prevents adults from laying eggs. Another tactic is to cure the harvested beans by heating them to 135°F. for three or four hours, or by hanging bean plants up to dry, intact, for six weeks or so.

Bio-control. Parasitic nematodes will control any ground-level infestations of root weevils (soil-dwelling, root-eating weevils) or other weevils that come in contact with the ground.

Sprays and Dusts. Dusting with diatomaceous earth will deter vegetable weevils, or cabbage curculios before they enter stalks.

WHITEFLIES

Physical Description

Adults are very small, mothlike flies, from $\frac{1}{20}$ to $\frac{1}{10}$ inch long. Milk white, they are covered with a waxy powder. There are several stages of nymphs, the first and most active feeders appearing as greenish white, six-legged

Whitefly

specks. Tiny eggs ($\frac{1}{100}$ inch) are yellowish when laid, fading to gray, and left attached to the underside of leaves.

Habits

Nearly constant greenhouse occupants, whiteflies move in as the fall temperatures drop. They're also prevalent in outdoor gardens. Both nymphs and adults feed on tender growth, sucking out plant juices. They congregate in thick crowds on the undersides of leaves and flutter like tiny snowflakes when disturbed. Whiteflies in all stages produce a sugary honeydew.

Whiteflies on leaf

Range and Habitat

These pests are most common in warm, sheltered areas, indoors or in greenhouses. Found worldwide, they will inhabit gardens in the southern United States year-round, and claim northern territories for the summer as they are introduced via infested nursery transplants.

Garden Targets

Almost everything in the garden is subject to whitefly attack. Plants deficient in magnesium and phosphorus seem especially vulnerable.

Damage and Signs

Feeding weakens plants, which may turn yellow and dry, and may even die. Fungal growths often accompany the honeydew secretions and contribute to sickening the host.

Deterrents

Cultural Practices. Check nursery transplants thoroughly for pests. Nasturtiums, marigolds, and nicandra will help repel whiteflies, while catnip draws hordes of them and makes a fine perennial trap crop.

Bio-control. One parasite, *Encarsia formosa*, attacks the larval stages of whiteflies. It is native to the United States and Canada, and is available commercially. Lacewings and ladybugs also wolf them down.

Traps. Traps made from bright yellow boards (safety yellow) covered with a sticky coating (Tanglefoot, etc.) will attract and catch loads of whiteflies. Place the traps at plant level, either in the garden or greenhouse.

Sprays and Dusts. The many sprays to try range from a blast of plain water to the more extreme. Soap sprays will kill whiteflies. A mix of 4 parts water to 3 parts rubbing alcohol, plus a squirt of liquid soap, can be used to mist plants, indoors or out. This will desiccate these pests as well as many others. Wettable sulfur, at the rate of 1 tablespoon per gallon of water, with a few drops of liquid soap, is highly effective, but exposure to sulfur may carry health risks for humans.

WIREWORMS

Physical Description

Adults, commonly called click beetles, are about ⅝-inch-long, murky dark beetles with broad stripes on the wing covers. The larvae, wireworms, have hard, shell-like jointed skins that may be yellow to dark reddish brown. Some grow as long as 1½ inches. They are distinguishable by three sets of legs attached just behind the head.

Click Beetle

Habits

An adult beetle can right itself if overturned by flinging itself with all its might into flips, until it happens to land right side up. The

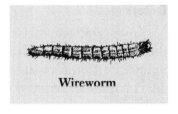

Wireworm

flip causes the beetle to strike the ground with a loud click.

Wireworms chew on germinating seeds and underground plant parts throughout their larval period.

Range and Habitat

Wireworms are often more of a problem in garden plots converted from sod within the previous two years and in soils with poor drainage.

Garden Targets

Dinner may include seedlings of corn, beans, and peas; tubers of potatoes, sweet potatoes, carrots, rutabagas, radishes, and turnip; and the roots of cabbages, cucumbers, tomatoes, onions, watermelons, and others.

Damage and Signs

Attacks on germinating seeds destroy the young plants. Crops with root damage are less vigorous, less productive, and may wilt or ultimately die. Damage to root crops results in gnawed produce that is subject to disease.

Deterrents

Cultural Practices. Till the soil several times in the fall and if necessary leave the ground *totally* bare (this means weeds, too) for a season. Working in organic matter or even sand to improve drainage is helpful. Cover crops such as clover, alfalfa, or buckwheat are highly recommended.

Buckwheat and white mustard are unpleasant to wireworms, making them good repellent plants to mix with other crops.

Bio-control. The commercially available beneficial nematodes *Heterorhabditis heliothidis* and *Neoplectana carpocapsae* attack and destroy these as well as other soil-dwelling pests.

Traps. Traps made by burying a chunk of potato or a handful of sprouts a few inches under the soil and covering with an old board will draw a crowd of wireworms. Set several out, a few feet apart in the garden. Every few days dig them up and destroy the worms.

Anthracnose

Description

Fungus disease that may overwinter on infected seed, plant debris, or in the soil.

Plants Affected

Beans, cantaloupe, cucumber, melon, pepper, and tomato.

Damage

Appears as dark brown circular sunken spots on pods or fruit. The centers of the spots may ooze pink spores. On the leaves, anthracnose shows up as reddish discoloration of the veins. Disease favors areas of high humidity, plentiful rain, and warm temperatures.

Controls

Home Remedies. If you have trouble with anthracnose, don't save your own seed for planting. Use western-grown seed because anthracnose is not a problem there. Be sure to rotate your crops. Avoid working in the garden when it is wet as this encourages disease spread.

Commercial remedies. Treat seeds with a fungicide. Fungicide sprays or dusts help prevent this disease. Start spraying vine crops when runners are 6 to 8 inches long.

Bacterial Blight

Description

This disease is usually spread by infected seeds.

Plants Affected

Beans, peas.

Damage

Brown and water-soaked spots appear on the leaves and pods. Infected areas often turn yellow, then brown, and finally die. Spots on the pods enlarge and often exhibit reddish markings.

Controls

Home Remedies. Rotate crops and clean up old debris. Don't work among wet plants, as this may help the disease spread. If you have a problem, do not save any seed.

Commercial Remedies. None.

Bacterial Wilt

Description

Wilt organisms live within cucumber beetles and are transmitted to the vine crop through their feces. The bacteria clog the water and nutrient transport system of the plant.

Plants Affected

All vine crops.

Damage

First appears as wilting of a few leaves or a small portion of the vine. The rest of the vine wilts within a week or so. When the vine is cut, a white substance oozes from the stem. This disease is most severe east of the Mississippi River.

Controls

Home Remedies. Pull out and destroy infected plants before the disease spreads. Keep cucumber beetles away.

Commercial Remedies. Spray with rotenone, pyrethrum, or neem to control cucumber beetles.

Blackleg

Description

Blackleg is caused by a fungus that is carried on seed and lives in the soil.

Plants Affected

Broccoli, Brussels sprouts, cabbage, and cauliflower.

Damage

Lower stem blackens and is completely girdled. Young plants yellow, wilt, and die.

Controls

Home Remedies. Practice crop rotation. Clean up plant debris at the end of the season.

Commercial Remedies. None effective.

Clubroot

Description

A fungal slime mold causes this disease, which lives in the soil and enters the plant through the roots.

Plants Affected

Cabbage family crops.

Damage

Roots become enlarged and swollen (clubbed), often cracking or rotting. Young plants are killed, while older, larger plants have reduced yields. The above-ground portion of the plant will yellow and wilt during the day, but recover at night.

Controls

Home Remedies. Use a 4-year crop rotation plan as spores can survive in the soil a long time.

Commercial Remedies. The disease thrives in acid soil so it is helpful to keep soil pH above 6.0.

Downy Mildew

Description

This fungus disease overwinters in crop residues and spreads through infected seeds.

Plants Affected

Lima beans, lettuce, onions, spinach, all vine crops.

Damage

Lettuce and spinach have pale spots on the leaves with furry whitish growth on the underside.

Lima beans have white, felt-like growths on the pods, with a possible reddish discoloration around the white areas. Mostly eastern United States because high humidity and cool to warm temperatures help it spread.

Controls

Home Remedies. Pull up and destroy infected plants and all crop residues. Plant resistant varieties. Be certain to rotate crops yearly.

Commercial Remedies. Spray or dust with a fungicide.

Early Blight

Description

Early blight is a fungus disease.

Plants Affected

Potato, tomato.

Damage

Leaves develop spots that are dark brown with a series of concentric rings within each one, giving it a target-like appearance. These spots usually appear on the older leaves first. Under favorable conditions, especially in warm, wet weather, the disease will spread rapidly over the entire plant. Serious infections will cause reduced yields and defoliation of the plant.

Controls

Home Remedies. Rotate crops, remove plant debris to prevent the disease from overwintering, and be certain to use healthy seed potatoes and tomato seedlings.

Commercial Remedies. Spray with all-purpose tomato/potato dust or a fungicide every seven to ten days. Begin early in the season.

Fusarium Wilt
(Verticillium Wilt)

Description

Fusarium wilt is a fungal infection of vascular

tissues. The fungus lives in the soil and infects plants through the roots. Very similar to verticillium wilt.

Plants Affected

Potato, tomato, eggplant, pepper, okra.

Damage

Leaves and stems turn yellowish. Plants wilt and have a brown discoloration inside the stems. Plant growth is stunted and yields are reduced. Fungus develops during hot dry weather.

Controls

Home Remedies. Crop rotation is important as well as the planting of resistant varieties where available. Practice a 4-year rotation plan for okra.

Commercial Remedies. None effective.

Late Blight

Description

Late blight is a fungus disease that first appears as wet-soaked or light spots on the leaves. As it progresses, these spots turn black and a white fungal growth may be seen on the underside of the leaf.

Plants Affected

Tomato, potato.

Damage

The disease spreads rapidly under cool, wet conditions causing all the above-ground parts of the plant to become soft and blighted. At this stage there will be a strong odor characteristic of this disease.

Controls

Home Remedies. Use resistant varieties, rotate your crops. Don't follow either tomatoes or potatoes by each other. Clean up all crop debris at the end of the season. Use clean seed potatoes.

Commercial Remedies. Spray or dust with an all-purpose potato/tomato dust every seven to ten days starting early in the season.

Leaf Spot

Description

Fungus disease that overwinters on seeds or infected crop debris.

Plants Affected

Beets, chard.

Damage

The plant leaves are dotted with small, tannish spots. These spots have purplish borders. The disease may cause leaves to drop later in the season and is most troublesome east of the Rocky Mountains.

Controls

Home Remedies. Practice crop rotation. Till in all crop residues at the end of the season.

Commercial Remedies. Spray or dust with a fungicide.

Mosaic

Description

This virus disease overwinters in perennial weeds. In the spring it is transmitted by aphids to vine crops and other host plants.

Plants Affected

Beans, cucumber, melon, pepper, squash, tomato.

Damage

Shows up as a yellow and green mottling of the leaves. Plants are stunted and yields are greatly reduced. Infected fruit is mottled, bumpy, and misshapen.

Controls

Home Remedies. Plant healthy seeds of mosaic-resistant varieties. Control aphids. Pull and destroy plants that become infected. Keep weeds down around the garden.

Commercial Remedies. Apply dormant oil sprays to control aphids on fruit trees and roses. You can also control aphids with rotenone and diatomaceous earth.

Neck Rot

Description

Neck rot is a fungus disease. It usually attaches onions in storage and overwinters in infected bulbs.

Plants Affected

Onions

Damage

Onions have brownish, dry rot areas around the neck. If the disease has progressed the entire bulb may be rotten. Neck rot usually appears in storage.

Controls

Home Remedies. Allow onions to mature completely in the field before harvesting. Cure and store them properly. Don't try to store bulbs that have been bruised or damaged. Sweet varieties tend to be most susceptible.

Commercial Remedies. None.

Root Rot

Description

Root rot is caused by fungi that live in the soil.

Plants Affected

Peas.

Damage

Root rot causes yellowish, unhealthy looking plants, often with withering of the lower stem.

Controls

Home Remedies. Rotate your crops yearly. Plant in well-drained soil. Raise your beds if the soil is too wet.

Commercial Remedies. None.

Rust

Description

This fungus overwinters on infected plant residue.

Plants Affected

Asparagus, beans, sunflowers.

Damage

Numerous tiny, rust-colored spots appear on the leaves, turning darker in color as they mature. Leaves turn yellow and then die. High humidity or wet weather causes more rapid growth of the disease.

Home Remedies. Plant rust-resistant varieties, cut and burn infected ferns as well as removing all crop debris at the end of the season.

Commercial Remedies. Spray with sulfur or dust with undiluted sulfur.

Scab

Description

Fungus disease that overwinters on seed, infected crop debris, and also in the soil.

Plants Affected

Cucumber, melon, squash.

Damage

Scab appears as dark, sunken spots on fruit. In severe cases, these will be like small craters over the entire fruit. There may be ooze or a fungus growth from infected areas. Cool, wet weather is favorable to disease development.

Apple scab

Controls

Home Remedies. Plant resistant varieties. Practice crop rotation. Clean up all plant debris.

Commercial Remedies. None.

Smut (Corn)

Description

Fungus disease that overwinters on crop debris and in the soil.

Plants Affected

Corn.

Damage

First appears as whitish-gray galls on the ear or other part of the plant. As galls mature they turn black and finally burst, releasing thousands of spores. This disease occurs throughout the United States and favors warm, dry seasons.

Controls

Home Remedies. Remove and destroy smut galls before they break open and spread spores. Be sure to clean up all crop debris. Rotate your crops. Plant varieties of corn that are somewhat resistant.

Don't use diseased plants in compost.

Commercial Remedies. None.

Yellows (Aster)

Description

Aster yellows is caused by mycoplasmas that overwinter in weeds and other perennial plants.

Plants Affected

Celery, lettuce, spinach.

Damage

Plants will be yellowed and stunted. Yields are reduced, infected plants usually don't head. This disease is spread by leafhoppers.

Controls

Home Remedies. Control leafhoppers. Keep weeds down around the garden. Plant lettuce in sheltered areas as leafhoppers prefer open spaces.

Commercial Remedies. Spray or dust with rotenone or pyrethrum, or a combination product to control leafhoppers. Start when plants are small and repeat treatment once a week.

VEGETABLES

It is a good idea to start your vegetable garden with a plan, just as if you were designing a flower bed. Lay it out on paper, using tracing pads of graph paper, available from any place that sells engineering and drafting supplies. You'll have a choice of several grid sizes; probably four squares to the inch is most practical for laying out a garden to scale.

The advantage of using graph paper on tracing stock is that you can overlay this year's vegetable garden on last year's (and even that of two years ago) to plan crop rotations easily. Note each vegetable variety in the layout and, after you plant, the date of planting. The plan will ensure proper spacing in the garden and will make it possible to calculate how much seed to purchase.

You will also want to keep in mind the best combinations of companion plants (chapter 1), trap crops (chapter 1), and insect deterrent plants (chapter 5) to ensure a healthy garden. See chapter 1 for more on garden planning and chapter 3 for planting techniques.

A Simple Lay-Out

To get maximum sun, plant tallest crops on the north side of the garden, so they don't shade shorter ones, or have your rows run north and south.

Plant vegetable families together in order to aid planning the rotation of crops in subsequent years:

■ Legumes: peas, beans, limas
■ Brassicas: cabbage, kale, broccoli, collards, cauliflower, kohlrabi, Brussels sprouts
■ Vine crops: cucumber, melons, squash
■ Nightshade family: peppers, tomatoes, potatoes, eggplant
■ Root vegetables: beets, carrots, turnips, salsify, parsnips, radishes, rutabagas, onions, garlic, leeks
■ Corn
■ Leafy greens: spinach, chard, lettuce

Take advantage of all the space you have by utilizing vertical cropping, intercropping, and succession planting.

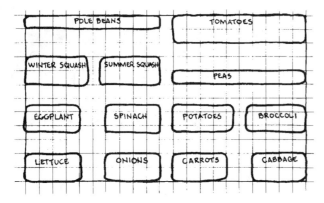

Garden layout

Vertical cropping means training sprawling plants to grow up (see pages 13–18). Try it with cucumbers, squash, tomatoes, and melons. Intercropping means planting quick-maturing vegetables such as lettuce and spinach between widely spaced rows of a slow-maturing crop such as tomatoes, or growing squash in with corn. Succession planting means making a second planting, such as putting in beans where you've just harvested early spinach. Make sure to dig in compost or fertilizer before you replant.

Here's a look at the common, and some not-so-common, vegetables for your garden.

BEANS

Beans are warm weather vegetables. Plant when the danger of frost is past and the soil has warmed up.

Beans are not too choosy about where they'll sink their roots as long as it's sunny. They'll give you a good crop in soil that's loamy, sandy, rocky, rich, or poor. Beans don't like wet soil, but if you grow them on raised beds, they'll probably do fine.

Beans

Because they are legumes, able to take nitrogen from the air and fix it on their roots, beans don't need much fertilizer to produce abundantly. Inoculate your beans just before planting to help them gather as much nitrogen from the air as they can. Bean-seed inoculant is available at most garden stores. Try block plantings of beans if you have the room and want a big harvest. Block planting is good for growing dry beans because they are a "plant and pick" crop. You don't have to do much while they're growing, just harvest them when the season's over.

Types of Beans

Beans are divided into three types: snap, shell, and dry, though there's quite a bit of overlap among these. For example, red kidney beans (usually thought of as a dry bean) and French horticultural beans (usually considered a shell variety) can be eaten first as a snap bean, later as a shell bean, and even as a dry bean at the end of the season.

Green and Yellow Snap Beans. These beans used to be called "string" beans because they had fibrous strings that ran the length of the pods. The string has been bred out of most varieties. Snap beans come in bush and pole varieties. They are harvested when the pods are young and tender, when they still "snap" into pieces easily.

Shell Beans. Lima beans, southern peas, and horticultural beans are the best examples of shell beans. To harvest, you have to open the pods or shells, and collect the soft beans inside.

Dry Beans. Dry beans come from plants that have completed their growth and produced hard, dry seeds inside their pods. When mature, the beans are packed with protein. All you have to do is separate the beans from their hulls and store them.

Common Bean Problems

Bean Insects. Bean plants can withstand a lot of insect damage before the yield is affected, so be careful about spraying them. Many times you can wait until the first big harvest is over.

■ The Mexican bean beetle, a 16-spotted ladybug type, is one of the most common bean

12 TIPS FOR GROWING VEGETABLES AND HERBS

■ Spread a thick layer of manure on the asparagus patch after the ground freezes in fall. It does double duty as winter protection and an early source of nutrients in spring.

■ Fill a shaker with borax and sprinkle on soil next to beets (provides boron).

■ To provide magnesium for faster development of tomatoes, peppers, and eggplants, mix two tablespoons epsom salts to 1 gallon of water. Apply one pint to each plant just as bloom begins.

■ For cucumber flavor without cucumber vines, plant the annual herb borage or the perennial salad burnet. Mince and add to salads.

■ Crushed egg shells mixed into soil around brassicas (cabbage, broccoli, cauliflower, etc.) provide extra calcium, which they need.

■ Sprinkle coffee grounds over carrot plantings to repel the root maggot.

■ Herbs like lime and gritty soil. If you live in an area where ground oyster shells are available, mix one handful into each planting hole for herbs.

■ If you do let winter squash trail, leave a minimum of 5 feet between plants. Fewer plants well spaced give more squash, and they are much easier to pick more quickly.

■ Plant cucumbers between corn plants to give them some light shade, which they like. Both crops like heat and moisture.

■ Aim for a three-year rotation in your garden, in terms of the plants' needs for nutrients.
   Year One—Heavy feeders: corn, squash, brassicas, tomatoes, melons.
   Year Two—Heavy givers: legumes, which return nitrogen to soil—peas, beans, alfalfa, clover, vetch.
   Year Three—Light feeders: root crops—beets, onions, carrots, turnips, kohlrabi, parsnips.
   Or interplant the three types of crops in the same bed.

■ Make sure onion necks are exposed to sun and not covered with dirt. By harvest time, they will already by partly dried.

pests. The adult and the orange-to-yellow larvae feed on bean leaves, often working from underneath.

■ The bean leaf beetle, a yellowish bug with six spots, feeds on leaves, too, but it's not as common as its Mexican cousin.

■ Many people find Japanese beetles on bean plants, but they can be brushed into a can and destroyed before doing much damage.

Bean Diseases. Anthracnose, bacterial blights, common bean mosaic, and rust are the most common bean diseases. Try to grow varieties resistant to these diseases. A good seed catalog will point these out.

- Before planting, use a seed inoculant on your beans, especially those you plant early when the soil is a little cool.

- Stay out of the garden when plants are wet, because water is often the carrier of diseases.

- Rotate the bean crop each year to avoid soil-borne diseases.

- Well-drained soil is important for growing beans. If soil stays wet, raised beds are your best bet.

- Use mulch for walkways and wide-row growing to prevent raindrops from splashing soil and disease spores on the plants.

CABBAGE FAMILY

Popular members of the Cabbage Family, also referred to as brassicas, include cabbages, broccoli, cauliflower, Brussels sprouts, turnips, and mustards. Brassicas like it cool. You can plant them early, at least three or four weeks before the last spring frost date, and also replant later in the season so they can mature in the cool weather of fall. The light frosts and cold weather of fall don't hurt the cabbage family vegetables. In fact, a light frost adds tangy sweetness to Chinese cabbage and Brussels sprouts maturing in fall.

Cabbage

Growing Tips

Fall Crops are Nearly Pest-Free. Fall crops rarely have disease or insect problems. Most pests hit hardest in late spring and early summer. By the time the cool weather of fall rolls around, pests are more interested in finding a home for the winter than going on a picnic, so they do little or no damage to your crops.

Pinch Leaves Off Transplants. When transplanting cabbage family members, pick off some of the lower leaves on each seedling. Trimming them gives the plant a much better start, especially when they are transplanted late in the summer. The soil then is more apt to heat up and dry out, and whatever you can do to take the strain off the roots will help.

Plant Cabbage Family Plants Closely. People put their cabbage family crops much too far apart in the rows, but they can be planted as close as 10 inches apart. Several good things happen when you plant closely:

1. **You can fit more plants in each row.** This results in a much bigger harvest from the same space.

2. **Leaves of the plant quickly reach out to their neighbors and shade the ground.** This blocks out weeds and keeps the soil moist and cool.

3. **You get a continuous harvest** of cabbage, Brussels sprouts, broccoli, and Chinese cabbage. Because these crops are in a wide row, they will mature over a long stretch of time, not just within a few days as often happens with many widely spaced plants in single rows.

In a wide row, some plants get ahead of the rest and grow faster. They take a good share of the nutrients, which keeps their neighbors growing at a slower pace. When the biggest plants are harvested, though, neighboring plants suddenly have more sun, food, and water. They put on a spurt and are soon ready to pick.

Pest and Disease Control for Cabbage Plants

Insect Pests. Cabbage worms are the worst pests for cabbage family plants. They can devour leaves, stems, and broccoli heads, too. The worst feeling

WHEN TO PLANT A FALL CROP

Vegetable	Weeks before first fall frost date*
Broccoli	10–12
Brussels sprouts	12–16
Cabbage	10–12
Cauliflower	10–12
Chinese cabbage	8–10
Kohlrabi	6–8

*For sowing seed directly in garden. All crops may be started close, perhaps in a short wide row, and (except for kohlrabi) transplanted when 4 to 6 inches tall to another row. (Don't transplant kohlrabi; it grows like a root crop where it is seeded.)

Rotate Crops to Avoid Diseases. The cabbage family crops are susceptible to several diseases — yellows, blackleg, black rot, clubroot, and root knot. Avoid planting members of the cabbage family in the same place two years in a row. Move them to a spot where beans, peas, tomatoes, or other vegetables grew previously.

When you buy transplants, check for disease symptoms such as stunted plants, blemished or yellowing leaves, or wilted foliage. If you discover badly diseased plants in the garden, pull them up, burn them, or toss them in the trash. Don't put them in the compost pile. For more information on pest control, see chapter 5.

Broccoli

The center head must be cut before it blossoms, even if it's on the small side. How do you tell when the head is ready to blossom? A head of broccoli is a cluster of flower buds. When the head is young, its individual buds are packed very tightly. As long as the buds stay tight, let the head grow. But when the buds loosen up and spread out, they are about to pop up and produce little yellow flowers.

The heads may be very small when the buds loosen, but harvest anyway. Because of hot weather, lack of water, or some other stress, the plant is determined to send up flowers and try to make seed. The only way to stop this is by harvesting.

Once you cut out the center head, many smaller heads, or side shoots, will form on other parts of

Harvesting broccoli main head

in the world is finding them in a dish of cooked broccoli. But there is a safe, natural non-chemical worm killer. The spray is a naturally occurring bacterium, *Bacillus thuringiensis*. It causes a fatal disease in the worms but does not hurt plants, people, or other animals.

Start using it on your garden as soon as you see those white butterflies. Spray all the cabbage family crops and repeat the spray every 7 to 10 days until the harvest is over. This safe regular coverage guarantees that you'll never see a worm in your cabbage family crops.

This non-toxic substance can end your worries about cabbage loopers, the big tomato hornworm, corn earworms, and many other common pests. Even in a small garden with just a few cabbage family crops, it's worth it. You can mix the spray in an old Windex bottle or plant mister and apply it in just minutes. For more information on pest control, see chapter 5.

the stems. These may not be large, but often there are so many of them you can top up your harvest basket in no time. The smaller shoots also will try to send up flower stalks and blossoms. If you let a plant blossom, it will go to seed and stop producing. It's important to keep them picked.

Harvesting side shoots

Brussels Sprouts

The sprouts form where a leaf grows out of the thick stalk. They'll appear on the bottom of the stalk first, the oldest part of the plant.

To encourage early sprouts to grow big in a hurry, break off all the branches, starting from the lowest and continuing up 6 or 8 inches as soon as you see tiny sprouts begin to form. The sprouts stay in place, but all the branches near them are gone.

Stripping the stalk stimulates the plant in

Brussels sprouts

two ways: It grows taller so it can add more leaves and sprouts, and it directs energy to the tiny sprouts at the bottom of the stalk, which grow in a hurry. In five or seven days they will be ready for picking. As you harvest, snap off more branches higher up on the stalk. This helps the next harvest grow.

The plants will get pretty tall if you continue to strip the branches. They'll keep growing until winter knocks them out or until some of the sprouts send out seed stalks and blossoms.

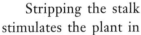

HOW CLOSE IS CLOSE ENOUGH?
Planting spacing guidelines:

Broccoli	12–16 inches
Cauliflower	12–16 inches
Brussels sprouts	16–18 inches
Cabbage	10–12 inches
Chinese cabbage	10–12 inches

Cauliflower

Cauliflower is less tolerant of hot weather than its relatives, so it's important to set your plants out very early or plan on a fall crop. If the heads mature in the heat, they're apt to have a bitter taste or go by very quickly.

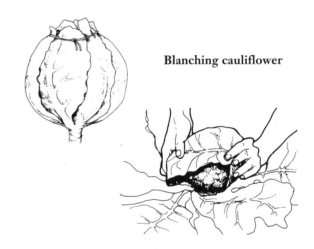

Blanching cauliflower

For your first crop, set out some plants three or four weeks *before* the average date of the last spring frost. Pinch off a couple of the lower leaves.

As cauliflower heads get to be 4 to 5 inches across, they should be blanched by preventing sunlight from reaching the heads. Blanching keeps the heads creamy white and sweet tasting. Normal blanching takes four to eight days, but it may take a little longer in the fall. Cover the heads either by tying the leaves up around the head or by taking an outside leaf from the plant, breaking it partially at the stem, laying it over the top of the cauliflower, and tucking it in on the other side of the head. Do this on all sides of the plant. This lets air in but keeps the sunlight out. The folded leaves also shed the rain, so you have fewer problems with rot.

When cauliflower heads are about 6 inches across, you can begin to harvest them. Depending on the variety, you can let them get as large as 12 inches across. Be sure to cut the heads before the tight flower buds open. Cauliflower loses its fine texture and taste when the buds start to loosen. Unlike broccoli, cauliflower does not produce side shoots, so once a head is cut, that's it.

Cabbage

To have a continual harvest of cabbages, set out the plants in wide rows three or four weeks before the last spring frost date; they can take a light freeze. In the early part of summer, sow more cabbage seeds, some in the garden and some in flats in partial shade outdoors. In midsummer, set the seedlings out in the garden; these will produce eating-sized heads from late summer right up until the end of the season when the ground freezes.

Cabbage heads, like all vegetable heads, grow from the inside out. If yours start to crack, this probably means that the cabbages are growing too fast in the center. (This condition is frequently caused by heavy-handed fertilizing.) If you let the cracking continue, the head will split wide open and send up a seed stalk.

If you see a crack, hold the head and twist the whole plant halfway around, like turning a faucet. This breaks off many of the roots and that slows the inner top growth of the plant. Give the plant another quarter turn in a few days if the cracking continues.

Chinese Cabbage

Sow Chinese cabbages eight to ten weeks in ad-

vance of the expected first fall frost. Use a wide row and gradually thin out the row (or transplant seedlings to *another* row) to leave 5 to 8 inches between plants. Watch out for flea beetle damage when the crop is young. Later the plants may be bothered by cabbage loopers (for controls, see chapter 5). When plants are 8 to 10 inches tall, blanch them for milder flavor by slipping half-gallon milk cartons (both ends torn open) over them.

Chinese cabbage

Chinese cabbage grown beyond maturity is worthless. Harvest the heads when they are full and tight, much as you would Romaine lettuce. Once harvested, the heads will keep for a couple of weeks in the refrigerator.

Michili is the most popular variety of Chinese cabbage. It matures in about 70 days, grows well in partial shade, and will withstand a few autumn cold snaps. *Bok choy* produces short, compact heads with a mild flavor and is more tender, sweeter, and crisper than *Michili*. The heads also have wider stalks, which is good for Chinese style cooking.

Mustard, Collards, and Kale

Kale, mustard, and collards are the tasty greens of the cabbage family. But since they grow like other greens and because most people think of them as greens, they are included with the other greens, pages 128–129.

CORN

Corn is a member of the grass family. If you think of it as a great big, fast-growing, tasseled grass, you will appreciate what a hearty appetite it has. To support the rapid development of its stout stalk, long stiff leaves, and heavy ears, corn needs a ready supply of plant food, especially nitrogen, which fosters leaf growth. Most gardeners sensibly plant corn in the richest soil on the place.

Enriching the Soil

Enrich the soil well in advance of planting. If possible, plow under a 1-inch layer of manure the preceding fall. You can also grow a green manure crop, such as buckwheat, oats, clover, rye, winter wheat, or vetch. In the spring, before planting corn, turn this cover crop under.

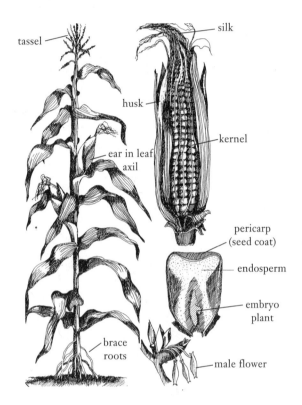

Tips for a Full Season of Sweet Corn

Timed Planting. There are two good ways to have fresh corn week after week. Plant early and mid-season varieties the same day. Early varieties will usually produce after eight or nine weeks; later ones need 10 to 12 weeks or more. The result is five or six weeks of steady eating. Also, stagger planting dates. Sow a block of corn every 10 to 14 days for about a month.

Plant late varieties for best flavor. Some gardeners, tempted by the short growing times of the extra-early varieties, plant them all season long. They'll be disappointed. They'll get ears to harvest but they will definitely not be as tasty as late

varieties which need 12 or 13 weeks to mature.

Location. Corn does best with a full day of sun, so plant it away from trees or buildings. Think about the height of your corn varieties. Will they shade any plants? In hot climates a little shade from your corn can *help* many crops. If you plant your corn rows on the north side of the garden, they won't shade any smaller crops, and provide the added benefit of blocking the wind.

Plant Spacing. For sturdy corn, plant your seeds 10 inches apart in a furrow or trench, then hill the plants as they grow. This supports the plants and also gets rid of weeds.

Plant sweet corn in blocks of at least four rows. This assures good pollination.

Separate Varieties. If you're planting popcorn, keep it at least one hundred feet away from your other corn. Popcorn tends to "dominate" and if it crosses with your sweet corn, the sweet corn could taste anything but sweet.

Care of the Growing Crop

Thin the seedlings to their proper spacing — 8 to 12 inches apart. Crowded corn plants shade each other and compete for soil nutrients. Leave the tillers (those extra stalks growing from the base of the plant) on the plant. Although their function is not completely understood, it is generally agreed that corn grows better if the tillers are not removed.

Cultivation

When the plants are small, weeds should be eliminated — or at least kept under control, because they use up soil nutrients, and the fast-growing weeds can shade out young corn seedlings. When chopped down young and tender, weeds contribute a certain amount of green manure. If weeds are hoed down until the plant is knee-high, it is usually not necessary to do much cultivating after that. Some gardeners hill up the rows — draw soil toward the plants from the middle of the rows — when plants are knee-high. This helps to encourage strong root formation. Once they have reached that height, corn plants have extensive roots, which could be damaged by hoeing too close to the plant.

Water

Irrigation is not always possible — many corn patches are far from a hose outlet — but in a dry season it can boost your corn yield. Watering is most effective at the time of tasseling and when the kernels are forming. If you do irrigate your plants, soak the soil at least 4 inches deep. Surface dampness only encourages the development of shallow roots, which quickly die when the soil dries again.

Fertilizing

For really spectacular corn, side-dress the plants twice during the growing season with liquid plant food, such as diluted fish emulsion (available in most lawn and garden stores) or manure tea.

Soak the soil around each plant with the manure tea or fish emulsion once just after the final thinning, when the seedlings are about 8 inches high, and again when the plant is knee-high. Many gardeners think such side-dressing is worth their while, both to give the plants a boost and to maintain soil fertility. In good rich soil, though, you should get a good corn crop without this extra step.

Harvesting

Sweet corn is at its tender, sweet, juicy best for only a few days. That moment of perfection occurs 18 to 20 days after the silks have been pollinated. This is the milk stage, when the kernels contain as much moisture as they will ever have. The juice in the kernels is milky, and the usual test of readiness is to puncture a kernel with your fingernail to see if milky juice spurts out. If you are too early, the juice will be watery. Too late (about 28 days beyond pollination),

Checking corn ripeness

and the kernels will turn doughy as the moisture recedes and sugar turns to starch. Here are some other signs of ready-to-pick corn.

- **Dark green husks.** If the husks are yellow, the corn is probably old and tough.

- **Brown, but not brittle, silks.**

- **Well-filled ears.** It is important to know your variety here, though. The varieties Wonderful and Candystick, for example, have very slim ears and can be ready before you realize it, if you are waiting for those ears to fill out.

EGGPLANT

Eggplant is a tender crop. It can't stand frost. Set out a few transplants before your last frost date and surround them with plastic or cover them with hot caps. The rest of the plants can go in the garden when there's no threat of frost and the ground is warm. Set the plants in the soil just slightly deeper than they were in its flat or pot.

Eggplant

Put eggplants in a sunny spot because they thrive on sun and lots of heat. Eggplant is one of the most heat-tolerant and drought-tolerant vegetables.

Eggplants don't need a lot of fertilizer. A tablespoon of 5-10-10 at planting time and another when you see blossoms or the first little eggplants is about all they need.

Harvest When Glossy

Eggplant tastes best when young. Start harvesting when the fruits reach one-third their full growth — anytime after their skins appear glossy. The eggplants are past their prime when the outside skin turns dull and you find lots of seeds inside.

GREENS

There are greens you can grow in every season — even winter. Some garden greens, like spinach, grow quickly and last just a short time. Others, such as chard, remain ready for picking all season long. Heat lovers, such as New Zealand spinach, need warm weather to grow in; but they are the exception. Most greens thrive in cool weather. Some, in fact, such as kale, are at their best after frost.

Spinach

Succession Planting

The secret to a continuous harvest is succession planting. You might, for example, plant early spring spinach, followed by green beans that ripen in August, and then a quick crop of radishes put in after the beans finish. Your summer greens can be grown in the rows where spring peas or scallions have finished. For a fall harvest, you can transplant kale, cabbage, and other good fall greens into spaces left by early radishes or beets. Fall spinach and escarole can follow summer-harvested onions. Most green vegetables do well when seeded right in the row, but you might want to raise some seedlings in flats and have them ready for transplanting to the garden, both to get an early spring start and to save growing time in midseason.

Intercropping

Another way to fit more greens into your garden is to tuck a quick-maturing leafy vegetable, such as spinach or leaf lettuce, in the wide space between your tomato, melon, or squash transplants. By the time the spreading vegetable needs all the room you have allowed for it, the leafy vegetable will have been picked and eaten. Shade from larger vegetables nearby sometimes helps to keep some spring vegetables, such as spinach, producing for an addi-

tional week before going to seed in the summer warmth and longer days.

Rich Soil

Since they grow quickly and leafily, greens need plenty of nitrogen — a pretty rich soil. Chard and parsley, both deep-rooted plants, are exceptions here. They do well in soil that is not especially rich, perhaps because their roots can delve deeply to find nourishment in the subsoil that other more shallow-rooted plants miss.

Compost, animal manure, and turned-under green manure plantings, such as clover or rye, will boost both fertility and humus content of the soil. Humus is especially helpful to shallow-rooted greens because it holds moisture at root level, available when the plant needs it. For a quick boost during the growing season, you might also want to give your leafy greens an extra dose of manure tea, blood meal, or diluted fish emulsion (available at garden stores and hardware stores).

Water

For tenderness, rapid growth, and mild flavor, greens need a good supply of water. They require at least an inch of rain or water each week. Shallow-rooted greens, such as lettuce, are more adversely affected by drought than deeply rooted chard or parsley.

Fertilize After Crew Cut Harvest

Many greens are best harvested by cutting them to an inch above the ground. Because the roots are left intact, the plants will quickly put on new growth, which means another tasty harvest for you. Just sprinkle dehydrated manure or other natural fertilizer around the plants. The next rain will carry the nutrients into the soil to provide some pep for the plants as they come back.

Insect Control for Greens

The most troublesome insect pests of greens are

the small leaf miners which feed on spinach, chard, and mustard (and beets and turnips as well). They are hard to control because they feed inside the leaves, not on them. Tear off the areas of the leaves with miners *before* you harvest; it's easier done in the garden than in the kitchen.

Because they are part of the cabbage family, mustard, collards, and kale can be bothered by the cabbage worm. Routine sprayings with *Bacillus thuringiensis* once you spot the white cabbage moth should prevent any problems.

Aphids can be a problem with greens if they become too numerous. They are small, come in all colors, and hurt crops by sucking plant sap from leaves and stems. In a bad case, the plants will become stunted. Luckily, there are many natural predators of aphids—ladybugs, lacewing larvae, and some wasps. If you notice an unusually large group of aphids feeding on your greens, spray the plants with a soapy mixture until predators bring the aphid population back to a level you can live with.

ONIONS

The key to growing onions successfully is to *start early in the season*, well before the last spring frost date. There are two reasons to get going early: The cold won't hurt onions, and they need as much time as possible to grow big, lush green tops. The more top growth your onions produce, the bigger the bulbs they will form on the bottom.

After onions have been growing a while, they suddenly stop putting energy into their tops when Mother Nature gives them a signal, or "trips" them. This signal is a combination of increasing temperature and the number of hours a day the sun shines. It's complicated, but the point is that suddenly the onions shift gears and the energy from the leaves is transported down to

Onions

make a bulb. If you have a healthy onion plant with a lot of green tops, you should get a good-sized bulb. If you plant late, the onions may be short on top growth, which means smaller bulbs.

You can start your onions by sowing seed, by buying started plants, or by planting sets (little bulbs started from seed the previous season). Starting onions from seed gives you the widest choice of varieties, but it takes 100 to 120 days for mature bulbs to develop. You can, of course, use the immature onions as scallions (green onions) sooner. Buying plants gives you a smaller choice of varieties, but enables you to produce an edible crop more quickly. Planting sets gives you even less choice of varieties (unless you've grown your own) but you will get green onions very quickly, and the bulbs will mature three or more weeks before those grown from seed.

Preparing the Soil

Onions prefer a friable, well-worked soil, ideally with a pH of 6.0. The fall before planting, compost and/or manure should be dug or tilled in, at the rate of 20 pounds per square yard. If you wish, you may also incorporate fertilizer (5-10-10 is recommended by many) at the rate of 3 to 4 ounces per square yard.

In order to give the onions a long period of growth, seed should be planted in late August in areas where winters are not too severe. In colder areas, seeds should be started indoors. However, if your season is long enough to give you 100 to 120 days for the onions to grow and mature (the actual length of time needed will depend on the variety you are growing), you can sow seeds outside a month before the final spring frost.

Allow ½ ounce of seed for every 100 feet of row to be sown. Seeds should be placed at a rate of two per inch, in a row to be covered with ¼ to 1 inch of soil, with the greater depth for soil that may dry out quickly.

Many gardeners thin their rows twice, the first time when the seedlings are very small and can be transplanted into another row, and the next time when the plants are large enough to be enjoyed as scallions. The mature plants should be 3 to 4 inches apart, depending upon the size of the mature onion.

Planting

Whether you have raised your own plants or bought them, they can be planted outdoors as much as a month before the last frost date. Be sure to harden them off first. Sets, too, can be planted at this time.

Plants should be set out at about the same level they were growing. Press sets into the soil so they are not more than 1 inch below the surface, and 4 to 6 inches apart. You will need about 4 pounds of sets per 100 feet.

For scallions, you can plant the sets more closely, planning to thin the rows until the maturing onions stand 6 inches apart, and to use the thinnings as scallions. If you prefer not to thin the onions, then plant the sets 6 inches apart. In this case you will need about 2 pounds of sets per 100 feet of row.

Care During Growth

Whichever way your onions are started, they will all need the same care. Keep them free of weeds. Onions are far less tolerant of the crowding of weeds than many other vegetables. Water them regularly until the tops start to yellow, then withhold the water and ease them partially out of the ground. Bend the tops over away from the sun so that the bulbs get all possible sunlight. At no time while they are growing should soil be drawn up around the plants. Onions do better growing on or near the surface. For the maximum-sized onions, pull away the soil from the upper two-thirds of the bulb. Because onions have a root growth close to the surface, cultivation should be shallow.

Harvesting

When the tops are quite dry, the bulbs may be lifted, and left in the sun to dry, long enough so that any dirt on them is dry. The onions can now be prepared for storage either by braiding the long dry

Braiding onions: (1) loop string around onion top. (2) Braid in second onion around the string. (3) Repeat with third onion and others.

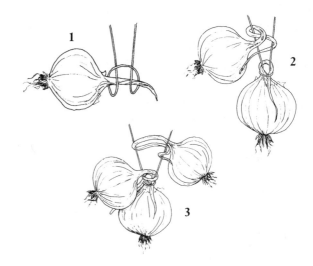

tops and hanging them, or the tops may be cut off, leaving an inch of stem on each bulb, and the onions placed in slatted crates, netted bags, or old nylon stockings.

Curing should be continued for several weeks by keeping the onions in a shed or under cover where air can circulate freely. While the weather is still dry and before frost is expected, move the onions into a dry, cool, frost-free, and (preferably) dark storage place. Use thick-necked onions first. They are not good keepers.

Everlasting Bunching Onions

For the tastiest, earliest scallions you can imagine, plant a bunching onion variety. These onions will not form a bulb. The bottoms stay thin all year long. Plant them where you won't be tilling, such as next to a perennial planting.

Plant the seeds thickly in early spring. Thin them a little with a rake when they come up, then let them grow. Harvest some of them when the stems are as big as a pencil, but leave plenty alone. Let them go right into the fall and

Scallion

winter. Don't mulch them — they don't need it.

In the spring they'll come back and you'll be able to harvest some very early scallions. Again, be sure to leave plenty of plants in the row. These will go to seed before too long. When they do, don't do anything except admire the beautiful blossoms and watch the bees work them. You want the plants to reseed the row. A whole new group of onions will start to grow. They'll winter over and send up early greentails the next spring. They're about the very *first* thing you can eat from your garden. You can pull some from the bed anytime, but you'll find that the first handfuls in early spring have the best flavor.

Garlic

Buy a few garlic bulbs from a garden store or supermarket and break each one into individual cloves.

Plant each clove 3 or 4 inches from the next one in a wide row. Push them in to their full depth, pointed end up. Plant them as early as you can, like onion sets, and give them two or three side-dressings during the season. Keep the soil loose around them, and don't let them get dry.

For big garlic bulbs, the plants need to grow

Garlic cloves

mostly in cool weather. That's why some folks plant garlic in the late summer or early fall and mulch the plants over the winter. The plants grow during the cool fall and spring weather before making their bulbs.

When the garlic tops fall over and die, pull up the bulbs, let them dry in the sun for a few days, and cure them in an airy place as you would onions. Store them in mesh bags or braid the tops.

Leeks

Start leeks indoors quite early along with onions, and set them out in the garden as transplants.

Instead of planting in a wide row, you can set them in the bottom of a narrow furrow 4 to 6 inches deep. Set the plants an inch deeper than they were in their flat. As the plants grow, gradually fill the furrow with soil. In this way, 4 inches or so of stem beneath the soil will be white — and that's what leeks are all about!

You can keep a bed of leeks growing year after year with a bare minimum of effort. Harvest mild, small leeks each spring and they continue to seed and multiply. The tastiest harvest is in the spring when the plants put on quick, new growth. After the spring

Leeks

harvest, toss a few handfuls of compost around remaining plants. These go to seed in early summer and the bed soon starts adding plants.

Onion Problems

Insect Pests. Thrips are tiny insects that feed on onion leaves and cause white, blotchy areas. The plants weaken, and the yield is reduced.

The onion maggot is the offspring of a small fly that lays her eggs near the base of the plant, or on the bulb itself late in the season. The maggots kill the plant by burrowing into the stem and the bulb. Pull up and destroy any plants with maggots before they mature into flies.

Disease. Neck rot is probably the most common onion disease. It often hits just after the harvest or while the bulbs are in storage. All onion varieties can develop neck rot, but the mild-flavored, Bermuda-type onions are especially susceptible. Drying the onions at warm temperatures with good ventilation and then storing them in a cool, airy spot can help prevent this disease.

PEAS

For an extended pea season, plant early, midseason, and late varieties at the same time, as soon as the soil can be worked. This gives better results than successive plantings of one variety. Peas of one variety tend to catch up with brethren planted earlier. Two weeks difference in planting may mean only one day's difference in harvesting.

Peas

Getting Started

The secret to "no-work" peas and a good harvest in warm climates is to plant them in wide rows. Choose a dwarf variety such as Little Marvel, Progress No. 9, or Wando (which fills its pods well in warm weather). Snow peas also do well in wide rows without fencing.

Because peas are legumes, they don't need much fertilizer — especially nitrogen. A day or two before planting, broadcast 1 or 2 pounds of 5-10-10 commercial fertilizer over each 100 square feet of garden space and work it into the top 2 to 3 inches of soil.

Don't worry about cold weather — peas will stand many freezes. Treat the seeds with inoculant and sow them in rows at least 16 inches wide. Tamp them down and cover with soil from alongside the row, or simply rototill them in a few inches.

Growing and Harvesting

When the peas come up, they'll quickly screen out the sun from hitting weeds which are trying to grow up through the peas. You never have to weed a good wide row of peas. Most important for southern gardeners, the shade keeps the soil cool and moist.

With a dwarf variety like Little Marvel you'll find that the plants in a wide row won't need staking. The only pods in the wide rows that sometimes hit the ground are those on the outside of each row. Most of the peas will be in the air, dry, and easy to get to when you're picking.

INGENIOUS PEA SUPPORTS

- Prop up vines with piles of hay, a tip from Ruth Stout.

- Plant dwarf peas, those that grow only 15 to 18 inches high, in rows 5 to 6 inches apart or in a 6-inch wide trench. Plants will intertwine and hold each other up.

- Use pea brush, as our forefathers did. Just after planting, stick twigs of deciduous trees or shrubs into the pea trench. Place them close together so they form a natural latticework for pea vines to climb.

- For conventional pea fencing, stretch chicken wire on metal fence posts. Make it 3 to 4 feet high for regular peas and 6 or more feet high for the edible-podded variety.

PEPPERS

Peppers — both hot and sweet — seem to grow much like eggplant. They like a sunny area and soil that is warm, dry, fertile, and slightly acidic. Don't plant them where you have used a lot of lime.

Getting Started

If you start peppers indoors, put your flats in a warm place. Peppers need more heat than other crops to get going. They are one of the best crops for raising under fluorescent lights inside, because they never get leggy, which can be a problem with other crops.

Peppers need fertilizer, but they don't appreciate getting it in large doses. It is a good idea to put compost or manure under them when they are transplanted. Side-dress them with rich, organic commercial fertilizer when they blossom.

Approaching Harvest

When the plants start to blossom, take an empty spray bottle and put in a spoonful of epsom salts — a form of magnesium. Fill the bottle with lukewarm water, shake it, and then spray the mixture right on the leaves of the plants. The leaves turn dark green, and soon you will have an abundance of peppers.

Bad weather can plague peppers. Sometimes blossoms will fall off in a cold spell. Nothing can be done about this; you have to wait for more blossoms to appear.

Peppers

There's no special trick to growing red peppers. Leave the pepper on the plant and it will turn red. A few varieties will turn yellow or orange when they mature, but most peppers, including the popular California Wonder bell pepper, will turn red.

POTATOES

A good potato crop starts with good seed potatoes. A garden store will have certified seed potatoes that are free of disease. These are the best. Don't rely on old potatoes from your root cellar because they could be carrying disease organisms without showing it.

Irish Potatoes

Planting Stock. When you buy seed potatoes, you'll get some small ones. Plant these whole. Cut the bigger ones into two or three blocky pieces, being sure to cut them so that each piece has two or three buds, or "eyes." Cut up seed potatoes a

day or two before planting and leave them in a warm place. This gives the cut surfaces time to heal over and dry out a little.

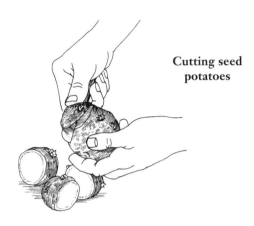

Cutting seed potatoes

You can douse seed potatoes with sulfur immediately after cutting them up. Sulfur powder is a cheap, natural protectant available at most drug stores. Two ounces will protect 10 pounds of seed potatoes from rot. Put the cut and whole potatoes in a paper bag. Add 1 or 2 tablespoons of sulfur and shake the bag to coat the potatoes. The sulfur also will lower the soil pH around the potatoes a bit, which is good because potatoes like an acid soil.

You can plant your earliest potatoes five to six weeks before the last expected frost and use Red Norland potatoes because they will produce early. A frost before the plants come up is no problem. The soil will insulate them. But if the young leaves have popped through the soil and there's a frost warning, push the soil from the walkways up over each plant. In a few days the leaves will grow back up through the soil as if nothing happened.

After the average last frost day in your area, plant your main crop of potatoes. This second planting can go into the root cellar just before the first frost of early fall.

Preparing the Soil. A silt or sandy loam, high in organic matter, with good drainage, is the ideal soil for growing Irish potatoes. But if you are not blessed with the ideal, it is not a sign that you should deprive yourself of good homegrown spuds.

Plenty of organic matter — leaf mold, manures

— will do much for a clay soil. A few cubic feet of sand will help lighten an otherwise heavy soil. Soils that are too sandy can be improved with organic matter.

Be sure you have good drainage. Poor drainage will promote rot in the seed before it sprouts, and possibly in the forming of young tubers.

But authorities recommend a pH no higher than 6.5 for Irish potatoes. A higher soil pH reading may promote potato scab. Your potatoes will tolerate a low pH better than a high pH, so avoid any use of lime.

If your soil test has shown a marked deficiency in phosphorus and potash, an application of 10 to 15 pounds of rock phosphate and an equal amount of greensand or granite dust per 100 feet of row is recommended. The nitrogen needed can come from the manure, or from compost, made without the addition of lime.

Avoid spreading fresh manure on land to be used for potatoes. An ideal way to prepare the land is to grow soybeans or some other legume on the site the previous year, then rototill this crop under in the fall and add compost or rotted manure, spreading as much as 10 wheelbarrow loads per 100-foot row.

The rock fertilizers can be applied in the previous summer or fall, but if applied the year you grow potatoes, they should be spread several weeks before planting time to give the ingredients time to be broken down into a form the plants can use.

Bed Planting. Plant Irish potatoes under straw, hay, leaves, or mulch of some other material, called the "lazy bed" method in some gardening circles. This method eliminates practically all cultivation after sowing, permits a significant increase in space utilization, is safe in soils where scab may be a threat, and permits easy harvesting on an as-needed basis.

The lazy bed is set up on a rectangle not more than 6 feet wide (less if your reach is short) to allow you to reach the middle from the sides without stepping on the bed. The length is determined by the amount of potatoes you wish to plant, or the available space.

When preparing the bed, cultivate the soil deeply and, if heavy rains are a problem in your area, give the final bed a slightly rounded contour or a slight slope to permit drainage. Place the potato chunks, cut side down, 12 inches from the sides and ends, spacing them 12 inches apart in each direction. Thus, for example, on a 6 x 12 foot bed, you can place four chunks across and ten on the length, or 40 plants.

After the chunks are in place and pressed down firmly in the soil — no need to bury them — spread a layer of straw, hay or shredded leaves on top of them. If you use baled hay, 6-inch pads will do the job. If you use loose hay, spread it 12 to 18 inches thick. That loose hay will pack down and disintegrate gradually, and if it isn't deep enough, there's a danger of potatoes showing through, greening, and thus becoming inedible. And, once the plants have come up and spread, it's difficult to add additional mulch.

If there's a chance the mulch will blow away, weight it down with wire, wooden slates, or a sprinkling of soil. The first rain will usually mat down this layer and hold it in place.

After that chore is completed, forget about cultivation and weeding. (That's why some call this the "lazy bed" method.) The lazy bed method may not be practical in large scale growing because of the need for large quantities of mulch, but its advantages in the home garden will become apparent. The mulch requirement is not on a scale that the gardener can't meet. If it is necessary to buy the hay, one or two bales will be sufficient for the average small garden.

Row Planting. If you wish to plant your potatoes in rows, hoe or dig a trench about 12 inches wide and 6 inches deep. If there's a question about the richness of the soil, put a 2-inch layer of compost in this trench and work it into the top layer of soil. Plant potato chunks, cut side down, 12 inches apart and 3 inches deep. As plants emerge, hoe soil up to them, gradually filling the trench and building a row-long hill about 8 inches high. If you desire, you can mulch at this time, to keep the soil cool and to discourage the weeds. By hilling the potatoes, you give them an ample area of loose soil in which to spread out and grow. The rows in this method should be about 28 inches apart.

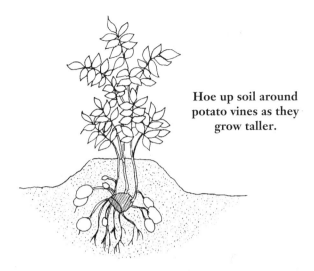

Hoe up soil around potato vines as they grow taller.

If heavy rains are a problem in your area, make certain that standing water does not remain between rows after these rains. Hoeing the mounds higher will help with this problem, and protect the potatoes from rotting underground due to the standing water.

Harvesting and Storage. Pick a relatively dry period for your final harvest. Wait until the vines are dead and dry. This is a sign that your potatoes are fully matured.

Use a potato hook or fork on plants in a row, and work carefully, trying to avoid puncturing or otherwise damaging the potato skins. If you used the lazy bed method, pull or rake back the layer of mulch and pick up your crop. Dig under the top several inches of soil occasionally, to see whether any potatoes have hidden there.

Let the potatoes dry for one or two hours, then move them into storage. If the potatoes are to be used in the next four to six weeks, they can be stored in a dark area with temperatures as high as 70°F. For winter storage, fully mature potatoes should be stored in the dark, at temperatures of 38 to 40°F., and with a relative humidity of 85 to 90 percent. They will keep this way for at least five or six months. Darkness is essential for these potatoes. Light will promote greening, making them inedible. Higher temperatures cause early sprouting and shriveling.

The storage area should have some air circulation. You will get good results with a homemade storage box with 1-inch holes in the sides and ends. You might want to layer the potatoes in straw, so air can circulate around them.

Growing Sweet Potatoes

The sweet potato is a major commercial product in Louisiana, North Carolina, Texas, and Virginia, but the growing area for home gardeners has spread, aided by the development of more hardy varieties, and the use of such aids as black plastic to raise the soil temperature, and hot caps to protect the emerging plants. Northerners may find it an interesting challenge to grow sweet potatoes in their gardens.

Ideally the crop should have 130 to 150 frost-free days, with most of them up to 80 to 85°F. and with moderate to high humidity. Planting should be well after the last frost, when the soil has warmed to about 70°F.

Getting Started. Sweet potatoes are started by using the whole potato to grow plants, and these plants are transplanted to the potato bed. About seven to eight weeks before the average last frost date, get some sweet potatoes from the market. Cut them in half lengthwise and lay the pieces cut-side-down in aluminum pie plates filled with moist peat moss, put a shallow covering of moist peat moss over the potato pieces and wrap the works in a plastic bag.

As soon as the slips (tiny sprouts) appear, take off the plastic and put the plants in a sunny window. After the last frost date, pull each slip and plant it separately. It will grow to a full-sized sweet potato plant.

You can also get slips by sprouting a section of sweet potato in a jar of water. Like sprouting an avocado pit, most of each piece should be submerged in water on the kitchen windowsill.

In warm climates, start slips from sweet potatoes planted in cold frames or in soil at the edge of the garden. In case of a very cold night, make sure they're covered up.

You can also send away for sweet potato slips. Specify the date you want to receive them — when your soil has warmed up and the danger of frost is about past. (Northern gardeners: try the Centennial variety first. It does best in cooler summers.)

Plant the slips in raised beds, about 6 to 8 inches high. Fertilizing is a delicate matter with sweet potatoes, as too much plant food, especially nitrogen, will produce skinny potatoes and lush vines, yet too little fertilizer cuts down on the harvest. When using commercial fertilizer, the basic guideline is about 4 to 5 pounds of 5-10-10 broadcast over each 100 feet of row.

Set the slips 12 to 15 inches apart in the row, and about 5 to 6 inches deep. Make a little hole for them. Set them in and gently water after firming the soil around them. If you have some short slips, put them into the soil with one leaf showing above ground; they'll do fine.

Care. Watering is very important in the next few days. Keep the soil around the slips wet, so the roots can expand quickly. Once the roots have anchored the plants, sweet potatoes can be considered drought-hardy.

After the plants take hold but before their vines really start to run along the ground, you should give them more fertilizer as a side-dressing. Try a tablespoon of 5-10-10 for each plant. Bonemeal, high in phosphorus, is also a good side-dressing fertilizer; apply 1 cup for each 10 feet of row.

Harvest Before the Frost. Sweet potato plants will grow as long as the weather stays warm. Their vines don't die and signal the harvest as white potatoes do. Most gardeners wait until their sweet potatoes are pretty large, then harvest all of them, although they can be eaten when they're not much bigger than your finger.

A fall frost can hurt sweet potatoes even though they're underground, so harvest them before cold weather. When frost kills and blackens the vines above the ground, decay spreads to the roots.

Dig the sweet potatoes on a dry day. Dig gently around the hills, starting from a few feet away; you don't want to slash any wandering potatoes with your shovel or fork.

Dry the potatoes on the ground for an hour. If you dig late in the day, don't leave them out overnight. Never wash the potatoes after the harvest, either.

Select any badly cut or bruised potatoes to eat first; they won't keep well. Sort the rest according to size in boxes or baskets to cure before storage.

Curing, which is important for sweet potatoes, takes 10 to 14 days. Keep them in a warm, dark place with some ventilation. The temperature should be around 70 to 80°F. with high humidity.

Sweet potatoes bruise easily and suffer in storage when handled roughly. The less you handle the crop, the better. They won't keep long.

Potato Problems

While the Irish potato attracts many insects, viruses, and fungi, all are not likely to attack at the same time. Many of these Irish potato enemies appear in certain regions and not in others. For controls of these common pests, see chapter 5.

Insect Pests. The Colorado potato beetle might appear throughout the United States, except California and Nevada, but its principal appearance is in the eastern states. Wherever it appears it is always hungry, eating all the foliage it can sink its teeth into.

Remove any beetles as soon as they appear, crushing them under foot. Keep a close eye on the underside of leaves, and crush any of those orange clusters of eggs these beetles lay. Handpicking beetles and crushing egg masses is not an exhausting or time-consuming task in the family garden, and is effective if done often enough.

Be on the look out, too, for flea beetles, which leave tiny holes in the potato leaves. The small, green and lively potato leafhoppers often associated with leaves that curl and die, are found in the eastern United States and parts of the Southwest. Aphids can also be a problem.

Diseases. The diseases that may strike potatoes are many. The prime defense against them is to buy certified seed stock, which is inspected by government officials both while growing and when harvested. This stock is thus certified free of such diseases as rot, blackleg, ring rot, and early and late blight. Resistant varieties can be selected to avoid mosaic and other virus diseases. This certified seed stock is more expensive than potatoes for eating, but freedom from diseases makes them worth the price.

In the South, the most damaging diseases to the Irish potato are early and late blight. Since humidity seems to promote blight infestations, it appears in other humid sections of the United States as well. Prevention is the best control. Always plant clean stock. Wait until plant tops are dead and dry before harvesting, then rake and burn all plant residue.

Since this is a fungus that lives in the soil, rotating the area each year where potatoes are planted helps to control it. If chemical control becomes necessary to save complete destruction of the crop, use a fungicidal dust or spray.

ROOT CROPS

The key to growing the best root crops — beets, carrots, parsnips, spring and winter radishes, salsify, turnips, and rutabagas — is in proper soil preparation. Root crops need a loose, friable soil that is deeply worked and drains well. They also require more phosphorus and less nitrogen than leaf and cole crops and heavy feeders like corn and melons. An overabundance of nitrogen, in fact, causes some root crops to produce bushy tops and hairy, spindly, or forked roots.

Till the seedbed to a depth of 6 to 8 inches. As you do so, work in plenty of organic matter to improve the soil. This is particularly helpful if you have a clay soil. Then rake the soil to remove all rocks and clods.

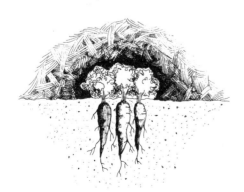

Root crops under mulch

If you use a commercial fertilizer, select 0-20-0 (also known as superphosphate) for your root crop bed. Rock phosphate is an excellent source of phosphorus, and superphosphate is simply rock phosphate treated with acid to make the phosphorus more accessible in the soil. Sprinkle the fertilizer over the bed, about 8 pounds per 100 square feet of garden, and rake it into the top inch of soil where young feeder roots can best use it. Bonemeal is also high in phosphorus but releases its nutrients slowly over the season. Use it with long-season root crops like parsnips and salsify.

Root crops produce best in raised beds, planted in blocks rather than single-file rows. If you have a heavy clay or shallow soil, growing long root crops like carrots, parsnips, and salsify is next to impossible without a raised bed.

Beets

Beets thrive in cool weather, so plan spring and fall plantings. Although they can't tolerate scorching summer heat, they can stand a light frost. Plant beets about two weeks before the last frost in spring (garden conditions permitting), sowing them in succession every two weeks until June. Then make one large planting about 90 days before the first frost in the fall.

Beet

Getting Started. A beet "seed" is actually a fruit containing several seeds. When they germinate, a small clump of plants results, requiring thinning. Sow the seeds about 2 inches apart in square-foot blocks, about ½ inch deep. The seedlings sprout in about two weeks if the soil temperature is below 50°F.; one week at 75°F. To avoid pulling up whole clumps of seedlings, carefully pinch out the unwanted plants when thinning. Thin the beets to about 3 to 4 inches apart (closer for Cylindra beets), then mulch with clean straw.

Maintenance. The quality of homegrown beets

depends on rapid, uninterrupted growth with a steady moisture supply. If your soil is heavy, soften it by working in plenty of sand and organic matter. Otherwise, the beets will be spindly and as tough as bullets. Beets like a pH of 6.5 to 8.0 and won't produce well in acidic soil. Sweeten the soil with about a pound of lime for each square yard of bed.

Hot, dry soil toughens the roots, making them fibrous. Keep the soil moist, not saturated, for the best-tasting beets. A light mulch around the young beets also hinders weeds and helps the soil retain moisture for plumper, juicier beets.

Common Problems. Beets are especially sensitive to boron deficiency. To avoid blackspot, sickly growth, and poor taste, make sure your soil contains this trace element. It's difficult to test for boron, but only minute amounts are needed. Mulching with compost is all that's necessary. Use a variety of organic materials and you shouldn't have boron problems.

Beet roots are rarely attacked by pests and diseases. Wireworms occasionally cause problems, but crop rotation and a fertile, well-prepared soil keeps them under control.

Beet greens, on the other hand, are routinely attacked by leaf miners and flea beetles. The safest way to protect the greens is to cover the entire beet bed with a spun-bonded row cover, like Reemay, to keep the insects from laying eggs on the plants.

Harvest and Storage. The best beets are young, only 1 to 2 inches in diameter, about the size of a golf ball. The only exception is Long Season. The large roots may develop woody centers, but these slip out easily after cooking.

Storage beets, harvested in late fall, shouldn't be pulled until a frost threatens, preferably after a dry spell. Where winters are mild, store the roots right in the ground under 8 to 12 inches of straw to keep the soil from freezing. Otherwise, pull the beets and let them cure in the sun for a few hours. Top the roots, leaving about ½ inch of stems above the crowns, then pack them in moist sand. Stored beets need high humidity and a temperature just above freezing, about 35°F. If properly handled, they'll store for three to four months.

Carrots

Carrots need a stone-free, deeply worked soil that drains well. During early stages of growth, the carrot's taproot must meet no resistance in the soil. If a root meets a rock or impenetrable clay, it will branch or simply stop growing. Too much water and the carrots may develop cavity spot — black spots near the crown of the root which break down, leaving unsightly rooting cavities. Improper soil conditions account for most of the problems experienced with carrots.

Carrot

Getting Started. Carrots produce best in raised beds. Till the soil to a depth of at least 8 inches, adding plenty of compost but no manure, unless it is well rotted. Excess nitrogen causes branching and hairy, fibrous roots. Potassium, on the other hand, promotes solid, sweet carrots. Wood ashes contains highly soluble potassium, which reaches the plants quickly. As you prepare the bed, work wood ashes into the top 4 inches of the soil, where feeder roots thrive. Then rake the bed smooth of rocks and clods.

Carrots are cool-weather vegetables, so start sowing about two weeks before the last expected frost in your area, garden conditions permitting. Make successive plantings every three weeks until July. Make furrows about ¾ inch deep, spacing the furrows 4 inches apart.

When sowing the seeds, try to space them ½ inch apart — no easy task but worth the effort when it comes time to thin. Because carrots are slow to germinate, gardeners often mix radish seeds with the carrot seeds to mark the rows.

Place a ½-inch layer of sifted peat moss in the bottom of each furrow, sow the seeds sparingly on top, then cover the seeds with about ¼ inch of the peat moss. To help germination, cover the bed with burlap bags, soak them, and keep the bed moist until the carrots sprout. Remove the burlap and water the beds daily until the seedlings are well established, then mulch with clean straw.

Maintenance. The first few weeks after sowing determine if you'll have a bumper or a bummer crop. Carrots can't tolerate a deep planting in a dry bed, so the trick is to offer them a shallow sowing with even moisture. The seedlings grow slowly and can't compete with weeds. Hand weeding is recommended until the carrots are 2 inches tall. Thin the carrots to 3-inch spacings, then mulch with chopped leaves, pine needles, and compost to keep the weeds at bay. Mulching also helps the soil retain moisture and prevents "green shoulder," which is caused by exposing the crowns of the carrots to the sun, making the roots bitter.

Common Problems. The insect terror of the carrot world is the rust fly. Carrots planted after the first week of June often escape the first generation of rust flies, and those harvested before September usually escape the second generation. Interplanting onions or garlic in the carrot beds will also ward off the villainous flies.

Compost and wood ashes will also scare off not only rust flies but carrot weevils, wireworms, and other carrot pests. Probably the best organic way to get rid of pests is to soak the bed once a week with a thin mixture of wood ashes and water. A watering can will do the job fine.

Most carrot pests and diseases are soil-borne and can be controlled by crop rotation.

Harvest and Storage. Most varieties are ready for harvest in less than three months. The largest carrots will have the darkest, greenest tops, but don't leave the roots in the ground too long or they'll be tough. Most carrots are at their prime when they're about an inch in diameter at their crowns.

When harvesting, drench the bed with water first, making the carrots easier to pull. When you find a carrot large enough, grasp the greens at the crown and gently tug with a twisting motion. If the greens snap off, carefully lift the roots with a spading fork. Use damaged roots first and store unblemished roots for later use.

There are three ways to store fresh carrots: Leave them in the ground under a heavy mulch, store them in a root cellar or underground barrel,

or keep them in the crisper bin of the refrigerator. The thick-cored varieties store the best.

Parsnips

Parsnips should be planted in early spring, about the same time as peas and radishes. Like carrots, they require a deeply tilled, well-prepared soil, raked smooth of rocks and clods. Like other root crops, parsnips thrive in a soil rich in potassium and phosphorus, so work in a dusting of wood ashes (potash) for good measure.

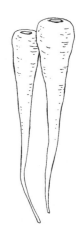

Parsnips

Getting Started. The seeds germinate slowly (up to three weeks), even in the best garden conditions. To hasten germination, some gardeners soak the seeds overnight or treat them with boiling water before planting. You can start the seeds indoors between moist sheets of paper towels. Presprouted seeds have a better chance of survival. When the tiny white roots of the sprouted seeds are about ¼ inch long, they're ready to plant. Be careful not to break the small roots or allow the seeds to dry out.

A trick for growing monster parsnips is to plant them in conical holes. Drive a crowbar into the soil to a depth of about 2 feet, rotating the bar in a circular fashion until the hole is about 6 inches across the top. Then fill the conical hole with a mixture of sand, peat moss, and sifted soil, leaving a slight depression at the top of the hole. Place two or three sprouted seeds in the depression, then cover with ½ inch of sifted sphagnum moss and water. Space the holes 8 inches apart each way in the bed.

Maintenance. As the seedlings grow, keep the beds evenly moist, but not saturated, until each plant has three or four leaves. Then thin to one strong plant per hole and mulch the beds. A 2-inch or 3-inch straw mulch will control weeds, help the soil retain moisture, and maintain a cool soil temperature.

Parsnips grow slowly, and mulching is the best way to pamper them.

If the parsnips receive inadequate moisture during the summer, they'll be tough and likely to split and rot with the fall rains. During dry spells, water the beds deeply once a week.

Common Problems. Parsnips are attacked by the same pests that favor carrots, particularly the carrot rust fly. Parsnips are also occasionally afflicted by a fungal disease called canker, which causes dark, sunken pits on the shoulders and crowns of the roots. Proper drainage and crop rotation generally keep canker at bay.

Harvest and Storage. Aside from mulching and regular waterings, the plants can be left alone until harvest, which isn't until winter or after a few frosts. The colder temperature changes starches in the roots into sugar. Store the roots right in the ground where they grew, digging them as you need them throughout the winter, knowing they'll be sweet and delicious. Mulch the parsnips with up to 12 inches of straw to keep the soil soft enough to dig. Even if there's snow on the ground, you can have fresh, tasty parsnips.

Harvest the roots before the soil warms in the spring, before new tops start to grow, or the roots will be bitter and tough.

When harvesting parsnips, don't try to pull them as you would carrots. Use a spading fork to loosen the soil and lift the roots from the ground. Leave the dirt on the roots until you're ready to use them, for the roots tend to shrivel when exposed to air.

Radishes

For the best radishes, give them a friable soil, cool weather, uninterrupted growth, and constant moisture. To provide a steady supply of radishes, make small weekly plantings during April and May, then again in August and September. (In warmer regions, plant them a little earlier in the spring and a little later in the fall.) Most radishes are ready for harvest in less than a month.

Getting Started. Till the radish bed to a depth of 8 inches (especially if you plant to sow the longer varieties like White Icicle), mixing in plenty of organic matter. Then make furrows with a yardstick, spacing the furrows about 3 inches apart. Sow the seeds at a depth of ½ inch, trying to space the seeds about 1 inch apart.

Early radish

When making succession plantings, keep in mind that the longer the radish, the better it tolerates heat. Plant the round varieties first (Sparkler, Cherry Belle), the blunt radishes next (French Breakfast), and finally the slender, tapered one (White Icicle). In the fall, reverse the process, planting some winter radishes like Black Spanish and China Rose in late August. The fall varieties, if mulched with straw, can remain in the garden through the winter to be harvested as you need them.

Maintenance. When the seedlings are about 2 inches tall, thin them to 3-inch spacings. If you don't thin them, you'll end up with lush greens and shriveled, inedible roots. Mulch the bed with compost to maintain stable soil moisture, which could mean the difference between perfect and pitiful radishes. If

Late radish

the soil is too dry, the radishes will bolt and become pithy and pungent; too wet and the roots will split and rot. Never let the radish bed dry out, but don't keep it mucky either.

Common Problems. The worst invader in the radish bed is the root maggot. As with most soil-borne pests, root maggots are best controlled with a proper crop rotation schedule. Radishes shouldn't be planted in a bed that hosted a cabbage or other brassica crop for at least three years. In the small garden, however, this may be unrealistic. If you're incorporating generous portions of wood ashes in the soil, maggots shouldn't be a problem.

Radishes are rarely troubled with diseases. The long radishes occasionally develop black root, which produces dark regions at the bottom of the root. If this is a problem in your garden, grow only the round radishes.

Harvest and Storage. When the radishes mature, check them frequently. When the radishes are ready, pull them whether you need them or not, cut off the leaves, then put the roots in a plastic storage bag in the vegetable bin of the refrigerator. Don't leave them in the ground too long.

Winter radishes are excellent winter keepers. Although they can be stored in moist sand in a root cellar, they're best left in the garden under a heavy straw mulch and harvested as needed.

Salsify

Salsify has a culture similar to parsnips, requiring a long growing season and a deep, friable soil worked to a depth of about 10 inches. Avoid using fresh manure or high-nitrogen fertilizers with salsify, or you're likely to harvest hairy, forked roots. Like parsnips, salsify is a low-maintenance crop; once established in the garden, the plants need only occasional weeding and watering.

Salsify

Getting Started. Sow seeds in the spring, around the same time as you would parsnips. Use fresh seed each year. Salsify germinates slowly, so plant thickly at a depth of ½ inch. When the seedlings are 3 inches tall, thin to 4-inch spacings.

Maintenance. Be careful when thinning and weeding, for the seedlings resemble blades of grass and are often eliminated by unknowing gardeners. Once

thinned, mulch the salsify bed with clean straw. Unlike other root crops, salsify tolerates drought without loss of quality, but grows best in a soil that's watered deeply once a week.

Harvest and Storage. Like parsnips, salsify is a biennial, perfectly hardy left in the bed until needed. The roots improve in flavor after a few heavy frosts. Cut off the tops, then mulch with straw to keep the soil from freezing solid. As with parsnips, it's best to dig the roots with a spading fork rather than trying to pull them like carrots. Harvest salsify before new growth begins in the spring, unless you intend to use the young shoots.

Although salsify can be stored in moist sand in a root cellar, it tends to get tough and shriveled, and the oyster flavor deteriorates with long storage. The roots can be stored for a few days in plastic bags in the refrigerator, but for the best eating, dig the roots fresh from the garden just before kitchen preparation.

Turnips and Rutabagas

Turnips are easy to grow in cool weather. Spring and fall crops are usually possible, although a fall crop is preferred. They'll tolerate light frosts, so plant early in the spring, about a month before the last frost if possible. An early heat wave, however, will make the roots bitter. This is particularly a problem in the South. A fall crop, when turnips mature in cold weather, results in more tender,

Rutabaga

sweeter roots and greens. Sow eight weeks before the first fall frost, even later for fast-maturing varieties like Tokyo Cross and Market Express.

Getting Started. Turnips are excellent for planting in spaces where other crops — beans, spinach, peas — have come and gone. Although the main turnip root goes no deeper than the topsoil, many finer roots reach as far as 4 feet into the ground.

Before sowing, loosen the soil in the bed to a depth of at least 10 inches, working in plenty of compost, sand, and wood ashes. Don't use highly nitrogenous material unless you only want greens.

The easiest way to sow turnips is to broadcast the seed over the bed, then thin the seedlings later. Sow thinly, for germination is high, almost 100 percent. After broadcasting the seeds, lightly rake the bed to just barely cover the seed, no deeper than half an inch, and water well to get them started.

Maintenance. When the seedlings are 3 inches tall, thin them to 3-inch spacings for the smaller varieties and 5-inch for the larger Purple Top types. Use the thinnings for greens. (Don't thin the turnips if you're growing them for greens only.)

The key to growing tasty turnips is to grow them fast and give them regular waterings. After thinning, mulch the turnip bed with shredded leaves, well-rotted sawdust, and grass clippings. The roots require constant moisture but won't tolerate waterlogged soil. Water deeply once a week, more often during drought periods. Shallow, erratic watering causes bolting. If you use a drip irrigation system, you'll have no problem.

Rutabagas should be grown only as a fall crop, maturing in cold weather and stored in the root cellar for winter enjoyment. Plant them in mid-June or about 90 days before planned harvest shortly after the first frost. Sow the seeds about ¼ inch deep at 8-inch spacings. Provide plenty of moisture until the seedlings are growing strong, then mulch well and water deeply once a week.

Common Problems. Turnips and rutabagas are attacked by the same pests that favor other brassicas. In the South, aphids, flea beetles, and cabbage loopers can ruin a crop of turnip greens. These pests can be controlled by dusting the plants, especially the undersides of the leaves, with rotenone or diatomaceous earth.

The scourge of the turnip patch is the cabbage root maggot. Work plenty of wood ashes into the soil before planting, then dust the turnips every week with the ashes to keep the maggots at bay. Some gardeners plant radishes in the bed before the turnips to trap the maggots; the flies lay their eggs on the radishes, which are then pulled and destroyed. The most effective method of handling root maggots is to completely cover the bed with fine cheesecloth or a spun-bound material, preventing the adult flies from laying their eggs on the plants.

Turnips and rutabagas are virtually pest-free when grown in late fall, as the weather gets colder. Avoid growing them in a bed that recently contained other brassicas. Rotate crops to prevent the spread of soil diseases like blackleg and black rot.

Harvest and Storage. Most turnip varieties mature in two months or less. The plants seem to double in size each week, so watch them carefully. Although most varieties will grow to be 6 inches in diameter, they're tastier and more tender when they're no larger than a golf ball. Harvest the greens before hot weather in the spring, or they'll be too strong and tough to eat.

Turnips don't store as well as rutabagas. Because of their high water content, turnips dehydrate quickly when exposed to air. In some parts of the South, turnips can be left in the ground for most of the winter under a mulch of straw and harvested as needed. In the North, however, turnips should be pulled before a hard freeze and put into storage. Don't clean the roots if you keep them in a root cellar or the refrigerator. They'll store longer and won't bruise as easily. Ideally, turnips should be stored in high humidity with a temperature between 30 and 40°F.

Harvest rutabagas after a few frosts, but before the ground freezes. Cut the tops and store them like carrots in a root cellar or basement. Good roots will keep for up to six months if stored just above freezing with 90 percent humidity.

TOMATOES

The tomato is actually a perennial; if the weather never got cold and if summer or tropical conditions continued to prevail, it would keep on growing for a long time. But as it is grown in virtually every part of the United States, the tomato is treated as if it were annual; it has to make it from seed to seed in a single growing season.

Tomatoes are a heat-loving crop. They don't do well until the soil warms up to 65°F. or more, and until nighttime temperatures get up into the 50s.

Tomatoes thrive in soil rich in organic matter with a pH of about 6.5. If you are adding lime to your soil, it is a good idea to use high-magnesium lime, as long as you don't have a magnesium test to tell you you don't need it.

Tomato

Starting Plants Indoors

Start plants from seed six or seven weeks before the frost-safe date. Little is gained in the long run by starting plants any earlier than that as they will grow leggy and spindly.

Setting Out the Plants

Don't forget to harden off the plants before setting them out in the garden.

Spacing in the garden will vary with your method of growing. If you are going to let the plants sprawl on the ground, each plant needs a space of 4 square feet. For those that are to be staked and trained, 3 square feet is adequate.

If your soil tends to be on the wet side, set each plant out on a mound 4 to 6 inches higher than the surrounding soil. If the land is particularly dry, set the plant down in a depression, hoping that rainwater may concentrate around its roots a bit. Water plants well an hour or two before transplanting so that they will be turgid.

If you have nice sturdy plants, set them straight into a hole dug with your hands or a trowel. Set them about two inches deeper than they are in the

Tomato cage

pot. Don't disturb the roots any more than necessary. If they are in a peat pot, tear the peat pot so that roots can escape easily. After planting, remove a couple of the lower leaves by picking them off. This brings the top into balance with the roots which you may have injured a little in your transplanting manipulations.

If your plants are long and leggy, much stem and few leaves, then lay the plant down on its side and bury part of the stem along with the roots. Prune the lower leaves off, leaving just the top leaves of the plant exposed. Roots will soon form on the stem, and at this stage the growth of the top will take care of itself in rapid fashion.

Immediately after planting, water the plant well. Some folks water the plant after it is placed in the hole and again after it has been covered. This is called "mudding-in" and is common when planting woody plants. It forces all the air away from the roots. After the initial watering, go back and water only plants that show wilt. Otherwise, leave them alone. They don't need to be drowned.

A thick mulch around tomato plants, especially staked ones, will help them get a steady supply of water, but it could hurt if you mulch too early.

Wait at least four to six weeks after you set out your plants before mulching them. By that time the soil will be warm. If you mulch too early in the season, you insulate the ground and keep it from warming up. This can delay the harvest two or three weeks.

Slugs and mice visit the garden when you use hay or other natural mulches. If you let the tomatoes sprawl on the ground, a mulch isn't necessary.

If you've mulched to even out the water supply between rains, don't water tomatoes until you see wilt. Then water them well. Frequent light watering makes shallow root growth and weak roots. At any stage of the tomato's growth, overwatering is undesirable. Roots need a balance of both soil gases and nutrient solutions in the soil pores.

Pruning Tomatoes

It's not necessary to prune tomatoes. But staked and trellised plants will be easier to train if they

SUPPORT METHODS FOR TOMATOES

Advantages	**Disadvantages**

Staking

■ Staking saves space. You can grow more tomato plants in a row, staking them as close as 18 inches from each other.	■ It takes time and effort to set the stakes, train the plants up the stakes, and prune them.
■ Keeps vines and tomatoes off the ground so the harvest is cleaner and there's less rotting. No slugs either, and that's a big plus for many gardeners.	■ Tomatoes are more prone to cracking, blossom end rot, and other problems because they are standing up and are much more exposed.
■ Earlier harvest. The pruning that staked tomatoes need forces more of the plant's energy into ripening the fruit. Tomatoes tend to be larger when a plant is staked. Again, this is the result of pruning: more energy goes into fewer tomatoes.	■ Decreases yield.
	■ Plants usually need plenty of mulching.
	■ Staked plants need *more* water than unstaked ones.
■ Easier to pick tomatoes and to work around the plants.	

Trellising

■ Like staking, trellising holds tomatoes off the ground for cleaner, easier-to-pick harvest.	■ Trellising can be hard work, especially for a big planting. Poles, wires, and braces usually needed.
■ Usually doesn't require as much pruning as staked tomatoes. Most common trellising methods let you grow two or three main stems.	■ Requires weekly maintenance to keep plants running up the trellis. Often the plants need to be tied to trellis wires.
	■ Takes time at end of the season to disassemble the trellis and store parts.

Letting Plants Run

■ Very little time spent caring for crop. Little or no pruning, no staking and training, no supports to build or buy.	■ In wet weather many gardeners will have rot or bug problems with tomatoes on the ground. Slugs can be bad news around free-growing tomatoes.
■ Total yield seems to be higher than staked or caged plants.	■ Requires more room in the garden. Sprawling plants will bush out quite a bit.
	■ Sometimes it is hard to find those tomatoes close to ground or hidden by thick growth.

Cages

■ Cages are set up as soon as seedlings are transplanted to the garden. No additional work is necessary.	■ Store-bought cages are expensive, though you can make your own from galvanized wire mesh.
■ No pruning is involved, so leaves shade the tomatoes and protect them from sunscald and allow them to ripen evenly.	■ A lot of work is required in setting up the cages and securing them to small stakes.
■ Like staking and trellising, cages hold the tomatoes off the ground for easier harvest.	■ It takes time at the end of the season to disassemble the cages and store the parts.

have only one or two main stems.

Pruning means pinching off the shoots, or suckers, that grow out from stems right above leaf branches. By restricting the vine growth somewhat, you'll get bigger tomatoes. If you let these suckers grow, each becomes another big stem with its own branches, blossoms, and fruits — even its own suckers.

In a very hot, sunny area, you can let some of the suckers put on a couple of leaves and then pinch out the top to stop its growth. The extra foliage will help the plant manufacture food and will help shade tomatoes.

Side-Dressing

Plants that are dark green and vigorous don't need more nitrogen. A general yellowing or pale green indicates nitrogen need. It is strictly normal, if not inevitable, that some of the lower leaves on the tomato plant turn yellow and wither or drop off for a couple or three weeks after planting; this does not necessarily mean the plant needs a shot of nitrogen. Don't side-dress with nitrogen until after flowering is well under way. It promotes leafy growth in excess and delays flowering. Once flowers appear, side-dressing a little can result in more vigorous plants and more fruit, providing there isn't already enough nitrogen present. You can side-dress with an ounce or so of 5-10-10 in a ring around the base of the plant. Don't get it on the leaves; it may burn. Or you can use a quart of manure tea, made by mixing one-third manure and two-thirds water, and stirring daily for a couple of weeks.

Tomato Diseases and Pests

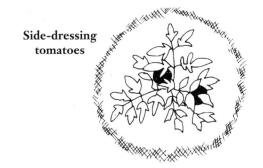
Side-dressing tomatoes

Blossom End Rot. Your tomatoes may be growing just fine and starting to ripen, when suddenly there's a hot, dry spell. After a few days you notice large brown or black spots showing up on the bottom side of all your tomatoes. This is blossom end rot and it will spread.

There is no cure for blossom end rot once it hits your tomatoes. The best thing to do is pick the tomatoes that have been hit and toss them on the compost pile. No use wasting any of the plant's energy on damaged goods.

You can avoid blossom end rot only by expecting it. A steady moisture supply is crucial, because the rot starts when there isn't enough moisture in the ground to travel all the way through the plant out to the ends of the tomatoes. Mulch staked plants or watch them regularly in dry times because end rot hits them first. And make sure *all* your tomatoes get the water they need during a dry spell.

Catfacing. This is a type of scarring. Tomatoes develop unusual swelling and streaks. It is not a disease, it's caused by abnormal development of the tomato flower. Cool weather is believed to cause the problem.

Blossom Drop. Some years early blossoms will fall off. This is caused by temperatures below 55°F. at night. Some varieties, such as Pixie, will keep their blossoms and set fruit in cool weather, but most varieties won't. Some blossom drop will also occur when night temperatures get above 75 or 80°F. in the summer.

Curling of Leaves. Curling, or leaf roll, is very common, but don't worry, it does not harm production. Heavy prunings may promote curling.

Sunscald. This occurs when green or ripening tomatoes get too much sun. At first, a yellowish-white patch appears on the side of the tomato facing the sun. The area gets larger as the fruit ripens and becomes grayish-white. If this is a problem for you, grow varieties that develop heavy foliage. To guard against sunscald, don't overprune plants. Or grow them in cages where they'll develop lots of protective foliage.

Early Blight. One of the most common and most

harmful diseases, early blight is caused by a fungus. It appears first as a brown spot, surrounded by yellow, that spreads outward on the leaves. The lower leaves wither. Higher leaves are hit, too, and the crop can be badly damaged. To control early blight, mulch to reduce splashing and use an all-purpose tomato dust.

Late Blight. A serious disease in areas east of the Mississippi, late blight is more pronounced in cool, moist weather. Leaves develop large, brown spots and wither. Spots on tomatoes turn brown and harden.

Leaf Spot. A fungus disease that is often a problem in the Southeast and some northern areas that have warm, moist weather. The leaves have small spots with light centers. They may turn yellow and drop off. The fungus that causes the disease lives on old tomato vines, in the soil, and on perennial weeds. Rotating crops is important to keep the disease in check.

Pests that trouble tomato plants include flea beetles, blister beetles, Colorado potato beetles, aphids, hornworms, tomato fruitworms, and stinkbugs. For controls, see chapter 5.

VINE CROPS

The squash family encompasses a wide variety of plants, including cucumbers, melons, squashes, and pumpkins. Although they may have different uses, their culture is very similar. Plants are generally grown in mounds and send out vines that run over the ground. Many people grow bush or compact strains that do not require much space. Even if you are very short on ground space, you can grow many vine crops on trellises. Even heavy vine crops, like pumpkins and melons, can produce as they crawl over a sturdy trellis. The trick here is to be sure the fruit is supported and won't break off the vine under its own weight.

Cucumber vine

All squashes are tender to frost (some are even more tender than others), and most require a fairly long season to mature. They thrive in well-drained, rich, light soil and full sunlight.

Squashes

Getting Started

Since they resent transplanting, squash seeds are best sown where the plants are to remain. You can start seeds in inverted sod squares or peat pots indoors and transplant them with relatively little root damage.

Ordinarily, vine crops are planted outdoors after the last frost date because they are so tender and need warm soil. You can get an early start by planting them under hot caps or plastic tunnels which trap a lot of heat.

To plant early, work the soil once or twice a few days before planting and then one last time right before sowing the seeds. Plant either treated seeds or presprouted seeds, which will come up quickly. After planting the seeds, covering and tamping them down, put the tunnels or hot caps over them.

Once the plants sprout and start to get big, check the hot caps regularly. On sunny days it's wise to take them off for part of the day.

When the weather warms up for good and the danger of frost has passed, lift off the hot caps and tunnels, and the vine crops will be well on their way.

Mound Planting

For most squashes, seeds should be sown outdoors after it is sufficiently warm (at least 60 to 70°F.).

Prepare slightly raised mounds of soil 1 to 2 feet in diameter, leaving at least 3 feet (more for pumpkins and larger squashes) between mounds for the vines to run. Depending on your soil quality, it may be a good idea to mix a shovelful of well-rotted manure in with the soil a few inches below ground level and then build the mound up on top of it.

The plants should be spaced evenly around the mound at least 6 inches apart and thinned to one or two plants per mound as needed. Pumpkins and larger varieties of squash will require more room.

Water deeply at least once a week if there is no rain. Avoid wetting the leaves, since this encourages disease. Cultivate soil lightly to keep weeds down until the plants are big enough to shade them out. A mulch of hay between the mounds helps to keep out weeds and to keep the fruits clean and dry.

Trellising

Cucumbers grow well on a trellis and so do gourds, some varieties of winter squash, and even pumpkins (with a little bit of extra support).

The most sensible trellis is one that lasts. You can easily make one out of sturdy posts and tough 3-foot or 4-foot chicken wire. Install your trellis on or before planting day. (If you pound stakes into the ground later, you may injure the roots.)

Place the trellis on a slight slant so that the prevailing winds will push the plants onto, and not away from, the trellis. Slanting the trellis also makes it easier for the plants to climb.

Trellises are not maintenance-free. You have to guide the plants up the trellis and sometimes tie

Cucumber trellis

vines to it. Heavy gourds, small pie pumpkins, or some acorn squash may need additional tie-ups to hold the vegetables against the trellis.

There's always open soil on the back side of the trellis early in the season. It's a good spot for a crop of lettuce, onion sets, or a quick crop of greens like turnips or chard.

If you grow vine crops on a trellis, watch their water supply. Trellised plants, because they are more exposed to wind and sun, can lose moisture quickly.

Side-Dressing

Side-dress your vine crops when they blossom if you want the best harvest. The energy they get then will help produce good sized fruits and new vine growth.

To side-dress, place about a tablespoon of 5-10-10 or similar fertilizer in a band 3 to 4 inches from the stems of the plants. It's important to cover the 5-10-10 with soil so that the leaves don't flop down on it and get burned.

Pests and Diseases

The worst pests of vine crops are the striped cucumber beetle and the spotted cucumber beetle. See chapter 5 for controls. The beetles hatch three or four broods of eggs, so you may have to repeat the spraying every week or so. However, if you get rid of the beetles early, you avoid repeated sprayings.

Two other insects to watch for are the squash bug and the squash vine borer. Squash bugs can be controlled by trapping adults under boards placed near the plants. The borer is tough to control. You can avoid a serious problem by staggering your plantings over several weeks or a month.

A good way to prevent disease, besides stopping the cucumber beetle, is to select disease-resistant varieties. Normal gardening cleanup practices, too, go a long way toward preventing problems. If you notice a diseased plant, pull it to keep the disease from spreading to healthy plants. Diseases move quickly among vine crops, especially cucumbers, and speed up in wet weather.

PERENNIAL VEGETABLES

Perennial vegetables will last for years with proper care. An asparagus bed can still be productive after 30 years. Likewise rhubarb will keep going for a long time. Horseradish and Jerusalem-artichokes seem to grow forever. The biggest job with them is how to keep them from invading the rest of the garden.

Asparagas

To grow one or more of these crops, put the bed where it won't be in the way of tilling and planting your annual vegetables and flowers. Your perennials will have to live in one spot for a long time, so it pays to work a lot of organic matter and compost into the soil before planting.

One of the biggest problems in growing perennials is not pests or diseases (those are rare) but moving before you've harvested much of a crop. It's most serious with asparagus which needs about 3 years in the garden before you get a decent harvest.

Weeding is the main difficulty for those who do stay put. You can avoid a lot of weeding by planting in a part of the garden which is relatively weed-free. This might be where you have grown several thick green manure crops in succession.

Asparagus

The best way to grow an asparagus bed is to plant 2-year-old roots which you can order from a seed catalog or pick up at a garden store. One-year-old roots may be cheaper, but the savings are not worth waiting an extra year for your first harvest, and the 2-year-old roots are more reliable in transplanting.

Planting. If you live in the North, set out asparagus roots in the early spring. In the South, set them out in the fall because it can be so dry and hot in the summer that the plants may not make it through.

Asparagus will grow in most types of soil, but it does best in soil that drains well. Place the plants about 2 feet apart with 5 feet between rows. Once the bed is established, which takes three seasons, 25 to 30 crowns will produce enough asparagus for a family of four.

Dig a trench 12 to 18 inches deep, the length of your row, and add 6 or 7 inches of aged manure, or compost, or a little peat moss. Sprinkle on a dusting of 10-10-10, add a couple of inches of soil from beside the trench, and mix everything together.

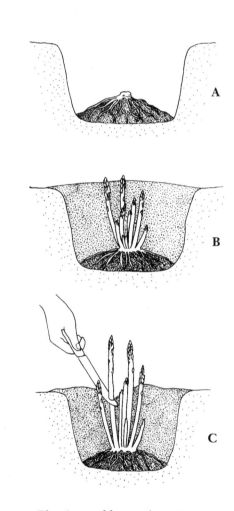

Planting and harvesting asparagus

With this mixture, build up mounds at the bottom of the trench about a foot apart. Set each crown on top of a mound and drape the roots down just the way you'd put a wig on a head (A). This enables the roots to get moisture and food throughout a depth of 4 or 5 inches of soil. If you place the roots flat on the ground they can feed only at one level and it will be a while before they grow down and get water and food from a deeper level.

Place the top of the crowns at least 4 inches below the soil surface. Fill up the trench to cover them with a couple of inches of soil. This puts the soil level of the row a little below the rest of the garden. When the shoots grow up, fill in the trench with a little more soil to give the stalks excellent support (B).

First Year Care. You may want to put a thick mulch around the small spears *after* they come up to keep the weeds down and hold in moisture. Let the new plants grow through the summer and fall without cutting the shoots or ferns. Let the tops die down in late fall. Don't do a thing to them.

Second Year Care. Every spring, starting with the second year, you'll have to do a little maintenance on your asparagus bed *before* it starts to grow again. Cut the old ferns that died over the fall and winter and clear them out. Remove any mulch that's left. Then fertilize the plants. Use a cupful of 10-10-10 or similar fertilizer for each 3 feet of row. Cultivate a couple of times between the rows each spring. If you are using a tiller, till at a shallow depth to avoid cutting any spreading roots.

As the weather warms, the asparagus will poke through the soil. Don't harvest the second year. When the spears are tall enough to mulch, weed and then mulch around them.

Third Year Care. Early in the third spring, again cut away old ferns, pull the mulch back, and fertilize. You'll probably be able to harvest some spears. They are at their prime when 6 to 8 inches tall. If they are as thick as your finger, pick some. If they are skinny, let them grow into ferns.

Harvest with a knife and cut the spears a hair below the soil surface (C). Cut with care. Another spear may be about to come up right next to the one you're harvesting.

Care During the Following Years. As your asparagus plants get stronger and stronger over the next few years, you can harvest for 5 to 8 weeks each spring before letting the plants concentrate on growing ferns.

Keep asparagus fresh in the refrigerator by storing in a jar with the bottoms standing in about an inch of water.

After the last harvest, pull all the weeds. Fertilize the bed again, and mulch heavily around the spears. This halts all weed growth.

Once your bed is established, there's a simple way to stretch out the harvest period. Early in the spring, pull the mulch away from only part of your patch. The asparagus will come up faster when the soil is exposed to the warmth of sunlight. The mulched soil in the rest of the bed will stay cool longer, delaying the growth of the remaining asparagus. Wait a couple of weeks and then pull the mulch off the rest of the row. If you see spears poking through the mulch before the two weeks are up, pull the mulch back. Otherwise, some of the asparagus spears may curl over when they come up.

Rhubarb

Rhubarb grows from root divisions which you can buy in a garden store or from a seed catalog. Often the best way is to get some roots from a neighbor. Three or four root crowns will produce all you can eat.

Rhubarb

Planting. In the spring, dig planting holes several inches deep and 18 inches apart. Put some compost or fertilizer in each hole. Place a single piece of root in each hole, covering it with about an inch of soil. Do not harvest from these plants the first year. Give them a few side-dressings through the season so they'll grow lots of tops and in turn nourish the developing root system.

Care and Harvesting. The next season you can harvest some stalks. When they get 8 to 10 inches tall, gently pull out and up on the ones you want to tear away from the plant. Harvest the largest stalks first. Don't eat the leaves. They are toxic.

During the second year, the rhubarb plant may put out tall seedpods. Remove these so the roots will produce tasty stalks all season. The more stalks you harvest, the more the plant will produce.

To keep your rhubarb plants thriving for many years, they must be divided every four or five years. You can do it in the fall or in the spring before growth starts.

Drive a shovel down into the middle of the plant and dig up half the root. Fill in the hole with compost. This forces the plant to produce younger, better crowns the following year. With young crowns you'll have tender, flavorful rhubarb. The half of the plant you dig up can be saved in the root cellar, planted right away, or given to a friend.

Horseradish

To start a bed, get some roots from a friend who has one. A horseradish grower won't mind because the plants expand quickly; unless you till around it several times a year they will try to invade neighboring crops.

Horseradish

Planting. You'll need only six root pieces. Plant them as early in the spring as you can. Till or spade the area to a depth of 6 to 8 inches. Dig a hole or furrow 4 to 6 inches deep and put a handful of fertilizer or compost at the bottom. Cover this with 2 inches of soil.

Push each root piece in the soil at a 45° angle rather than straight up and down. This way, the roots that form along the length of each cutting can grow straight down without getting tangled up. The top of the root cutting should be 2 inches below the soil surface.

(Note: if you buy roots at a store, one end will be cut on a slant. That slanted end should be planted downward. If you dig roots in a friend's garden, cut them the same way so you'll get the right end planted downward.)

Jerusalem-artichokes

Jerusalem-artichokes are closely related to sunflowers, but grown for their underground tubers which are delicious and low in calories. They will grow almost anywhere in the United States and can be planted either in the fall or as early as the ground can be worked in the spring.

Jerusalem-artichoke flower

One of the nicest things about Jerusalem-artichokes, besides their taste, is that they are almost completely free of diseases and pests. They are so prolific that if you do not watch them closely, they will take over the whole garden, your lawn, your woods, and any nearby roadside ditches. Any tuber left in the soil will sprout the next year and send out roots.

Planting. Start Jerusalem-artichokes by planting tubers which you can buy or dig from a friend's garden. You will need six pieces, cut in quarters, for a 25-foot long row. Cut the tubers into pieces with an eye in each and plant them about 4 inches deep, spacing them a foot apart. Leave 3 to 4 feet between the rows so you can till next to them. When Jerusalem-artichoke plants are mature, they will be 6 or more feet tall, so plant them where they will not shade other plants.

Harvest. Jerusalem-artichokes need a very long growing season — about 126 days. Start harvesting in late fall or after the frost has killed the tops. They also can be harvested in the spring before they sprout again.

Jerusalem-artichoke tubers

THE HERB GARDEN

Herbs are often grown more for culinary, medicinal, and aromatic purposes than for their beauty. People who enjoy cooking, plant those that are used for flavoring and savoring, such as sweet basil for pesto, tarragon for vinegar, and spearmint for tea. Others concentrate on plants for medicinal salves and ointments; and still others choose to specialize in the fragrant herbs.

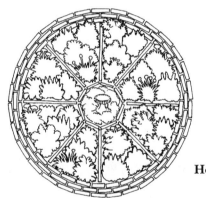

Herb garden

Learning about the lore, history, and uses of herbs is nearly as much fun as cultivating them. Owners of a vintage home, for example, often research the plants in common use when it was built, and feature them in a border; someone in the clergy might design a bed using herbs mentioned in the Bible. Other herb gardens have featured such varied historical themes as Shakespeare, medieval and colonial periods, as well as brides' gardens, saints' gardens, plots with only silver- or gold-colored plants, gardens filled completely with fragrant geraniums, cutting gardens for dried bouquets and wreaths, and much more.

DESIGNING AN HERB GARDEN

Herbs are so versatile that they are at home almost anywhere — along pathways, as landscape plants or ground covers, in rock gardens, terraces, vegetable beds, or containers. But they usually give the most gardening pleasure when planted in a well-designed herb bed. It may be as informal as a tiny plot outside the door of a country cottage, or as formal and elaborate as a classic medieval wheel, knot, butterfly, stained glass window, or some other geometric design.

The ideal site for most herbs is in the sun, although a few, such as the mints, watercress, and lemon balm, grow well in shade. Some will thrive in almost any type of soil, but most prefer it to be well drained, with a pH that is neutral to sweet, rather than acidic. In a sunny spot outside a kitchen door you might plant a small salad garden of culinary perennial and annual herbs, and a few salad greens.

In small, informal beds minimal planning is necessary — primarily the arrangement and proper spacing for the plants you've chosen. Consider the ultimate size of each plant, and arrange it so

A traditional knot garden pattern constructed in a formal, intricate design that resembles knotted rope.

that the small species, such as parsley and thyme, are not hidden and shaded by lovage, comfrey, or other tall growers.

If you choose to create a larger, more ornamental bed, it is desirable to plan it first on graph paper. To attain the necessary symmetry and balance, the different species must be orderly and neat, colors and sizes arranged to balance each other, and edgings are essential. Pathways, which are integral to the design of most geometric-type gardens, should be in place before any planting is done. Paths of flagstone, brick, pebbles, or mown grass form the skeletons of such beds. Each path should be 3 or 4 feet wide to provide plenty of room to move about and work in each area.

The different colors of herb foliage make them fun to arrange in interesting patterns. Blooming times are not especially important because most of their flowers are rather inconspicuous. Rows of compact, low-growing plants (chives and parsley, for example) can be used to separate various groupings and to edge the paths.

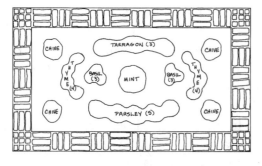

Kitchen herb garden

Whether your garden is formal or informal, position any spreading varieties where they will not become invasive. Weedy species are best kept within bounds by planting each one in a separate soil "pocket." These can be large plastic pots sunk into the garden or sunken clay tiles such as those used for chimney liners.

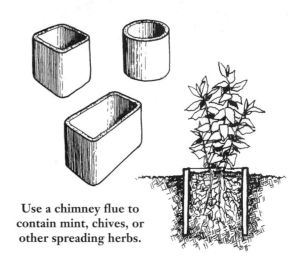

Use a chimney flue to contain mint, chives, or other spreading herbs.

PLANTING THE HERB GARDEN

Prepare the Soil

Herbs will prosper in most types of good garden soil, especially a fertile, well-drained, sandy loam. Since most herbs are native to the poorer, rocky soils of the Mediterranean, they are able to make a fine showing under less than optimum conditions. Most herbs require well-drained soil (the exception being some types of mint). Do not plant in poorly drained areas unless you plan to build raised beds.

If you are considering a long-term perennial bed, it is advisable to make your soil the best possible with the addition of organic matter such as compost, chopped leaves, or peat moss. The more humus, the better, in an herb bed. Mix manure and compost with the soil and prepare it as thoroughly as if you intended to plant a flower or vegetable garden. After the surface is smoother, take your design in hand and outline the spaces for each herb with white flour or lime. After planting, spread a mulch around each plant to help prevent erosion and to keep the plants clean. It's annoying to find herbs that you intend to use in a salad or potpourri splattered with dirt from the latest rainstorm.

Getting Plants Started

From Seed. Many annual and biennial herbs are easily started from seed sown directly in the garden. Or you can get a jump on the growing season by starting your plants (except tarragon) from seed indoors, then transplanting when the soil warms up. Prepare the soil in the early spring, as soon as the ground warms up and is easily worked. Rake over the seedbed and break up any clumps of soil or organic matter. After you have a fine granular surface, scatter the seeds lightly on the top of the soil. Most herb seeds are very small and need only a fine covering of soil. Mist the seedbed with water and do not let it dry out until germination.

Most perennial herbs can be started from seed, although it is far easier to buy started plants in order to get quicker results. A few, such as French tarragon and lavender, should be started by division rather than by seed to obtain good plants. Also, the different strains of oregano and the mints can vary so much in flavor that it is best to taste or smell each variety before planting it in your garden.

Division. You can also expand your garden by propagating by division, layering, or cuttings. A neighbor with an established herb garden may be able to provide you with plants this way. To propagate by division, dig up a section of the roots of an established plant (A) in the fall or early spring. Separate them into smaller clumps with a shovel, or small knife, or by hand — depending on the size of the clump (B). Replant divided clumps in a new location, taking care to set plants at the proper depth

Dividing plant clumps

A

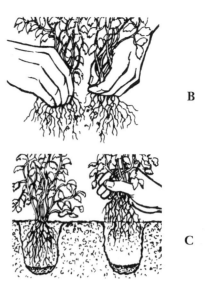

B

C

(C). It's a good idea to add compost or well-rotted manure to the soil in the planting hole. Chives, mints, oregano, rosemary, sage, tarragon, and thyme lend themselves to root divisions.

Layering. Some herbs form roots along stems that touch the ground. These herbs can be propagated by layering. Simply secure the middle of a long, flexible stem to, or slightly below the surface, and mound soil over the stem to encourage rooting.

Layering to start new plants

Woody plants sometimes root faster if you make a slight cut in the stem where it touches the ground. When the stem takes root, it can be cut from the Mother plant. Layering is effective with mint, oregano, rosemary, sage, and thyme.

Cuttings. You can also propagate herbs with cuttings. Take a 3-inch to 4-inch shoot cut from the tip of the current season's growth. Strip all but the top two leaves from the shoot, dip the cut surface into a hormone rooting powder and plant in a loose growing medium. Once the plant is established, transplant it into the garden, if desired. This method works for marjoram, mint, oregano, rosemary, sage, tarragon, and thyme.

Transplants

Many kitchen herbs are set out from transplants or young seedlings that have been growing for 8 to 12 weeks. These plants get off to a faster start and may be larger at the end of the season than the directly seeded herbs.

Space the transplants at the distance recommended on the seed package for each herb. Small herbs are usually planted 8 to 12 inches apart; larger types may be separated by as much as 3 feet. Although the spacings may look too roomy at first, in no time the plants will fill out the area.

MAINTAINING AN HERB GARDEN

Once established, most perennial herbs are hardy and will live for years, but in northern zones, tender plants (rosemary and bay) must be treated as annuals or potted and taken in for the winter. In addition to perennials, you may want to reserve spots in your garden in which to plant some of the many excellent annuals. A culinary herb garden wouldn't be complete without basil, dill, borage, anise, chervil, coriander, sweet marjoram, nasturtium, rocket, and summer savory. Seeds of biennials such as parsley must be resown each spring along with the annuals. The seeds can either be sown directly in the garden, or, for an earlier harvest, seedlings set out.

Fertilizers and Mulch

Most herbs require only small amounts of fertilizers and are sensitive to overfeeding. The best time to fertilize herbs is in the early spring, just as they are planted or when they start to put on new growth. You can use organic fertilizers, such as compost, alfalfa meal, bonemeal, blood meal, or cottonseed meal. Well-rotted or dehydrated manures can also be used. Fresh manure contains too much ammonia and may burn plants. If the plants look as if they could use a lift later in the season — indicated by yellowing foliage and sparse growth — give them a shot of a liquid fish emulsion or seaweed mixed with water.

You can use a complete chemical fertilizer such as 5-10-10, if you desire. Add a couple of tablespoons around each perennial shrub in the early spring. Mix it into the soil and water well to send the nutrients down to the roots.

Most perennial herb gardens benefit from a layer of mulch to maintain even soil temperatures and moisture content. It also discourages weed growth. Mulching the herb garden cuts out a large percentage of the time you would ordinarily spend watering or weeding.

HERB SELECTION GUIDE

Basil (*Ocimum basilicum*). Basil is a tender annual, very sensitive to frost. It is easily propagated by seed sown directly in the garden after the soil has warmed up. Basil likes a soil rich in organic matter and thrives on an extra dose of compost. Plant it in full sun and be sure to water it weekly in dry weather.

This fast-growing plant reaches about 2 feet in height and has large, egg-shaped leaves that curl inward. In midsummer, small spikes of white flowers shoot up from each  stalk. Pinching out the blooms, or the tips of each stem before they flower, will make the plant bushy. The leaves can be harvested throughout the summer from the growing plant.

Basil

There is a 'Dark Opal,' or purple, variety of basil that beautifully offsets the greens and the grays of the kitchen herb garden. It also imparts a rich magenta color to white vinegar.

To dry basil, harvest just before it blooms. Hang, screen dry, or freeze.

Bay, Bay Laurel (*Laurus nobilis*). Slow-growing evergreen shrub with aromatic leaves. Sun-loving, it is a tender perennial and must be taken indoors during the winter in cold climates. Difficult to propagate. Can grow to a height of 10 feet.

Burnet *(Sanguisorba minor).* Cucumber-flavored leaves are used in drinks, soups, and salads. Easily grown from seed. Grows 1 to 2 feet tall in sun or light shade and slightly alkaline soil.

Camomile *(Anthemis nobilis).* Tea made from the blossoms is used as a soothing tranquilizer; also used as a tonic. Grows easily from seed or divisions. *A. nobilis* grows up to 10 inches with a spreading growth habit.

Caraway *(Carum carvi).* Biennial culinary herb used to flavor cheese, rye bread, and pastries. Seeds ripen in fall of second year. Plants grow up to 2 feet. Likes sun and ordinary garden soil.

Catmint, Catnip *(Nepeta cataria).* Beloved by felines and used in tea by humans as a cough remedy and aid to digestion. Plants are 2 to 3 feet high. Easily grown in sun or light shade, and in most soils.

Chives *(Allium schoenoprasum).* Small onionlike plants, useful in salads, soups, and egg dishes. Easily grown from plants or seeds. A nice kitchen pot plant that grows to a height of 1 foot.

Chives are a hardy perennial, reaching 12 to 18 inches in height. The leaves — dark green, hollow spears — poke up through the soil in the early spring, almost before anything else. Mauve-blue flower balls bloom on hard, green tendrils from midsummer on. These should be cut to keep the plant growing but can be left later in the season to keep foraging bees happy.

Chives prefer full sun, rich soil, and plentiful water. Mulching around the plants is helpful to keep competitive weeds and grasses at bay.

Propagate by seeds or root divisions. A small plant will quickly enlarge and should be divided every three or four years to keep the plant healthy. Simply cut through the plant with a shovel or sharp knife in the early spring, allowing at least ten small, white bulbous roots per new clump. Set the divisions ten inches apart.

Harvest chives as soon as the spears are a few inches long. Snipping out entire spears encourages tender new growth. Chives do not dry well. Freeze for winter use.

Comfrey *(Symphytum officinale).* Vigorous herb with large leaves, sometimes used as a poultice to aid in the knitting of broken bones. Recent findings suggest it may be harmful if ingested in more than small amounts. Also grown for animal food. Usually started from divisions. Plants are 2 to 3 feet high. Grows easily in sun and ordinary garden soil.

Costmary, Bible Leaf *(Chrysanthemum balsamita).* Its fragrant leaves with a minty flavor were pressed and used as bookmarks in Bibles during Colonial days. Used today as a garnish, in tea, and for potpourri. Propagated by root division. Plants grow 2 to 3 feet high. Likes a sunny spot and ordinary garden soil.

Dill *(Anethum graveolens).* Dill is a hardy annual that closely resembles fennel. However, it usually develops only one round, hollow main stem per root, and the feathery branches are a bluish green. Yellow flowers bloom in clusters of showy umbels. The dill seeds are dark brown, ridged, and strongly flavored. Dill grows 2 to 3 feet tall and can be planted in groupings to keep the plants supported in windy weather.

Dill

Propagate by seed sown directly in the garden. It does best in full sun in sandy or loamy, well-drained soil that has a slightly acid pH (5.8 to 6.5). Enrich your soil with compost or well-rotted manure for best dill growth. Once you have grown dill, it will reseed in the following years.

Dill weed and dill seed are both used in cooking; the weed is mild and the seeds are pungent. Dill weed can be harvested at any time, but the volatile oils are highest just before flowering. The seed heads should be cut when the majority of seeds have formed, even though some flowers may still be blooming. The seeds can be threshed from the heads after drying.

Fennel *(Foeniculum)*. There are two types of fennel grown: Florence fennel *(F. dulce)* or finocchio, grown for its anise-flavored foliage, seeds, and fleshy base, is usually harvested as an annual. Common or herb fennel, *F. vulgare*, more weedy, is grown primarily for its seed and foliage. Both are used in salads and stews and, less commonly, as a medicine to reduce appetite and to treat various ailments.

Fennel

Herb fennel is a hardy biennial that often becomes a perennial in favorable climates. The plant reaches 3 to 5 feet tall and has thick, shiny green, hollow stalks; feathery branches; yellow flowers that bloom on showy umbels; and sweetly flavored, ridged seeds.

Fennel prefers a rich, well-drained soil in full sun. Add lime if the pH is below 6.0. Propagate by seed in the early spring to give it sufficient time to flower and go to seed. The leaves should be harvested just before the plant flowers.

Fennel is easily grown from seed, but best kept isolated, as it is reputed to adversely affect the growth of other plants nearby. It is closely related to dill and the two should not be interplanted because they may cross-pollinate, resulting in dilly fennel or fennelly dill!

Feverfew *(Chrysanthemum parthenium)*. Biennial or perennial. Hardy medicinal herb credited with many beneficial characteristics. Easily grown from seed or division; grows 2 to 3 feet tall. Best in sun or light shade and a well-drained soil.

Garlic *(Allium sativum)*. Grown for the flavor of its corms (or cloves). See chapter 6 under Onions and Other Alliums for growing information.

Ginseng *(Panax quinquefolium)*. Medicinal plant with roots that are said to have many miraculous powers, everything from a tonic to an aphrodisiac. In this country it is valued mostly as a cash crop. It needs acidic soil, heavy shade, and frequent applications of fungicides as protection against disease.

The plants grow slowly, and it may take up to ten years for the roots to reach harvestable size. Plants grow up to 15 inches.

Hops *(Humulus lupulus)*. Perennial vine that produces flower pods used for flavoring beer. Propagated easily from seeds, layers, or root division. Likes full sun, grows rapidly, and often becomes rank. The tops may die to the ground over the winter in cold areas, but roots are hardy.

Horehound *(Marrubium vulgare)*. Leaves are dried for tea and used fresh in candy and cough syrup. Grown from seed, cuttings, or division. Plants grow 1 to 2 feet. Needs full sun and dry, sandy soil.

Horseradish *(Armoracia rusticana)*. A hardy perennial herb grown for the pungent flavor of its roots. See chapter 6 under Root Crops for growing information.

Hyssop *(Hyssopus officinalis)*. A hardy, ancient herb used as a purifying tea and for medicine, it is said to cure all manner of ailments from head lice to shortness of breath. Started by seed or division. Grows to 3 feet. Prefers full sun and well-drained, alkaline soil.

Lavender *(Lavandula)*. Aromatic herb used either fresh or dried, in sachets and pillows. Grows from seeds, cuttings, or divisions. Plant in a protected location in the North. Prefers lime soil. English lavender *(L. vera)* produces the loveliest blossoms and the most fragrant oil. Plants grow 1 to 2 feet.

Lemon balm *(Melissa officinalis)*. Lemon-scented leaves are used for tea, jelly, or flavoring, either dried or fresh. Attracts bees. Start from cuttings or division. Plants grow 1 to 3 feet high. Plant in sun or light shade and well-drained soil.

Lemon verbena *(Aloysia triphylla* or *Lippia citri-odora)*. Tender, aromatic perennial that cannot stand frost, so must be used as a houseplant during the winter in northern climates. Loses its leaves in the fall, but they promptly return. Most often enjoyed for its fragrance. Height: 10 inches.

Lovage *(Levisticum officinale)*. The celery-flavored leaves and stalks are used in soups, salads, and similar dishes. Grows well from seed. Mature plants may be 4 to 6 feet high. Grows best in partial shade and moist, fertile soil.

Marjoram *(Majorana hortensis,* sometimes listed as *Origanum majorana).* Marjoram is a tender perennial native to the warm Mediterranean. In colder climates, it is grown as an annual. The plant reaches 8 to 12 inches in height and has short, branched, squarish stems. The small, oval leaves are grayish green and covered with a fuzzy down. Little balls or knots grow out of the leaf clusters and the end of the branches in the midsummer. From these, white or pink flowers emerge.

Marjoram

Marjoram thrives in a light, rich soil in full sun. It prefers a neutral pH. Since it has a shallow root system, mulching around the plant helps to retain soil moisture and keep the weeds down.

Marjoram seeds can be sown directly in the garden after the soil has warmed up. Germination is slow — usually about two weeks. Keep the seed bed moist until the plants have sprouted. Marjoram can also be started from cuttings, layering, or division. Set transplants about a foot apart.

Marjoram is highly aromatic and its flavor improves with drying. Harvest just before the flowers open.

Mint *(Mentha).* Peppermint and spearmint are the most popular, but orange, apple, lemon, and others are also widely grown. Mint is known by its squarish stems and its tooth-edged leaves. Clusters of white or purple flowers bloom off the terminal ends of the shoots.

Mints are hardy perennials often attaining 3 feet in height. They are notorious spreaders and will invade the surrounding garden territory if they are not confined. They prefer a moist, rich soil and will do well in full sun to partial shade.

Although they may be grown from seed, it is a good idea to buy small plants of your choice to be sure of getting the variety you want. Mints are easily propagated by divisions. Older mint plantings can be divided up every four or five years. Separate the roots into foot-sized clumps with a sharp shovel. These divisions are a nice present for a gardening friend.

The leaves can be harvested and enjoyed fresh throughout the summer. To dry mint, cut the stalks just above the first set of leaves, as soon as the flower buds appear. Hang to dry for 10 to 14 days.

Oregano *(Origanum vulgare).* Some confusion has arisen about the relationship between oregano and marjoram. They are close relatives and oregano is often called wild marjoram.

Oregano is a hardy perennial, growing 18 to 30 inches tall. The oval, grayish green, hairy leaves grow out from the nodes. White or pink flowers make their showing in the fall.

The plant grows in ordinary garden soil, but does best in a well-drained, sandy loam soil. If the pH is below 6.0, add lime before you set out the plants; oregano likes a sweet soil and a plentiful supply of calcium. Oregano strives in full sun in a location sheltered from high winds. Mulch over the plant if winters are severe.

Oregano

Oregano may be propagated by seed, divisions, or cuttings. Because the seeds are slow to germinate, you will get best garden results by setting out young plants spaced 15 inches apart.

To dry oregano, cut the stems an inch from the ground in the fall, just before the flowers open. Hang to dry. The herb is used in soups, salads, meat dishes, and pizza, especially in Italian and Mexican cuisine. Because there are many species, test the plants you buy for strength of the flavor.

Parsley *(Petroselinum)* Probably the most commonly grown culinary herb today, parsley is used as a garnish, and in salads, soups, and such. There are two main types of parsley: Italian (*P. hortense*) and French or curly (*P. crispum*).

Parsley is a hardy biennial, often grown as an annual. During the first growing season, the plant develops many dark green leaves that are grouped in bunches at the end of long stems. Italian parsley leaves are flat and fernlike; French parsley leaves are tightly curled. Umbels of yellow flowers are borne on long stalks. The plant reaches 12 to 18 inches in height.

Curly parsley

Plants thrive in moist, rich soil, endowed with plentiful organic matter. Parsley prefers full sun for optimum growth, but it will survive in partial shade. It can be planted from seed sown directly in the garden. However, since it takes three to four weeks to germinate, it is often more reliable to set out young plants. Space parsley transplants about 8 to 10 inches apart.

Parsley can be picked fresh throughout the season. To preserve for winter use, cut the leaves in the fall and dry or freeze them.

Pennyroyal (*Mentha pulegium*, English; *Hedeoma pulegioides*, American). Old-time medicinal herbs used for flavoring and to cure a variety of illnesses. The American Indians and early settlers also used it as an insect repellent. Grown from seed, cuttings, or root divisions. Plants grow to 1 foot high. Prefers a shady location and moist soil.

Rosemary (*Rosmarinus officinalis*). Used both as an aromatic and flavoring herb, it is useful in sauces, soups, teas.

This perennial evergreen shrub grows 2 to 6 feet high, depending on the climate. It has woody stems, bearing thin, needlelike leaves that are shiny green on the upper surface and a powdery, muted green on the un-

Rosemary

der surface. Blue flowers bloom on the tips of the branches in the spring.

Rosemary is a tender plant and must be sheltered or grown in containers and taken indoors for the winter in northern latitudes. It makes a nice potted plant and can be grown as a bonsai. It thrives best in a warm climate and prefers plenty of moisture in a well-drained, alkaline soil. Apply lime or wood ashes to acid soils testing below pH 6.5. Plants are susceptible to insect problems.

Rosemary is usually started from cuttings, root divisions, or layering because seed germination is slow and poor.

Harvest any time for fresh use. Hang to dry for winter supply.

Rue (*Ruta graveolens*). A bitter medicinal herb used for thousands of years as an antidote to all kinds of poisons. Easily grown from seed, but the ancient Greeks believed that a plant stolen from a neighbor's garden had more power than one acquired honestly! Plants grow 2 to 3 feet high and thrive in an alkaline soil, in sun or partial shade.

Sage (*Salvia officinalis*). One of the most common culinary herbs with many ornamental varieties available.

Sage is a hardy but short-lived perennial, native to the Mediterranean. It grows 2 feet or so in height and has velvety, textured, patterned, grayish green leaves. The stems become woody as the plant matures and should be pruned out to keep the plant producing. Lavender flower spikes bloom in the fall.

Sage can be started from seed, cuttings, or divisions. Since the

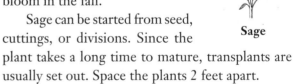

Sage

plant takes a long time to mature, transplants are usually set out. Space the plants 2 feet apart.

Sage prefers a well-drained soil in full sunlight. Enrich the soil with compost before planting, and add lime if the pH is below 5.8. Water well while the plants are young.

Harvest sparingly the first season and increase your quota yearly. The leaves can be picked any

time; but it is recommended that two crops a year, one in June and another in the fall, be harvested to keep the plants less woody. Hang to dry in small bunches.

Scented geraniums *(Pelargonium)*. Numerous varieties, each with a distinctive fragrance, flower, and leaf. Not frost-hardy. The leaves of rose geraniums are used in jelly or to make tea. Most varieties are grown primarily as scented houseplants. Started from cuttings. Prefers full sun and well-drained soil.

Sorrel *(Rumex)*. The leaves have a sour, acidic, citrus flavor and are used in soups and salads. French sorrel *(R. scutatus)* is most often planted, but garden sorrel *(R. acetosa)* is similar. Prefers acidic soil. Grows easily from seeds or division and often becomes a weed. Plants grow to 2 feet, in sun to partial shade.

Sweet woodruff *(Asperula odorata)*. Used in Germany for many centuries to flavor May wine, it has also been used as an ointment, in perfume, and as an internal medicine. Placed in drawers, it repels insects and gives sheets and towels a pleasant scent. Likes acid soil. Difficult to grow from seed, so buy plants instead. The top may be cut and dried anytime; the delightful fragrance appears only after drying. Plants grow to 8 inches high.

Tansy *(Tanacetum vulgare)*. A strong-smelling plant used as a fly and ant repellent, and in tea as an aid in digestion. Its yellow foliage may be dried for bouquets. Grows well in full sun and ordinary garden soil from seeds or divisions; can become weedy. Height: 2 to 3 feet.

Tarragon *(Artemisia)*. Tarragon is a perennial plant, the best varieties coming from the European countries. The French variety *(A. dracunculus)* has the best flavor and is much preferred to Russian tarragon *(A. redojwski)*, which is weedy and lacks the essential oils. One way to distinguish between varieties is this: the Russian tarragon produces viable seed, the French rarely does.

Tarragon grows 2 to 3 feet tall and tends to sprawl out late in the season. The long, narrow leaves, borne on upright stalks, are a shiny, dark green. Greenish or gray flowers may bloom in the fall. Since it rarely sets seed, tarragon should be propagated by cuttings or divisions.

Tarragon

Tarragon prospers in fertile soil with plentiful water and sunlight. It is advisable to mulch over the roots in the late fall to protect the plant from winter injury. Since tarragon becomes a rather large plant, it is often divided up every three or four years to make it easier to manage.

This herb may be harvested throughout the summer. To dry for winter use, cut the stalks a few inches from the ground in the early fall. Hang or screen dry.

Thyme *(Thymus vulgaris)*. Native to the Mediterranean, this aromatic, perennial herb has many well-known varieties including lemon thyme, creeping thyme, and garden or common thyme. Most varieties have ornamental, culinary, and aromatic qualities. Thyme is a favorite plant of bees.

Thyme is a short plant, various kinds growing only 8 to 12 inches tall, and often used as ground covers or rock garden plants. The leaves are small and narrowly oval, usually a dull grayish green. The stems become woody after a few years. Pink or violet flowers arise from the leaf axils in the early fall.

Thyme

Thyme flourishes in sandy, dry soils in full sun. It is an excellent candidate for rock gardens.

Propagate thyme by seeds, divisions, or cuttings. The seeds are slow to germinate, so it is best to set out transplants. Space thyme 15 inches apart. Older, woody plants can be rejuvenated by digging up the plant and dividing it in the early spring. Fertilize with compost or seaweed.

The leaves can be harvested for fresh use throughout the summer. To dry thyme, cut the stems just as the flowers start to open. Hang to dry in small bunches. Harvest sparingly the first year.

Wormwood (*Artemisia absinthium*). A bitter, strong-smelling, medicinal herb. Toxic in large doses. An attractive plant with gray foliage, it is easily grown from seed and may quickly become a weed, so be wary of planting it in your garden. Plants grow 2 to 5 feet high. Ordinary garden soil is fine, and so is a location in the sun or light shade.

Watercress (*Nasturtium officinale*). Used for garnish and flavoring. If you have a shallow, slow-moving stream or pond where there is a no threat of flood, you may want to try growing this flavorful herb. Watercress can be easily transplanted from one stream to another. Propagated by division. Low-growing.

BERRIES AND GRAPES

Fruit plants are not much of an initial investment in light of all the future dividends you get from them. A fruit tree can cost as little as a bushel and a half of good fruit, and berry plants are only a few cents each. Even a small family with their own garden and orchard can easily save several hundred dollars a year on their annual food bill. Why buy tropical fruit drinks when you can make your own? Why spend hard-earned money on commercial wines and all the taxes?

If you have only a small lot, you can still grow fruit. Many dwarf trees grow to full size within an 8-foot circle. Strawberries grow in crocks, hanging baskets, pyramids, and barrels. A few feet of raspberries will produce quarts of fruit every year. Blueberries and other fruit-bearing shrubs can be substituted for ornamental foundation plants and hedges around the house. Fruit trees can replace flowering trees and shrubs, and nut trees can be planted instead of shade trees. While your orchard

may bear little resemblance to Kew Gardens, you will find a satisfying pleasure in growing something that is beautiful in all seasons and also produces a product that can be put into a tasty pie or a tantalizing jug.

STRAWBERRIES

If there is one fruit every homesteader and suburbanite should cultivate it is easy-to-grow strawberries, the first fruit of the season and the quickest to bear of any fruit.

And no matter where you live, there is a variety that will thrive and do well in your region. Though they do best in the cooler, moist regions, they can be grown in hot, dry climates, especially where windbreaks can be provided and supplemental watering is possible during the critical months of July, August, and September.

STRAWBERRY VARIETIES FOR SPECIAL REGIONS OR PURPOSES

For areas with little frost: Fresno, Headliner, Pocahontas, Tioga.

For the Northwest: Fresno, Goldsmith, Shasta.

Hardiest: Catskill, Dunlap, Empire, Fairfax, Premier (same as Howard 17), Sparkle.

Everbearers: Gem, Mastodon, Ozark Beauty, Rockhill.

Excellent flavor: Albritton, Dunlap, Empire, Fletcher, Midland, Sparkle, Suwanee.

Best for home freezing: Earlibelle, Earlidawn, Marshall, Midland, Midway, Pocahontas, Redglow, Sparkle.

Largest fruit: Atlas, Catskill, Guardian, Jersey Belle, Sequoia, Tioga.

Most resistant to late spring frosts: Catskill, Earlidawn, Midway, Premier (same as Howard 17).

Earliest: Atlas, Blakemore, Dunlap, Earlibelle, Midland, Premier, Sequoia, Sunrise, Surecrop.

Midseason: Apollo, Catskill, Empire, Fairfax, Fresno, Guardian, Marshall, Midway, Raritan, Redchief, Robinson.

Latest: Albritton, Armore, Badgerbelle, Columbia, Garnet, Hood, Jersey Belle, Ozark Beauty, Redstar (very late), Sparkle, Tennessee Beauty, Torrey, Totem, Vesper.

Strawberry plants respond for the gardener in direct proportion to the care they receive. Larger yields of high quality fruit await those who improve the soil, devote extra attention to cultivation, provide irrigation if needed, and mulch the planting properly.

Buying Strawberry Plants

Because of the popularity of the strawberry, a great many new varieties have been developed during the short time it has been in cultivation. There are now kinds that grow well all over the United States as well as in parts of Alaska, Canada, and even in the really warm parts of Florida. Because of the wide range of varieties, be careful to choose the right ones for your region. And try to locate some that are grown nearby and are freshly dug. Be sure to buy only those plants that are certified virus-free. By doing so you are likely to save yourself a great deal of distress later on.

Preparing the Soil

Since your strawberry plants will be growing in the same spot for at least two years, it is extremely important to have the ground very well prepared. The plants are small and shallow-rooted compared to all other fruit plants, so they get all their moisture and nourishment from the top few inches of soil.

This soil should be light, rich, slightly acid (pH of 5.5 to 6), and full of rich humus (manure, compost, or peat) that will hold moisture even during the driest weather. Generally, soil that will grow a good crop of potatoes is also good for strawberries. In fact, it is always important to plant strawberries on land that has been used first for cultivated crops for a year or more previously in order to get rid of the grass, weeds, and white grubs. These are the worst enemies of the strawberry, and well-prepared soil helps eliminate all three. White grubs live mostly in grass-covered soils, and one of their favorite foods is strawberry roots. Grass and weeds compete with the shallow-rooted berry plants for nutrients and moisture, and they crowd and shade the plants as well. You can wage war on weed competition by frequent cultivation, hoeing, and hand-weeding or applying a heavy mulch.

Planting

How many plants do you need? Gardeners usually plant from 25 to 100 plants in their first strawberry bed. Later on you will know better whether to plant more or less. The number you choose will depend on your yield and how many berries you eat, freeze, preserve, and give away.

When should you plant? Spring is usually regarded as the best time, the earlier the better. There doesn't seem to be much gained by fall planting, even if the plants survive — and many don't.

Once your plants have come and the soil is tilled to a depth of nearly a foot and is loose, crumbly, and rich, you're ready to plant. You have two planting methods to choose from: the matted row or the less-used hill system.

To plant a strawberry plant, use a trowel to

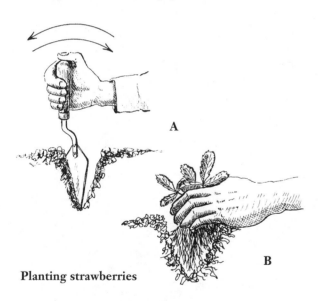

Planting strawberries

make a hole 5 to 7 inches wide and deep enough to accommodate the roots of the plant (A). Set the plant in the hole, gently spreading out the roots and setting the plant with the top of the crown just above ground level (B). The roots should be completely buried in soil. Firm the soil around the plant, being sure that the crown remains just above ground level.

The Matted Row. In the matted row method, set the plants about 18 inches apart in the row at the proper depth as described above. Water them well. If you plant more than one row, keep the rows at least 3 feet apart, or even wider if you plan to use a power tiller for cultivation. In this method the plants are allowed to produce runners freely (runners produce new little plants). You'll have to steer them so they will grow toward their adjoining plants, take root, and fill in to make a row matted with strawberry plants.

Matted row

In this system, the crop is treated like a biennial and is planted one year, harvested the next, then plowed under. If kept for a third year, so many new plants are produced that the bed becomes overcrowded, the fruit crop is small, and the berries are usually small and hard.

The Hill System. The hill system takes more plants and usually more attention, but it saves annual replanting and is ideally suited for home gardeners with little growing space. Those who like raising plants organically with a deep mulch also prefer it.

The plants are set 12 inches apart in three rows, which are also 12 inches apart. The plants are mulched. If you want more than three rows, leave 3 or 4 feet of walking space between the beds.

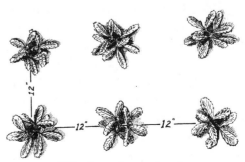

Hill-planted strawberries

After setting out, keep the plants well watered. Unlike the matted row system in which you let the runners grow freely, in this system you cut off all runners as soon as they form and permit no new plants to grow.

In other words, the strawberry plant is treated as a perennial, which it is. When grown this way it will keep producing for six years or more. Since none of the plant's energy goes into setting runners and making new plants, both plant and fruit get quite large.

Whichever method you choose, be sure to set your plants at the correct depth. If the crowns are planted under the soil, the plant will smother and die. If the crowns are set too high above the soil, they will dry out. If you cultivate or hoe the bed, it is important never to hoe soil up around strawberry crowns as you would around corn or beans.

Rotate Your Crops

Although the hill method of growing strawberries has much to recommend it, most home growers use the more familiar runner method. In the spring they set their plants alongside the vegetable garden and cultivate them as they do the other plants. The next spring they plant another bed on the other side of the garden. Berries are picked in the second year from the first bed planted. After bearing, it is plowed under and the bed is planted with winter rye or oats; or if you don't want to plant a cover crop, the bed can be heavily fertilized and covered with mulch or black plastic to keep it weed-free.

The next spring, strawberries are again planted for the following year in another spot in the garden. The quick plowing under of the old plants and continual change in location of the new plants aids greatly in disease and insect control. The annual planting of virus-free plants means a good crop of large fruit from brand new plants each year.

You may wonder why you shouldn't save money and dig extra plants out of your own patch for planting. Of course you can, but unless you are absolutely sure they are disease-free and insect-free it's a lot smarter to get them each year from a certified virus-free nursery.

Weed Control

Weeds and grass are a real problem in growing strawberries. To keep them out, hand-weeding, hoeing, cultivation, or mulching with organic material or black plastic are all used. Some growers use chemical weed killers. Others allow geese to run in their berry beds to eat the grass and dandelions.

For homegrowers, hand-hoeing, cultivation, or mulching are safest and do less damage to the plant. Chemicals are often tricky to use, and geese are very dirty and not always selective as to what they eat. If you hoe or cultivate be sure you do not "hill up" around the plant and suffocate it. As when planting, the crown must never be buried.

Pick Off Blossoms the First Year

Whichever planting arrangement you choose, be very sure not to let any fruit develop on your strawberry plants the first year. Growing and ripening even a berry or two will weaken the plant so much that the following year's production will be drastically curtailed. To prevent fruiting, simply pick off all blooms as fast as they form.

Everbearing strawberries are an exception to this rule, however. If you plant everbearers, the blossoms should be kept picked until midsummer the first year, but from then on the plant can be allowed to flower naturally. By that time it is well-enough established to support its fall crop.

Everbearing Strawberries

Everbearing strawberries produce a light crop in early summer, a few more fruits off and on throughout the summer, and another heavier crop in late summer or fall. They're ideal for summer home gardeners who preserve very little fruit but like to pick a few berries now and then all season. They are the best kinds to plant in pots, jars, barrels, and pyramids. They begin to bear quickly and look nice all season.

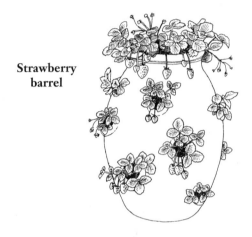

Strawberry barrel

Everbearers are a bit tricky to grow in some areas. Most kinds don't do well in southern regions, and they're usually not recommended where growing seasons are unusually short. That leaves zones 5 to 8 as their ideal growing spots.

Winter and Frost Protection

In almost every spot north of the Mason-Dixon line — and in some to the south — some sort of winter protection is necessary for best strawberry production. The fruit buds, even before they begin to show in the spring, are easily hurt by below-freezing temperatures.

Straw is the preferred winter cover. It doesn't mat hard or contain lots of weed seeds like so many other covers. Also, when the plants are uncovered in the spring the straw makes a nice mulch that both conserves moisture and keeps the ripening fruit clean and away from the soil.

You should cover the plants about the time the hard frosts start (15 to 18°F. above zero) and the ground is beginning to freeze slightly. The covering should be left on all winter and not removed until all medium-hard frosts (25°F. above zero or under) have finished. When you remove the covering, it's best to do it on a cloudy or rainy day, or at least late in the afternoon, so the bright sun won't hit the tender shaded shoots before they have had a chance to toughen up a bit.

Besides needing protection from winter's cold, the plants will probably need to be protected from late spring frosts that sometimes hit when strawberries are blossoming. This is the time you quickly rip the quilts off the bed to cover them up, or set out kerosene flares. Small patches of strawberries can be protected by running lawn sprinklers over them all night. It may also help to cover them with plastic sheets, newspapers, or cardboard cartons or to move the straw mulch back over the blooms.

Harvesting

Strawberries should always be picked on the day they ripen, which usually means daily picking during the harvest season. Overripe fruit spoils quickly, on the vines or off. Early morning is the best time to pick; gathering the fruit while the air is still cool and rushing it to a cool place will help keep the berries fresh longer. But even in a refrigerator it's hard to keep strawberries for more than a few days. Wash them just before you use them, because when they are wet they spoil faster.

Insects and Diseases

Some manuals on growing strawberries list dozens of bugs and diseases that bother them. If you read those bulletins first, you may never find the cour-

and buzz around lights on early summer nights.

Cyclamen Mites. These small, hard-to-see insects also bother delphiniums, house plants, and other ornamentals, causing leaves and buds to curl tightly. It's hard to find safe sprays to use for control of this pest; natural parasitic insects often control them best.

Weevils. Weevils are one of the most serious problems for many growers. They lay their eggs in the bud cluster, causing it to be partly severed from the plant. If an insecticide has to be sprayed to control these weevils, care must be taken to use it before the blooms open so it won't also kill the pollinating bees.

It is always better to rely on organic controls, but if spraying becomes necessary for these insects, a general-purpose orchard spray can be applied at intervals of 10 to 14 days from the time the leaves begin growing in the spring until a week before the flowers open. This will control most strawberry diseases and insects.

Some strawberry growers plant a marigold between every plant to help repel certain insects. Since these are annuals, they never become weedy and they do dress up the patch.

age to plant at all. Most of these pests are no serious problem to the home gardener, fortunately, and only when large plantings are grown on the same lot for years do they sometimes become a serious threat.

Buying virus-free plants is the best insurance against disease. Leaf spot, leaf scorch, verticillium wilt, red stele, and other virus diseases are most common, but you may never encounter any of them.

Fungicides can be used to control many of the berry diseases if they become real problems. Fungicides are expensive, though, and ordinarily they shouldn't be necessary for home growers.

As for insects, you very likely will encounter at least a few. Many garden insects also attack strawberries. The Japanese beetles, aphids, thrips, leafhoppers, slugs, grasshoppers, spittlebugs, and leaf rollers that sometimes bother garden and flower plants often lunch on strawberries as well.

White Grubs. These root-eating pests are more likely to be a problem on new ground that was only recently in sod. The grubs develop into those big May (or June) beetles that bang on the windows

BRAMBLE FRUITS

The brambles, raspberries and blackberries, are among the most popular of all bush fruits, ranking second for most families only to the strawberry. They are easy to grow and very rewarding, for they produce the most fruit with the least amount of effort.

Raspberries

Classes of Raspberries

Red raspberries are by far the most familiar bramble. The reds come in both one-crop and two-crop varieties. The one-crop variety matures in midsummer in most areas, on canes grown the previous season. Two-crop raspberries are often called "everbearers," which they are not, or "fall-bearers," which they are. They bear a crop during the regular season on canes grown the year before and another one in the fall on canes grown the current year.

Yellow raspberries are closely related to the reds and vary in color from yellow to pale pink. These are so fragile they are seldom seen in stores, but they're ideally suited for home gardens. Many fruit lovers regard the yellow raspberry as the finest fruit in the world. A handful of them tossed together with the bright red variety makes an elegant dessert.

Black raspberries are dark in color, with an unusual flavor and odor. Some people like them very much, while others don't care for the slightly musky aroma and taste.

Purple raspberries are closely related to the blacks, with a similar flavor and similar growth habits and uses.

Classes of Blackberries

Blackberries come in three types: the *upright*, the *trailing kinds* called dewberries, and the *semi-upright*. The growth habit of the upright is very similar to that of the red raspberry. The canes of dewberries grow very long and vinelike, trailing on the ground unless supported. The third group has some of the growth characteristics of both.

Hardiness

Many varieties of red and yellow raspberries can be grown far up in Canada. Black and purple raspberries are nearly as hardy as the reds, with some varieties being suitable for Zone 3. Other varieties have been developed for milder climates. As with all other fruits, you should buy whichever plants are suitable for your area and those that are grown as nearby as possible. Here again it is wise to check

HARDINESS OF BLACKBERRY VARIETIES
by temperature zones

Variety	Zone
Alfred	4(a), 5, 6
Aurora(b)	8
Austin Thornless	7(a), 8
Bailey	5, 6
Boysen	7, 8
Brainerd	6(a), 7, 8
Brazos	8, 9
Cascade(b)	7(a), 8(c)
Chehalem(b)	7(a), 8(c)
Cory Thornless(b)	7(a), 8
Dallas	6(a), 7, 8(c)
Dewblack	6(a), 7, 8(c)
Early Harvest	6(a), 7, 8(c)
Early Wonder	6(a), 7, 8
Ebony King	5(a), 6, 7
Eldorado	5, 6, 7
Erie	5, 6, 7(c)
Evergreen(b)	8(c)
Flint	7, 8
Flordagrand	9
Gem	8
Georgia Thornless	9
Hedrick	5(a), 6, 7(c)
Hillquist	6(a), 7, 8(c)
Himalaya	7, 8
Jerseyblack	6, 7
Lawton	6(a), 7, 8(c)
Logan	6(a), 8(c)
Lucretia	7, 8(c)
Mammoth(b)	7(a), 8(c)
Marion(b)	8(c)
Mayes	7(a), 8
Midnite	6(a), 7, 8(c)
Nanticoke	6, 7, 8
Oklawaha	9
Olallie(b)	8(c)
Ranger	6(a), 7
Raven	6(a), 7
Smoothstem	7, 8(c)
Snyder	5, 6
Thornfree	6(a), 7, 8(c)
Williams	8
Young	6(a), 7, 8

(a) Subject to winter injury in some years if not protected.
(b) Not adapted to States east of Arizona.
(c) Adapted to northern part of zone or higher elevations.

NORTH AMERICAN HARDINESS ZONES

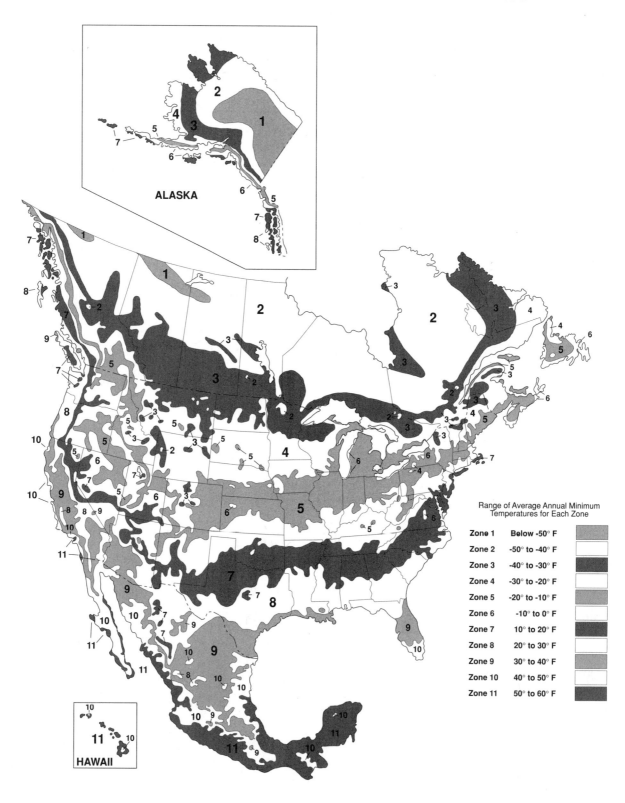

ALASKA

HAWAII

Range of Average Annual Minimum
Temperatures for Each Zone

Zone 1	Below -50° F
Zone 2	-50° to -40° F
Zone 3	-40° to -30° F
Zone 4	-30° to -20° F
Zone 5	-20° to -10° F
Zone 6	-10° to 0° F
Zone 7	10° to 20° F
Zone 8	20° to 30° F
Zone 9	30° to 40° F
Zone 10	40° to 50° F
Zone 11	50° to 60° F

with your local extension service for their recommendations.

Many fall-bearing red and yellow raspberries are winter-hardy, but if you decide to plant them in Zones 3 or 4, make sure the variety you choose will mature before early frosts destroy the berries.

Most cultivated upright blackberries are not as hardy as raspberries, although some have been developed that do very well in Zone 3. Because very few nurseries carry these, growers in cold areas may have trouble locating a blackberry worthy of growing. Snyder is one of the hardiest, but unfortunately its size and quality are much inferior to other kinds.

Trailing blackberries are even more tender, and most can be grown only in Zone 6 and warmer. Lucretia, one of the hardier varieties, is sometimes successful farther north and might be worth a trial in Zones 4 and 5. Like the other dewberries, it needs a long growing season to properly harden the wood before the first fall frost.

Planting

First prepare the ground thoroughly, as you would for a vegetable garden. It is important that grass and weeds be eradicated as completely as possible to get the brambles off to a good start. Since red raspberries and blackberries sucker badly, you won't want to plant them near a vegetable garden, strawberry bed, or flower patch. The best location for them is a place where you can mow around the bed or have some other certain way to keep the suckers under control.

Mail-order plants are likely to be shipped bare-rooted and may be dry when they arrive. Unwrap them and soak their roots for several hours in a tub of water as soon as possible to help them recover from their trip.

If you purchase the plants from a local nursery or garden center, the plants may be bare-rooted or in small pots. The potted ones, although more expensive, will probably get off to a better start because of their established root system and be well worth the extra money.

Plant raspberries and blackberries 2 feet apart,

STEPS FOR SUCCESS IN THE RASPBERRY AND BLACKBERRY PATCH

First Year

Prepare the soil carefully and plant the berries 2 feet apart. If bare-rooted plants are used, cut the tops back to 2 inches above the ground after planting. Mulch heavily.

Second Year

Spring. Cut back all plants to 2 inches above ground level in early spring. This encourages maximum cane growth for big crops.

Fall. Cut tops of plants back so canes are about 4 feet tall. This makes a stiff plant that doesn't fall over in winter's snow and wind.

Third Year and Each Year Thereafter

Summer. Mulch, cultivate, mow, or pull out tips or sucker plants that grow in the wrong places and make the row too wide. Keep each row only 2 feet wide for ease of picking, weeding, and pruning. Cut off and burn wilted tops as soon as they appear. Dig or pull out any sick-looking plants and destroy them (far away).

Late Summer. Cut to ground level the canes that bore fruit and now look sick. Remove and destroy them. Thin the new canes to 6 inches apart. Cut out any weak canes that won't produce.

Fall. Cut back canes to 4 feet in height for winter. Put up wire for support if necessary. Add mulch and manure. Spray with ferbam if spur blight is a problem.

setting each plant to the same depth as it grew in the ground or pot. Water heavily so that each plant sits in a muddy mixture and is therefore free of any air pockets around the roots. Continue to water the newly set plants thoroughly every two or three days for two weeks unless it rains heavily. Water is cheap

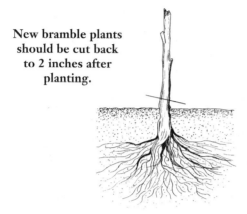

New bramble plants should be cut back to 2 inches after planting.

fruit insurance.

If potted plants are used, no pruning is necessary at planting time. With bare-rooted plants, however, you should cut back the canes to 2 inches above the ground to encourage new root growth. If the canes are not cut back enough, the tops will grow too rapidly with not enough corresponding root growth to support them. The result is a weak plant that will most likely give up or take years to get going.

Mulching

Grass and weeds can be one of the worst enemies of your brambles. They compete with the plants for nutrients, limit their growth, and reduce berry production, to say nothing of giving the garden a messy appearance. Since rototilling or hoeing can

easily damage the shallow bramble roots, heavy mulching is a better way to control grass and nourish your plants at the same time.

Thick layers of shredded bark, maple leaves, shavings, or wood chips are all excellent mulches. Paper and hay can also be used. Sawdust is not a good mulch for berries because it packs too tightly and has a bad habit of taking nitrogen from the soil as it rots. If the mulch around the plants is several inches thick, enough shade will be provided to suffocate new weed and grass seedlings, which are always desperately trying to get started, yet the new berry canes will push through easily.

Sometimes black plastic or sheets of old metal roofing are laid between the rows to keep berry plants as well as weeds from growing there. Never use asphalt or roofing paper, for asphalt is not good for plants.

Supports for Bramble Berries

Probably you'll have to provide some means of support to keep your bramble fruits from falling over. Some berry growers like to tie the canes to stakes or posts placed every 2 or 3 feet along the row.

Others put up a fence consisting of strands of smooth wire on each side of the row. Still others never support the plants at all but simply cut all the canes back to a height of 4 or 5 feet in late fall, making them stiff enough so that they're less likely to fall over.

Whether you give any support to your plants or not may depend partly on the variety you grow. The short-growing Newburgh raspberry is less likely to need staking than the taller-growing Viking

FRUIT PRUNING GUIDE

Blackberry	After bearing and in summer	Remove at ground canes that bore last crop. In summer cut back new shoots to 3½ feet high.
Raspberry	After bearing and in summer	Remove at ground in fall canes that bore last crop. In summer head back new canes to 20 to 22 inches high.
Currant	Early spring	Remove old unfruitful growth. Encourage new shoots. Same as currant. Cut back new shoots to 12 inches high and side shoots to two buds.
Gooseberry	Early spring	Requires heavy pruning of old wood to encourage new bearing wood.
Grape	Late winter or early spring, before sap starts	Remove all old branches back to main vine. Cut back the previous year's new growth to four buds.

and Latham. Trailing blackberries (dewberries) always need some kind of fence or trellis to keep them off the ground, and upright blackberries and black raspberries are apt to fall over when they get loaded with fruit unless they're supported in some way.

Pruning Brambles

If pruning is neglected when you grow the bramble fruits, the plants will deteriorate rapidly. The brambles, both raspberries and blackberries, are unusual in that while their roots are perennial, their canes are biennial. So while the roots of these plants often live for many years, each cane sprouts and grows to its full height in one year, bears fruit the following year, then dies. Because of this, after a few years wild raspberries and blackberries become a jungle of dead canes, and soon the entire patch dies off. Cultivated canes that are neglected will do the same.

This is fairly easy to avoid: Simply cut off each dead cane to ground level after it has finished bearing in late summer. You'll recognize the dead ones by their pallid color and brittle appearance. Hand-held clippers are ideal tools for this job, and you'll

probably want to wear thick gloves to handle the thorny canes. Because insects and disease enjoy wintering over in the old canes, it's a good idea to remove them to the local landfill or to burn them as soon as possible.

Cut old canes at ground level after they finish bearing.

As the berry patch ages, more pruning becomes necessary. Usually too many new canes are produced each year, so all the weak ones should be cut off at the same time the old dead ones are removed. Berries will be larger if all the weak canes are removed and even the strong, healthy canes are thinned sufficiently so they are at least 6 inches apart.

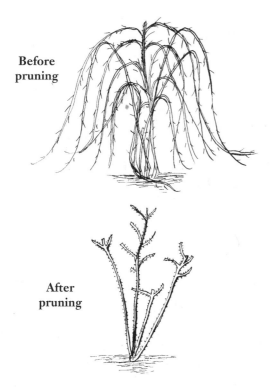

Before pruning

After pruning

Remove weak or dead canes annually to promote strong, healthy plants.

Black and purple raspberries do better with even more room than the red ones. Space their canes even farther apart, probably 8 to 10 inches. Also, while the rows of red or yellow raspberries or upright blackberries may be permitted to become 2 or 3 feet wide, those of black or purple raspberries or of trailing blackberries should be kept to a width of no more than 12 to 18 inches. The extra room between plants and between rows allows air circulation, which will reduce the plants' likeliness to contract spur blight, mildew, and other diseases. It also will help increase berry size and add to your ease in pruning and picking.

Harvesting Raspberries and Blackberries

Both raspberries and blackberries taste so good and have so many uses it is hard to get an oversupply of them. Furthermore, since they ripen over two or three weeks, you can enjoy the berries daily over a relatively long season.

Fruit picked on sunny days has the best vita-min content, but no matter what the weather, the berries should be picked when they are ripe. Usually this means picking at least every other day during raspberry season. Early, midseason, and late varieties can be planted if you want to extend the season even more.

Be sure to handle the tender berries with care so that you don't bruise them. Use only small picking dishes because too many berries in the same container will crush the bottom ones badly. Avoid handling them any more than necessary, and move your freshly picked berries out of the sun as soon as possible.

Diseases of Bramble Berries

The viral diseases — leaf curl, mosaic, and orange rust — are especially serious since there is no apparent cure. Both plant and fruit get smaller and sicker-looking each year until the bushes finally die.

Leaf curl. New leaves curl down and inward.

Mosaic. If you find that the leaves on your new canes are marbled green or have a greenish-yellow mottled look, mosaic might be the cause.

Orange Rust. This one is especially bad on blackberries. Look for bright orange spores during the summer on the undersides of leaves and on the canes. This is a fairly common disease and one of the reasons so many blackberry plantings fail. Some nurseries still sell infected plants, and many wild blackberries have it.

Anthracnose. This blight shows as gray blotches with purple edges on the bark. Black raspberries are most susceptible. Captan sprays control it.

Root (Crown) Gall. Fleshy growth on roots. Plant only certified plants in soil not previously infected with diseased plants.

Verticillium Wilt. This is the same disease that strikes tomato plants, maple trees, and many others. There's not much you can do about it, unfortunately. The canes wilt suddenly, usually in midsummer. It's best to plant the brambles away from potatoes, peppers, and tomatoes if you've noticed that these plants have ever shown signs of this disease.

Insect Pests

When you consider how many pests bother the tree fruits, it is surprising that so few insects attack the brambles. The cane borer is one of the most troublesome, and rare is the bramble grower who doesn't encounter this one sooner or later. Happily, it is easy to control without poisons. The sudden wilting of the tops of the new canes is evidence that this critter is at hand. Inspection will reveal two complete circles near the top of the cane. If you open it at this point, the larva will be found sitting quietly here as though it had every intention of making this plant its own. If undisturbed,

the borer will go down the cane, killing it and continuing on to infect other canes with increasing damage to your patch in future years. Control is easy. As soon as the wilted, infected ends appear, simply cut them off below the bottom ring and burn them. Exit borers.

Tree crickets, crown borers, sawflies, and raspberry beetles may attack the plants in certain areas of the country and may be especially troublesome at times to commercial growers. All-purpose orchard spray (see chapter 9) can be used to control these pests if necessary, but large bug colonies seldom show much interest in small-time berry growers.

BLUEBERRIES

Highbush blueberries can be grown in most areas of the United States; however, don't plant them in an area where winter temperatures frequently fall below -20°F. Also, because they need winter chilling, don't plant blueberries in areas where there is not at least 800 hours (about 2 months) of temperatures below 40°F. You can extend these limits somewhat by planting new cultivars especially developed for extreme northern and southern areas. In most cases these cultivars are crosses between highbush blueberry and rabbiteye for southern locations and low bush blueberry for northern locations.

Blueberries

Beating the Climate Limitations

You can extend the general temperature area limitations if you select a location within your area which is known to be warmer or cooler than the surrounding area — this is called a microclimate.

For instance, if you have an area protected from

BLUEBERRY VARIETIES

For a longer season and a better crop, plant early, midseason, and late-ripening cultivars. Although blueberries are considered self-fruitful, you will get a greater yield and larger fruit that ripens earlier if you interplant several cultivars.

This listing is based on United States Department of Agriculture recommendations. Approximate order of ripening is indicated by the letters "e" for *early*, "m" for *midseason*, and "l" for *late*. There are many cultivars that are not included in this list, so consider suggestions from your local extension agent, too.

Geographic Area 1: North Florida, coastal plain of Georgia, South Carolina (south of Charleston), Louisiana, Mississippi, Alabama, East Texas, lower Southwest, and Southern California (Los Angeles and south)

Cultivars: Flordablue, Sharpblue (for trial only)

Geographic Area 2: Mountain and Upper Piedmont regions of Area 1

Cultivars: Morrow (e), Croatan (e), Harrison (e), Murphy (e), Bluetta (e), Patriot (m), Bluecrop (m), Berkeley (m), Lateblue (l)

Geographic Area 3: Richmond, Virginia, south to Piedmont and coastal plain Carolinas, Tennessee, lower Ohio Valley, east and south Arkansas, lower Southwest, and mid-California

Cultivars: Morrow (e), Croatan (e), Harrison (e), Murphy (e), Bluecrop (m), Patriot (except in coastal plain areas)(m)

Geographic Area 4: Mid-Atlantic states, Midwest, Ozark highlands, mountain regions of Area 3, northern California, Oregon, and Washington

Cultivars: Bluetta (e), Collins (e), Patriot (m), Bluecrop (m), Blueray (m), Berkeley (m), Darrow (l), Lateblue (l), Elliott (l), Herbert (l), Elizabeth (l)

Geographic Area 5: New England and cooler areas of the Great Lakes States

Cultivars: Bluetta (e), Collins (e), Patriot (m), Bluecrop (m), Blueray (m), Meader (m), Berkeley (m), Northland (m)

---

the cold northern winds, it will be warmer than an exposed area. It will also reduce drying injury. You can create an area like this by providing a windbreak by planting trees or putting up a fence on the north side of the planting. Frequently, you can also take advantage of existing windbreaks provided by buildings — yours or your neighbors.

Any structure — even a driveway — near your plants which absorbs and/or reflects heat, may help to maintain higher temperatures. If you are looking for a cooler area, select an exposed area with good air movement. A northern slope or an area which is shaded from the late afternoon sun (after 3:00 p.m.) will provide a cooler environment.

Reduce Frost Damage

If you live in an area where late spring frosts are likely, locate the plants on a northern slope. This will delay the bloom in the spring and reduce chances of frost damage. A gentle slope is also recommended because it will provide better air drainage, help dry the air, and reduce fungus diseases. Do not plant in areas surrounded by buildings or dense stands of trees because both will cause poor air circulation.

Provide Full Sunlight

For best production, plant your plants where they can receive 8 hours of sunlight per day. Too much shade results in spindly growth, reduces yield, and decreases the quality of the fruit.

Provide a Good Soil Environment

The best plants are grown on soil that is acidic (sour) and fertile, with plenty of organic matter worked in. It must also have good water drainage.

The best soil pH (acidity) for growing blueberries is between 4.5 and 5.6. This is also good for rhododendrons and azaleas. If your soil pH is higher than 5.6, you should add powdered sulfur. You may have to experiment a little with amounts for your soil condition. In general, 24 pounds of sulfur for each 1,000 square feet should lower acidity by 1 full pH point. If your pH is too low, your soil is too sour; limestone should be added to sweeten it. Again, the exact amount will depend upon your location, but about 150 pounds per 1,000 square feet will raise the pH by 1 point.

You must have good soil drainage with a water table no closer to the soil surface than 18 inches. A good way to test this yourself is simply to dig a hole about a foot deep and fill it with water. If the water disappears within about an hour and a half, the drainage is okay. If it doesn't, you'd better find another spot. But remember, swampy areas can be planted as a last resort, if you either install a costly system of drainage ditches or plant the bushes on small mounds as they grow naturally in swamps.

Preparing the Soil

Preparing the soil for highbush blueberries means building up organic matter and adjusting the soil pH. The best way to start is to plant a green ma-

nure crop of buckwheat in the early summer prior to planting the blueberries the following spring. In late summer, measure the soil pH and adjust it to be between 4.5 and 5.0 by spreading either ground limestone (to raise the pH) or ground sulfur (to lower the pH) just before turning the buckwheat under. In early September, till the area again, and plant a crop of winter rye. This will reduce soil loss from erosion during the winter months, as well as add additional organic matter. In early spring, turn under the winter rye and whatever other organic materials you can find — rotted manure, compost, and peat moss — and bring the soil to a fine texture by thorough harrowing or rototilling. Complete this and let the soil settle for at least 2 weeks before planting.

If you are only planting a few bushes, you can prepare individual planting holes. In the early spring, dig the holes approximately 2 feet in diameter by 2 feet deep. Use a mixture of equal parts of loam, sand, and organic matter, such as rotted sawdust, compost, or peat moss, to fill the hole when planting. A word of caution! Be sure the sawdust or compost component of the mix is well rotted. Undercomposted organic matter, such as fresh sawdust, can severely stunt the plant.

Selecting Plants

Blueberry plants are available from nurseries as rooted cuttings or as older plants. Generally, we recommend buying dormant, vigorous 2-year-old plants, 12 to 18 inches high. Younger, smaller plants may be less expensive, but they require greater care, while the cost of older plants frequently is not justified.

Blueberry plants are generally self-fruitful, but interplanting cultivars will improve yields because some cultivars, such as Earliblue and Coville, do not produce enough good pollen.

Estimating Quantities

You can figure out how many bushes you need by remembering the following points.

■ A plant 6 to 8 years old or older can produce

up to 10 quarts of fruit per bush, if you take good care of it.

- Each mature bush may have a total spread of 4 to 5 feet.

- Bushes are usually spaced about 6 feet apart within rows and about 8 to 10 feet apart between rows.

- In hedgerows, space bushes 4 feet apart.

Planting

You can obtain blueberry plants from the nursery bare-rooted, canned (potted), or balled-and-burlapped. The latter 2 are best because they usually can be planted without disturbing the roots too much.

Bare-rooted plants often are shipped in plastic covers. Remove these as soon as the plants arrive. If you can't plant immediately, heel the plants in by placing the roots in a trench and mounding soil around them. If the ground is frozen, put them in a cool, protected place, such as a garage, and cover the entire plant with damp peat moss or sawdust.

Try to plant during the afternoon of a cloudy day.

Although blueberries can be planted in the fall, spring planting is safer and is recommended in most areas. Do this as soon as the ground can be worked in the spring. This means as soon as the ground has dried out enough. Prune off any damaged or excessively long roots, any weak or broken wood, and all flower buds, since fruiting the first year may stunt the bush.

Plant your bushes 1 to 2 inches deeper than they were in the nursery and 4 to 6 feet apart in rows spaced 8 to 10 feet apart. In large plantings, do not separate cultivars by more than 2 rows from others with similar ripening seasons. After you put the plants in the hole, fill it three-fourths full of either soil or a loam-peat-sand (1 to 1 to 1 proportions) mixture, and flood it with water. After the water has seeped out, fill the remainder of the hole and pack firmly with your feet. Water the plant thoroughly with a starter solution to encourage rapid growth. A layer of mulch will help hold in moisture and discourage weeds.

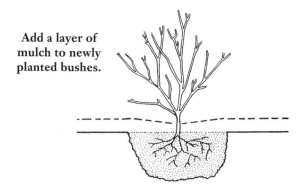

Add a layer of mulch to newly planted bushes.

Caring For Your Blueberries

Highbush blueberries are easy to grow. All you have to do is fertilize them 2 or 3 times a year, prune once a year, and make sure they have enough water. A mature, vigorous bush should have dark green foliage and should produce 2 or 3 new shoots from the base of the plant each year. About half of the new growth on the bush should be longer than 5 or 6 inches and a few new shoots should be 12 to 18 inches long.

Irrigation

Blueberry plants require a constant moisture supply for best growth. The relatively shallow, fine, fibrous root system is susceptible to drought stress under poor soil conditions.

When should you water? First, try the "feel test" to determine whether the soil needs moisture. Squeeze a soil sample in the palm of your hand. If

Soaker hose

the ball formed is weak and easily broken, soil moisture is adequate. If it is not easily broken, the soil is too wet; if no ball is formed, then it is too dry.

If irrigation is necessary, water during the early morning, but don't wet the bushes when berries are beginning to ripen. If you wet the berries at this time they may split. You can use ground flooding or soaker hose. This will conserve water and prevent wetting of the bush. Apply about an inch of water during each watering.

Fertilizing Blueberry Plants

Periodic application of fertilizer is necessary to maintain plant vigor. Make the first fertilizer application about a month after planting. Apply about ½ cup of 5-10-10 or 10-10-10 per bush. Just spread the fertilizer around the plant in a broad band at least 6 inches but not more than 12 inches from its base. Repeat the application in early July. If the plants show low vigor, fertilize again in the fall when the leaves drop. Make the last 2 applications at the same rate as the first. If you have mulched around your bushes, double the rate of the first application and omit the second.

You should increase the rate of fertilizer each year until mature plants (after 6 to 8 years in the ground) are receiving about 1 pound per plant, two-thirds applied at the beginning of bloom and the other third applied 5 to 6 weeks later. Since most fertilizer nutrients move vertically in the soil, proper fertilizer placement is important.

If your mature plants are not vigorous, a late autumn application (when the leaves drop) of about 1 pound of fertilizer per bush will increase nutrient reserves in the plant and promote an early spurt of growth in the spring. Don't try this on your vigorous bushes, and do not apply the fertilizer too early in the autumn, since an early application could encourage late autumn shoot growth that will winterkill. When possible, rake in the fertilizer after application.

In sandy soil, where leaching is rapid, additional fertilizer may be required. This can, however, present a danger of root injury from the higher salt concentrations. You can offset poor growth in sandy soil by burying up to 3 bushels of a peat moss/soil mix (1 to 1 proportions) or compost per plant beneath the dripline — if you only have a few bushes to worry about. Plant roots will grow into these areas, invigorating the plant.

Be sure to fertilize every year regardless of whether a crop is produced.

As an alternative to commercial fertilizers, you can use blood meal, cottonseed meal, tankage, or well-rotted manure. Most of these will also provide valuable organic material that will improve soil texture and aid plant growth. You should use combinations of these materials to provide for a more balanced fertilization. Don't use bonemeal or wood ashes, because they tend to sweeten the soil.

Don't apply organic fertilizers after the early summer, because they could stimulate late fall growth of the plants if applied too late. The amount to apply will be determined by the plant vigor.

Soil Management

Blueberry plants do not compete well with weeds for water and nutrients. Therefore, they should either be cultivated frequently or thoroughly mulched. In most areas of the country, mulching is perhaps the wisest and best soil management practice. Nearly any organic material — grass clippings, pine needles, straw, peat moss, buckwheat hulls, or wood chips — can be used.

Pruning

Planting Time. Remove all weak, diseased, and broken wood and all flower buds.

After One Year. Again prune any diseased or broken wood. Vigorous plants may be allowed to bear up to a pint of fruit (20 to 30 flower buds). Remove any additional buds.

After Two to Five Years. Continue similar pruning practices for the next two to five years. If the plants appear vigorous, do not remove more flower buds than is necessary during pruning. During this time, the emphasis should still be on producing healthy bushes and not on fruit production.

Older Bushes. Blueberry bushes that have been neglected for several years may be rejuvenated and returned to good production by severe pruning. Cut these back to the ground, leaving only short, 2-inch to 3-inch stubs. The whole bush may be done at once (1-year method) or half the bush may be done one year and the other half in the following year (two-year method). By using the one-year method, the entire crop is lost for one season. The two-year method does allow the plant to bear a portion of the crop each year of the rejuvenation process.

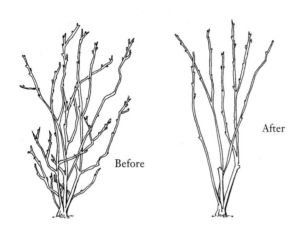

Pruning a blueberry bush after
2–5 years in the field.

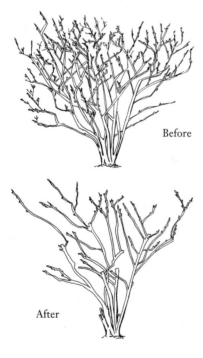

Pruning a mature blueberry bush
using the two-year method

Blueberry Problems

In many areas blueberries can be grown without the use of sprays. This is especially true if plants are maintained in vigorous condition, are planted in an optimum location, and are grown under good, sanitary conditions. This includes removing old leaves, berries, and prunings from the site and practicing good weed control.

Rotenone, *Bacillus thuringiensis*, and handpicking the larger insect pests will provide control for most blueberry pests. If diseases are present, you will have to use a fungicide, if you want to produce any fruit at all. Make sure you observe the specified time interval between last application and fruit harvest.

Disease Control

Blueberry Stunt. Plants are stunted, with leaves turning first yellow, then brilliant red or mottled red in August or September. This symptom appears well before normal fall coloration. Berries are small and unpalatable. You can control this disease only by destroying infected plants and by controlling sucking insects which transmit this disease.

Stem Canker. New cankers appear in late summer as reddish swellings on new shoots. These swellings enlarge in the second year, lose their red color, and become fissured, blistered, and grayish. Eventually the cankers will girdle and kill the cane. Remove infected branches and maintain plants in good vigor.

Mummyberry. Ripening fruit turns a creamy pinkish color instead of blue. Berries shrivel, become hard and dry, and drop to the ground. They provide an overwintering body for the fungus. Spring rains provide for the release of the fungus, which then attacks the new growth and swelling buds. This is the "twig blight" stage of the disease, which is recognized by blackened and wilted new growth.

Additional spores produced in this stage infect the flowers and fruit, thus completing the cycle.

Controlling this disease may require several applications of a fungicide. Apply this just as the flower buds begin to swell in the spring. Additional applications of fungicide may be required. Follow label directions on commercial products carefully. Also, applying at least 2 inches of additional mulch will help control this disease.

Botrytis Blight. New growth in the spring appears watersoaked and discolored. Later, some may become covered with grayish-white mold. Often infection begins in the flower, moves into the fruit cluster and then into the shoot, resulting in a few inches of shoot dieback. Leaves may become infected when they contact infected flowers or shoots. Very little infection occurs late in the season.

Apply a fungicide just as the buds show green, but before the blossoms open. Removal of fallen blueberry leaves may also help control this disease.

Witches Broom. The disease appears on the shoots only, producing a "broomlike" development of many deformed shoots arising close together on a swollen stem. This disease is found on the edges of woodlands where the balsam fir is present. This fir is an alternate host for the disease. Eliminate the nearby balsam fir trees and remove infected plants.

Red Ringspot Virus. The symptoms become very obvious in the autumn, when characteristic red, often irregular, rings appear on the leaves. Rings may also appear on the stems. Removing affected plants is the only control.

Insect Pests

Tip Borer. Newly hatched worms bore into the soft, new stems of the plant. The tunnels may reach 6 to 10 inches in length by autumn and destroy the stem. New shoots will wilt, arch over, and discolor, with leaves turning yellow with red veins. Stems will turn purple. Prune off affected shoot tips and begin applying an insecticide spray, such as rotenone, when blossoms begin to drop. (When using rotenone, it is best to spray in the evening to avoid harming bees that aid in pollination.)

Red-Banded Leaf Roller. The greenish larvae feed on foliage during the early summer, often folding or rolling leaves together. Later larvae feed on the fruit surface near the stem. Pupae overwinter and moths emerge in the spring to lay eggs on the plant bark in flattened clusters. Most leaf rollers can be controlled with insecticidal sprays, such as rotenone, beginning when about three-fourths of the blossoms have fallen. These may have to be repeated over a 4-week to 5-week period.

Sharp-Nosed Leafhopper. The adult is dark chocolate in color with a pointed extension of the head. Eggs begin hatching in midspring and adults develop in early summer. This insect is very important, not so much for its actual feeding damage, but because it is the only known agent capable of transmitting blueberry stunt disease. Control these as you would the leaf rollers.

Scale. The winged adult is about 1/25 inch in length and bronze in color. The female secretes a grayish-brown waxy covering which envelops and protects her. The young (crawlers) move to other sites and begin to feed by sucking the plant juices. Further development takes place, and the scale overwinters under its waxy protection. Development begins anew when spring temperatures reach 50°F. Feeding injury appears as red specks on the plant part, usually a shoot. The plant will usually decline in vigor and productivity in cases of severe infestation. Control with delayed dormant oil sprays (use oil with a viscosity of 60 to 70 sec.) and remove heavily infested branches.

Blossom Weevil. The long-snouted adult beetle emerges in the spring and begins feeding on the plant, boring into the side of swelling buds and flowers. Injured buds usually do not open, or they open deformed. Egg-laying begins during bloom, when the female weevil punctures the flower to place the eggs. Hatching in a few days, the grub eats the flower, often destroying over half of the crop. Watch carefully for these signs, and remove and burn affected growth. For additional control treat with insecticide when flower buds show white.

Cherry Fruitworm. The adult dark gray moth emerges in late spring, and lays its eggs on the undersides of leaves and on the fruit. These hatch in about a week, and the larvae enter the fruit through the blossom end and feed on the pulp for a few weeks. Larvae will hibernate in pithy weeds or small prunings near the base of the bush. Control is the same as suggested for leaf roller.

Cranberry Fruitworm. The night-flying adult moths become active when the largest berries are about one-fourth grown and lay eggs in the blossom end of the fruit. In about a week, the young green caterpillars hatch and enter a berry. Up to six berries may be webbed together during feeding. Following feeding, the mature caterpillar crawls to the ground and overwinters in a soil-encrusted cocoon under weeds or trash. Control as suggested for leaf roller.

Plum Curculio. The adult beetle has a long snout and is brown to steely gray with whitish patches. It has four bumps on its wing. Beetles usually become active when early cultivars begin to bloom. The adults feed on buds and flowers, making a small hole about ⅛ inch deep. When berries are about ¼ inch in diameter, the female lays eggs in the fruit. Punctures in the fruit in which eggs are laid are typically half-moon or crescent shaped. The eggs hatch in late summer in about six days, and the worm feeds on the fruit. Infested berries usually fall to the ground, worms remain in the berries for about three weeks, and then move into the soil. After about a month, new moths emerge to feed on the foliage before moving into trash or soil to winter over. Control with insecticide, as suggested for leaf roller.

Blueberry Maggot. The adults become active in midsummer. They resemble houseflies except for their characteristic black wing bands. The female punctures the fruit skin to lay her eggs. After a short period, the eggs hatch into small maggots which feed on the flesh of the fruit. The berries will often decay or ripen prematurely and become inedible. In mid-June, apply an insecticide and continue spraying at recommended intervals.

Yellow-Necked Caterpillar, Acronicta Caterpillar. Caterpillars need little description, but the damage they do by chewing the leaves cannot go unattended. Handpick the colonies.

Fall Webworm. The pale yellow, black-spotted hairy caterpillar forms large colonies in a tightly spun web. Caterpillars feed on foliage inside the web until it is consumed, then make another web. Handpick the colonies.

Stem Borer. Grubs emerging during warm weather bore into the stems about 3 to 6 inches from the tip. If left undisturbed, they will emerge as large, conspicuous, long-horned beetles after three years. The infested canes will have small piles of sawdust near their bases and will appear weakened. Remove the wilted canes below the injured area. Do this as soon as injury appears.

Protection from Birds

Birds present one of the worst problems of any pest. Nearly any kind of bird will destroy the ripening fruit and, at times, will even eat the flower buds on the dormant plant.

The most effective type of bird control device is netting. You can cover entire plantations or individual bushes for nearly 100 percent bird protection. A durable, synthetic netting, often made of nylon and treated to resist deterioration from ultraviolet radiation, will usually last for several seasons. Place the netting over the bushes as the first fruits begin to ripen, and remove it after harvest is completed. When protecting individual bushes, envelop the plant completely with the netting, tying the netting around the base of the plant and using scrap lumber supports to keep it off the bush. Whole plantations can be enclosed with netting, but it does require support posts and wires to keep the netting sufficiently high over the plants to allow easy access to the bushes.

An alternative to the complete use of netting is to construct a "cage" for the plants from 1-inch-mesh poultry fencing. A combination of the two materials, with poultry fencing on the sides and flexible netting on the top, is quite frequently used.

GRAPES

Grapes have the reputation of being fragile and difficult to grow. Many northern gardeners, convinced that all grapes are too tender for their fierce winters and uneven spring temperatures, do not even consider trying to grow them, yet some vines will flourish in regions of every state and in several Canadian provinces. A good rule of thumb is that if wild grapes grow in your area, you can grow plump and tasty domestic grapes of some kind.

Grapes

Planning Your Vineyard

Grapes need an abundance of heat and sun to grow and to produce well. Because of this they are one of the last fruit plants to start growth in the spring, and they bloom much later than any of the tree fruits. If you live in one of the cool northern states, you will want to plant them in heat pockets whenever possible. Places where buildings, walls, or hills form corners that face and trap the southern and eastern sun are best, especially when they are protected from the cooling north and westerly winds.

In some areas you may have to create your own heat trap. Fiberglass fences, plastic tents, and other artificial structures have all been used to increase and hold the heat for the sun-worshiping grape. It can also be beneficial to mulch with black plastic or crushed rock, which attract and hold heat better than organic mulches.

Soil

Grape vines will grow in many different soil types. Well-drained, deep, fertile loams are excellent, yet grapes will thrive on soils containing clay, slate, gravel, shale, and sand. Gravelly, stony soils generally drain well, and they absorb and reflect the sun's

GRAPE VARIETIES

Probably even the apple has fewer named varieties than the grape. In millenniums of culture, thousands of kinds have appeared and disappeared. Varieties that are usually easily available and suitable for home gardeners are the only ones mentioned in this list.

Dessert and white table grapes: Golden Muscat, Himrod, Interlaken, Niagara, Seedless.

Blue grapes: Beta, Buffalo, Concord, Fredonia, Moore's Early, Schuyler, Stark Blue Boy, Steuben, Van Buren, Worden.

Red grapes: Brighton, Catawba, Delaware.

Wine grapes: Aurora, Baco-Noir, Cascade, Catawba, De Chaunac, Delaware, Dunkirk, Foch, Moore's Diamond, Seyval Blanc, Siebel (No. 1000, No. 5279, No. 5898, No. 9549), Steuben.

Earliest: Alpha, Beta, Moore's Early, Ontario, Seneca, Van Buren.

Next earliest: Brighton, Buffalo, Fredonia, Schuyler, Worden.

Hardiest: Alpha and Beta, two of the hardiest early grapes are both more suitable for processing than eating fresh. Concord is a high-quality, easy-to-grow, very hardy grape, but it ripens too late for most northern areas. Others are Delaware, Hungarian, Jonesville, Moore's Early, Van Buren, Worden.

Seedless: Concord Seedless (blue), Himrod (yellow), Interlaken (pink-yellow).

For the warmest climates: Black Spanish, Blue Lake, Chapanell, and the Muscadine grapes — Cowart, Magoon, Roanoke, and Sugargate.

warmth to give the vine bottom heat.

Very dry and very wet soils are bad for grapes. A soil that drains poorly is quite unsuitable, as are shallow soils underlaid by hard-pan, gravel, or sand. Very rich soils with high levels of organic material tend to make vines with excessive foliage, or bearing a heavy crop of late-ripening, low-sugar fruit. Leaner soils are more desirable as they give comparatively modest crops of fruit that mature earlier and have considerable sugar in the berry.

Have your soil tested *for grape growing*. A complete soil test will tell you the pH level, levels of mineral and trace elements, and make the necessary recommendations for soil improvement.

Grapes do not tolerate weeds or competitive grass. Therefore, land intended for a vineyard is usually plowed, disked, and planted to some row crop the year before the vines are set out. This reduces the number of weeds substantially.

The vineyard should be plowed deeply and should be very well disked, so that the soil is thoroughly pulverized before the vines are set out. Since grapes are usually grown on a slope in "clean cultivation" (no plant competitors allowed nearby), *the risk of erosion is considerable*. If your slope is more steep than gentle, your local soil conservation service specialist can help you plan the most advantageous contour rows for your vines.

Building a Trellis

Grapes require some system to support their eager vines. While grapes can be grown ornamentally along fences, for best harvest results, the vine should be trained to grow on a trellis system designed for ease of pruning and maximum sunlight. An overgrown, dense vine will not receive enough sunlight to ripen the fruit.

The trellis should be built for sturdiness and longevity. It is particularly important that the posts which support the trellis wires be strong and well-set. The end posts must be the strongest; they should be heavy and well-braced, set three feet deep and angled outward so they will not be pulled over by the weight of the mature vines. In each row the end posts should be positioned four feet from the last plants in the row. Every two or three vines, set in the line posts to carry the trellis. Remember that the posts must support the weight of the heavy foliage and fruit, and during windstorms the stresses can be powerful.

Grapevines should never be set right up against a post, for the plants will outlast any wooden post, and the roots will be disturbed when the post has to be replaced. Long-lasting wooden posts are made of black locust, white oak, red cedar, and osage orange. Posts made of other wood may be treated to make them last longer, but the preservatives can harm your vines.

Better than wooden posts, but quite expensive, are steel or concrete posts. But, steel posts also act as lightning rods in a vineyard on an exposed hill. Lightning has been known to run along the trellis wires and destroy a row of fruiting arms. Grapegrowers who live near granite or other stone quarries may be able to get their hands on stone posts that are beautiful and last forever.

Once the posts are set, putting up the trellis wire is not unlike putting up a fence. The standard trellis consists of two or more strands of no. 9 wire stapled to cross arms on each post. The staples are not driven snug, but allow the wires to slide back and forth beneath them, so that the wires may be tightened at the end of the row with a turnbuckle when the weight of the vines causes them to sag.

Planting the Vines

Grapes should be planted as early in the spring as the soil can be worked north of Arkansas, Tennessee, and Virginia. Farther south the vines can be planted in the autumn. It is important that the plants make themselves at home and get established before the long hot days of summer begin.

Order your grape stock from a nursery as nearby as possible; if you can, pick out and pick up the plants yourself. The best stock is strong, sturdy, one-year-old plants with large fibrous root systems; two-year-old plants are more expensive, and they will not bear any sooner.

Dig a good hole in the worked-up soil, large enough to spread out the vine's roots comfortably.

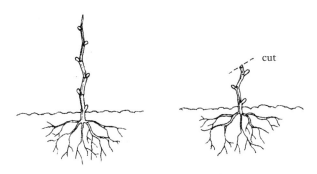

Plant the vine at the same depth it grew in the nursery. Prune it back to a single or three buds tall.

Never stuff a grapevine into a cramped miserly hole. Pack the soil firmly around the roots, leaving no air spaces that can increase the chances of disease. Plant the vines at the same depth they grew in the nursery, then prune them back to a single stem two or three buds tall. If it is early spring and the soil is moist, you need not water at planting. Later in the spring you may want to water well after planting. Watering helps the soil close in around the roots.

Space most hybrid cultivars eight to ten feet apart in the row, with the rows ten to eleven feet from each other. Less vigorous vines, like Delaware, can be closer together — seven or eight feet apart in the row. Although most grapes are self-pollinating, you will need to keep this in mind. If your grape selection is not self-pollinating, it will need a partner nearby to produce well.

Pruning: The Kniffen System

Pruning is probably the most important part of grape culture. Because of the grape's tendency to grow so vigorously, a lot of wood must be cut away each year. Grape vines that are overgrown become so dense that the sun cannot reach into the areas where fruit should form. Those grown on lattice-work and trellises are particularly hard to prune, but it can be done. Usually grapes grown in this way are more ornamental than productive.

The best and easiest way to grow grapes for fruit is on a two-wire fence in a method known as the Kniffin System.

First Year. Vines should be planted about 8 feet apart, with a post midway between each plant and one on each end. String two strands of smooth 10-gauge wire on the posts, the first 2 feet above the ground and the second about 3 feet higher.

After planting, cut back the new vine so it is only 5 or 6 inches long and contains two or three fat buds. This encourages additional root growth. Allow the vines to grow freely the first year.

Second Year. Very early in the spring, before the buds swell, cut them back to a single stem with no branches. This will encourage more vigor.

During the year allow four side branches to grow (two in each direction) and train them along the wires. Pinch off all other buds that are inclined to grow in other directions.

By the end of the second year if growth has been good, the space along both wires should be filled. These vines should then bloom and produce a few grapes the third year.

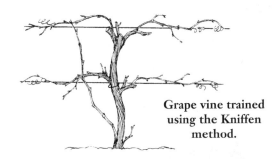

Grape vine trained using the Kniffen method.

Third Year. During the year, four more canes (only) should be allowed to grow from buds along the main stem. These should parallel and eventually replace the first four.

In late winter following the third year, cut out the old canes that produced and tie the new ones to the wires to replace them. Trim off all excess growth except the four new canes.

Treated in this way, each mature vine should produce from 12 to 15 pounds of grapes or 30 to 60 bunches per year. If more bunches than that are produced, remove them before the grapes develop, to avoid overbearing and thus weakening the plant. With this renewing process, your vines should go on producing for 50 years, and often they last even longer.

The soil around the vines can be either cultivated or mulched, but whatever you do, don't allow weeds and grass to choke them.

Like peaches, even the hardy varieties sometimes have trouble terminating their rapid growth in time to harden up before the first frost. Because of this, all fertilizing should be done early in the season. And be careful never to overfeed the vines, especially with nitrogen fertilizers.

Harvesting

It is a mistake to pick grapes too early because, unlike most other fruits, grapes don't continue to ripen after they are picked. Ripe grapes separate easily and the seeds are brown. If they are to be used for jelly they can be picked before they are completely ripe, but if you want them for eating or for juice, they should be left until fully ripe. Don't let them freeze, though.

Like berries, you will want to pick them on a dry day, because wet grapes don't keep well. It's a good idea to clip the bunches from the vine rather than break them, so there will be less chance of damage.

Grapes must be refrigerated to keep for any length of time. A temperature of just above freezing is best.

Grape Diseases

When you are growing grapes in an isolated home garden you usually don't have many problems with either insects or disease. Life is never simple, though, and sooner or later one of the following diseases is likely to show up.

Anthracnose. This will appear as spots on the fruit. It also affects leaves and the new sprouts. A fungicide usually helps.

Black Rot. This disease affects the fruit and turns it black, rotten, and shriveled. Leaves are covered with brown spots and black pimples. Spraying with a fungicide gives good control.

Dead Arm. A fungus is the cause of this disease; it gradually kills the plant. Cutting and burning the infected parts is about the only cure, although a fungicide applied early in the season may help to control it.

Downy Mildew. Another serious disease, especially in the East. Leaves and new shoots as well as the fruit become covered with a gray down. Bordeaux mix or powdered sulfur were often used to control mildew in times past. Other commercial fungicides are now available also.

Insect Pests

Hundreds of insects attack grapes in different parts of the world, and even isolated vines may be visited by some of them. Many, such as the Japanese beetle, are familiar names to growers of other fruits. Others bother only the grape.

All grape insects can be controlled by good sanitation and, when necessary, careful spraying. The botanical insecticide rotenone gives good control and is usually safe for the beginning orchardist if directions are carefully followed. It is important to time your spraying so that bees will not be harmed. If chemical pesticides seem the only solution, spray shortly before blossoms open, just after fruit has begun to form, and, if necessary, twice more at two and four weeks after the fruit appears. Isolation, sanitation, and encouraging birds are better than spraying, however, and should be used whenever possible for insect control.

Curculio. Attacks the grapes the way its relatives attack other fruits.

Cutworms. Feed on opening buds at night.

Flea beetles. Similar to other flea beetles. Attack the vine and leaves.

Grape berry moths. The main source of wormy grapes. Their larvae eat the pulp of the grape.

Phylloxera. Small sucking insects, similar to aphids. They attack European grapes mostly.

Rootworms. Small, grayish-brown beetles that attack leaves. Their larvae eat the grape vine roots.

Rose chafers. Eat blossoms, buds, newly formed fruit, and leaves. Usually they are most troublesome to vines grown on sandy soil.

Thrips. Sucking insects that also attack other small fruits.

TREE FRUITS

When you are involved in a home orchard that will quite likely last a lifetime or more, you naturally want to do it right. Mistakes made early have a way of coming back to haunt us. If you plant your vegetable garden with the plants growing too close together or in the wrong spot, or if you choose the wrong seeds, you lose only one season. But if you make a similar mistake with fruit trees, it may be years before you find it out, and decades before you can remedy the damage.

Even if you can't plant everything you want the first year, it's an excellent idea to make a plan so you will have the best possible trees growing in the best possible locations. Then put the plan in a safe spot where you can always find it. Keeping your plan up-to-date throughout your gardening or orchardist career will pay dividends because labels will no doubt be lost, and whenever a tree begins to bear you'll want to know what it is. Also, if a tree does poorly or dies, you'll want to know the variety so you can decide whether to replace it with the same kind or try another.

If you have only a small lot, you might not have much choice about where the trees will be planted. But within the boundaries you have, you will want to place them where they will have full sun and plenty of room to grow. Also make sure that they have well-drained soil; tree roots can't grow well in heavy, wet soils.

Another point to keep in mind is that certain fruit trees are susceptible to disease and insects and may need spraying during the summer. If vegetables and berries which may be ripening at that time are planted too close, it may be difficult to avoid spraying them when you spray the fruit trees.

PLANNING THE ORCHARD

Before you start making a blueprint of your future fruit garden or orchard, you have to do some careful planning. First, decide roughly how many trees you are going to plant. If space is limited, you should resist the temptation of crowding in too many trees. Keep in mind that a few trees well cared for will be far more productive and satisfying than a larger orchard partly neglected.

It's almost impossible to suggest the right number of trees for every family's needs. Each family has a different taste preference. And it makes a difference, too, whether all the fruit will be consumed fresh or if some is to be preserved. No two gardeners would ever have the same reasons for choosing their assortment.

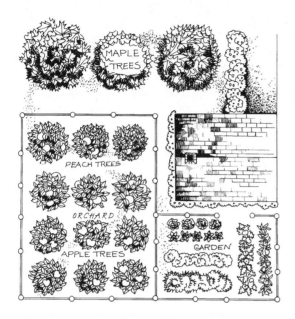

Planting Distances

Different varieties of fruit trees grow in quite different ways, so it's difficult to say for sure how wide each tree will eventually grow. Some grow upright, like the Yellow Transparent apple and the Dolgo crab. Others are very spreading — the McIntosh, for instance. And trees grow differently in varying soils and climates. Catalogs often give estimated sizes of mature trees, but check with your supplier before buying just to be sure.

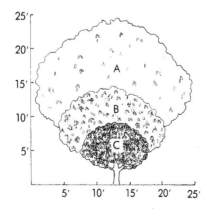

Relative tree sizes.
(A) Standard. (B) Semi-dwarf. (C) Dwarf.

The following are approximate diameters of some full-grown fruit trees. When you plant them, allow enough additional room so that you can walk between them and light can reach all the outside of the tree.

Fruit Trees

	Crown Diameter
Apple	
(standard size)	25 to 35 feet
(semi-dwarf)	15 to 20 feet
(dwarf)	7 to 10 feet
Apricot	
(standard)	18 feet
(dwarf)	8 feet
Peach	
(standard)	18 feet
(dwarf)	8 feet
Pear	
(standard)	18 feet
(dwarf)	8 feet
Plum	
(standard)	18 feet
(dwarf)	8 feet
Quince	12 feet

Nut Trees

Butternut and Black Walnut	35 feet
Chestnut (Chinese)	30 feet
Filbert	15 feet
Walnut and Hickory	35 feet

Plan your orchard so that no tree will touch any other tree, even when they are full grown. They should also be planted so that they will not eventually rub buildings or overhang highways, sidewalks, or property lines.

FRUIT VARIETIES SUGGESTED
FOR BEGINNING GROWERS

Zone 3

Apple: Astrachan, Connell, Dolgo Crab, Duchess, Peach Apple, Prairie Spy, Quinte, Wealthy, Yellow Transparent
Peach: None
Pear: Golden Spice, Luscious, Mendall, Parker, Patten
Plum: La Crescent, Pipestone, Redcoat, Waneta
Plum Cherry: Compass, Sapalta
Sour Cherry: Meteor, North Star
Sweet Cherry: None
Nut: Butternuts

Zone 4

Growers in this zone should be able to grow everything listed for Zone 3 plus:

Apple: Cortland, Imperial, Lobo, Lodi, McIntosh, Northwest Greening, Regent
Cherry: Richmond
Peach: Reliance (in favored spots)
Pear: Flemish Beauty, Kieffer, Seckel
Plum: Green Gage, Monitor, Stanley
Sweet Cherry: None
Nut: Black walnuts (hardy strains)

Zone 5

Growers in this zone should be able to grow everything listed for Zones 3 and 4 plus:

Apple: Delicious, Empire, Gravenstein, Northern Spy, Prima, Priscilla, Rhode Island Greening, Yellow Delicious

Peach: Stark Frost King, Stark Sure Crop, Sunapee
Plum: Burbank, Damson, Earliblue, Italian, Santa Rosa, Shiro
Sour Cherry: Montmorency
Sweet Cherry: Bing, the Dukes, Stella, Windsor
Nut: Carpathian walnuts, filberts, hickory

Zones 6-8

Many varieties that will grow in the colder zones will also do well here, although certain kinds of fruits developed especially for the colder climates may not be satisfactory for these zones.

Apple: Grimes, Golden, Rome, Stayman, and Winesap should all do well here, too. Apples that grow best in Zone 3, including those of the McIntosh family, are not recommended
Cherry: All should do well
Peach: Candor, Elberta, Halehaven, Madison, Redhaven
Pear: Anjou, Bartlett, Bosc, Clapp Favorite
Plum: Most should do well
Nut: Chestnuts plus the hardiest pecans and walnuts are worth a trial

HOW MANY TREES

For a family of four who will do some preserving the following suggestions are a good start.

Fruit	Number of Trees
Apples (full size or semi-dwarf)	3 to 6
Apples (dwarf)	4 to 10
Apricots	2 to 4
Cherries	2 to 3
Nectarines	2 to 4
Peaches	2 to 4
Plums	3 to 5
Quinces	1 to 2

If standard (full-size) trees are used, the space between them need not be wasted the first few years. If necessary spraying is done carefully, vegetables, strawberries, or other temporary crops can be grown there. As long as adequate fertilizer is used, you'll do no harm to the fruit trees.

CHOOSING VARIETIES

If you're a beginning fruit grower it's wise to choose fruits that are easy to grow. While it may be tempting to try Granny Smith Apples, Red Peaches, Sweet Cherries, Japanese Plums, and English Walnuts, it makes more sense to start with varieties that need less painstaking care. For your first attempt at growing tree fruits, you may want to try some easy-to-grow apples and plums.

After you have decided on the fruits you want to grow, the next step is to pick out the varieties of that fruit best suited for your geographical region. Be sure to consult the agricultural extension service nearest you. It's always an excellent idea to talk with local fruit growers who have been at it long enough to know what they are doing. They are of-

ten better sources of helpful information than all the books, extension pamphlets, and fruit magazines ever written. They can help you decide which trees are best for your climate and give you advice on what insects and diseases are bad in your area so you can buy the best suited varieties for your area.

Even resistant varieties can sometimes have problems, however, and you should keep in mind that fruit gardening, like every other form of agriculture, is a legal way to gamble. You are only stacking the odds a bit more in your favor by planting disease-resistant varieties.

MAPPING THE ORCHARD

Once you have chosen the number and variety of trees that you want to plant and determined the amount of space each tree willl require, it helps to sketch the orchard on paper ahead of time. It is much easier to move a pencil line than a crowded tree.

First, measure the area where your orchard will be and match it up to the gridlines of graph paper. Note objects that you will have to work around, such as buildings, large boulders, property lines, walkways, inhospitable neighboring plants, and anything else that might influence your planting decisions.

Pollination is an important consideration in planning your orchard. You might even consider hiring a hive for the season or keeping bees yourself to insure a good harvest.

Draw in each tree based on the crown diameter of the mature tree, and leave enough space for them to grow without crowding. Keep in mind as you sketch which trees need to be near each other for cross-pollination. Also note, more hardy or tender species may benefit or suffer depending on their placement in relation to other trees, structures, and so on.

PLANTING TREES

Most mail-order trees will be shipped bare-rooted, packed in moisture-retaining wrapping. Trees purchased at a local nursery or garden center may also be bare-rooted, or they may be potted or balled. Balled or potted trees can be planted successfully at any time of the year when the ground isn't frozen. It's best to plant bare-rooted trees in the spring before growth starts in northern areas. In Zones 6 and warmer they usually can be safely planted in the fall.

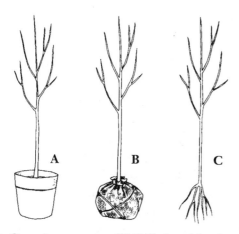

(A) Container-grown. (B) Balled-and-burlapped. (C) Bare-rooted.

Bare-rooted trees are almost always the cheapest to buy. They were probably dug in the fall, stored in controlled temperature and humidity during the winter, then wrapped and shipped in the spring. They are likely to be quite dry when they reach your doorstep. Your first and very important step when they arrive is to unwrap them at once and soak the roots for several hours in a tub or a pond of water. Don't worry if they arrive on a cold day. Even if the roots are frozen, there is no problem as long as they thaw slowly. Put the package in a cool basement or garage and let the tree warm up gradually. Then soak the roots. After a few hours of soaking, the tree should be planted.

Soaking bare-root trees

The planting is done in much the same way for each tree, whether it comes to you bare-rooted, balled, or potted. Since presumably you've already chosen a good location, the next step is to dig a hole much larger than necessary — one the size of a bushel basket should be adequate. Put all the soil that has been taken out in two heaps, with the good topsoil on one side and the poorer subsoil on the other.

Mix generous amounts of compost and manure or dried blood with the topsoil. About half soil and half organic matter is a good proportion. A bushel of this mixture is about right for an average-size tree, and should adequately fill the hole you have dug. (Do *not* use any dry granular chemical fertilizer at this point because it is much too strong for a tender new tree.) Enough of this mix should be put back in the hole so that the tree can be set at about the same ground level as it grew in the field or pot. On a bare-rooted tree you can find this level on the tree bark just above the roots. Planting a tree too deep smothers the roots and usually kills the tree; or, if you are planting a grafted tree, the wrong stock may start growing in the wrong direction. Planting it too shallow causes the roots to dry out.

Remove any plastic wrapping or containers from balled or potted trees, but be sure that the soil that is surrounding the roots is kept intact. For bare-rooted trees, you should cut away any broken

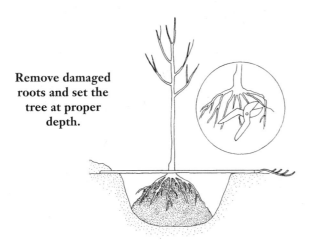

Remove damaged roots and set the tree at proper depth.

the tree to trap rain and future waterings. Unless it rains really hard, a newly planted tree should be thoroughly watered two or three times a week. Each time it will take a whole pail of water poured on slowly to reach the bottom of the roots. Keep watering until the tree is well established, at least a month. This watering cannot be emphasized too heavily. It is the cheapest, quickest, and most dependable way to get your tree off to a fast start.

If you like you can add manure or a small amount of liquid fertilizer such as fish emulsion or

or damaged roots.

Now hold the tree carefully, making sure it's standing straight and at the right planting depth, with the roots well spread out. Then put back enough of the soil mix to barely cover the roots. Fill the hole completely with water. Allow the water to soak into the soil mix and drive out any pockets of air that could dry out the roots.

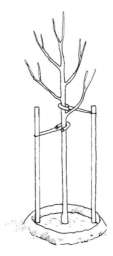

A slight depression directs water toward the roots.

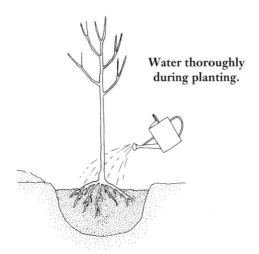

Water thoroughly during planting.

manure mixed with water to every other watering to feed the tree and give it a faster start.

A good deep soil is very important if you want a healthy tree. If you hit a rock ledge or hard clay when you dig the hole for it, seek out another location. The tree's roots can find their way around small rocks, but if the soil is too shallow, your planting will be doomed from the start. Digging a pocket in a shallow vein of clay to plant the tree is not recommended either. Water is likely to collect there and drown the tree. Attempts to break up subsoil are usually frustrating and should be done as a last resort only if no other location is available. If absolutely necessary, iron bars, pickaxes, tractor subsoilers, and even dynamite can do the job.

With the rest of the soil mix, finish filling the hole to nearly ground level. Be careful not to damage the tree with the shovel during the process — the young bark is tender and can't stand rough treatment. It may be necessary to use a little of the subsoil you've dug up too, but most of it should be carted away and discarded. Giving your tree's roots the best start possible is very important.

The tree should be staked if necessary and a slight depression or saucer should be left around

Pruning at Planting Time

After the tree has been planted it should be pruned immediately if you received it balled or bare-rooted. (If the tree has grown in its pot for a year or more, no pruning is necessary.) The reason for pruning at this early stage is so the top will balance the roots. When the tree was dug before you got it, some of the roots were cut off and a corresponding amount of top should be cut back to compensate for this loss. If the tree is not pruned, a lot of little branches and leaves will begin to grow faster than the roots are growing to support them. By holding back this top growth you encourage the roots to keep ahead of the top and thereby make a stronger tree.

Trim away all the weak and broken branches, cut back the strong ones at least by half, and then cut back the top to about three-fourths of its original height, just above a strong, fat bud. The tree will look pretty well chopped up, but it will grow and thrive far better than if it were planted with all its branches intact.

Staking

Newly planted, standard-size fruit trees seldom need staking if they are carefully set in and pruned back. However, in very windy areas the trees may lean with the prevailing winds unless they are given some help in their early years. Another exception is dwarf trees, which are extremely shallow-rooted and often benefit greatly from staking. If you need to stake, first drive a large post in near the tree. Wrap a strip of burlap around the tree trunk — use cloth or a piece of strong plastic or even stockings or pantyhose. Then secure the wrapped part of the tree to the post. Avoid using any kind of string or wire that may cut into the tender bark of the tree. As soon as the trees begin to grow and their roots become well anchored, staking will probably no longer be necessary.

Mulching

Unless your tree is living in a well-manicured lawn, you will probably want to mulch around it after it is planted. A mulch will help hold moisture, suppress grass and weeds, and help feed and protect the tree. Mulches are best made of organic matter that can rot and gradually add fertility to the soil.

GRAFTING FRUIT TREES

Most fruit trees that you purchase are probably grafted, because hardy roots and prime fruit don't always start out on the same tree. It's not uncommon for a third variety to be grafted between the root and top to add more desirable growth habits.

Suppose you covet a nifty Delicious apple tree in your neighbor's backyard, and you find, in your own flower border, a small, 2-foot-tall apple tree that accidentally grew from a seed in the core some-

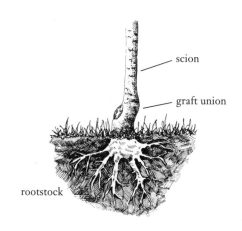

scion

graft union

rootstock

one threw out. On a warm day in late winter, catch your neighbor in a good mood, make him an offer he can't refuse, and under his watchful eye, snip off a small branch called a scion (pronounced sigh-on). By grafting, you can acquire a duplicate of his Delicious tree for your own yard.

Cleft Grafting

For the home gardener, cleft grafting is probably the most practical and easiest of the many types of grafting. It can be used for grafting small trees or for grafting new varieties onto the limbs of larger trees. The latter is often called top working.

The best time to graft is in early spring just as the leaf buds are swelling and beginning to turn green. Sap is flowing at that time so the new branchings cut for grafting — the scions — are less likely to dry out before they begin to grow. Here's how to do it.

Prepare the rootstock. The graft is made by cutting off the small tree that you're using for the rootstock a few inches above the ground, or by cutting off the branch of a larger tree wherever you want to put the graft. Be sure to make the cut straight across the branch or limb with edges as smooth as possible (A).

A. When cleft grafting, make the cut straight across the branch or limb.

Split this cut end in the middle about ¾ inch deep with a sharp knife or grafting tool. Cut carefully so the knife won't get away from you and completely split the trunk (B).

B. Split the cut end, making a vertical cut one and one-half inches deep.

Prepare the scion. Cut a piece from the branch of the good fruit tree you want to propagate. The scion should be 3 to 6 inches long and contain not more than 2 or 3 buds (C). It should be about the same diameter of the limb or stem it is to be grafted upon, or it can be slightly smaller. In any case, it should never be larger.

It is important that the scions do not get dry before the operation. You may want to collect your scions the day before and put the cut ends into a pail of water so the new grafts will be turgid. Some gardeners like to dip all of the scion, except for the

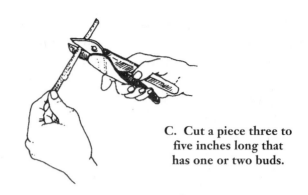

C. Cut a piece three to five inches long that has one or two buds.

cut end, into melted wax before it is grafted to protect it from drying out.

Sharpen the cut edge of the scion to a neat wedge shape (D). Again, use a sharp knife so the edges will be smooth. Don't drop the scion or allow the cut edges to touch anything that could infect it, not even your fingers. Don't stick it in your mouth either; you don't want to get any bacteria into the incision.

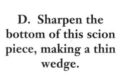

D. Sharpen the bottom of this scion piece, making a thin wedge.

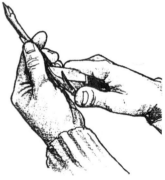

Insert the scion into the rootstock. Open the split part of the tree trunk with a knife and slide the wedge-shaped scion down into it (E). Since your scion is not likely to be exactly the same diameter as your rootstock, take great care that the cambium layers of each are perfectly aligned on one side. This is where the sap is going to flow from one to another.

Cover the wound. When the scion is solidly in place, cover the wound to keep the air from drying it out (F). Regular grafting wax is usually used for this purpose, but it's a bit messy since it has to be melted and brushed on. You can also use a tree wound sealer, such as Tree Kote, or wrap it in strips of rubber electrical tape. Don't use plastic tape as that will constrict the tree as it grows. The rubber tape stretches and eventually weathers away.

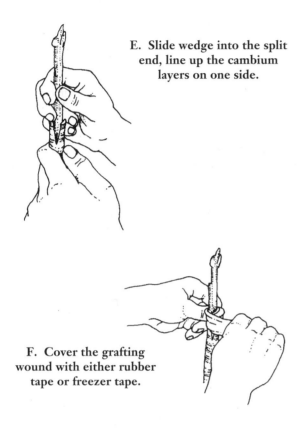

E. Slide wedge into the split end, line up the cambium layers on one side.

F. Cover the grafting wound with either rubber tape or freezer tape.

Grafting Tips

■ You can gather scions a couple of weeks before they are to be used and keep them sealed in a plastic bag in the refrigerator. The scions will stay dormant while the rootstock begins to grow. Then after the graft is made, the scions are less likely to dry out before the new sap gets to them.

■ Keep all sprouts below the graft rubbed or cut off so all growth energy can be directed into the new scion.

■ Stake the tree if necessary. The graft union will be fragile for a few weeks. Staking may prevent it from breaking off in a high wind.

■ Keep records. It is easy to forget varieties and when the tree begins to produce, you'll want to know its kind and where it came from.

■ Don't be impatient. The new graft is unlikely to start growing for a week or two after all the other buds. Not all grafts start at once, either. Give them all a chance. Even experienced grafters sometimes have failures, so don't expect 100 percent success. It is a precision operation.

After-Care of Grafts

Grafts take longer to start growing than do the branches already established, and can sometimes look pretty dead among all the green sprouts. They often start to grow three or more weeks later, so don't give up too soon. In the meantime, don't touch the graft or allow anything to knock it out of alignment. Even after it starts to grow, a new graft is still very fragile, and the wind or a slight touch can snap it off easily. Because all the strength of the root system is supplying a small scion, the growth is often very rapid once it gets going, however, and this makes the fragile union even more brittle. On trees grafted close to the ground, it is good insurance to put a small stake nearby and tie the graft to it as soon as it has grown tall enough. Trees grafted higher, on the branches, are harder to protect.

Pinch off all the side sprouts that form the first summer on grafted fruit and shade trees, and encourage the new graft to grow straight with a single stem. On all grafts, the sucker shoots that sprout from below the graft should be pinched or snipped off. Otherwise, because they are so vigorous, they will quickly crowd out the grafted top.

If your grafts are in pots, the nutrients are likely to leach away rapidly because of frequent waterings, so some liquid feeding or other fertilizing during the growing season will be necessary for good growth. If the plants are in the ground, however, and the growth of the new grafts appears good, it is not a good idea to feed the plants at all the first year. Top growth that has grown too fast is not only very brittle, but in the North it can fail to harden before the first frost, and be injured by sub-freezing temperatures.

ORCHARD CARE

In the spring, check over the orchard frequently to see that insects, disease, animals, or any other dangers are not threatening it. Insects and disease can increase rapidly with favorable warm weather conditions, and scavenging animals can swiftly pass the word to their many friends to come and join in the feast of young succulent twigs and forming fruits.

Also make sure the trees have a good supply of nutrients at this time when they are growing their fastest. And not only should plenty of fertilizer and moisture be available, but be sure the trees get first chance, before the weeds and grass.

A light pruning is usually beneficial to keep young trees growing in the right direction and to stop them from getting too wide, from developing too many tops, or from growing lopsided. And all sucker branches springing from the roots and the lower part of the trunk should be removed as soon as they sprout.

PRUNING IS ESSENTIAL

After its initial pruning your young tree will need very little additional pruning until it begins to produce fruit. Only some frequent minor clipping or pinching of branches is necessary to get it to grow into a good shape. Although there is something special about a gnarled, spreading, twisted old dooryard fruit tree, if you want it to attain its maximum fruit production, some shaping is essential in infancy.

Some varieties seem to grow naturally into a nice shape with little care. The Dolgo crab apple, for instance, shapes itself beautifully. Other trees, such as the Yellow Transparent apple, seem bent on growing as many tops as possible. The extra tops should be pruned back to encourage a more spreading tree. Many plum trees grow so wide that the outer branches hang on the ground unless they are snipped back occasionally.

Frequent light pruning is ever so much better than having to cut off large limbs that have grown in the wrong places. Frequent pruning also condi-

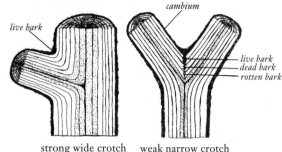

Wide crotch angles insure strong branch structure. The angle of the crotch on the left is wide. Note the relative thickness of six layers of wood laid down by the cambium in this crotch angle.
On the right, the angle is narrow and the bark in the crotch angle comes together before the crotch is filled with woody tissue. This results in a weaker joint and encourages decay. A narrow crotch tends to split with heavy loads of fruit and is often associated with winter injury on adjacent bark.

tions the orchardist to the pruning habit by developing both his attitude and skill.

How to Cut

The cardinal rule of pruning is to cut cleanly and leave no stubs. A dead stub will rot, die, and is vulnerable to infections that can spread to the rest of the tree. Either cut close to the main branch or immediately above a bud.

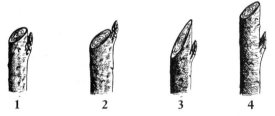

In cutting or heading back, make cuts just above healthy outward-facing buds.

1. correct cut
2. too close to bud
3. too slanting
4. stub too long

When cutting above a bud, which will stimulate new growth, make the cut just above a bud that grows in the direction the new growth is desired. A bud on the outside of a branch will grow out; one on the inside of a branch will grow in toward the center of the tree — usually an undesirable direction. The cut should be made close to the bud so it does not leave a long stub, and it should be angled, but not so sharply that it leaves a long, exposed surface.

When sawing off a sizable limb, the main danger is that the limb will split off before you have completed your neat and clean saw cut. There is a simple three-step cutting method that avoids this hazard. Make a cut about one-third of the way through the branch, 10 to 15 inches out from the main trunk. Saw from the bottom up. A second cut is made farther out on the branch, this time from the top down and cutting all the way through. The limb will often break off, but the jagged edge will extend no farther than the first cut you made. Then cut the remaining stub flush and parallel to the main trunk.

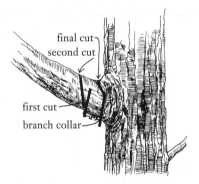

Removing a large limb.

After performing the cutting operation, any loose bark should be trimmed back to the point where it is sound and firmly adhered to the wood. For the quickest healing results, the wound should be trimmed clean with no ragged edges. Use your knife to smooth over the wound and surrounding bark.

Every cut of more than 1½ inches in diameter should have a protective coating of wound dressing. The primary reason for coating a large wound is to keep out moisture and to accelerate the healing process. Healing is quicker if the wound is trimmed in an oval shape. It sometimes takes years before a wound is covered with bark, so a seasonal repainting is advisable. Although any paint will seal out the insects and the effects of weather, a commercial tree-paint preparation contains antiseptic as an additional protection against disease.

PRACTICAL PRUNING TIPS

- Cut off a diseased, dead, or broken branch from any tree or plant at any time.

- Prune the weaker of two rubbing or interfering branches that are developing bark wounds — the quicker the better.

- Always prune flush to the parent branch or trunk. If only the end of a branch is dead, cut just beyond and close to a bud. **Note:** Be sure the branch is dead — not dormant — by slicing the bark and looking for green wood.

- In pruning, don't leave stubs or ragged cuts. Always use sharp, clean-cutting pruning tools.

- All bark wounds over 1½ inches in diameter should have a protective coating of dark paint.

- Pruning top terminal branches produces a low spreading tree. By pruning lateral or side branches the tree will grow upwards — less bushy.

- Burn what you cut to avoid spreading disease and attracting rot organisms.

- Keep pruning shears sharp and well-oiled, and use the right tool for the job.

- Keep trees out of foundation plantings. Never let trees and shrubs block windows of the house.

- Keep your feet on the ground. Don't use step ladders, chairs, or other makeshifts to prune the upper branches — use long-handled pruners or tree pruners and pole saws.

CONDENSED PRUNING GUIDE

Fruits	When	How
Apple	Winter or early spring	Train tree for low head. Prune moderately. Keep tree open with main branches well spaced around tree. Avoid sharp V-shaped crotches.
Cherry	Winter or early spring	Prune moderately, cut back slightly the most vigorous shoots.
Peach	Early spring	Prune vigorously — remove one-half of the previous year's growth, keep tree headed low, and well thinned-out.
Plum	Early spring	Remove dead and diseased branches, keep tree shaped up by cutting back rank growth. Prune moderately.
Quince	Early spring	Cut back young trees to form low, open head. Little pruning of older trees required except to remove dead and weak growth.

Shaping Trees

Direct all of your early pruning to guiding the tree into the desired shape. Fruit trees are usually trained in one of three forms: central leader, modified leader, or open center.

Central Leader. Trees that bear heavy crops of large fruit, including apples and pears, are usually best pruned to grow with a central leader, or trunk, at least in their younger days. With only one strong trunk in the center of the tree, branches come strongly out from it at fairly wide angles and can safely bear abundant loads of fruit.

Thin out the branches growing from the central leader as necessary to allow open space between the limbs. Thin also the branches that come from these limbs, and so on to the outermost branches. Sunlight produces colorful, flavorful, vitamin-enriched fruit. Sunlight and circulating air also help to prevent scab, mildew, and a host of other diseases that thrive in shade and high humidity.

Eventually you will have to remove the top of

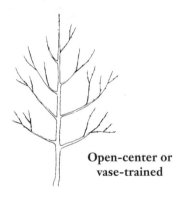

Open-center or vase-trained

the central leader because this high-growing leader will gradually sag under a load of heavy fruit, forming a canopy over part of the tree that will shut out the light. Cutting back the top helps prevent a canopy from occurring while also keeping the tree from growing too tall.

Modified Leader. The modified leader method is initially the same as the central leader method, but eventually you let the central trunk branch off to form several tops. This training ensures that the loads of fruit at the top of the tree are never as heavy as those at the bottom where limbs are larger. Cut back the tops of larger trees from time to time to shorten the tree or to let in more light. Although the central leader method is preferred by most orchardists for growing apples and pears, the modified leader method is easier to maintain simply because most fruit trees grow that way naturally.

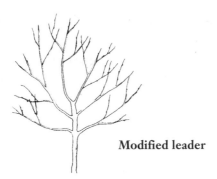

Modified leader

Open Center. The open center method, also known as the open top or vase method, is an excellent way to let more light into the shady interior of a tree. Since this method produces a tree with a weaker branch structure than if it had a strong central leader, the lightweight fruits are the best subjects: quinces, crab apples, plums, cherries, peaches, nectarines, and apricots.

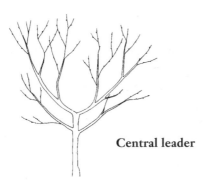

Central leader

Prune so that the limbs forming the vase effect do not all come out of the main trunk close to each other, or they will form a cluster of weak crotches. Even with the whole center of the tree open, you'll have to thin the branches and remove the older limbs eventually, just as you would with a tree pruned in the central leader method.

Pruning Hints

Prune for good crops of quality fruit. Good fruit needs plenty of sunshine. Because of its tight branch structure, only 30 percent of an unpruned tree gets enough light, while another 40 percent gets only a fair amount of light. When only the top exterior of the tree produces good fruit, you are getting the use of but a third of your tree, and all that fruit is grown where it is most difficult to pick. Even the most careful pruning won't bring the light efficiency to a full 100 percent, but you can greatly increase it.

Prune to keep your trees from getting too large. Since standard-size fruit trees can grow to 25 feet or more, they are often pruned to keep them at a more manageable height. A tall tree is difficult and dangerous to work in. And, because so much of the tree is shaded, it often produces poor fruit.

Of course it's best to prune regularly so that your tree doesn't get too tall in the first place, but if this advice comes too late, consider shortening them. The tree should be healthy enough to stand major surgery. Make sure that there will be enough lower branches left on the tree to sustain it after its upper level has been removed: the leaf surface remaining must be adequate to supply nutrients to the tree.

If these conditions can be met, begin to prune back the top in late summer or early fall. Make the cuts in small stages, cutting off only small pieces of limbs at one time, so that the limb weight will be lightened before you begin the heavy cutting. These small cuts lessen the danger of splitting limbs, and also help insure that you won't drop heavy pieces of wood onto the lower branches. If possible, have a helper handy to catch the limbs as they fall or to guide them away from the tree.

Don't cut off more than one large limb in any one year. Make sure that some regrowth has started on the lower branches before you make any further cuts.

Prune to keep your tree healthy. Even young fruit trees occasionally need to be pruned because of some mishap: limbs get broken, tent caterpillars build nests, and as the tree gets older, rot and winter injury often take their toll on the branches.

As soon as you notice any damage, clip or saw off the injured part back to a live limb or the trunk. Even one deteriorating limb is not good for the tree's health, and the accumulation of several sick limbs will rapidly speed up the decline of the tree.

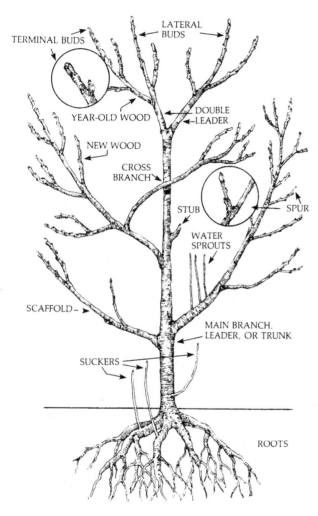

Anatomy of a tree.

Thin out and open up old trees to permit sunshine to enter and ripen the fruit. Air will circulate to discourage disease, and it will be easier for birds to spot and pick up preying insects.

Cut off crossed branches or branches that might rub to cause wounds in the bark.

Water sprouts are those upright branches that grow in clumps, often from a large pruning wound. They are usually unproductive, and they can weaken the tree by causing additional, unwanted shade. You should remove water sprouts promptly.

Suckers are the branches that grow on the lower part of the tree trunk or from the roots of the tree. Usually they grow from below the graft, so if you don't remove them, they'll grow into a wild tree or bush that will crowd out the good part of the tree within a few years. A lot of sucker growth results on fruit trees when a slower-growing variety is grafted onto a vigorous-growing rootstock. Usually the suckers appear as a cluster of branches close to the base of the tree trunk, but sometimes (especially on plum trees) they may pop up out of the roots anywhere under the tree, even a distance away from the trunk. Mow or clip them off at ground level as soon as they appear.

When to Prune

Spring. Most people agree that pruning a fruit tree when it is just beginning to make its most active growth is one of the worst times. The tree will probably bleed heavily, and it may have trouble recovering from the loss of so much sap. Also, infections such as fire blight are most active and easily spread around in the spring.

The only pruning you should do in the spring is to remove any branches that have been broken by winter storms or injured by the cold. Immediately tack back onto the wood bark that has split from the trunk, and seal the wound with tree dressing to prevent air from drying the bare wood.

Late summer. Late summer is a favorite time for many people to prune their fruit trees. By pruning after the tree has completed its yearly growth and hardened its wood, and before it has lost its leaves, you stimulate less regrowth. You still have to take care of any frost injury in late winter, but this late summer-early fall pruning works well if extensive winter damage is not likely.

Wherever growing seasons are short and the extreme cold or heavy snow and ice loads may cause injury to the trees, late-winter pruning is best. Don't cut back the tree in late summer if there's a good chance that the remaining branches will be winter-killed. You'll have to prune away too much of the tree.

Late fall and winter. Late fall or winter is a favorite time to prune in the warmer parts of the country. Orchardists have more spare time then, and the trees are bare, so it is easier to see what needs to be done. You should choose days when the temperature is above freezing, however, to avoid injury to the wood. Because frozen wood is very brittle, it breaks easily when hit by a ladder or pruning tool.

However, if you live in a cold part of the country, or if you are growing tree varieties that are inclined to have winter injury, wait until the coldest weather is over before pruning.

Late winter. This season is probably the most popular time for northern gardeners to prune. As in late fall and winter, the tree is completely dormant, and since the leaves are off, it is easy to see where to make the cuts. You can repair any winter injury, the weather is usually warm enough during the day, and most orchardists are not too busy during this season.

If you prune your trees regularly each year, late winter is a satisfactory time to prune because you don't have to remove large amounts of wood. However, if the trees have been neglected for a few years and are badly in need of a cutback, late winter is not the best time to prune. Excessive pruning in late winter usually stimulates a great deal of growth the following spring and summer, because the tree tries to replace its lost wood. Branches, suckers, and water sprouts are likely to grow in great abundance. If a major pruning job is necessary, do all or at least a large part of it in late summer or early fall so that you won't cause a great amount of regrowth.

ORCHARD INSECT PESTS AND DISEASES

If a tree is not happy with its climate, moisture, soil, fertilizer, or light conditions, or if it is starved

ORCHARD SPRAYS

For a long time, orchardists relied on nasty chemicals, particularly malathion, methoxychlor, and captan, to control pest and disease problems. But one of the greatest benefits of growing your own fruit is the assurance that your produce will be free of harmful chemicals.

In addition to all the home remedies that organic growers have known about for years, new pesticides are introduced every year that are safer and more effective than the existing ones. A few points to keep in mind are:

- Pest control is an important consideration in all phases from planting and pruning through harvesting and orchard cleanup.

- Before you spray, consider what you are spraying for. Sprays, dusts, and other control measures are far more effective when carefully timed and targeted at a specific pest.

- Spraying or dusting with chemicals is only one part of a thorough pest control plan and may not, in itself, be enough to curb insect and disease problems.

- Preventive measures and dormant sprays are usually more effective than spraying after insects and disease have damaged trees and fruit.

by weed and grass competition, it is not going to do well, and no amount of spray can help. Likewise, if a tree has been damaged by animals, chemicals, salts, or machinery, it is going to look less than healthy and again, even the best all-purpose orchard dust will do no good. So diagnosing the problem correctly is most important.

When you've determined that a tree has problems not caused by its environment or by things such as animals or machinery, check the leaves and bark for insects. Sometimes insects can be easily seen, sometimes not. Tent caterpillars, Japanese beetles, and even aphids can be spotted easily and identified. Others, such as mites and scale, are very small and hard to see, even though the damage they do can usually be recognized. Still other insects spend a lot of their life out of sight either underground or beneath the loose bark of a tree. Then there are those that fly around the orchard at night, laying eggs that hatch inside the fruit. Naturally, every insect that you see in your orchard is not an enemy. Most will be quite harmless, and some even beneficial.

Diseases are easier to identify. Whoever named them used terms so descriptive that even beginners can often recognize them. How could you not identify brown rot, powdery mildew, leaf curl, scab, sooty blotch, fire blight, black knot, rust, or leaf yellows?

Before you reach for the spray can, spend some time trying to determine which problem you have, and then you can aim your control measures at the right target.

Natural Controls to Fight Insects and Diseases

Rather than spray, you can use natural controls and orchard sanitation to fight insects and disease. For instance, releasing ladybugs or praying mantises (warmer areas only for mantises) will control aphids and certain other insects. They can be purchased from many mail-order nurseries.

Another natural control has the descriptive name "Tanglefoot." A sticky goo, usually available in garden stores, it can be spread in a band around each tree a foot or so from the ground. This will prevent the insects that usually crawl up the trunk from doing so. It particularly discourages ants from carrying aphids up to the leaves.

Planting insect-repellent herbs and flowers throughout the orchard is another natural control method you can use. Plant tansy, wormwood, marigolds, peppermint, nasturtiums, petunias, or horseradish.

Sanitation Methods

Whether you prefer chemical or natural pest control, or a combination of both methods, you will probably want to follow these sanitation practices.

Pick up all unused fruit. Bury it in the compost pile or destroy it. Many bugs and diseases overwinter in old fruit.

Prune fruit trees regularly. Cut out all infected wood and dead or broken branches where trouble can start.

Thin out branches to allow better air circulation, which helps cut down scab, particularly in humid or wet summers when the disease is at its worst.

Rake up and compost leaves where scab and other diseases may linger. Fruits, leaves, and twigs that are already infected should be burned or otherwise destroyed.

Keep loose bark scraped from the trees so insects can't overwinter in it.

Isolate the planting if possible. If you have the only fruit trees within miles, the worst bugs and disease may never find you. Small growers have it easier than commercial orchardists because large plantings are very attractive to insects. If there are other small orchards in your area, see if you can all work together to discourage bug hospitality.

Mix up your plantings. Like isolation, it's another way to make things tough for the bugs. Whereas large growers want all their varieties together for convenience in picking and spraying, small growers don't need to group them.

Bug Traps

Electric bug traps are quite successful at trapping flying insects, particularly those that move by night.

MAJOR INSECTS AND DISEASES

Disease	Enemy of	Attacks
Apple scab	Apple	Leaves, twigs, fruits
Black knot	Plum, cherry, other stone fruits	Branches
Brown rot	Peach, plum, apricot, nectarine	Fruits
Canker	All trees, some bush fruits	Trunks, limbs
Cherry leaf spot	Sweet and sour cherry	Leaves
Fire blight	Apple, pear, quince	Branches, twigs
Peach leaf curl	Peach and nectarine	Leaves
Peach scab	Peach, plum, nectarine	Leaves, fruits
Powdery mildew	Many fruits, berries	Twigs, leaves
Root gall	Tree fruits	Roots
Rust	Apple, quince	Leaves, twigs
Wilt	Tree fruits, berries	Leaves, branches

Insect	Enemy of	Attacks
Aphid	All fruit trees, especially apple	Leaves, fruits
Apple maggot	Apple	Fruits
Borer	All fruits, especially peach	Trunks
Cherry fruit fly	Cherry	Fruits
Codling moth	Apple, pear	Fruits, leaves
Curculio	All fruits, except pear	Fruits
Mites	Apple, peach, plum, nectarine	Fruits, leaves
Oriental fruit moth	Peach, apricot, plum	Leaves, fruits
Pear psylla	Pear	Leaves
San José scale	All fruits	Trunks, twigs, fruits, leaves
Tent caterpillar	All fruits	Leaves

Many companies have them for sale, or you can make your own by shining a light bulb with a reflector on it into a shallow pan of water that has a film of kerosene. The light will attract the insects and they'll subsequently die in the kerosene.

People who object to electric bug traps say that they kill good and bad bugs alike and also attract insects from great distances. Also, many insects, such as the apple maggot, may not show any inter-

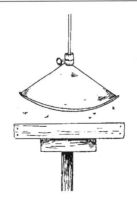

Homemade bug light

ORGANIC PEST AND DISEASE CONTROLS

With the rising concern for the health and environmental side effects of agricultural sprays, many alternatives to dangerous chemicals have become more popular. These alternatives include bands, traps, barriers, botanical sprays, introduced predators, and bacterial controls.

The thing to keep in mind is that anything that kills insects might have other side effects. Always shop carefully, read labels, and follow package diretions for best results. If you have any quetions or doubts, ask for advice from your local agricultural extension service or plant nursery.

Physiological Controls

The first and simplest thing to do when you see an unwelcome bug in your garden or orchard is squash it. It's easy and usually has no harmful side effects. On a larger scale, traps, bands, and other barriers placed between the pest and the plant may be effective.

Traps can be a jar or cup containing molasses and water, vinegar, or even beer, depending on the insect you're after. Place the trap in the neighborhood of the bug, monitor it carefully, remove and destroy captured insects, and replenish the lure as needed.

Bands can be as simple as a folded strip of fabric tied around a tree. When crawling insects get caught in the fabric, remove and destroy them. It is important to check bands frequently; if neglected they can end up harboring pests. Other bands can be made of tar building paper painted with sticky material, such as tar or molasses, which stops crawling insects in their tracks. A commercial product called Tree Tanglefoot was developed specifically for this purpose and can be painted on bands or, in some cases, directly on tree trunks.

Abrasive Substances

Scratchy materials can be effective when applied in dust form to surfaces that insects frequent. The greatest advantage is that these generally have no toxic side effects.

Wood ashes were used by old-time gardeners who tossed them through their trees when the dew was on in the morning. They claimed this controlled disease and insect problems, and was a good fertilizer as well. While this may be a bit of an exaggeration, it may serve as a repellent because many insects don't like gritty textures under foot.

Diatomaceous earth, made from needle-sharp fragments of seashells and fossils. Spread on leaves, fruit, and branches, it scrapes and pierces the bellies of cutworms, grubs, and caterpillars. Even if they are not immediately killed by these wounds, the scratchy material will repel them.

Botanical Insecticides

Various plant parts are used in manufacturing insecticides. Though most botanical preparations are relatively safe, commercial formulas are often mixed with more dangerous chemicals, so it is important to pay attention to what you are buying and to follow label directions carefully. Because they are made from plant parts, botanical formulas tend to break down more quickly and tend to have fewer side effects, but even pure botanical formulas can have toxic properties and should be handled accordingly. Other effective mixtures can be made from herbs and plants that you just might have in your house or garden.

Herbal Formulas. Insects normally avoid especially strong herbs, such as parsley, tansy, garlic, hot red peppers, and others. Effective sprays can be made at home by grinding the leaves, adding a little soap and water, letting the mixture steep, and then straining to make a spray. The mash can be buried in the garden to enrich the soil while discouraging soil-borne pests.

Rotenone and Pyrethrum are derived from plants and commonly used in commercial insecticides because they kill a large range of insects. They wash off easily and have a relatively low toxicity, which is both good and bad, because it means they need to be applied frequently to be useful. However, they are harmful to bees and should be used after bees have returned to the hive for the evening. They may also be harmful to fish, so keep them away from ponds, streams, and other water sources.

Ryania is derived fom the roots of a South American shrub. It is effective in controlling codling moths, corn borers, cranberry fruit worms, aphids, and Japanese beetles and can be used fairly safely as harvest time approaches. For really serious infestations, stronger sprays may be needed.

Sabadilla usually comes in dust form and is good against many types of beetles, web worms, army worms, codling moths, grasshoppers, and aphids. It may be irritating, but it is relatively nontoxic to humans and wildlife. However, some people have an allergic reaction to it, and it is toxic to honeybees.

Dormant Oil Sprays

Organic gardeners sometimes use dormant oil sprays to control the first infestations of many diseases, and often this is enough if they follow other safeguards. Dormant oil spray can be bought ready to mix at many garden supply stores or can be prepared at home by mixing 2 quarts light motor oil (not kerosene or fuel oil) with 1 pound fish oil soap or ½ cup liquid detergent. Mix 1 part of this mixture with 20 parts water as needed. Use at once after you have mixed it with water, because the oil and water will separate if stored for any length of time.

Dormant oils can be used safely on the trunks and branches of trees early in the spring before any growth starts. It should never be used on green leaves, however.

Other Sprays

Soap. Commercially produced insecticidal soaps are effective against many pests. Even a spray of water mixed with a small amount of soapflakes can clean away aphids, whiteflies, and other insects.

Bacterial Controls. *Bacillus thuringiensis* (Bt) is a bacteria that sickens chewing insects like caterpillars and other wormlike larva. Bugs swallow the disease organism along with bites of your leaves. *Bacillus popilliae* (milky spore disease) is useful against Japanese beetle grubs and other ground-dwelling pests.

est in them at all, since they're more likely to be abroad in the daytime.

Gallon glass jugs with a pint or so of vinegar in them attract and trap large numbers of fruit flies.

Paper cups with a bit of molasses in the bottoms, hung among the limbs of apple trees, are used successfully to trap egg-laying codling moths in the spring.

Black paper tied around tree trunks will provide a shelter for some harmful insects. By removing the paper at intervals you can kill the insects under it.

A hedgerow helps encourage insect-eating birds. Birdhouses, feeders, and water also help bring birds to the area.

Keeping the grass mowed discourages places where insects and disease can hide out and increase.

Toads eat vast quantities of insects that spend part of their life cycle on the ground. Clay pots with a hole broken in one side and pans of drinking water encourage these beneficial and friendly fellows.

Insect Pests

Here are some insect problems that may show up in your orchard. There are many types of insects, and they attack fruit plants and trees in different ways. Some chew leaves or burrow into the wood or bark. Others suck nutrients from the leaves or branches.

Aphids. Various kinds attack bark, leaves, or fruit of almost every tree. Scores of insecticides have been formualted to control them, but organic controls are usually safer and, in the long run, more effective. Many of the leaf aphids are spread far and wide by ambitious ants who like the sweet substance they secrete. The tight curling of new leaves at the end of branches on young trees is often a result of heavy aphid colonies sucking out the plant juices. Small infestations can often be knocked out with a steady stream of water from the hose. Insecticidal soap sprays are effective, as are homemade sprays of lime, or garlic, or teas brewed from rhubarb leaves or larkspur. The introduction of lady bugs,

Aphid. Newly hatched insects on a bud, injured fruit, and leaf.

lacewings, or parasitic wasps has been highly effective in some cases. Dormant oil sprays applied in early spring will suffocate eggs before they hatch. For a quick rescue in midseason, you can try applications of garden rotenone dust. Treatment should be in two installments. A week after the first treatment you should repeat it, to catch any new insects that may hatch later.

Apple Maggots. Easily one of the meanest insects in the fruit world, these persistent pests have wrecked many a crop of apples. They're known as the "railroad worms" and can quickly reduce a beautiful apple to a pulpy brown mess. The damage is caused by an insect closely resembling a house fly but slightly smaller, which lays its eggs in the growing fruit by piercing the skin. The larvae, often in large numbers, hatch and tunnel through the fruit. Larvae live in fruit that falls to the ground in the orchard during the fall, then burrow underground

Apple maggot. Adult fly and maggot tunnels in apple.

for the winter, ready to emerge the following summer. Swarms of these flies can often be seen under fruit trees in late summer in neglected orchards. Cleaning up all the old fruit is one of the best controls. An effective trap can be made by mixing 1 part molasses to 9 parts water and 1 teaspoon of yeast in a wide mouth, gallon jar. Cover with coarse-mesh hardware cloth to keep bees out. Let this mix ferment for 48 hours, then hang one jar in each tree where the sun will strike it. A good spraying program carried on through most of the summer will almost completely control this maggot if the problem becomes serious.

Borers. The apple-tree borer is the flat-headed larva of a copper-colored beetle that appears in late spring to midsummer. A similar pest attacks stone fruit trees. These small worms burrow into the trunks of trees, often near or just above ground level. A pile of sawdust and jelly-like excrement, together with the weakened condition of the tree, indicate the presence of this fat, alien invader. Usually brutally punching or digging out the fat grub with a wire or pen knife is the most effective means of disposing of it, since sprays frequently fail to reach it. It is important to monitor these wounds for signs of disease. Tree wraps can help discourage this creature and keep it from getting started, but unfortunately trees received from nurseries occasionally already have the young larvae in them. Better look closely at the trunks of all new trees when they are first received to make sure no borers are at work. Even one can soon weaken a tree enough so it will break off at ground level. Examine trees in June and September for signs of dam-

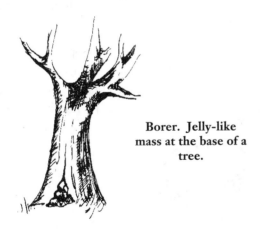

Borer. Jelly-like mass at the base of a tree.

age. A whitewash applied to the trunk and main branches up to 3 feet off the ground discourages borers and may also destroy their eggs. Large-scale infestations can be treated with insecticides to kill the adult beetles in June, July, and August.

Codling Moths. A fat white or grayish grub and its excrement about the hole in the fruit are solid indicators of the insect at work. The codling moth is fond of laying its eggs in the flower at blooming time, an effective way to control this pest is to spray with an insecticidal soap or botanical insecticide between the time the bees leave — when the petals have fallen — and the time the new fruit has formed protection for the hatching egg. Dormant oil sprays are also helpful. Sometimes there is a second or third generation the same year, all infecting the crop. Codling moths like to overwinter in sheltered

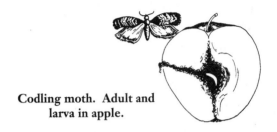

Codling moth. Adult and larva in apple.

spots, a favorite one being the space under the loose bark on older fruit trees, so it helps to scrape off loose bark to remove those hiding places. Sticky barriers, like Tree Tanglefoot, will trap adult moths and migrating larvae. Dusting with diatomaceous earth will discourage egg laying. Milky spore disease (*Bacillus thuringiensis* or Bt) is lethal to most caterpillars. Parasitic trichogramma wasps and woodpeckers are also your allies here.

Curculios. These small insects puncture developing fruit and lay eggs, often causing the fruit to drop prematurely. Dark blotches around the punctures are clearly visible on the fruits that remain on the tree.

When disturbed, curculios and other snout beetles often curl up and play dead. They can often be controlled by the jarring method, which involves spreading a sheet under the tree and shaking or hitting the tree with a padded mallet, and destroying the insects that fall into the sheet. It is most effective if you do this.

Bands of cloth treated with tar or other sticky substances will trap beetles and other crawling insects. Tree Tanglefoot can be applied directly on the bark of mature trees.

Clean cultivation around trees and removal of dropped fruit are important cleanup measures.

Wild hawthorne and crabapples, the curculio's native food, should not be planted within a half mile of the orchard.

Plum curculio. Adult beetle and larva in fruit.

Mites. Small sucking insects that attack leaves and fruit, mites may never become a nuisance in most home gardens, or they may show up some dry summer. Orchard cleanup and ordinary orchard sprays control them.

Oriental Fruit Moths. Occasionally these become real pests on peaches and nectarines. They attack twigs and fruits, often having four or five generations in a summer in warmer climates. The caterpillars can be controlled by the same methods as codling moths.

Pear Psylla. The most common pear insect, this small creature can strip the leaves off a tree and soon ruin a crop unless it is controlled. It can also beget several generations each summer, so early spraying is important. Black sooty secretions cover the fruit and leaves when psylla is present.

San José Scale. An insect so tiny you need a magnifying glass to see it, this bug works under a scale it has built up for protection. Along with its numerous relatives, scale sucks nutrients from the twigs in such quantities that the branches often die. Few fruit trees are immune from this pest. The most common include scrubbing or squashing the pests, dormant oil sprays, and introduction of predatory lady beetles. For extreme cases, a contact insecticide may be necessary.

San José scale. Adult scale and young crawler.

Tent Caterpillars, Cankerworms, and Webworms. The cobweb masses that are a familiar sight in hedgerows are usually caused by one of these. All of them cause similar injury to leaves during the summer months. The big webs may be cut off and burned if you choose. Controls described to combat codling moths are also effective here.

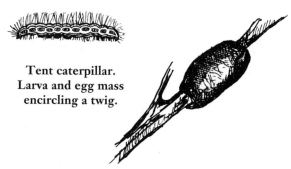

Tent caterpillar. Larva and egg mass encircling a twig.

Diseases

Diseases can be spread by wind, rain, insects, and pruning tools. Like human genetic diseases, they may also be inherited and passed on through scion or rootstock. Some are very hard to control — fire blight, for instance. Others, such as certain scabs and rots, are quite often easily kept in check by destroying affected limbs or fruit along with carefully timed spraying.

Apple Scab. The most common apple disease, scab attacks both leaves and fruit. It forms olive-colored splotches on the leaves, often making them warped and curly. Fruits are covered with dark, hard, un-

Scab. Fruit and leaf damaged by apple scab.

sightly blotches, and sometimes with cracks. Fruit infected early in the season may fall before maturing. Those infected later are often unfit for use. Because the disease overwinters in old leaves on the ground, cleanup is important. Control requires carefully timed spraying with a fungicide to prevent these later infections, which are frequently spread by rain.

Scab may not be a problem at all in dry years. In seasons with a lot of rain, spraying may have to be continued until a week or two before harvest. Dormant oils can help prevent early infestations, but fungicides will likely be the only way to have good control all season. The disease often overwinters in apples and in leaves on the ground.

Black Knot. Recognized by the thick, fleshy excrement on limbs of cherry, plum, and other stone fruits, black knot begins in summer as sticky secretions, but is most noticeable in winter when trees are bare. The best control is to remove infected limbs in summer as soon as it is spotted. All wild plums and cherries nearby that are infected should also be removed.

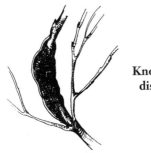

Knots. Black knot disease on plum branch.

Brown Rot. This fungus attacks the growing fruit of all the stone fruit family. Plums and peaches are often affected the worst, with the fruit becoming a mushy rot just before it ripens. Like scab, it is spread by rain, so is worse in wet summers. It also overwinters in decaying fruit on the ground. As with scab, cleanup of fallen fruits and leaves, along with regular spraying with a fungicide gives good control.

Brown rot. Fungus spores and mumified fruit.

FUNGICIDES

Specialized sprays are available to combat fungi that cause plant diseases. Fungicides may be *eradicants*, which kill or neutralize fungi living in the soil or on the plant, or *protectants*, which prevent the growth of fungi on susceptible plant parts.

While there are a wide variety of products on the market, it is difficult to find effective, all-purpose fungicides that meet the safety standards demanded by organic gardeners. In the past, orchardists routinely used sulfur preparations like Bordeaux mixture (a mix of lime and copper sulfate discovered by French vinyardists in the 19th century). Similar commercial preparations are still readily available.

Promising new products use beneficial fungi to fight more harmful species.

Canker. In its various forms, canker may bother fruit and nut trees as well as small fruits. Apple blister canker, bleeding canker, blueberry canker, butternut melanconis dieback, camellia canker, currant canker, grape dead arm disease, and nectria canker are some of them. While the list sounds rather depressing, probably none will ever bother your orchard.

Canker is a very noticeable diseased section of the woody part of a tree or bush, and it may even be an open wound. In some cases it may spread all around the trunk and kill the tree. Often it results from injuries that were left untreated. If canker does get started, the best method of treatment is to cut out all the diseased wood and seal the cavity with a tree sealer or cement. Sterilize all tools after use with a bleach solution.

Cedar Apple Rust. One of the worst of several rusts that bother fruits, cedar apple rust attacks

SPRAY SCHEDULE FOR MOST HOME ORCHARDS

Before you begin, there are times when you definitely should *not* spray. First, never spray when the trees are blooming, in order not to harm pollinating insects. Second, do not spray within two weeks of picking — humans are important too.

Since trees bloom at different times, the first four sprayings may be at irregular intervals, according to the flowering period of specific trees. After that fourth spraying, the whole orchard may be sprayed at one time. In order to coordinate these sprays, you may allow 7 to 12 days between petal fall and summer sprays. If you wish, dormant oil spray can be used instead of orchard spray for the first spray. After that, use the orchard spray or your choice of organic sprays.

Sprays for Tree Fruit

1. **Dormant spray.** Use when tips of buds are swelling but before they begin to turn green.

2. **Bud spray.** Use when leaf buds are just beginning to open.

3. **Pink spray.** Use when blossom buds show pink and are nearly ready to burst open.

4. **Petal fall spray.** Use when nearly all petals are off tree.

5. **Summer sprays.** Two or more additional sprays may be needed in some areas and in some years. If so, they may be continued at intervals of 10 to 12 days until two weeks before harvesting begins.

leaves and fruit. The disease needs nearby wild juniper (red cedar) to complete its cycle, so elimination of that plant when feasible controls it beautifully. Where this is difficult, a fungicidal spray may help.

Cherry Leaf Spot. As its name implies, the disease attacks cherries. It overwinters on fallen leaves and is spread by spring winds. It is worse in damp weather. Raking and composting leaves each fall helps prevent this problem from spreading. A fungicidal spray may help, also.

Fire Blight. This deadly disease presents a real problem only to certain fruit trees. Many varieties of pears and some apples are very vulnerable. Planting disease-resistant kinds is the best precaution. You can also control it by promptly sealing all new tree wounds with a tree compound and pruning away all infected parts as soon as they appear.

Fire blight. Wilted leaves and gummy cankers on branches.

Most other plant diseases are caused by virus, but fire blight is caused by bacteria, which are spread most often by wind, insects (especially bees), and pruning tools. An especially prepared inoculant is sometimes used in commercial orchards for treatment. The disease is curious in that it can be very bad in certain years and then disappear entirely, apparently for no reason, even with no treatment.

Peach Leaf Curl. This disease overwinters on the tree twigs, spreading rapidly in the spring. Infected leaves are curled, crinkled, and thickened. Orchard cleanup in the fall helps prevent problems. A fungicidal spray may offer some control, and should be applied after trees go dormant in the fall or before the buds begin to open in the spring.

Peach Scab. Attacking both peaches and plums, peach scab causes velvety blotches to appear over the mature fruits. Orchard cleanup and fungicide sprays give good control.

Powdery mildew. A white velvety disease, powdery mildew covers leaves, twigs, and fruits of tree fruits, currants, and grapes. Wettable sulfur has long been the standard control. Sanitary measures, not crowding the plants, sufficient pruning, and careful disposal of infected parts are the best controls.

Root (Crown) Gall. This bacterial disease causes large swellings on roots of fruit trees and bramble fruits. There is no known cure. Plant only certified healthy trees and plants, and cut and burn infected plants immediately to prevent the problem from spreading.

Wilt. Wilt occurs in several varieties that may bother tree fruits. Besides the obvious one that occurs when there is not enough water in the soil, there are others caused by diseases that suddenly shut off moisture to part of the plant. Verticillium wilt is most common, attacking fruit trees and berries, vegetables, and shade trees. Control is especially difficult. It is well to plant fruits and berries away from vegetables if the disease is present in the garden, and to cut out the diseased limb and burn it at once. All pruning tools and shovels used in digging out infected plants should be sterilized immediately after using, to prevent spreading the disease. A good disinfectant can be made by mixing 1 part bleach with 9 parts water.

THINNING

Here's a trick little used by home gardeners that can make you the envy of your neighbors: If you want your tree to produce its best fruit and bear big crops every year, don't ever neglect to thin the fruit.

Mother Nature herself does a lot of thinning. Immediately after the fruit sets, a mature tree will usually drop hundreds of tiny fruits, and a few weeks later, when the fruits are the size of marbles, another drop usually occurs. This is known as the May drop, June drop, or July drop, depending on where you live. Don't be alarmed. The tree is merely getting rid of the extra fruit it can't grow to maturity.

Some apples such as the McIntosh do a pretty good job of thinning themselves with early summer drops, if they have been properly pruned. On the other hand, many apples such as Wealthy, Yellow Transparent, and others have a tremendous desire to overproduce, and heavy thinning is almost always necessary, not only to ensure large fruit but sometimes even to save the tree from bearing itself to death.

Thin peaches to leave one fruit every six to eight inches.

Peaches, apples, pears, and the large fruited plums all benefit from thinning, but don't bother to thin cherries, crab apples, the small canning pears, and small fruited plums.

Besides producing better fruit, thinning provides other benefits. One of the frustrating things about fruit growing is the fact that many varieties bear fruit in alternate years. With some trees such as York Imperial and Baldwin apples this tendency is normal. Even severe thinning doesn't completely correct it. With most trees, though, pruning excess branches and thinning the surplus fruit will promote fairly regular bearing every year.

Toward the end of summer, fruits begin to rapidly increase in size. Insects and disease may still be a problem, especially in years that are unusually wet or dry, so spraying may still be necessary. Check your bearing trees frequently to see that the crop is not overloading the branches. Some years a large tree may produce nearly a ton of fruit, so take a look now and then to see that the limbs are not in danger of breaking from the weight. If this seems likely, wide boards or planks of the proper length can be stood upright on the ground to prop up sagging branches until the fruit is harvested.

Be sure to resist any temptation to use fertilizers in the late summer to increase the size of the fruit. Tree growth must not be stimulated at that time since the tree is getting ready for its long winter nap.

HARVEST

The flowers have bloomed and faded. You've won the war against insects and diseases. And now it's time for your reward. Except for actually eating the fruit, harvesting is probably most people's favorite part of maintaining an orchard.

The home grower's greatest advantage over commercial orchards is the opportunity to pick each fruit at its peak ripeness. Tree-ripened fruit usually tastes better, and often has more vitamins. A little practice will tell you when each fruit is ready for picking. Get to know the exact color your fruit variety ripens to. Not all apples are red; some turn yellow, green, or even brownish. When fruit separates from the branch with an easy twist, it's usually ready.

Pears and certain kinds of peaches should be picked a little before they are fully ripe. They'll soften and rot if left on there too long. Store them in a cool place after picking, and they should be ready to eat in a few days.

GARDENING WITH FLOWERS

The impact that flowers make is a measure of professionalism in the home landscape. Regardless of the size and space available, you probably have room for at least a few bright splashes of color that will add magic to an ordinary lot. New plantings of annuals allow you to redecorate your yard every year. Or, give yourself something to look forward to as the season progresses by setting spring bulbs that flower before summer annuals and perennials. By incorporating succession of bloom into your planning, you can have flowers almost as long as snow doesn't cover the ground.

START WITH A PLAN

It's easy to let your imagination run wild on paper. Sketch out the existing landscape, and then use colored pencils or crayons to fill in green foliage with splashes of color. Remember in your planning that not all plants bloom at the same time, and not all plants bloom from early spring through fall. It may help to add your color on different tracing-paper overlays according to blooming seasons.

Designing with Flowers

Design is the first step in creating your colorful world. Decide where you need some shape and color, then choose plants that conform to the surroundings as well as your desires. Small beds or edgings along low hedges or beneath foundation plantings demand a low-growing choice, such as ageratum, alyssum, or begonias. In larger areas, you can vary the height to make the effect more interesting, especially if the ground is flat. In a freestanding bed, place taller plants in the center, stepping

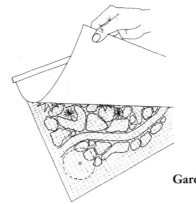

Garden plan

down to an intermediate-sized plant and then to a ground-hugging plant in front. For a border against a fence or wall, use the tallest in the back and work down to the front.

For a mixed bed or border, choose three sizes of plants. This can be done by combining three varieties of the same plant, such as zinnias or marigolds, in different heights; or by combining three different plants, such as tall spider flowers and medium-sized dahlias trimmed with a carpet of low-growing petunias.

Flower Shapes

Plants also grow in many different shapes, a mixture of which is most attractive in a mixed bed. Imagine a combination of spiked snapdragons intermingled with mounded begonias and edged with low-growing lobelia. Flowering plants also grow upright and bushy (African marigolds) or in an open, informal manner (cosmos). Again, try to work in groups of three.

spike

globe, rounded

open, informal

Flowers also come in different shapes, and combining them will make a mixed bed or border more interesting. Examples could be plumes of snapdragons, globes of marigolds, trumpet-shaped petunias, and a wide assortment of single, double, round, daisy-shaped, frilled, or irregularly shaped flowers.

Although combinations are most attractive, they are not a design necessity; mass planting of one variety of impatiens, for example, in one shape or color, is just as appealing. The decision depends on the effect you want to achieve; a massed planting is sleek and modern in appearance. If the ground is flat, building berms (mounds of soil) for mass plantings will give them height and more perspective.

If space is tight, plant in areas that are most visible. For example, plant beds or borders along the walkway or driveway to greet you when you come home, or place them in the back yard where you will be relaxing on weekends.

The shape of the planting area can be influenced by the surroundings. A stately Georgian or very modern house would demand a formal, straight-lined bed. A Colonial home would call for a closely packed, cottage-garden style. Most of today's architecture is complemented by semi-formal, contoured flower beds or borders.

Wherever space permits, flower beds and/or borders should be incorporated into the overall design. Flower beds are those plantings that are accessible from all sides. An example is an island planting in the middle of the lawn. Borders, on the other hand, are at the edge of an area, be it the lawn, walkway, driveway, foundation, shrub planting, or fence.

Because borders can usually be worked from only one side, do not plan them any deeper than 5 feet at the most, or maintenance will be difficult. Up to that point, they can be as wide as space and looks permit. Beds should be planned in relation to the surrounding area; don't try to situate too large a bed in a small grassed area, or it will be out of proportion.

You can locate beds and borders anywhere on your grounds, uniting plantings of evergreens and flowering trees and shrubs with ribbons of living color.

Besides adding aesthetic value, beds and borders can be used to either highlight or camouflage areas or even to direct foot traffic. If you want to draw attention to your front door, frame it with color. If you want to conceal your trash cans, let an annual vine climb on a trellis in front of them. If you don't want the children cutting across the front lawn, plant a border to make them walk around the lawn to the path.

Coloring Your World

Color is probably the most striking aspect of flower bed design. It reflects the personality and mood of your home. Warm tones of yellow, gold, orange, and red attract attention to those sections of the garden where they are used. Blue and violet, on the other hand, create a quieter, more tranquil mood. Warm colors make a planting appear smaller than it actually is, while cool colors make it appear larger.

Keep color schemes simple. Use more than one or two colors only in a bed of the same plant, such

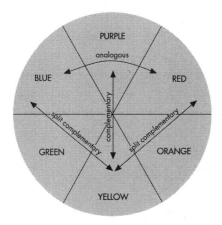

as zinnias, impatiens, dahlias, or celosia.

There are a number of possible harmonies you can select. Choose *complementary* (opposite) colors such as orange and blue (calendula with lobelia), or violet with yellow (two different varieties of pansies). *Split complementary* color combines one color with the color to either side of its opposite. Examples would be red with blue (salvia and ageratum), or red with yellow (red geraniums with yellow dahlias). Treat pink, a tint of red, the same way as red when designing. Treat violet the same way as purple. *Analogous* color harmony is three colors in a row on the wheel, such as yellow, yellow-orange or gold, and orange (marigolds). *Monochromatic* design is different tones of the same color (pink and/or red geraniums, zinnias, or impatiens). Select one harmony and stay with it throughout the bed or border for best effect.

White can blend well with any other color or be effective alone. Like pastels, especially light pinks, white is most effective when viewed at night, as it reflects moonlight, street lights, and garden lights. It is best used massed alone or as a unifying border to other annuals. White used as buffers between two conflicting colors can often make the design look spotty and disjointed. The same rules apply to white, silver, and gray foliage plants, such as dusty miller.

ANNUALS FOR INSTANT BEAUTY

Instant beauty and spectacular and diverse color — these are the advantages and charms of annual flowers. By definition, an annual is a plant that grows, flowers, sets seed, and dies in the same season. The term "annual" is also applied to tender perennials that survive the winter only in the mildest of climates, but are grown during the summer in other areas.

Garden Design with Annuals

The same design principles apply to gardening with all flowers. But when you shop for bedding plants or seeds, you will notice that many annuals come in a "series." For example, there are 'Super Elfin Pink,' 'Super Elfin Red,' and 'Super Elfin Blush' impatiens; 'Pink Pearls,' 'Azure Pearl,' and 'White Pearl' petunias; and 'Inca Yellow,' 'Inca Gold,' and 'Inca Orange' marigolds. If you are planning a massed bed of the same plant in mixed colors, you will achieve greater success if you use plants from the same series. They will be more uniform in height, plant shape, and bloom size.

Planting

Choosing Stock. If you purchase bedding plants instead of growing your own annuals from seeds, look for deep green, healthy plants that are neither too compact nor too spindly. It is better if they are not yet in bloom. Most annuals will come into full bloom faster in the garden if they are not in bloom when planted.

Most bedding plants are grown in individual "cell packs," although they may be in flats or individual pots. If you can't plant them right away, keep them in a lightly shaded spot and be sure to water carefully.

PLAN A SUCCESSION OF BLOOM

The blooming times noted here are for zones 5 and 6. If you garden in a warmer or colder zone, the plants will bloom at different times, and you will need to adjust the schedule accordingly. Check with experienced local gardeners or nurserymen to find out when the plants in each category are likely to blossom. In zone 3, for example, almost nothing blooms until May, and all spring-blooming and early summer-blooming perennials flower a few weeks later than noted in the list. By midsummer the long days have enabled most of the summer- and fall-blossoming perennials to catch up, so their flowers appear in the North at nearly the same time as they do farther south.

Plants marked with an asterisk are especially good choices for beginning gardeners because they are easy to grow and are desirable in the border. Some are extremely vigorous, however, and must be kept under control. Note too, that some species, such as *Veronica*, include many varieties that may bloom at different times.

Perennials That Bloom Over a Long Season

* *Campanula carpatica*, Carpathian bellflower
* *Centaurea montana*, mountain bluet
Coreopsis grandiflora, tickseed
Dianthus latifolius, long-blooming sweet William
* *Dicentra eximia*, fernleaf bleeding-heart
* *Gaillardia aristata*, blanketflower
* *Heuchera sanguinea*, coral bells
Kniphofia uvaria, torch lily
Myosotis alpestris, alpine forget-me-not
Physostegia virginiana, false dragonhead
* *Viola cornuta*, horned violet

February/March

* *Crocus angustifolius*, crocus
Eranthis hyemalis, winter aconite
Erica carnea, spring heath
Helleborus, Christmas rose
Iris reticulata, netted iris
* *Narcissus*, daffodil, jonquil, narcissus
Scilla siberica, squill

April

Ajuga reptans, bugleweed
Alyssum saxatile, goldentuft
* *Aquilegia*, columbine
Arabis alpina, rockcress
Aubrieta deltoidea, purple rockcress
* *Bellis perennis*, English daisy
Caltha palustris, cowslip, marsh marigold
* *Centaurea montana*, mountain bluet
* *Dicentra eximia*, fernleaf bleeding-heart
* *D. spectabilis*, bleeding-heart
Euphorbia polychroma, spurge
* *Iberis sempervirens*, candytuft
Iris chamaeiris, Crimean iris
Mertensia virginica, Virginia bluebells
* *Nepeta mussinii*, flowering catmint
* *Papaver nudicaule*, Iceland poppy
Phlox divaricata, blue phlox
* *Phlox subulata*, moss pink
* *Primula*, primrose
Saxifraga cordifolia, saxifrage
Thalictrum dioicum, meadowrue
Veronica pectinata, early veronica, speedwell
* *Viola*, violet, pansy

May

Achillea tomentosa, wooly yarrow
Actaea, Baneberry
Ajuga reptans, bugleweed
Armeica, thrift
Aurinia saxatilis, goldentuft
Asperula odorata, sweet woodruff
Aster alpinus, mountain aster
* Bellis perennis, English daisy
Cerastium tomentosum, snow-in-summer
* Chrysanthemum coccineum, painted daisy
* Convallaria majalis, lily-of-the-valley
* Dianthus barbatus, sweet William
D. plumarius, grass pink
* Dicentra, bleeding-heart
* Doronicum, leopard's-bane
Epimedium, bishop's-hat
Euphorbia cyparissias, spurge
* Geranium, crane's bill
* Helenium, sneezeweed
Hesperis, sweet rocket
* Iberis sempervirens, candytuft
* Iris, bearded iris
Linum perenne, flax
* Pulinus, lupine
Lychnis chalcedonica, Maltese cross
Malva moschata, musk mallow
* Mertensia virginica, Virginia-bluebells
* Nepeta mussinii, flowering catmint
Paeonia suffruticosa, tree peony
Polemonium caeruleum, Jacob's-ladder
* Primula, primrose
Ranunculus repens, dwarf buttercup
Saxifraga, saxifrage
Sedum, stonecrop
Thymus, thyme
* Trollius, globeflower
* Veronica, speedwell
* Viola, violet, pansy

June

Achillea tomentosa, wooly yarrow
* Althaea rosea, hollyhock
Alyssum rostratum, yellowhead alyssum
Asclepias tuberosa, butterfly weed
Callirhoe involucrata, poppy mallow

* Campanula, bellflower
* Chrysanthemum coccineum, painted daisy
Coronilla, crownvetch
* Delphinium, larkspur
* Dianthus barbatus, sweet William
Dictamnus, gas plant
* Digitalis, foxglove
* Echinops ritro, globe thistle
Erodium manescavii, heron's-bill
Geum, avens
Gypsophila, baby's-breath
* Hemerocallis, daylily
* Heuchera, coral-bells
* Iris
Lychnis, campion
* Lythrum, loosestrife
* Monarda, bee balm
* Paeonia, peony
* Papaver, Iceland and oriental poppy
Penstemon, beardtongue
Thermopsis, false lupine
* Veronica, speedwell

July

* Achillea, yarrow
* Aconitum, monkshood
Adenophora confusa, ladybells
* Althaea rosea, hollyhock
Anchusa italica, bugloss
* Anthemis, yellow daisy
Aruncus sylvester, goat's-beard
* Chrysanthemum coccineum, painted daisy
* C. maximum, shasta daisy
* Delphinium, larkspur
* Digitalis, foxglove
Filipendula ulmaria, meadowsweet
* Gaillardia, blanketflower
Geum, avens
* Hemerocallis, daylily
Lychnis, campion
Penstemon, beardtongue
* Phlox maculata, 'Miss Lingard'
Platycodon, balloon flower
Scabiosa caucasica, Caucasian scabious
Stokesia, Stokes' aster
Tradescantia virginiana, spiderwort
* Veronica, speedwell

Succession of Bloom (continued)

August

* Anthemis, yellow daisy
* Artemisia, silvermound
Chelone, turtlehead
Cimicifuga, bugbane
Coreopsis grandiflora, tickseed
Gypsophila, baby's-breath
Helenium, sneezeweed
Heliopsis, false sunflower
Hibiscus moscheutos, rose mallow
* Hosta, plantainlily
* Liatris, gayfeather
Linum, flax
Lobelia, cardinal flower
Macleaya cordata, plume poppy
* Monarda, bee balm
Phlox paniculata, border phlox
Physostegia, false dragonhead
Platycodon, balloon flower
Scabiosa, pincushion flower
* Veronica, speedwell

September

Aconitum autumnale, autumn monkshood
Anemone japonica, Japanese anemone
Artemisia lactiflora, white mugwort
* Aster
Boltonia, false starwort
Chelone, turtlehead
* Chrysanthemum
Cimicifuga, bugbane
Echinacea purpurea, purple coneflower
Eupatorium, mistflower
* Gaillardia aristata, blanketflower
Helenium, sneezeweed
* Helianthus, sunflower
Heliopsis, false sunflower
* Hibiscus, rose mallow
* Lathyrus, flowering pea
Liatris, gayfeather
Lobelia, cardinal flower
* Phlox paniculata, border phlox
Physostegia, false dragonhead
Rudbeckia, gloriosa daisy
Salvia, sage
Sedum, stonecrop
Stokesia, Stokes' aster
* Veronica, speedwell

When to Plant Outdoors. Do not try to jump the gun at planting time! Tender annuals cannot be planted until after all danger of frost has passed and the soil is warm. Half-hardy annuals can be safely planted if nights are still cool as long as there will be no more frost. Hardy and very hardy plants can be planted in early spring as soon as the soil can be worked.

How to Plant. Just before planting, the bedding plants should be well watered, as should the soil in the bed or border. Carefully lift plants from cell packs or pots, keeping the root ball intact in order to avoid damage. The best way to do this is to either gently squeeze or push up the bottom of the container if it is pliable enough, or turn it upside down to have the plant fall into your hand. If the plant does not slide out easily, tap the bottom of the container with a trowel. If the root ball is moist, as it should be, it should slip out easily without being disturbed.

Occasionally, you will find plants in a flat without individual cells. If you do, just before planting separate the plants gently by hand or with a knife so that the roots do not dry out. Other times, plants may be growing in individual peat pots. In this case, either peel most of the pot away, or be sure the top of the pot is below soil level after planting.

If roots are extremely compacted, loosen them gently before planting. Dig a hole slightly larger than the root ball, set the plant in place at the same level at which it was growing, and carefully firm

To set a container-grown plant in place, make a hole large enough to accommodate the roots without crowding and deep enough so that the plant sits at the same height it grew in the pot.

the soil around the roots. Water well soon after planting, and again frequently until plants are established and new growth has started. Then an application of soluble fertilizer high in phosphorus will encourage root growth.

To reduce transplanting shock, plant on a cloudy or overcast late afternoon. Petunias are the most notable exception to this rule, tolerating planting even on hot and sunny days.

Reseeding. Some annuals, notably impatiens, portulaca, salvia, and nicotiana, will reseed from one year to the next. As many annuals are hybrids, the seedlings may not be identical to the parent and will often be less vigorous. It is best to remove these seedlings and replant all flower beds and borders each year for maximum effect. In most areas, the seedlings will never grow large enough to be showy.

Fertilizing

Most annuals do not require high levels of fertilizer, but will do much better if adequate nutrients are available. Notable exceptions are nasturtium, spider flower, portulaca, amaranthus, cosmos, gazania, or salpiglossis, all of which do best in poor, infertile soils. With these, the fertilizer incorporated before planting is adequate. With other annuals, you can fertilize once or twice more during the growing season with 5-10-5 or a similar ratio at the rate of 1 to 2 pounds per 100 square feet. As

an alternative, you can use a soluble fertilizer such as 20-20-20, following label directions and applying every four to six weeks. Overfertilizing will cause a build-up of soluble salts in the soil, especially if it is heavy soil, and result in damage to the annuals. Overfertilizing can also result in heavy foliage growth and few flowers.

Watering

Heavy but infrequent watering encourages deep root growth. Annuals should be watered only as often as the lawn. Keep foliage dry during watering. Using soaker hoses is a good way to achieve this. However, if overhead sprinklers must be used, as early in the day as possible you should water those annuals that are disease-prone (zinnias, calendula, grandiflora petunias, and stock, in particular) so that the foliage will dry out before nightfall, lessening the chance of disease. When you use annuals for cut flowers, not watering them overhead will prevent water damage to the blooms. Where dry soil and dry skies prevail, and irrigation is not possible, choose drought-resistant annuals such as portulaca, celosia, cosmos, sunflower, amaranthus, candytuft, dusty miller, gazania, spider flower, sweet alyssum, and vinca.

Mulching

After your annuals are planted, adding a 2-inch to 3-inch layer of mulch will not only add a note of attractiveness, it will also reduce weeds and conserve soil moisture, resulting in better growth. The best mulches are organic and include bark chips, pine needles, shredded leaves, peat moss, or hull of some kind. The following year, the mulch can be incorporated into the soil before planting, thereby enriching it. Additional mulch can be added each spring, resulting in better soil structure and therefore better growth as years pass.

Weeding

In addition to supplying the basic requirements for good growth, you will want to weed your plants in order to keep beds and borders as appealing as possible. Remove weeds carefully, especially when the annuals are young, so you do not disturb the annuals' roots.

Manicuring

Some annuals, chiefly begonias, impatiens, coleus, alyssum, ageratum, lobelia, vinca, and salvia, require little care. Their flowers fall cleanly from the plant after fading and do not need to be removed by hand. Others, such as marigolds, geraniums, zinnias, calendula, or dahlias, will need to have faded flowers removed. This is known as deadheading and it keeps the plants attractive and in full bloom, while preventing them from going to seed or becoming diseased. Deadheading can be performed with pruning shears or sometimes with the fingers.

To be kept compact and freely flowering, a few annuals, primarily petunias, snapdragons, and pansies, may need to be pinched back after planting or after the first flush of bloom. As new hybrids are

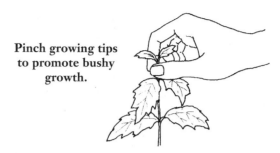

Pinch growing tips to promote bushy growth.

created, this is becoming less of a maintenance requirement. Sweet alyssum, candytuft, phlox, and lobelia may tend to sprawl and encroach on walks, the lawn, or other flowers. They can be headed back with hedge clippers. This shearing will also encourage heavier blooming.

In the fall, after frost has blackened their tops, annual plants should be removed so that the beds will not be unsightly through the winter. Better yet, turn plants under in the fall so their foliage becomes green manure to enrich the soil; if you wait until spring to do this, the dried-out stems won't decompose readily and most of their nutrients will be lost.

ANNUAL SELECTION GUIDE

Flower	Planting Distance	Maintenance	Plant Height	☀ Light	O Moisture	Ⓦ Temperature	❄ Hardiness
African daisy	8–10"	medium	10–12"	S	d	c	H
Ageratum	5–7"	low	4–8"	S, PSh	a–m	m	HH
Amaranthus	15–18"	medium	18–36"	S	d	m–h	HH
Anchusa	8–10"	medium	9–18"	S	d–a	m–h	HH
Aster	6–18"	high	6–30"	S, PSh	m	m–a	HH
Balsam	10–15"	low	12–36"	S, PSh	m	h	T
Begonia, wax	7–9"	low	6–8"	S, PSh, Sh	a	m	HH
Black-eyed Susan vine	12–15"	medium	3–6"	S, PSh	m	m	HH
Browallia	8–10"	low	10–15"	PSh, Sh	m	c	HH
Calendula	8–10"	high	3–4"	S, LSh	m d–a	c–m	H
Candytuft	7–9"	low	8–10"	S	d	any	HH

ANNUAL SELECTION GUIDE

Flower	Planting Distance	Maintenance	Plant Height	☼ Light	☽ Moisture	☾ Temperature	❄ Hardiness
Celosia	6–8"	low	6–15"	S	d–a	m–h	HH
Clarkia	8–10"	high	18–24"	S, LSh	a–m	c	H
Coleus	8–10"	low	10–24"	PSh, Sh	d–a	m–h	T
Cornflower	6–12"	medium	12–36"	S	d–a	m	VH
Cosmos	9–18"	medium	18–30"	S	d–a	m	HH
Creeping zinnia	5–7"	medium	5–16"	S	d–a	m–h	HH
Dahlberg daisy	4–6"	low	4–8"	S	a–m	m–h	HH
Dahlia	8–10"	high	8–15"	S, LSh	a	m	T
Dianthus	7–9"	low	6–10"	S, PSh	d–a	c–m	HH
Dusty miller	6–8"	low	8–10"	S, PSh	m	m–h	HH
Flowering cabbage, kale	15–18"	low	15–18"	S	m	c	VH
Forget-me-not	8–12"	low	6–12"	PSh	d–a	c	H
Four-o'clock	12–18"	low	18–36"	S	m	any	T
Fuchsia	8–10"	high	12–24"	PSh, Sh	d–a	m	T
Gaillardia	8–15"	medium	10–18"	S, LSh	d–a	m–h	HH
Gazania	8–10"	high	6–10"	S	a–m	m–h	HH
Geranium	10–12"	high	10–15"	S	m	m	T
Gerbera	12–15"	medium	12–18"	S	a	m	HH
Gloriosa daisy	12–24"	low	18–36"	S, LSh	d	m–h	H
Gomphrena	10–15"	medium	9–30"	S	m	m–h	HH
Hibiscus	24–30"	medium	48–60"	S, LSh	m	m	H
Impatiens	8–10"	low	6–18"	PSh, Sh	a	m	T
Ivy geranium	10–12"	medium	24–36"	S	d	m	T
Kochia	18–24"	low	24–36"	S	a	m–h	HH
Lantana	8–10"	medium	10–12"	S	d–a	m	T
Lavatera	12–15"	medium	18–30"	S	m	m	H
Lobelia	8–10"	low	3–5"	S, PSh	a	c–m	HH
Marigold, African	12–15"	high	18–30"	S	a	m	HH
Marigold, French	3–6"	high	5–10"	S	d	m	HH
Mexican sunflower	24–30"	medium	48–60"	S	m	m–h	T
Monkey flower	5–7"	low	6–8"	PSh, Sh	d	c	HH
Nasturium	8–12"	low	12–24"	S, LSh	m	c–m	T

ANNUAL SELECTION GUIDE

Flower	Planting Distance	Maintenance	Plant Height	☼ Light	O Moisture	ⓦ Temperature	❄ Hardiness
New Guinea impatiens	10–12"	low	10–12"	S, LSh	m	m	T
Nicotiana	8–10"	low	12–15"	S, PSh	m	m–h	HH
Ornamental pepper	5–7"	low	4–8"	S, PSh	m	m–h	HH
Pansy	6–8"	medium	4–8"	S, PSh	d	c	VH
Petunia	10–12"	medium	6–12"	S	m	m–h	HH
Phlox	7–9"	low	6–10"	S	d	c–m	H
Portulaca	6–8"	low	4–6"	S	m	h	T
Salpiglossis	10–12"	medium	18–24"	S	a–m	c	HH
Salvia	6–8"	low	12–24"	S, PSh	m	m–h	HH
Scabiosa	8–12"	high	12–24"	S	a	m	HH
Snapdragon	6–8"	medium	6–15"	S	d	c–m	VH
Spider flower	12–15"	low	30–48"	S	d	m–h	HH
Statice	12–24"	medium	12–36"	S	m	m–h	HH
Stock	10–12"	high	12–24"	S	d	c	H
Strawflower	7–9"	medium	15–24"	S	d	m–h	HH
Sunflower (dwarf)	12–24"	high	15–48"	S	a–m	h	T
Sweet alyssum	10–12"	low	3–5"	S, PSh	m	m	H
Sweet pea	6–15"	medium	24–60"	S	d–a	c–m	H
Verbena	5–7"	medium	6–8"	S	m	h	T
Wishbone flower	6–8"	low	8–12"	PSh, Sh	any	c	HH
Vinca	6–8"	low	4–12"	S, PSh	d–a	m–h	HH
Zinnia	4–24"	high	4–36"	S		m–h	T

☼
Light:
S = Full sun
LSh = Light shade
PSh = Part shade
Sh = Full shade

O
Moisture:
d = dry
a = average
m = moist

ⓦ
Temperature:
c = cool (below 70°F.)
m = moderate
h = hot (above 85°F.)

❄
Hardiness:
VH = very hardy, will withstand heavy
frost
H = hardy, will withstand light frost
HH = half hardy, will withstand cool
weather, but not frost
T = tender, will do poorly in cool
weather, will not withstand frost

PERENNIALS FOR LASTING PLEASURE

Perennials offer longevity and beauty that is hard to achieve with annuals, shrubs, or bulbs alone. Some famous perennial gardens include huge beds of perennials, but a few strategically placed plants can do wonders for a small-scale landscape. A perennial garden, like a vegetable plot, is more beautiful, productive, and satisfying when kept to a manageable size. The Chinese have a saying to which all gardeners should pay heed: "Praise large gardens, plant small ones."

Most gardeners spend a lot of time mulching, weeding, deadheading (removing faded blooms), dividing, watering, feeding, coping with insects and disease, and getting the garden ready for winter. Although low-maintenance plants, such as hostas, peonies, and daylilies, need little attention if they have been placed in an ideal spot, even these are not completely carefree.

Choosing a Site

Since flowering perennials need practically full sun throughout the day, choose a sunny spot if you want a wide range of plants to thrive. Ideally, a perennial garden will continue to grow for years in the same location, so make a note not only of present light conditions, but also try to anticipate what may happen in the future. If you or your close neighbors have young trees growing nearby, the amount of shade will increase as they grow, and some pruning, or perhaps complete removal, of trees will be necessary to ensure adequate sunlight for continued good growth and flowering of your perennials.

It is interesting to note as well that certain flowers tend to face the source of light when they are planted in a garden that is shaded for part of the day. Daffodils, most daisy-type flowers, pansies, violas, members of the sunflower family, and spiky flowers such as penstemon all have this habit, so if you plan to grow more than a few of these, position your garden to take best advantage of this tendency.

Positioning Perennials

The concept of clumping is basic to good garden design. When each plant grows separately and does not touch its neighbor, the garden has an orderly look, and each plant is allowed to reach its full potential. To create the masses of color and the shapes that make perennial borders so attractive, plant clumps of the same variety at intervals throughout the garden. The eye of the observer is drawn from one to the next and a pattern is created. One large peony, shasta daisy, or lupine clump is often large enough to establish a block or mass of the same color and height; but with smaller plants, such as *Primula* (primrose) and *Heuchera* (coral-bells), three, five, or even seven may be used. Odd numbers seem to work best in garden design.

When spacing the plants, allow plenty of room for the healthy expansion of each clump so that it will not imfringe on neighboring plants. This takes some discipline because we all have a tendency to put new small plants too close together. It is difficult to know the amount of space a mature plant will need because each one grows so differently, but as a rule allow at least 1 foot between every plant in a clump, and 2 or more feet between each clump. One vigorous-growing plant, such as daylily, peony, or gloriosa daisy, may fill an area 3 or 4 feet in diameter within just a couple of years.

Even with generous spacing, most perennials will need to be divided from time to time and the clumps reduced to a manageable size. Overgrown gardens often appear messy, but even more important, crowded plants do not grow or blossom well.

Flowering Times

The sequence of bloom is a major factor in the design of a perennial garden since it is hoped that there will be blossoms throughout the bed from early spring until fall frosts, unless a seasonal garden is planned. Most perennials bloom for only a limited period in their annual life cycle.

Just as it is difficult to estimate the height of perennials, it is also hard to tell exactly when each species will blossom. Various soils, light conditions,

and climate varia-
tions can cause
identical plants to
flower at different
times. In addition,
identical plants
may behave dif-
ferently from one
year to the next. A

Perennial phlox

warm spring may accelerate the blooms, or an unexpected late winter or cool spring is likely to delay the flowering period.

Although charts are useful as broad guidelines
(see Sucession of Bloom Guide on pages 214–216),
the expertise of neighboring gardeners will be more
precise and valuable. After a season or two of observing perennial plants in your area you will better understand how they are likely to behave in your
garden. Even so, you will probably shuffle plants
around for as long as you grow perennials in order
to achieve a satisfying design and attractive garden
appearance.

Plant Size and Blossom Considerations

A garden is easier to plan if you first select a few
basic or accent plants for each of the four blooming seasons (spring, early summer, mid-to-late summer, and late summer to fall). Accent plants are
those prominent perennials that form the backbone
of your display — strong growers that are durable,
have attractive blooms, and furnish interesting foliage for most of the season. You can plant your
entire garden with such plants, of course, but most
growers like to set some of the smaller, less robust
plants among the stronger growers to supply additional beauty and interest to the garden.

Planting the Perennial Garden

Be faithful to your plan and resist the temptation
to fill up the bed quickly with easily available perennials that you may not like in the future. There
is rarely any reason to do all your planting the same
day; rather, do it in stages as you acquire new plants.

Most newly planted borders look sparse, but if you
want a full bed the first season stick in annual bedding plants as fillers.

Because potted perennials can be planted successfully throughout the season, it's best to buy the
varieties you want in containers; they suffer no
transplant shock because every root stays intact.
Mail-order plants that are shipped bare rooted, and
other bare-rooted perennials, are best planted during spring in northern zones so they will have time
to become well established before winter. South of
zone 5, either fall or spring planting is equally good.

Plants that are freshly dug from a nursery or a
friend's garden can be moved easily in the spring,
although most perennials can be transplanted all
summer if they are handled carefully. Those that
go into a short, partly dormant period directly after blooming — bearded iris, bleeding-heart, peonies, Madonna lilies, *Doronicum*, and oriental poppies, for instance — are best moved at that time.

Setting Out Bare-Rooted Plants. When a bare-
rooted plant arrives from a mail-order nursery, the
roots are usually covered with sphagnum moss or
other moisture-retaining material. Unpack it immediately and if it looks dry, soak it in a pail of
water for a few minutes. Then plant it according to
the enclosed directions. If you must wait a few days
before planting, store it in a cool, dark place in the
packing material, but never leave it soaking in water for long periods.

Evenings or cloudy days are the best times to
plant bare-rooted stock because it won't dry out
quickly. Treat plants that are out of soil like fish
out of water. Always keep the roots covered with
moist burlap or a wet towel to avoid the drying effects of sun or wind.

Check your planting stock for broken or withered roots or stems and remove them. Dig a hole
large enough to accommodate the roots without
bending them at all. Half fill the hole with water;
the muddy mixture will help force out any air pockets that might dry out the roots. Place some of the
soil back to form a mound in the bottom of the
hole. Heavy feeders may appreciate having a bit of
well-rotted manure or fertilizer mixed with the soil
at the bottom of the hole, but fertilizer above the

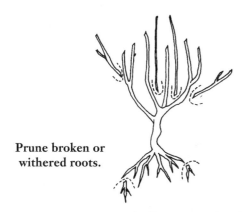

Prune broken or withered roots.

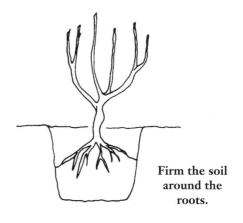

Firm the soil around the roots.

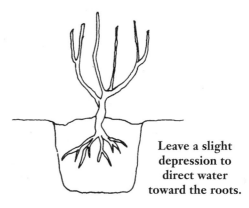

Leave a slight depression to direct water toward the roots.

roots may promote shallow root development. Gently spread the roots over the mound according to their apparent growth habit, either by spreading them outward or downward. Most perennials should be set at the same depth they were previously growing. If you aren't sure about the proper depth, arrange the plant so that the top of the root area — the bottom of the crown — is an inch below the soil. Notable exceptions to this rule are peonies and bearded iris. Set peonies so that the base of the red sprout on the uppermost part of the root is *not more* than three-quarters of an inch to an inch below the soil's surface. If it is deeper, the plant will not produce flowers for many years. Since iris roots, too, must be barely covered for best results, set the crown at ground level.

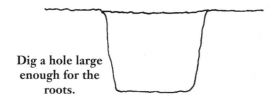

Dig a hole large enough for the roots.

Planting Balled Perennials. Dig a hole that is twice as large as the root ball; never try to squeeze the roots into a small hole. Mix a small amount of compost and a few tablespoons of manure with the soil you removed from the hole, and half fill the hole with water. Put a little of the soil you have prepared into the hole and set the plant into it. Fill the hole around the roots with the remaining soil. Firm the soil carefully, but leave a slight depression around each plant to catch the rain and future waterings.

Transplanting Potted Plants. If the soil in the pot is dry, water it thoroughly to soak the plant roots completely.

Dig a hole somewhat larger and deeper than the pot to accommodate a compost and soil mix around the root ball. Then proceed to plant just as you would with annuals (see pages 213–218).

Often perennial planting stock comes in larger individual pots. Usually the plant will pop out of its container easily if you turn it over and tap it gently on the bottom, but if it sticks insert a knife around the edge, just as if you were taking a cake from its tin. Keep the root ball intact and set it in the hole so that the top of the root ball is just beneath the surface of the soil.

EDGINGS

Edgings are needed to protect the bed from weeds which can invade the garden by sneaking their roots in subversively from the sides. An edging serves other worthwhile purposes. It defines exactly what is garden and what is not, and gives a bed a finished appearance, often making the difference between a fine garden and a mediocre one.

Install an edging when you first prepare the bed. If you want a straight-edged border use a taut string tied to stakes at each end as a guide. An irregular or curved bed can be created by using a rope, clothesline, or garden hose in a similar way.

In many gardens the edging is simply a narrow strip of bare earth about 8 inches wide between the flowers and lawn. These were once very popular and the edging tool used to create them — a sharp blade on a straight handle — was an indispensable piece of equipment for the serious gardener. Such a cut-out edging is attractive, but because it must be recut frequently, it is less used today.

Plastic, steel, or aluminum edgings take longer to install initially, but they make effective, long-lasting barriers. They are available at most hardware and garden stores, and can be bent easily to fit beds of any shape, which makes them useful for an island garden or a pathway, as well as for a straight border.

The depth of edging you need depends on the type of growth that surrounds your garden. A 4-inch depth will keep out shallow-rooted weeds and most lawn grasses, but 8 inches will do the job even better. Edgings that are 2 or more feet in depth are necessary to halt the deep-roving roots of shrubs and hedges. To install one — after marking the edge of the border — dig a ditch straight down to the necessary depth. Sink the edging vertically, but make sure the top edge is level with the soil so it won't be visible or interfere with mowing the lawn.

Many perennial beds are delineated with visible edgings, which are intended to add beauty to the garden. Bricks (placed either horizontally or at an angle), flagstones, paving blocks, tiles, concrete, wooden timbers, stone chips, and similar products are all used. If you decide to use a wood edging, choose cypress, redwood, or another long-lasting type. Treat less-durable woods with Cuprinol or another non-toxic preservative. Avoid using timbers such as railroad ties that have been soaked in creosote or other chemicals, such as pentachlorophenol, which are toxic to plants.

Attractive edgings can also be made with living plants such as a low, tight hedge of dwarf shrubs, perennials, or annuals. Boxwood, barberry, ivy, lavender, *Pachysandra*, candytuft, thyme, thrift, alyssum, and alpine strawberry are often used as edgings, especially in large formal gardens. Though beautiful, they require more maintenance than an inanimate edging, and they are not effective in keeping out weed roots.

You will find that a well-planned and maintained edging gives a finished touch to a garden, much as the right frame or matting enhances a fine painting or photograph.

Watering

Water both bare-rooted and potted plants immediately after planting. Add a bit of liquid seaweed, fish emulsion, manure, or liquid chemical fertilizer with the water to get the plant off to a fast start. After the initial watering, continue to water every day thereafter for a week or two, unless it rains hard. Once the plants are well established, water them only when the soil is dry.

Lupines serve as a good water register before and during their blooming period because, even though they have very deep roots, they are particularly sensitive to lack of water. You might want to plant a clump to provide a signal. When lupines begin to wilt, the whole garden needs watering.

Dividing Your Perennials

Each spring after the bed has become well established, some clumps need to be split up for a variety of reasons. First, the health of many types of plants will suffer if they become too large. As a plant expands, its outer roots may remain healthy, but

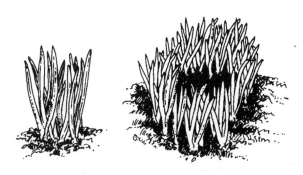

Perrenials need to be divided.

the middle portion will become crowded and starved for nutrients, moisture, and light. The roots of shasta daisies, phlox, and chrysanthemums deteriorate in the center as they grow larger, and others, such as iris and coral bells (*Heuchera*), push themselves out of the ground if they are too crowded. Another important reason for dividing is to control growth. Certain plants spread rapidly by nature, and the clumps must be divided regularly to

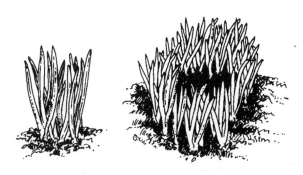

> ## MOVING DORMANT CLUMPS OF PERENNIALS
>
> 1. Prepare a hole, as for a potted plant.
>
> 2. Cut back tops to 2 inches.
>
> 3. With spade or fork, cut vertically, deep into the soil, encircling the plant, and taking with it a good-sized ball of soil.
>
> 4. Move clump to a new hole. If not planted immediately, keep the roots moist, and do not expose the clump to wind or sun.
>
> 5. Once in place, treat as a potted plant.

prevent them from crowding out their companions. A third reason for division is that you get lots of new plants to expand your own plantings, share with friends, sell, or donate to a community plant sale.

Perennials vary a great deal in their need to be divided. Most should be separated every two to four years, but some, such as chrysanthemum, *Monarda*, and *Anthemis*, need dividing every spring. Well-behaved species — *Dictamnus*, peony, hosta, and others — may thrive for many years in a clump without showing signs of deterioration.

There is some disagreement among gardeners as to what is the best time of year to divide, but those who live in the North (zones 3, 4, and 5) usually divide plants in early spring. The plants are still partially dormant then, so suffer less shock, and they'll have a long growing season ahead to become well established in their new location before winter. There are exceptions, however, *Doronicum*, *Primula*, *Pulmonaria*, daffodils, and other early-blooming plants are best divided immediately after their flowers have faded. The time to separate peonies, iris, and oriental poppies is likewise after their flowering period.

In warmer areas of the country, the general rule of thumb is to divide the spring-blossoming plants after they have bloomed, the summer bloomers in late summer or fall, and the fall bloomers in the spring, with the same exceptions as noted for peonies, iris, and oriental poppies.

Perennials are divided differently depending on how they grow. Most perennials fall into one of the following live categories.

Compact, shallow-rooted plants, such as Primulas. Dig up the entire clump and, with your hands, pull it apart into smaller plants. Pry them carefully so the roots will not be injured.

Solid clumps, such as *Aconitum, Centaurea*, day-lilies, *Dicentra*, peonies, phlox. When the purpose of your division is simply to make a healthy clump smaller, or to propagate one or two new plants, the easiest way is to cut away sections of the exterior with a spade so as not to disturb the interior. If the center of the clump is unhealthy and dying, however, the entire clump must be dug up and cut into pieces (or pried apart with a spading fork if the roots are intertwined). Discard the weak or diseased section and replant the good portions.

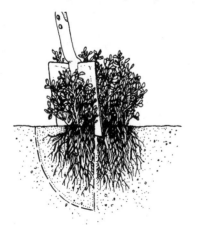

Bulbs, including lilies and spring-blooming bulbs, such as daffodils. Dig them up, separate by hand, and replant them at the proper depth. Place any tiny bulblets in flats or transplant beds for one season to allow them to come to maturity before they are planted permanently.

Ground covers and creeping plants, such as *Vinca* and *Phlox subulata*. Dig the plants up and cut them apart nearly anytime.

Plants with carrotlike roots, such as lupine and *Dictamnus*. Dig the entire plant in early spring, and cut apart each section with a sharp knife; if you do it carefully the injured plants will heal quickly.

In the spring you will find buds or sprouts on the crowns of perennials. Leave two to four in each division, as you split the clump apart. If you are dividing later, when the plant has live stems, cut them back by at least one half so there will be less foliage for the roots to support. Don't worry about the way they look; new stems and foliage will grow.

A PERENNIAL GARDENER'S CALENDAR

Obviously one garden calendar will not fit all the planting zones of the United States and Canada. Spring arrives in each zone at various time, as does the first fall frost, and each of these may differ from year to year even in the same locality. Therefore, the suggestions below — given for zones 5 through 7 — can serve only as a general guide, and must be modified to accommodate the area in which you live.

January/February

- Read garden books. Study the catalogs.
- Review your perennial record book.
- Design a perennial garden.
- Order plants, seeds, flats, starting mix, pots, labels, and stakes. Inspect new tools and equipment in hardware stores and garden centers.
- Plant perennial and biennial seeds in flats under grow lights.

March/April/May

- Clean up the garden as soon as the snow is gone.
- Uncover tender plants when the threat of hard frosts is past.
- Replant any plants that were heaved out of the ground by frost.
- Start weeding. If you use herbicides, apply the pre-emergent kinds early before new weed seeds sprout.
- Divide fast-growing perennials (*Bellis*, chrysanthemum, *Gaillardia*, geranium, *Hemerocallis*, *Kniphofia*, lily-of-the-valley, phlox, *Salvia*, shasta daisy) and others that are becoming too large.
- Transplant any perennials that you want to relocate.
- Expand the border, if necessary, and build any new gardens.
- Set out any seedlings and cuttings you started last summer, and when the weather warms up, all those you grew inside over the winter. Plant any newly purchased perennials. Be sure to label everything.
- Cultivate around the clumps and fertilize everything.
- Add mulch if the old layer is getting thin.
- Keep notes in your record book about new plantings, successes, and failures, and include comments and ideas for the future.
- Take cuttings from the tips of chrysanthemums and delphiniums to propagate new plants.
- Use a good fungicide to spray or dust hollyhocks, phlox, and any other plants that are susceptible to disease.
- Cut back the wilted flowers of early-blooming plants. Divide daffodils as soon as they die down if they are too crowded. Dig and store tulip bulbs in a cool closet for fall replanting.
- Ventilate greenhouses, cold frames, and hotbeds.
- Watch for early signs of aphids and other insects, and launch an attack if they appear.
- Stake tall-growing plants.
- Pinch back chrysanthemum sprouts to promote bushiness.
- Pick some of the buds off peonies for larger blooms.

June

- Keep fading flowers picked so the plants will continue to bloom longer, except for those you have chosen to produce seed.
- Cut back delphiniums after they have blossomed to encourage a fall bloom.
- Continue to pinch back chrysanthemums.
- Weed, spray, and water as needed.
- Layer the creeping phlox, dwarf pinks, and ground covers if you want more plants.

July

- Plant newly gathered seeds as soon as they ripen, or dry and save them for late winter planting indoors.
- Continue to weed, water, spray, and cut off all faded blooms.
- Apply liquid fertilizer or manure tea if plants are not growing well.
- Make a list of those things you wish that you'd done last winter when you were less busy and file it away for January reference.

August

- Continue weeding and deadheading as needed. Discontinue feeding.
- Be especially watchful for disease and insects; take steps to control them if necessary.

- Fill your home with perennial bouquets, share them with your friends.
- Divide and replant iris, Oriental poppies, and peonies if the clumps are too large.
- Transplant any seedlings into pots or transplant beds; or into the garden if they are large enough.
- Stake tall-growing chrysanthemums and other fall-blooming plants.

September/October/November

- Continue watering and using insect and disease control as long as necessary.
- Dig out, give away, or discard any plants that you want to replace.
- Prepare the soil for any new plantings.
- Cut back all perennials for neatness, disease control, and to prevent seeding. Leave a few inches of stem to hold snow for winter protection in northern climates.
- Do some final weeding; mulch between the plants with newly fallen leaves or other mulch.
- Cover tender perennials with evergreen boughs as soon as the ground starts to freeze lightly.

December

- Clean, oil, and store all your garden tools, Take an inventory of supplies so you can order necessary items before spring.

BULBS FOR THE GARDEN

The beauty of bulbs in the landscape is as dependable and as permanent as can be. Cut and brought indoors, bulb flowers offer color, form, fragrance and long-lasting qualities that welcome the end of winter or the glory of summer.

Crocus

Landscaping with Bulbs

Bulbs naturalized into an informal look are particularly appropriate in woodland settings. They can be planted to look natural and then left to multiply on their own to increase the colony. If you want to achieve this effect, select a spot for your naturalistic planting that will not have to be disturbed until after the flowers and foliage have faded away.

After bulbs have bloomed and the foliage has died down, you will be left with empty spaces. If you interplanted bulbs with ground cover, you have no further plans to make. In flower beds, add annuals as soon as they can be planted in spring. No harm is done to bulb plantings to overplant them with annuals.

Perennials also make excellent companions to bulbs, starting to come into bloom about the time the bulbs fade. If possible, divide and replant both the bulbs and the perennials in the spring when you can see the location of both, avoiding accidental injury to bulbs and roots.

Summer bulbs can be integrated into the landscape, filling in spaces that need color or adding a unique look to the flower bed or border. Since summer bulbs are dug up and stored each winter, you can plant them in a different spot each year, achieving a different design scheme as well.

Bulbs look best when planted in a clump. The number in the clump depends on the size of the bulb. The larger the bulb, the less you need in the clump. For large bulbs such as tulips and daffodils, you can use only three in a clump.

Formal or informal, bulb plantings look best when individual clumps do not contain more than one color and sometimes not more than one variety.

If you want your bulb plantings to look natural, arrange them in an informal design. Toss bulbs randomly onto the planting bed, and then plant them where they fall. You may have to adjust them slightly to maintain correct spacing, but the effect will not be as contrived as if you tried to arrange them.

Until you plant your bulbs, be sure to store them in a dark, dry, and cool, but not freezing, area so they will not grow, rot, or shrivel up. A good place to store them is in a covered box inside the garage; do not keep them in the house as the heat will cause them to start growing.

Spring vs. Summer Bulbs. You will hear and see the terms "spring bulbs" and "summer bulbs" whenever the subject is discussed. Spring bulbs are winter hardy; they are planted in fall, grow and bloom in spring, and then lie dormant for a year. They do not need to be dug out of the ground except when they need to be divided. Summer bulbs are not winter hardy; they are planted in spring, grow and bloom in summer, and are then dug from the ground and stored in a frost-free area over the winter until they are replanted the following spring.

When choosing bulbs for the garden, select a number of types so that you will have color from late winter until early summer. By ensuring the succession of bloom, you ensure continuous color.

Spring-Flowering Bulbs

Planting. You can plant spring-flowering bulbs any time in fall until the soil freezes; if you can't plant them all at once, start with the smaller, earlier flowering bulbs. Begin with crocus, squills, glory-of-the-snow, winter aconite, and other tiny bulbs; and with tulips and daffodils.

Bulbs in general prefer full sun to light shade. When you are planting, you may note that the bulbs seem to be in heavy shade if you are planting under a large tree. Since most bulbs bloom before trees leaf out, this shade is not a problem. However, if

BULB PLANTING DEPTHS

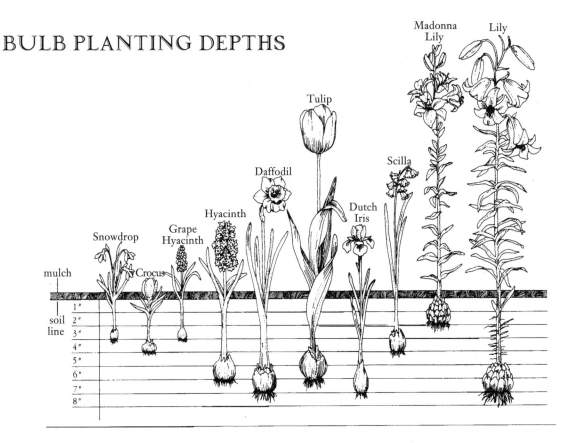

many hours of shade are cast from the side of the house, that will be a problem and the planting site should be moved.

Good soil preparation is critical to a successful bulb garden. Because bulb roots reach deep, you'll need to spade and prepare the bed to a depth of 12 inches.

The soil for all bulbs must have good drainage and aeration to prevent the bulbs and roots from rotting and to allow for pore spaces into which roots can grow. Before you plant, add organic matter equal to 25 percent of the soil volume. This organic matter may be peat moss, compost, leaf mold, or something similar.

You can either dig individual holes for each bulb, or you can dig out an entire area, put the bulbs in place and restore the soil. The latter is the better idea if you are planting a large number of bulbs.

When planting bulbs, you can use a narrow trowel or a special bulb planting tool. Some of these tools come with long handles so you do not have to bend over or kneel on the ground. Although bulbs contain their first season's food supply, fertilizing fosters future growth. To encourage root growth,

add phosphorus-rich bonemeal to the bottom of each planting hole and place the bulb on top of it. Then return the soil to the hole and tamp down gently.

One consideration with bulb plantings is the empty spaces they leave behind after blooming. If bulbs were planted into a lawn or shrub bed or under ground covers, there is no concern. A perennial border will start to fill in about the time the bulbs are finished, and annuals can be added on top of bulbs after danger of frost has passed. Be careful when planting annuals not to break or damage the bulbs in any way. Bulbs are particularly useful in rose beds as the rose foliage starts to fill out after the bulbs have passed their peak of bloom.

It's an especially good idea to mulch bulbs as mulch can help to keep the smaller bulbs from heaving out of the ground during the winter. Use an organic mulch such as leaf mold, compost, bean hulls, wood chips, or pine needles to enrich the soil as the mulch breaks down.

After Planting. If squirrels, chipmunks, or other small animals are a problem in your area and tend

ONE THING TO REMEMBER ...

True bulbs and corms should always be planted with the roots down and pointed end up.

to make breakfast of your bulbs, place the bulbs in a wire basket or cage and plant them inside this protection. Another method of keeping animals from digging up bulbs is to spread chicken wire on top of the bed after it's planted. Secure the wire at the corners, and cover it with mulch.

After planting, water the beds well and mulch them with oak leaves, bark chips, or other organic materials. One watering should be sufficient until growth starts the following spring. Label the bed so you know what's where, including the variety names. In spring, remove the mulch as soon as you see growth start, especially from low-growing varieties. Leaving mulch on too long in spring will cause foliage to be yellow and may smother the flowers of low-growing varieties.

Caring for Spring-Flowering Bulbs. Care requirements for spring-flowering bulbs are minimal, although a few chores in spring will keep bulbs at their blooming best.

You will need to add extra fertilizer each year to keep the bulbs healthy and flowering at their peak. When bulb foliage begins to emerge in spring, sprinkle fertilizer on the ground and water in. For maximum results, feed again as the foliage starts to yellow. Use an all purpose fertilizer such as 5-10-5 or a specially prepared bulb food.

Once bulbs start to poke their way through the ground in spring, they will need a lot of moisture, so water deeply if spring rain does not fall. Proper flowering and growth depend on sufficient water reaching deep into the root zone.

When tulips, daffodils, hyacinths, and other large bulbs have finished blooming, cut off the flowers (called "deadheading") to prevent seed formation and to direct energy to the bulb. Smaller bulbs can be left to go to seed, which will scatter and increase the colony. Never remove leaves until they have completely browned and pull away from the plant easily. Where neatness counts in a flower or shrub bed, braid the foliage of larger bulbs or twirl it into a circle until the foliage ripens. If the look is a natural one, the leaves can be left as is to mature. When bulbs are planted in a lawn, do not mow the grass until the foliage has browned.

Summer-Flowering Bulbs

Summer-flowering bulbs (which actually might be bulbs, tubers, rhizomes, roots, or corms) are sensitive to freezing temperatures. They must be planted in the spring and dug up and stored over winter each fall.

Summer bulbs are the perfect addition to the flower garden. They combine perfectly with annuals and perennials, offering a color, flower form, or uniqueness that completes the scene. Where a splash of red, green, pink, silver or white color is needed, fancy-leaved **caladiums** do the trick. **Canna** also has dramatic foliage and height along with its bright flowers, making it the plant of choice if you need an accent. **Gladiolus** make spectacular cut flowers. Their dramatic spikes can be grown en masse in a special cutting garden or in a mixed border. And for color all summer in the sun, whether for beds, borders, or cut flowers, **dahlias** do the trick.

Formal, frilly, rose, camellia, or carnation flowers in a painter's palette of colors describes the **tuberous begonia.** Perfect to brighten the shade, tuberous begonias do well in pots, hanging baskets, edgings, borders, and atop low walls. Often grown as houseplants, **calla** also do well in part shade.

In the **anemone** family are members which sport large poppy-like flowers. They make excellent cut flowers as well as adding very bright colors to the early summer. Paper-like swirls of petals make the **ranunculus** appear too perfect to be real. For good companionship, join them up with the fragrant, colorful and multi-flowered stems of trumpet-shaped **freesia.**

Several other lily-like bulbs can add an exotic look to the garden, including **montbretia, gloriosa lily,** and **acidanthera.** For other unusual touches, intermingle blue **agapanthus** with tricornered **tigridia.**

Planting. Soil with excellent drainage is required for summer-flowering bulbs. Before planting each spring, be sure the soil is rich in organic matter. Work the soil several inches deeper than the planting depth of the bulb.

While bulbs can be planted directly into the ground after all danger of frost has passed in spring, it is better to give some a head start indoors about four to six weeks before planting time outside. The ones most in need of this are tuberous begonias, caladiums, and calla. Start them in a flat with a growing medium of 50–50 sphagnum peat moss and perlite. Set in a warm spot with bright light but not direct sun, and keep moist. Plant outdoors after frost danger is past.

Large bulbs should be planted individually. Smaller bulbs look better planted in clumps for a massed effect.

Caring for Summer Bulbs. All summer bulbs like to be watered deeply and often. If possible, apply water to the soil, not to foliage or blooms, to prolong flowering and keep disease to a minimum. A mulch of organic material about 2 to 3 inches thick will help conserve moisture while keeping roots cool as temperatures climb. All summer bulbs also benefit from heavy feeding with a balanced fertilizer.

As cold weather approaches, all summer bulbs should be lifted from the ground and stored indoors. Tuberous begonias are best dug up before the first fall frost. Others should remain in the ground until the foliage is blackened by frost. Be careful when digging not to cut or damage the roots, corms, tubers, or bulbs.

After digging up bulbs, wash off as much soil as possible with a gentle spray of water, and dry them in a sunny spot for several days. Store bulbs in a dark, dry area at 40 to 50°F. A good method of storage is in dry sphagnum peat moss in a plastic bag.

Check the bulbs often to make sure they are in good condition. If they have started to grow, they need a cooler spot. If they have started to rot, allow the packing material to dry out somewhat.

Tulip

Some summer bulbs, primarily dahlias, benefit from disbudding. As flower buds develop, pinch out the side buds and allow only the center bud to develop. It will become much larger than if it had been left in a spray of flowers. To produce more compact, stockier plants with more flowering stems, pinch out the growing tip during the first four to six weeks of growth, encouraging side shoots.

Some taller growing summer bulbs, such as gladiolus and tall dahlias, will probably need to be staked. Stakes should be set into the ground at planting time so bulbs will not be injured later on. Stems can be secured to a stake with a twist tie; be careful not to injure the stem. Large plants or clumps of smaller plants can be staked with a hoop or cage.

Dividing. If your summer bulbs need dividing, do it in spring just prior to planting. Cut roots and tubers with a sharp knife, making sure that each division contains at least one growing shoot or eye. True bulbs and corms produce offsets called bulblets or cormels, which can be pulled from the parent and planted separately. They may not bloom during their first year of growth, but in time they will mature to full size.

BULB SELECTION GUIDE

Spring-Flowering Bulbs

Flower	Height	Blooming Time	Depth
Crocus	3–5"	Early spring	3–4"
Crown imperial *(Fritillaria imperialis)*	30–48"	Midspring	5"
Daffodil	12"	Midspring	6"
Darwin hybrid tulips	28"	Midspring	6"
Dutch iris	24"	Late spring	4"
Early tulips	10–13"	Early spring	6"
Grape-hyacinth *(Muscari)*	6–10"	Early spring	3"
Giant onion *(Allium giganteum)*	48"	Late spring	10"
Hyacinth	12"	Early spring	6"
Late tulips	36"	Late spring	6"
Snowdrop	4–6"	Early spring	4"
Windflower *(Anemone blanda)*	5"	Early spring	2"

Summer-Flowering Bulbs

Flower	Height	Planting Time	Depth	Spacing
Acidanthera	20"	Early spring	2"	5"
Anemones de Caen, St. Brigid	18"	South: Sept. – Jan.	2"	3"
Dahlia				
large varieties	48"	North: Early spring	4"	24"
dwarf varieties	12"	After last frost	4"	6"
Galtonia	40"	April – May	5"	10"
Gladiolus				
large flowering	60"	April – mid-June	3–4"	6"
small flowering	30"	Fall or early spring	3–4"	6"
Lily	3–7'	April – end of May	8"	8"
Montbretia	24"	South: Sept. – Jan.	4"	4"
Ranunculus	12"	Early spring	2"	8"
Tigridia	16"		3"	6"

BEAUTIFUL ROSES

Choosing Plants

Although roses are among the most adaptable of plants, being able to thrive in a wide range of climates from sub-tropical California to the deep-freezer climate of Alaska, some rose varieties are better adapted to certain regions than others. Also, some varieties are more disease resistant, more tolerant of neglect, and produce more flowers than others.

To find the best roses for your garden, visit local public rose gardens to see which plants are doing well in your climate. Talk with neighbors or others in your area who grow roses, discussing the ones that have done well for them. Joining the local rose society is a good way to meet these people. By joining the American Rose Society you gain access to rose gardeners and information both locally and nationwide. For information on membership, write the American Rose Society, P.O. Box 30,000, Shreveport, LA 71130-0030. The Society publishes a yearly-updated *Handbook for Selecting Roses*, which contains an alphabetical listing of rose varieties, each with a numerical rating from 1 to 10.

Based on these ratings, some of the best roses in each of the categories are:

Hybrid Teas: Mister Lincoln, First Prize, Dainty Bess, Pascali, Pristine, Granada, Peace, Precious Platinum, Duet, Color Magic and First Prize.

Floribundas: Europeana, Cherish, Simplicity, Sea Pearl, Anabell, Gene Boerner, Little Darling, and Iceberg.

Hybrid tea

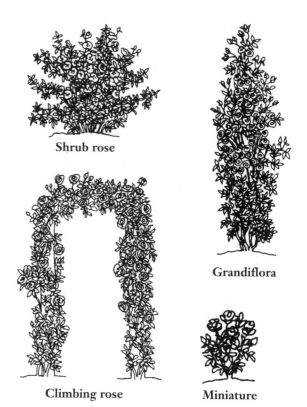

Shrub rose

Grandiflora

Climbing rose

Miniature

Grandifloras: Aquarius, Gold Medal, Pink Parfait, Queen Elizabeth, and Prima Donna.

Miniatures: Beauty Secret, Starina, Rise'n'Shine, Mary Marshall, Magic Carrousel, Holy Toledo, Lavender Jewel, Jean Kenneally, Minnie Pearl, and Pacesetter.

Climbers: Altissimo, Don Juan, Jeanne Lajoie, Sombreuil, America, Royal Sunset, and Handel.

Shrubs: Dortmund, Hansa, Ruskin, Will Scarlet, Wanderin' Wind, Golden Wings, Applejack, Cornelia, and Bonica.

Heritage: Souvenir d'Alphonse Lavallee, Apothecary's Rose, Celsiana, Crested Moss, Souvenir de la Malmaison, *Rosa hugonis*, Mme. Hardy, Nastarana, and Charles de Mills.

Location

The first consideration is sunlight. Roses need at least six hours each day for vigorous, healthy growth. If you have a choice between morning and afternoon sun, choose morning. It's important for the dew to dry off quickly as wet foliage is a breeding ground for disease. Furthermore, afternoon shade is beneficial in hot climates.

Roses are very tolerant of different soil types, especially if the soil is improved with organic matter. But good soil drainage is particularly important.

Avoid planting roses near large trees with shallow roots, such as silver maples or poplars. Also avoid planting under eaves or gutters where falling water, snow, or ice can be damaging.

An area with good air movement helps to quickly dry foliage from moisture of dew, rain, or sprinkler systems. Too much wind, especially in winter, can damage canes.

Ideal Soil

Roses grow best in a slightly acid soil with a pH of 6.0 to 6.5.

If you're going to plant roses among other plants that are growing well, then no special preparation is needed. For a newly planted area, first remove any sod. Next, till or dig the soil to a depth of at least 12 inches, removing any stones or large rocks. Spread a 4-inch layer of an organic material, such as peat moss, compost, leaf mold, or dehydrated cow manure evenly over the soil surface. Also spread on fertilizer. Till or dig this into the soil, incorporating well. The site is now ready for planting.

Planting Roses

Properly planting roses does not require any special know how. It is, however, helpful to plant bareroot roses at the correct time and to follow certain procedures to ensure success. In general, they can be planted using the same methods as other bare-rooted perennial stock. See pages 219–220.

Mulch Around Rose Plants

Mulching reduces the need for weeding and watering by inhibiting weed growth and slowing down soil moisture evaporation. Plus, over a period of time, it adds nutrients to the soil.

Before mulching, remove weeds and lightly loosen the soil surface. Spread 2 to 4 inches of mulch over the bed, leaving several inches of space unmulched around the base of each rose.

Over time the mulch will deteriorate, and some new mulch must be added at least once each year. There are a variety of materials that make effective mulches. Use whatever is locally available and cost effective. Some of the possibilities are wood chips and shavings, shredded bark, pine needles, cottonseed or cocoabean hulls, chopped oak leaves, partially decomposed compost, or ground corncobs.

These mulches will tie up soil nitrogen as they decompose, so use a fertilizer with a higher percentage of nitrogen than normally recommended for roses.

Another type of mulch that is becoming readily available is the porous black plastic or landscape-fabric mulches. These can be laid down first, then holes cut in them for planting, or they can be put down after the roses are planted. These mulches necessitate using a water-soluble fertilizer. To improve appearance, cover with a layer of bark chips or gravel.

Watering

An ample supply of soil moisture, coupled with excellent drainage, is essential for vigorous and healthy rose plants. Assuming you have well-drained soil, a good rule-of-thumb is never to let more than the top inch or so of soil dry out during the growing season. This may necessitate watering as frequently as every couple of days during the height of summer. Mulching plays an important role in conserving water, especially under these conditions.

Water in the early morning, so if foliage gets wet it can dry out before dark, thus inhibiting diseases. Water should be applied slowly to the base of the plant. Soaker hoses, drip irrigation systems, or a bubbler attachment for the end of the hose are various solutions; these also have the advantage of keeping water from splashing onto leaves and spreading diseases. Many gardeners create a basin, or dike, at the perimeter of the foliage spread to concentrate water at the roots.

Most importantly, water slowly and deeply. The soil should be soaked at least 12 to 18 inches deep. A light watering is almost worse than none at all because it encourages shallow roots that cannot adequately anchor the plant, are subject to fertilizer and cultivation damage, and need ever more frequent watering.

Roses grown in pots and tubs need very frequent watering as there is limited soil. Glazed pottery as well as wood and plastic containers lose moisture more slowly than unglazed pots. Check pots daily during the summer.

Feeding Roses

There are just about as many opinions on fertilizing roses as there are people growing them. The main agreement is that to produce that lush, healthy foliage and those gorgeous flowers, plenty of fertilizer is needed.

A basic fertilizer program for roses that repeatedly bloom throughout the summer includes three feedings. The first is in early spring, just as the buds begin to break. Plants should be fertilized again when flower buds have developed and, finally, about six weeks before the first fall frost in your area.

Additional or more frequent feeding will be needed if the soil is sandy or in warm climates with an extended growing season. Many expert rose gardeners also add several feedings of a water-soluble fertilizer during the summer.

A general-purpose dry granular garden fertilizer like 10-10-10 if plants are mulched, or 5-10-10 if they are not, will be sufficient for the first two feedings. Use a formulation without nitrogen, such as 0-10-10 for the last feeding before frost. Use about ½ cup for each rose bush. Scratch into the soil around the plant, without letting the fertilizer touch the canes or bud union, then water well.

If you decide to use commercial rose fertilizer or a water-soluble or foliar fertilizer, always follow manufacturer's directions.

The rose varieties that only bloom once, such as many of the species and heritage roses, only need to be fertilized once a year, in early spring.

Newly planted roses should not be fertilized until about a month after planting.

For those who like to use organic-type fertilizers, a popular recommendation is dehydrated cow manure and bonemeal in the spring, and fish emulsion or manure tea for the other feedings.

Pruning

Most pruning cuts are made at a 30 to 45° angle at a point ¼ inch above an outward-facing bud eye. A bud eye is a dormant growing point on the crotch between a leaf stalk and the cane, or stem. Pruning directly above a bud eye stimulates growth, which results in a new shoot. Because roses need good air circulation to prevent the spread of diseases, it's best to have most branches growing outwards from the center. This is why pruning cuts are made just above an outward-facing bud eye.

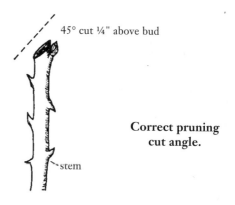

45° cut ¼" above bud

Correct pruning cut angle.

stem

A trick for minimizing injury to the plant is to have the cutting blade of the pruning shears on the lower side of the cut.

How much to prune depends on the result you want. Gardeners raising roses for competition usually prune back a great deal, as this produces a few very large flowers. Lighter pruning results in more flowers that are slightly smaller.

Pruning is done in early spring after the winter protection has been removed and just as the buds begin to swell (often about the time of daffodils blooming). Remove all wood that has died over winter. You've reached healthy wood when the center of the cane is white. As you prune, remove any

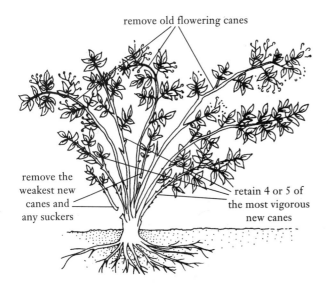

remove old flowering canes

remove the weakest new canes and any suckers

retain 4 or 5 of the most vigorous new canes

weak or crisscrossing canes, as well as any damaged or broken canes.

Through the growing season, the only other pruning necessary is to remove any diseased foliage or canes and the faded flowers, cutting the stem just above the first five-leaflet leaf below the flower. Keep in mind that taking cut flowers is another form of pruning and should be done with equal care.

cut above 5 leaves

Many of the new shrub-type roses need only minimal pruning of dead, diseased, or damaged growth. Most heritage and species roses, as well as climbing roses that bloom once a year, bear flowers on growth from the previous year. Prune these plants as soon as flowering is finished. Remove any small, twiggy growth. Cut the main shoots back by about one-third.

Most commercially available roses are produced by grafting a bud onto a special rootstock. Sometimes this rootstock will send up a shoot, called a sucker. These will have different looking leaves. Cut these sucker growths off as close to the rootstock as possible.

Preventive Pest and Disease Control

Just as with other garden plants, healthy, vigorous roses that are grown in humus-rich, fertile soil with plenty of water will be much less susceptible to pests than weak, untended plants. Also, try to choose varieties that are more resistant to pests and that are the best grade possible.

Preventive maintenance helps to keep pests in check. Immediately remove and destroy any diseased foliage and flowers during the growing season as well as in the fall before applying winter protection. Use the correct pest control as soon as pests are spotted, not after the infestation or disease has become a major problem. Many pests are prevalent just at certain times of the year, so learn to use control measures only when necessary. See chapter 5 for more on pest and disease control.

Winter Protection

Where winter temperatures do not go below 20°F., no winter protection of roses is needed. In areas with colder temperatures, varying degrees of protection are necessary to prevent the temperature around the plant from going below a certain point, to decrease the damaging effects of freezing and thawing, and to prevent canes from whipping about, which causes roots to loosen.

Preparation for winter should be done just before the first hard freezing weather in the fall or early winter. First, remove all rose leaves that have fallen to the ground around the plants as well as

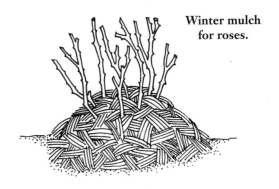

Winter mulch for roses.

any foliage still attached to the stems. This reduces places where diseases can overwinter. Apply a final spraying of fungicide. Work in a feeding of 0-10-10 around each plant, watering in well. Prune roses to one-half their height and tie the canes together with twine.

Many of the newer shrub roses, as well as some of the floribundas and miniatures, need only minimal winter protection. The following guidelines are for the widely available hybrid tea and grandiflora roses, as well as for any other rose varieties of questionable hardiness.

In areas where winter temperatures drop to 0°F., the base of each rose must be protected by an 8-inch mound of soil, coarse compost, shredded bark, or other organic material. If you are using soil, do not pull up soil from the rose bed; instead, bring it in from another part of the garden. This soil will have to be removed the following spring,

while organic materials can be spread out as mulch.

Where winter temperatures fall below 0°F., the mound is made progressively deeper, or up to 12 inches in the northern plains. Some gardeners cover this with another 8 to 10 inches of loose mulch, such as pine needles, oak leaves, pine branches, or straw. Where winds are severe, this can be contained in wire or paper cylinders. If temperatures stay below 15°F. for extended periods, caps, cones, or baskets over the two layers of mulch are recommended.

The large-flowered, repeat-blooming climbers need special care in areas with winter temperatures falling below -5°F. Put a mound of soil or organic material around the base of the plant, detach the canes from supports and lay them on the ground, covering with soil, pine branches, or mulch. A very hardy climber that does not need such protection is Dortmund.

ROSE PLANTING GUIDE

Region	Planting Time	Spacing Hybrid Tea/ Grandiflora	Floribunda
Pacific Northwest	February – March	3–4'	2.5–3.5'
Pacific SW Seaboard	January – February	3–4'	2.5–3.5'
Southwest	late December – January	3–4'	2.5–3.5'
South Central	late January – February	2.5–3'	2–3'
Mid-South	December – January	2.5–3'	2–3'
Sub-tropical	December – January	3–4'	2.5–3.5'
North Central	April – early May	2–2.5'	2–2.5'
Eastern Seaboard	March – early April	2.5–3'	2–3'
Northeast	April – early May	1.5–2'	1.5–2'

These planting times and spacing as well as rose-planting steps were developed by All-America Rose Selections, a national rose-testing organization.

CONTAINER GARDENING

Even if you happen to have large flower and vegetable beds on your property, the importance of having a few containers of plants for instant color and drama wherever it's needed can't be underestimated.

Of course, if you happen to live in a condominium or apartment or small home where space is at a premium, then container gardening takes on a new significance. Remember that you can, with patience and practice, grow almost any plants in any container that will hold soil. We are not just talking about a mix of petunias and geraniums for porch color, but anything you like: vegetables, fruit trees, lilies, shrubs, and even small trees.

The choice, in both containers and plants, is yours. And, one of the best parts of gardening in containers is that it's fun and easy to correct any mistakes. Instead of being faced with a huge drift of plants that don't work well together, if your color combination doesn't work out as you planned, you simply try again.

GETTING STARTED

Containers

Let your imagination run wild when you think about what to use for a container. You are not limited to clay and plastic flower pots. Whatever pot you choose for your garden, keep in mind that all containers should have adequate holes for drainage. Plants will eventually become weak if grown for any length of time in waterlogged soil. If you cannot drill holes in what you want to use as a planter, you can sometimes get around this by using another pot for the plants and placing that inside the container you prefer.

Another thing to remember is that a container must be the right size for the plant — or plants — that will be growing in it. This seems so obvious, but it is important. If a container is too small, the nutrients in the soil will be used up too quickly or a plant will become rootbound too quickly. On the other hand, if the pot is too large, a plant may spend all its energy on root production and not grow as it should.

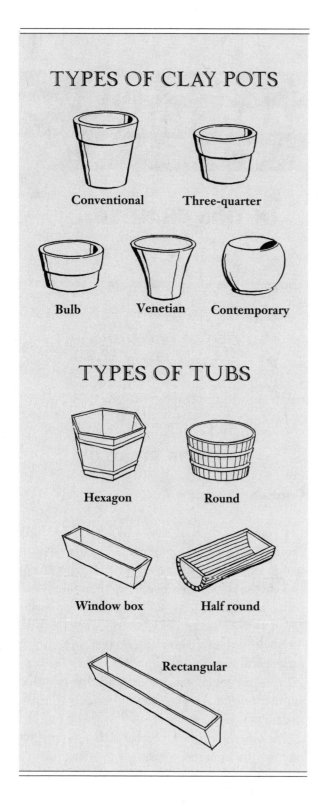

TYPES OF CLAY POTS

Conventional   Three-quarter

Bulb   Venetian   Contemporary

TYPES OF TUBS

Hexagon   Round

Window box   Half round

Rectangular

The weight of a container also needs to be considered. You don't want something that is so light that it will blow away in a strong wind or topple over, nor do you want something — if you plan on moving it — that will be too heavy to budge. Remember that once soil and compost are added to the container it gets heavier. Also, if you are in an exposed area that gets a bit of wind, be sure your container has a wide base to ensure stability.

Placing large containers on dollies makes them easier to move or rotate so that plants grow evenly towards the light.

If you are converting something to be used as a container, you may have to treat it so it lasts longer. For example, you can extend the life of a wooden container by treating it with a preservative. Avoid creosote, which is harmful to plants.

Many pots cannot be left out during a cold winter when the alternate freezing and thawing will cause them to crack. Pottery pots need to be moved inside or emptied and stored under cover. You may want to treat cast iron pots with an anti-rusting material.

Pot color is even a consideration. In warm climates, light colored containers are better. Black ones may absorb too much heat in the late-day sun.

Soil

You will need a good soil that is able to hold its nutrients and water even through hot, dry weather. Ordinary garden soil is not really suitable for container gardening. It is usually too heavy and it may contain all kinds of insects and disease. It also tends to dry out too quickly. You can use packaged potting soil made for containers, or you can make your own soil mix. A good container soil mixture includes soil, sand, peat, and other additives as needed.

The material of the container is important. The rate at which the potting mix will lose water is directly related to what the pot is made of. Soil in a terra-cotta pot dries out more quickly than it does in a plastic one.

A basic mix consists of the following:

1 part peat moss or compost
(run through a screen)
1 part garden soil
1 part builders' sand

The organic material in this mix provides body and the sand will improve drainage.

You can mix this easily in a large wheelbarrow or, if you aren't going to use all the mix at once, in a big plastic trash can. While you are mixing you will want to add a slow-release fertilizer to the soil.

You can add many things to your soil mixes. Some of the additives may be:

Humus or leaf mold. This retains moisture well and gives the soil a nice texture.

Manure. Use this in a dry, powdery form, otherwise it will overpower the mix. Filled with nutrients.

Peat moss. Holds water and any added fertilizer well.

Limestone. Reduces acidity of potting mix.

Limestone chips. Reduces any acidity and helps with drainage.

Sand. Good for drainage.

Perlite. Gives mix an open texture which improves aeration and drainage.

Vermiculite. Absorbs and retains any nutrients and moisture.

Sphagnum moss. Excellent water-retaining properties.

When you mix your own container fill, think about what you are going to plant and where you will plant. Use perlite instead of vermiculite if you get a lot of spring rain because it dries out faster.

Whatever combination you decide on, the mixing process is the same. Dump the ingredients in a pile — on the ground or in a big wheelbarrow and mix them roughly together. Dampen the mixture as you work on it. Then, as you mix, add in the ground limestone and fertilizer. The fertilizer you

choose should have nitrogen, potassium, limestone and the minor elements calcium, sulfur, iron, magnesium, zinc, copper, manganese, and boron.

Some gardeners prefer not using any garden soil in their mixes and choose instead a soil-less mix, which will be free of disease organisms and weed seeds. Mixes like Jiffy-Mix or Pro-Mix contain natural ingredients and are easy to use.

PLANTING IN CONTAINERS

It is best to wet any medium well before using it. If you buy a packaged mix you can wet it right in the bag that it comes packaged in. Put water into the bag and knead it through until evenly moist. Let the mix rest overnight before you use it. Your own soil mix needs to be moistened well before using it, too.

Planting is not difficult. You do want to try to get your plants into their new container as soon as you can after purchase.

Prepare potting soil mix before planting.

Gently tap the container to remove planting stock.

Firm soil around plants once they are in place.

Have the containers filled with the potting mix before you begin to plant — and if they are heavy be sure they are in their final position before you plant.

Remember these tips when you plant:

■ Leave 1 to 2 inches of headspace between the edge of the container and the top of the soil. This allows you to water heavily without washing soil out of the top of the containers.

■ Firm down the soil around the roots of the plants when you set them in place. This is simple to do with the heel of your hand or your fist.

■ Set plants back at least 2 inches from the edge of the container. This will help keep them from drying out in the future.

FERTILIZING POTTED PLANTS

You do need to pay more attention to plants growing in containers than to those in the borders or vegetable garden. Because of the limited volume of soil in the pot, it will dry out more quickly and need more added nutrients than the soil in the garden.

Usually, if you are using a mix that has fertilizer added to it, you will have to add fertilizer again about three weeks after you plant. And, if you have had to water frequently after planting, you'll have to begin fertilizing even sooner than that.

Once you have been gardening in containers for a while you will undoubtedly have your own system of fertilizing, but until that time, there are a couple of choices. Some people prefer to fertilize with a weak solution of fertilizer, applying it every other time they water. If you do this, use about ⅕ the amount called for on the directions for a monthly application. So, if the directions say to add 1 tablespoon to a gallon of water use the tablespoon but add it to 5 gallons of water.

Other gardeners fertilize less frequently, perhaps once a week, and still get good results. Other growers swear they have to fertilize every time they water to ensure good flowering.

These growers will often use a plant food such as Peters Professional Blossom Booster with a 10-30-30 rating and swear by it for lush flowers. You will have to experiment to see what you like. Hanging baskets sometimes benefit from more frequent feeding than other containers.

Most plants don't need large amounts of fertilizer but they do like to be fed on a regular basis. You may prefer using timed release fertilizers instead of feeding with diluted solutions. As the plant receives water, these fertilizers are released in small amounts. The easiest method is to mix a timed release fertilizer right into the soil you use. You can buy either 3-month or 12-month time-release formulas.

Organic fertilizers such as fish emulsion are also effective.

WATERING

Watering is necessary to keep container plants healthy. How much water your plants will need will depend on a number of factors: the nature of the soil, the temperature, the rainfall, the exposure of the plant to direct sun and wind, and the amount of growth of the plant.

It is usually best — if you are able — to water in the early morning or the evening. Water the plant thoroughly — until the water comes through the drainage holes. Repeat the watering again when the soil is almost dry. Use your finger to feel below the soil's surface to tell. When you water make sure you are watering the soil and not the plant's leaves.

Because of the increased heat and sunlight, you have to check container plants both in the morn-

ing and evening during the summer. But even in the spring and fall, pots can dry out quickly. Wind has a drying effect on plants, too.

The type of container has a bearing on how often a plant needs water. Plants in porous clay pots need water more often than those in plastic or glazed ones. Some gardeners like to solve this problem by planting in a plastic pot and sinking the plastic pot in a clay one, for aesthetic reasons. The space between the pots is insulated with peat moss, gravel, or perlite.

Another trick is to group small potted plants together in a larger box. This slows evaporation and decreases the need for watering often. You can, again, put peat moss or another material between the pots.

Watering cans are most often used for watering plants in containers and they are necessary to have around. On a larger scale, the garden hose is a necessary item and the many attachments for it are invaluable for the container gardener. Rigid extensions can be added to the hose to direct a flow of water above head height, which is useful for hanging plants. Mist spray nozzles can give plants the humidity they may need. There are also water breaker nozzles that deliver a high volume of water but don't disturb the soil in the container.

However you water, don't let the plants sit in a puddle. Always remove excess water from the dish under the plant — if there is one. If you cannot lift the plant to do this then get the water out with a baster or some other device. Root-killing mineral salts will build up in the water that sits there. You want to remove it quickly.

PESTS AND PROBLEMS

There's no predicting what could bother your plants, but, by taking preventive steps, you can often avoid many of the insect pests or diseases that could take over.

Of course, you need to start with healthy plants, plant them in a clean mix in clean containers, and then grow them in the conditions they prefer: sun or shade, etc.

If your container plants are attacked by bugs or disease you may have to be more ruthless in your handling of it than if you were tackling the same problem in a garden. If it is a problem found on one plant, it may be best to simply discard the plant — roots and all — before the affliction spreads. You will want to use clean soil before you re-plant.

With container plants it is often easier to pick off large pests — the caterpillars, snails, slugs — by hand and destroy them than to deal with poisons.

Problems caused by the smaller pests, such as aphids and whitefly, are harder to deal with and can cause stunted growth and can also spread viral diseases. These can be controlled by a variety of sprays made for the purpose; sometimes a stiff shower from the hose is enough to dislodge armies of tiny insects.

Mildew and black spot are apt to be found on some of your flowers, such as roses and nasturtiums, and can be controlled by spraying with a fungicide.

Water-seeking pests, such as earwigs and slugs, may be a particular problem, making a home under the dish that sits under the pot! If you use slug bait, you may want to put it on a leaf near the ground — lay your trap in the early evening after wetting the area around and underneath the containers. In the morning you can catch your critters and dispose of them.

Since container plants usually need to be watered daily, use this time to check over the leaves for any damage and under the pot for insect infestation and treat immediately. This way you should be able to avoid further more intensive damage. See chapter 5 for more on pest and disease control.

VEGETABLES IN CONTAINERS

If you don't have the space for a vegetable garden, you can rest assured that you can grow vegetables in containers. They'll be portable, they can be turned to face the sun and even brought inside if a sudden storm threatens to wreck havoc. And, vegetables are attractive while growing.

You can try almost anything in containers but you may not want to grow say, sweet corn, as the

CONTAINER VEGETABLES SELECTION GUIDE

Vegetable	Varieties	Season	Light	Space Requirements	Comments
Beets	Detroit Dark Red, Golden Beet	Cool, spring fall	Some shade	Grow in a container at least 8 inches deep	
Broccoli	Green Goliath, Bonanza Hybrid	Plant in spring	Full sun	Grow in a container at least 8 inches deep	
Cabbage	Ruby Ball, Stonehead Hybrid	Needs cool weather to mature	Full sun	Any kind of container 12 inches deep	
Carrots	Short-rooted kinds: Nantes Half-long, Royal Chantenay, Little Finger	Spring, summer, or fall		Thin early to 3 inches apart	Loose deep soil — at least 10 inches needed
Cucumbers	Bush types such as Spacemaster, with longer vines to train on a trellis	Grows well in summer	Likes full sun	Plant in a narrow, 8-inch-deep box	
Eggplant	Dusky Hybrid, an early variety		Needs full sun and warmth to grow well	Grow in a container that holds 1 to 5 gallons	
Kale	Many varieties available, check seed and nursery catalogs	Grows best in cooler weather	Will tolerate some shade	8-inch-deep container	Harvest whole plants or the outside leaves
Lettuce	Many varieties. Choose those that are slow to bolt in heat: Slobolt, Oakleaf, Summer Bibb	Early spring or fall	Will stand partial shade	Give head lettuce space, at least 10 inches apart in an 8-inch-deep box. Leaf lettuce can be closer together.	Harvest as needed.

Vegetable	Varieties	Season	Light	Space Requirements	Comments
Melons	Cantaloupes: Muskateer, Bush Star Watermelon: Burpee's Sugar Bush, Yellow Baby Hybrid	Needs summer heat	Full sun	One plant per 5-gallon container	
Onions	Many varieties	Plant in early spring	Green onions will take some shade; to mature you need full sun	Container needs to be at least 6 inches deep	You may harvest as green spring onions or let the bulbs mature.
Peppers	Many varieties of sweet bell and hot peppers.	Plant in late spring, early summer	Full sun	One plant per 3-gallon container	All varieties look good and are easy to grow in containers
Radishes	Cherry Belle, Icicle, and Scarlet Globe are old favorites that do well in pots	Plant in spring or fall	Sun	Any size container	Mix well with other plants, harvest early
Spinach	America, Melody Hybrid	Plant in spring or early fall	Need full sun — can stand some shade	Any size container	Mix planting with other greens or onions.
Swiss Chard	Rhubarb chard is good for containers and has attractive red stems	Plant in spring, summer, or fall	Will stand some shade	Any container that is at least 6 inches deep	Harvest again and again. Cut out leaves and more will grow. Good replacement for early spinach.
Tomatoes	Many selections suitable for containers: Burpee's Pixie Hybrid, Patio Hybrid, Small Fry, Super Bush, Tiny Tim		Full sun	One plant per 5-gallon container. Full size tomato plants can be grown in 25-gallon containers.	Train plant to stake and remove suckers to ensure tall growth. Harvest when small.
Zucchini, Summer Squash	Compact varieties: Black Magic, Gold Rush		Full sun	One plant per 5-gallon pot	One healthy plant will probably be all you will need.

yield isn't great and the space required is considerable. Think instead, of those vegetables with relatively small root systems: peppers, tomatoes, lettuce, onions, carrots, and eggplants.

Most tomatoes do well in containers.

Certain kinds of vegetables are made for container growth. Small, fast-growing greens such as lettuce, kale, swiss chard, and New Zealand spinach are all good choices. Fruiting vegetables that produce over a long period are also excellent choices: tomatoes, peppers, eggplant, and summer squash. Compact vined muskmelons also work well in container plantings.

Combinations in containers can work, too. Try fast-growing vegetables around the slower ones. For example, some leaf lettuce grown around an eggplant or tomato.

Vegetable containers tend to be larger than those used for ornamentals. Use something that holds from 3 to 30 gallons. Anything smaller may allow the plant to dry out too quickly, and there won't be enough room for root development.

Boxes that are 8 inches deep and 2 feet by 3 feet are good for vegetables such as beets, carrots, zucchini, and onions. For vegetables that will grow up a trellis, try an 8-inch-deep box that is narrow: 1 foot by 4 feet. And, for those crops you grow singly, such as tomatoes, peppers and eggplants, select pots that hold at least 4 to 5 gallons.

GREENHOUSE GROWING

IN THIS CHAPTER...

✔ Selecting Greenhouse Plants
✔ Greenhouse Designs
✔ Greenhouse Pest and Disease Problems

Healthy plants in a greenhouse can provide beauty and pleasure indoors and out. Plants in bloom can be brought into the house to be admired; a few weeks of dim light and dry air in the dining room won't hurt them. Hundreds of annuals can easily be started in the greenhouse to bloom outdoors from June to frost. And remember that healthy vegetables in the greenhouse can be as beautiful as any foliage plant.

Growing your own flowers and vegetables can make a big saving in cash. An inexpensive packet of seed can produce as many lettuces as a family of four could eat in a year. And a packet of celery seed could produce enough celery for a village. A pot of bulbs about to flower costs more than several dozen bulbs ordered in advance. And one bouquet would pay for all the flower seed you could use.

SELECTING GREENHOUSE PLANTS

Unless you are lucky, you will have to reach some sort of compromise between the requirements of different plants you want to grow and the conditions you can afford to maintain in the greenhouse. It is sensible to grow only those things that you are fond of, that are compatible with each other, and that do not make inordinate demands on your money or time. Local conditions — cloudy days, subzero winter weather, scorching summers — will have a strong influence on your choice of plants. But remember that different areas of the greenhouse can provide fairly different microclimates. Grow the heat-lovers at the apex, the light-lovers that can withstand cold nights at the front, the cold-sensitive light-lovers in the middle or against the back wall, and the shade-lovers down below.

Experiment with different types of plants and different regimes. You may find certain plants do better with less water or extra light or a greater drop in night temperature. Beg cuttings and young plants from your friends and see what grows well for you. You will almost certainly be able to pay them back in kind.

The tables of growing conditions included in this chapter are only a general guide; modify them as you go along. Every greenhouse has its own peculiarities of orientation, shading, ventilation, and/or soil composition. Only you can know what will grow well where and under what conditions in your greenhouse.

Tender Perennials

Tender perennials are the most common greenhouse subjects. These include most common houseplants, but also many flowering plants that could not stand the dry heat of an ordinary house. They are grown for the beauty of either their flowers or their foliage. Almost any attractive, hardy garden plants can also be brought indoors to bloom a few weeks early. You will appreciate them more indoors, and the blooms will be protected from the ravages of the weather.

Growing Conditions. Most ornamental plants will grow well in a mixture of two parts loam to one part peat to one part sharp sand. Variations from this are noted under individual entries. Seeds can be started in the same mix with some extra peat and sand. Cuttings do best in half peat and half sharp sand or in pure vermiculite.

The temperatures given are what the plants would prefer. They will accept the minimum temperature, but will often stop blooming or look unhappy if kept at that for long. If tender plants get frozen, spraying them with cold water before the sun hits them will sometimes save them.

"Good indirect light" ideally means a northern exposure with plenty of sky light and no direct sun, but partial shade cast by other plants or a place at the back of a greenhouse with a solid roof will do almost as well.

"Partial sun" ideally means shade for a few hours at midday and direct sun the rest of the time, but good indirect light all day will often do instead. Generally, foliage plants prefer, or at least accept, indirect light. Most flowering plants need lots of sunshine. (African violets, begonias, and impatiens are the major exceptions to this rule.) They will continue to grow with less light but will get long and spindly, and will soon stop flowering.

Keeping leaves clean will increase photosynthesis as well as make the plants more attractive. Wipe the leaves with a damp cloth whenever they begin to look dusty. Avoid hard water, which will leave lime spots. Half water and half skimmed milk gives the leaves a good shine. Large plants can be put outside in a gentle rain or even given a shower to clean them off.

The pot sizes given are those normally used for mature plants. Extra large specimens will of course need bigger pots. But don't put small plants into large pots. Wait till the roots have used up the available soil, then pot into the next size pot. If that is not convenient, just shake as much soil as possible off the root ball, cut a quarter to a third of the roots off with a sharp knife, and repot it with fresh soil in a clean pot of the same size. Prune the top back by about one quarter at the same time. Most plants need to be repotted or to have at least the top few inches of soil replaced annually in the early spring.

Annuals and Bedding Plants

In general, these plants are started in flats in the greenhouse to be planted out of doors in summer, but most of them can also be sown in late summer or fall to bloom indoors in winter or spring if sufficient light and heat can be given. If winter-flowering or indoor varieties are available, use them for forcing indoors in winter.

Starting Seeds. Sow the seed of annuals thinly and shallowly. Use ordinary potting mix with a bit of extra peat and sharp sand. If the seed needs light for germination, just press it gently into the surface of the soil. Otherwise cover it with a thin layer of fine peat or soil.

Cover the seed box with plastic or glass to retain humidity until the seeds have sprouted, then remove the cover and allow air to circulate. Most annuals germinate in about two weeks; bottom heat will speed them up by a few days. Transplant or thin them as soon as the leaves touch. Pinch out the growing tip to encourage branching. Gradually harden off those that are to be planted outside. Annuals are usually planted out two or three weeks after the last possible date of frost in your area.

GREENHOUSE DESIGNS

Although most people envision a free-standing building, greenhouses come in a variety of shapes and sizes. Large-scale growers may have huge glassed-in buildings, but the amateur horticulturist doesn't have to be left out. Smaller glass enclosures can be built or purchased to fit almost any circumstance. Regardless of the size of your greenhouse, plant cultivation should follow similar guidelines.

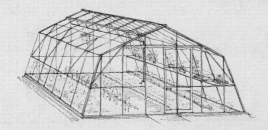

Traditional greenhouses are free-standing glass enclosures. This "Dutch" greenhouse has splayed sides, which are good for structural rigidity and increased ground planting area.

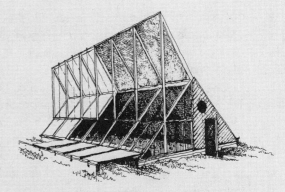

A wide-span A-frame solar greenhouse can be designed with reflecting shutters rigged to an external pulley system. This kind of shutter must be braced strongly to withstand high winds.

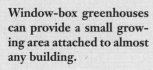

Window-box greenhouses can provide a small growing area attached to almost any building.

Lean-to greenhouses attach to the side of a building and may double as a sun room with roll-up shades to regulate light and heat.

Window greenhouses can be integrated into the design of a home to provide functional, attractive features that are ideal for plants and plant lovers, and visually interesting both inside and outside the house.

GREENHOUSE PEST AND DISEASE PROBLEMS

Your greenhouse provides good growing conditions for plants. Your greenhouse can also be a haven for many insects and diseases because their natural enemies are excluded. In an enclosed space, sprays and other cures that are effective in the garden may not be practical. A well-run greenhouse is much less susceptible to problems, so prevention is the best defense.

To Avoid Problems...

- Good ventilation discourages insects and prevents fungus diseases that thrive in stagnant, moist air.
- Clean up dead leaves, litter, and old pots that might harbor insect eggs and fungus spores.
- Check plants frequently for aphids and other small insects that cause injury *and* spread diseases.
- Once a year, disinfect the glass and surface areas with 10 percent bleach solution to kill growing fungi. Remove or cover plants that might be injured by drips or splashes. Cleaning the glass will also improve lighting and decrease the chance of condensation dripping on plants.

Whitefly

- Use only clean pots for repotting. Scrub and sterilize pots before reuse. Old clay pots should be soaked and scraped clean of any mineral crust that might keep air and water from passing through the clay.
- Use pasteurized soil for starting seeds and cuttings.
- When bringing potted plants in from outdoors, set the pots in water to the rim and soak them overnight to drown any insects in the soil.
- Do not handle plants when they are wet, because diseases are transferred more easily then.

When Problems Occur...

- If you have the space, quarantine unhealthy plants away from healthy specimens.
- Destroy badly infested or diseased plants before the problem spreads.
- After handling plants, especially after inspecting unhealthy plants for problems, wash your hands and any tools you used before touching other plants.
- For aphids and other small insects, often a good shower of water is enough to dislodge them.
- On a small scale, hand pick and destroy larger insects.

If You Have to Spray...

- Wear a respirator (not a dusk mask) and goggles. Even relatively safe pesticides and soap sprays can be dangerous in an enclosed environment.
- Spray in the late afternoon when the sun is off the plants and the greenhouse can be closed until morning.
- If your greenhouse is attached to another building, always shut any connecting doors and windows to prevent fumes from spreading to living areas.

Bulbs in the Greenhouse

In general, plants grown from bulbs, corms, and tubers will not come true from seeds. If you have extra space in the greenhouse, it is fun to experiment, but you are unlikely to improve on the parent variety.

Storing and Forcing Bulbs. Hardy bulbs (like crocus, hyacinth, narcissus, tulip) need a cold, dark rooting period. They can be forced to flower at any time of the year if the cold period can be given. Some people put pots of bulbs in the refrigerator in August or September to be sure of flowers by Christmas. For later blooming, bulbs are better left outside under a pile of leaves or straw once the weather turns chilly. You can buy specially preconditioned bulbs that need less time in the dark, so they will bloom earlier.

When the bulbs are well-rooted and leaves are 1 to 1½ inches tall, the base of the leaves should be fat with the emerging bud. At this point they are ready to come into the light, but some can be left for several weeks longer to give a succession of blooms. Give some shade for the first week indoors as the white leaves green up, then full sun at 45 to 50°F. After a few more weeks you can increase the temperature to 60°F. to speed them up, but never let them get really warm until the buds have opened. Even then, cold will prolong the life of the flowers.

Soil for Bulbs. Any good, free-draining greenhouse soil is suitable for growing hardy bulbs. Equal parts of peat, sand, and loam (or compost) is a good mixture. Many bulbs can be grown successfully in bulb fiber, peat moss with some charcoal, or even plain gravel, but they will use up all of their stored energy and are unlikely to survive to bloom another year outdoors. They are also more difficult to stake in these materials. When flowers fade, cut off only the flower head, leaving the green stalk to help feed the bulb for next year.

Vegetables in the Greenhouse

Just like garden plantings virtually all greenhouse vegetables require full sun for optimum growth. But those that are grown for their leaves or roots rather than for their fruit will usually grow moderately well, though more slowly, when partially in the shade. Winter vegetables should be well advanced by mid-autumn. They will stay in good condition but won't make much more growth in the depths of winter.

Soil. Most vegetables are grown in the standard soil mix of two parts loam to one part peat and one part sand. The depth of soil needed depends on the final size of the plant and whether most of its growth takes place above ground or below ground (carrots will obviously need deeper soil than lettuce, even though they take up less room above ground). Generally, 10 to 16 inches is sufficient, with a 2-inch to 4-inch layer of gravel or other free-draining material below.

Starting Seeds. Most vegetable seed will germinate at 50–60°F., though it will sprout sooner with more heat. A few plants absolutely require more heat to germinate; refer to the Greenhouse Plant Guide in this chapter for specifics.

GREENHOUSE PLANT GUIDE
Tender Perennials

Plant Name	Propagation by Seed	Vegetative Propagation	Growing Conditions	Comments
Asparagus Fern *Liliaceae* *Asparagus plumosus* *A. sprengeri*	Sow seed in April or May (60–70°F.). Soaking for 48 hours helps germination, which may take up to 2 months.	* Divide plants in spring.	55–70°F. (min 50°F.). Good indirect light. Keep moist except in winter.	Attractive, feathery foliage. New stems often bare at first.
Azalea *Ericaceae* *Rhododendron indicum*, syn *R. simsii* and others	Sow seed in early spring on moist peat, sprinkling sand over top (55–60°F.). Keep shaded and moist.	* Take 2–3" cuttings in spring or summer, inserting in 1 peat/2 sand (60°F.). Takes 2–3 months to root. Layer by making small slit in young stem and burying 2" deep. Sever after 2 years.	45–55°F. (min 35°F., max 70°F.). Partial sun. Does well in all-peat mixture. Keep thoroughly moist; avoid hard water.	Likes acid soil, moisture, semi-shade, and cool conditions. Prefers to be somewhat potbound. Spray daily when buds form, and keep atmosphere humid. Put outdoors in shade and keep moist in summer.
Begonia (fibrous-rooted) *Begoniaceae* *Begonia semperflorens* ("wax-leaved") and others	Sow seed in early spring (60–70°F.) on surface of soil in good light. Sprouts in 2–3 weeks. Blooms in 4–6 months. Or sow in August for winter.	* Take 3–4" cuttings any time. Root in peat-sand or water (60–70°F.). Flowers in 2 months.	60–70°F. (min 50°F.). Good indirect light. Add extra peat or leaf mold. Do not firm the soil.	Very easy to grow. Prefers warmth and indirect light, but very tolerant. Water well. Pinch back for bushy plants. Some tall species have dramatic stems and foliage. Look out for powdery mildew.
Begonia (rhizomatous) *Begoniaceae* *Begonia rex*, and others	Sow seed in early spring on surface of soil. (65–70°F.).	Divide plants in April. * Take leaf cuttings with 1" of stalk in spring (65–70°F.). For *B. rex*, nick underside of main veins and place flat on peat-sand mix; will root from each wound. When 2 or 3 leaves each, separate seedlings and pot. Take 2–3" stem cuttings of rhizomes.	60–70°F. (min 50°F.). Good indirect light.	Easy to grow. Culture as for fibrous-rooted begonias.

* Preferred method of propagation

Plant Name	Propagation by Seed	Vegetative Propagation	Growing Conditions	Comments
Begonia (tuberous) *Begoniaceae* *Begonia cheimantha* (Lorraine) *B. heimalis* *B. tuberhybrida*, and others	Sow seed on surface of soil in February (65–70°F.). Blooms in 4–5 months.	Divide tubers in March, one shoot per section. Take stem cuttings in early summer in peat-sand mix (65°F.). Pinch back and remove buds until November, then treat as ordinary tubers.	60–65°F. (45°F. in winter). 50–60°F. for Lorraine and *B. heimalis* varieties when flowering. Good indirect light. Add extra peat or leaf mold or use all-peat mix. Use high potash feed. Plant tubers concave side up, half their depth in soil.	When leaves die back naturally, overwinter tubers at 45°F. giving little water. Can store tubers in damp peat over winter. In March increase heat to 60° F. and increase watering to start growth. Keep atmosphere moist and avoid drafts. Stake large flowers. Some varieties become only semi-dormant and retain leaves. *B. heimalis* and Lorraine are winter-blooming.
Bougainvillea (paper flower) *Nyctaginaceae* *Bougainvillea* x *buttiana* hybrids *B. glabra* Other varieties take several years to flower		* 3–6" cuttings in spring or summer, with bottom heat (70–75°F.). Or 6" cuttings of dormant shoots in January (55°F.).	60–70°F. (50°F. in winter). Full sun. Water moderately; keep nearly dry in winter. 6–8" pot or deep bed.	Colorful bracts around insignificant flowers. Usually loses leaves in winter. Can get very large; prune by a third in early spring.
Bromeliads *Bromeliaceae* *Ananas* (pineapple) *Billbergia* and others	Sow fresh seed on surface in 2 peat/1 sand (80°F.). Germinates quickly, but takes many years to reach flowering size.	* Offsets produced after flowering; should be potted when leaves are 3–4" and have formed a rosette. Cut close to parent. Best done in early spring.	60–75°F. for most. High humidity; mist in warm weather. Full sun in winter, partial shade in summer. Thin-leaved varieties need less sun. Use half loam and half coarse leaf mold for soil mix. Avoid lime. Use rainwater if possible.	Most have watertight reservoir at base of leaves from which they absorb food, therefore need relatively small pots. Ethylene gas from ripe apples or banana skins will induce flowering. Most plants die after flowering.
Brunfelsia (yesterday, today, and tomorrow) *Solanaceae* *Brunfelsia paucifolra calycina*	Sow in summer.	* Take 3–5" tip cuttings in spring or summer (70°F.). When rooted, fertilize weakly, but do not pot for 3 months.	60–80°F. If you want the plant to rest, then keep nearly dry at 50–55°F. (min 40°F.) in winter. Partial shade in summer; full sun in winter. Maintain high humidity. 5–6" pot.	Flowers change color with age from purple to lavender to white; sometimes fragrant. Flowers better when rootbound. Replace soil in early spring without increasing pot size. Prune by a third to a half in early spring and pinch growing tips during summer.

* Preferred method of propagation

Plant Name	Propagation by Seed	Vegetative Propagation	Growing Conditions	Comments
Cactus (except epiphytes) *Cactaceae*	Sow fresh seed on surface of soil (70–80°F.). Sprouts in about 1 month. Transplant when ½" (may take a year). Some bloom in 3 years, some take much longer.	Divide varieties which produce offshoots in spring. Take cuttings in late spring or early summer. Cut at joint or 4" from tip. Dry for 24 hours then pot in sand or peat-sand mix.	55–70°F. (45°F. in winter) (min 35°F.). Full sun. Water moderately in summer; keep nearly dry in winter. Add extra grit for drainage. Feed only when in bud and flower; use high potash feed.	Likes well-drained soil and lots of light. Do not overpot. Make a paper collar to hold spiney plants with when repotting. Do not firm the compost, just tap the pot to settle it into place. Avoid repotting in winter. Needs very little plant food. Best outdoors in summer. Look out for soft rotting spots which must be cut away completely.
Cactus, epiphytic *Cactaceae* *Schlumbergera* (Christmas cactus) *Epiphyllum* (Orchid cactus) and others		Take cuttings at joints in spring or summer. Dry for 24 hours, then pot in ordinary cactus mix.	60–70°F., night 55°F. (min 50°F.). Partial sun in summer, full sun in winter. Add extra grit. Keep moist and maintain humid atmosphere when in bud and flower. Decrease water after flowering, but do not allow to dry out completely. Avoid hard water and excess nitrogen. 4–5" pot.	Tropical jungle plants with spectacular flowers. Good in hanging baskets when large. Can place outdoors in semishade in summer. Christmas cactus need long nights to set buds; beware of electric lights. A cold period at the end of summer will encourage bud formation of all epiphytic cacti. Do not turn plants in bud, as buds may drop off in effort to turn towards light.
Camellia *Theaceae* *Camellia japonica* *C. reticulata* *C. williamsii*, and many hybrids		* Leafbud cuttings or 3–4" cuttings of side shoots in summer (55–60°F.).	40–60°F. (min 25°F.; max 65°F.) Partial sun. Maintain humidity. Water well, but keep nearly dry for 6 weeks after flowering. Use lime-free soil, and add extra peat or leaf mold. 8–12" pots or deep bed.	Shiny, evergreen leaves with showy flowers. Early varieties will flower in winter. Will survive freezing, but buds may be damaged. Can grow to 12 feet. Trim if necessary in April. Look out for scale insects.

* Preferred method of propagation

Plant Name	Propagation by Seed	Vegetative Propagation	Growing Conditions	Comments
Carnations & Pinks *Caryophyllaceae* *Dianthus* See also Pinks, under Annuals	Sow carnation seed in late winter (65°F. until it sprouts, then 50°F.). Sow pinks seed in spring or in August for winter flowers (65–70°F.). Blooms in 4 months.	* Take 3" cuttings of perpetual carnations in winter (though will root anytime). Insert in sand (65°F. reducing to 50°F. when growth starts). Take 3–4" cuttings of pinks in summer. Pot in 1 peat/1 loam/1 sand mix. Keep in partial shade. Cuttings bloom in 4–8 months. Layer side shoots of pinks, border, and annual carnations in midsummer. Sever after 6 weeks, transplant 1 month later.	60°F., night 50°F. summer 5°F. higher (min 45°F. for perpetual carnations, others are frosthardy). Full sun.	Pinch young plants at least once (except for border and annual carnations) to ensure many flowers and bushy plants. Remove all but one bud on each stem if you want large flowers. Support stems with canes or string. Ventilate freely.
Chrysanthemum *Asteraceae* *Chrysanthemum frutescens* *C. morifolium*	Sow seed shallowly (55–60°F.). Sprouts in about 2 weeks.	Divide perennial species in early spring. * Take 2–4" cuttings and pot shallowly in sand or peat-sand mix (55–60°F.). Roots in 1–3 weeks. Blooms in 6 months.	50–65°F. (min 45°F.). Partial to full sun. Buds form only if continuous darkness for 10 hours daily. Maintain humidity. Give good ventilation. Water thoroughly, but allow to dry out between waterings.	Plant shallowly and support large plants with canes. Pinch out the growing tip for more flowers and bushier plant. Or, on standard mums, remove all but one main bud to produce a single enormous flower. Do not grow too close together or few flowers will appear. Time of flowering (2 months from beginning of 10-hour nights) can be accurately controlled by lengthening dark period in summer or giving extra light in fall. Outdoor plants are often lifted in fall to bloom indoors after frost.
Cineraria *Asteraceae* *Senicio cruentus* hybrids	*Sow April to July (55°F.) for flowers January to May. Prick out and grow outdoors over summer, avoiding hot sun.		45–50°F. until buds form, then 50–60°F. (65°F. max). Water well, but don't let them get waterlogged. 6–7" pots.	Usually bought in winter and discarded after flowering. Keep cool and humid. Look out for aphids and whitefly.

* Preferred method of propagation

Plant Name	Propagation by Seed	Vegetative Propagation	Growing Conditions	Comments
Clivia *Amaryllidaceae* *Clivia miniata*		* Remove 8–10" tall offsets after plant flowers. Insert in 4" pot of peat-sand (60–65°F.). Water sparingly. Flowers in 1–2 years. Old plants can be divided with a knife. Try to avoid damaging roots.	60–70°F. (45–50°F. in winter). Partial shade. Water and feed well in summer. Keep nearly dry in winter till buds appear. 8–10" pot.	Spectacular flowers in early spring. Prefers being pot bound. Replace top few inches of soil annually in late winter. Repot after flowering every 2–3 years. Remove fruits as flowers fade. For maximum effect do not remove offsets.
Coleus (flamenettle) *Coleus blumei* *Lamiaceae*	Sow seeds in late winter on surface of soil in good light (70–75°F.). Sprouts in 2–3 weeks.	* Take 2–3" cuttings in late summer or early spring (60–65°F.).	55–70°F. (not over 60°F. in winter). Good indirect light. Keep moist in summer, fairly dry in winter.	Brilliantly colored, fast-growing foliage plants. Pinch back for bushiness and remove any flowers which form. Best to start new plants from cuttings or seed each year.
Crassula *Crassulaceae* *Crassula argentea* (jade tree) *C. falcata* (propeller plant) *C. rupestris* (rosary vine) and others		* 2–3" stem cuttings or single leaf cuttings in spring (70°F.).	55–75°F. (45–55°F. in winter). Partial sun. Water moderately; keep nearly dry in winter. Add sharp sand to potting mix. 6–10" pots.	Succulents with unusual leaf forms. Need rest period in winter.
Crown of Thorns *Euphorbiaceae* *Euphorbia milii,* syn. *E. spendens*		* 3–4" tip cuttings. Dip in powdered charcoal and allow to dry for a day. Insert in barely moist peat-sand. Do not overwater.	65–80°F. (min 55°F.). Full sun. Water moderately; less if below 60°F. Add extra sand to soil mix and pack in firmly.	Very spiny plant with red or yellow bracts over a long period. Lower leaves eventually fall, leaving bare spiny stem.
Felicia *Asteraceae* *Felicia amelloides* *F. pappei*		* 2–3" cuttings. June for winter bloom; August for spring and summer.	45–65°F. (min 35°F.). 5" pots.	Sky-blue daisies all winter. Pinch twice before set buds. Remove flowers as they fade.
Ferns many genera and species	Reproduce by spores that produce prothalli that in turn produce little ferns.	* Some species can be divided. Best done in early spring. Take 2" tip cutting of above-ground rhizomes.	Tropical species, 65–70°F.; temperate species, 55–65°F. Medium indirect light. Humid atmosphere. Spray with fine mist in hot weather. Keep soil moist, except in cold weather. Use humusy soil.	Avoid direct sunlight. Many ferns are sensitive to air and water pollution, to chemical insecticides. Most become dormant below 50°F.

* Preferred method of propagation

Plant Name	Propagation by Seed	Vegetative Propagation	Growing Conditions	Comments
Ficus (fig) *Moraceae* *Ficus Benjamina* *F. elastica* (rubber plant) *F. pumila* (creeping fig) *F. sagittata* and others		* *F. pumila* and *F. sagittata* 4–6" cuttings in spring (60–65°F.). Larger ficuses are better air layered.	60–70°F. (min 50°F. for *F. Benjamina* and *F. sagittata*, min 35°F. for *F. pumila*). Indirect light. Water moderately (except *F. pumila*, keep moist).	An enormous range of foliage plants from trees to creepers. Shiny-leaved ficuses must be kept clean. To encourage branching of rubber plants, cut off tips and sprinkle with powdered charcoal to stop flow of latex sap. Variegated ficuses need more light.
Fuchsia *Onagraceae* *Fuchsia*	Sow seeds in spring (60°F.).	Take 3–4" cuttings. Pinch at 3".	50–65°F. (40–50°F. in winter)(min 35°F., max 70°F.). Partial sun. Feed well. 5" pots.	Pot lightly. Keep moist, but water less in winter. Too much heat will cause buds to drop, so give partial shade in hot weather. Cut back in fall or late winter. Keep cold and dry over winter. Will lose leaves. Standards need a little more heat to be sure the head is not damaged. Look out for whitefly.
Geranium *Geraniaceae* *Pelargonium domesticum* (regal pelargonium or Martha Washington geranium) *P. hortorum* (zonal or ordinary geranium) *P. peltatum* (ivyleaf geranium) and many scented-leaf geraniums	Sow seeds in early spring (60–65°F.). Flowers in 5–9 months.	* Take 3–4" cuttings in late summer or early spring, in sand or peat-sand mix (60–65°F.). Flowers in 6–8 months (3–4 months if taken in spring). Summer cuttings bloom all winter if not too cold.	60–70°F. (winter 45–50°F.) (min 35°F.). Full sun. Water thoroughly but allow to dry out between waterings. Keep almost dry in winter. Use high potash feed.	Shade only if necessary to prevent overheating in summer. Will stop flowering if too hot. Does well outdoors in summer. Cut back in fall before taking in. Pinch tips of young plants, except regals. Regals give best show of bloom but have briefer season and should be kept fairly dry for 2 months after flowering.
Gesneriads *Gesneriaceae* *Episcia* (flameviolet) *Saintpaulia* (African violet) *Streptocarpus* (Cape primrose) See also *Gloxinia* and *Achimenes* under Bulbs	Sow seed on surface of peat-sand mix (70°F.) in good light. Sprouts in about 3 weeks. Blooms in 6–10 months.	Take African violet leaf cuttings (70°F.). Blooms in about 1 year. Cut *Streptocarpus* leaves in 3" sections; insert top end up. Blooms in 6–9 months. Pot rooted *Episcia* plants at end of stolons. Divide mature plants in early spring.	60–75°F. (min 55°F.). Good indirect light. Maintain humidity. Water from below. Keep moist but not sodden. A light, free-draining, humusy soil is essential. Does well in all-peat mixture. Give very weak feed at every watering. 5–6" pots.	Does well under fluorescents. Likes warm nights. Pull off any damaged leaves; do not cut. Look out for aphids and mealybugs.

* *Preferred method of propagation*

Plant Name	Propagation by Seed	Vegetative Propagation	Growing Conditions	Comments
Hibiscus *Malvaceae* *Hibiscus rosa-sinenis*		* Take 3–4" cuttings, with heel if possible, in spring or summer (65°F.). Give weak feed for a month or two after rooting before transplanting.	60–70°F. (45–55°F. in winter). Partial sun. Water moderately when in growth; keep nearly dry in winter. 8–12" pots.	Big flowers on big plants. Pinch young plants. Can grow to 6 feet or more. Prune hard in early spring.
Impatiens *Balsaminaceae* (Busy Lizzie) *Impatiens sultanii, syn I. wallerana*	Sow seed in spring or summer on surface of soil in good light (65–75°F.). Sprouts in 2–3 weeks. Blooms in 3–4 months.	* Take 3" cuttings any time. Root in water or peat-sand mix (60°F.). Flowers in 1–2 months. 3 cuttings in a pot quickly makes a bushy plant.	60–75°F. (min 50°F., 55°F. to flower). Good indirect light. Keep moist, but water less if below 55°F. 5" pots.	Can bloom all year. Pinch back young plants. Prune old plants hard in early spring. Look out for spider mites and aphids.
Ivy *Araliaceae* *Hedera, Helix,* and others		Take 3–4" cuttings in summer. Root in water or peat-sand mix.	45–65°F. (50°F. in the winter)(min 30°F.). Keep only just moist in winter.	Will climb or trail. Wide variety of leaf shape and variegation. Look out for spider mites.
Jasmine *Oleaceae* *Jasminum officinale* *J. polyanthum*	Sow seeds in fall.	3–5" tip cuttings or heel cuttings after flowering (40–50°F.). Pinch 10". Will flower the following winter. Layer shoots in early fall; sever a year later.	5–6" pots. 40–60°F. (min 30°F.; *J. officinale* min 20°F.). Full sun. Keep moist, especially in summer. Ventilate well. 8–10" pots, or better in deep bed.	Fragrant climber. *J. polyanthum* is winter blooming. Train up wires or canes. Can be set outdoors in summer. Very vigorous. Can grow to 15 feet. Prune after flowering. For small plants, replace every 3 years.
Kalanchoe *Crassulaceae* *Kalanchoe blossfeldiana*	Sow on surface in light (70°F.). Sow February for winter bloom. May for early spring. Difficult.	3" tip cuttings in May.	55–70°F. (min 50°F.). Full sun in winter. Water moderately, less after flowering. 5" pots.	Bright red, orange, or yellow winter flowers with shiny succulent leaves. Usually bought in bud and discarded. Need long nights then short nights to flower. Look out for mealybugs and spider mites.
Lantana *Verbaenaceae* *Lantana camara*	Sow February (60°F.) for summer.	3" stem cutting in August (60–65°F.).	60–70°F. (winter 50°F.) (min 45°F.). Partial to full sun. Maintain humidity. Keep moist in summer, nearly dry in winter. 6–8" pot (up to 12" for standards).	Bright colored, fragrant summer flowers. Can grow as annuals. Pinch overwintered cuttings in late winter. Prune old plants hard in February. Look out for whitefly.

* Preferred method of propagation

Plant Name	Propagation by Seed	Vegetative Propagation	Growing Conditions	Comments
Orchid *Orchidaceae*	Propagation by seed is a difficult, highly specialized business.	Mature plants can be divided. Each piece of rhizome should have at least 1, preferably 2 or 3, pseudobulbs attached.	Temperature depends on species. Full sun in winter. Partial shade or good indirect light in summer. Terrestrial orchids — 1 coarse peat/1 loam/1 sand/1 sphagnum moss. Epiphytic orchids — 2 osmunda fiber or shredded bark/1 sphagnum moss, or 1 coarse peat/1 perlite/1 sphagnum moss. Allow soil nearly to dry between watering, then soak well. Needs little plant food. A foliar feed once a month should be enough.	Avoid stagnant air. Most species like a lot of heat if there is sufficient humidity (from 70 percent up to 100 percent for tropical species). Remove damaged roots and pack soil in firmly when repotting. Do not water newly planted orchids; mist daily for 3–4 weeks. Many orchids have a dormant period in fall or winter when they require very little water. Epiphytic orchids grow naturally on trees and suffer greatly if their roots are kept wet. Grow them on a piece of bark, a wooden basket, or special perforated pot for sufficient aeration.
Passiflora (Passion flower) *Passifloraceae* *Passiflora caerulea* *P. edulis*	*Sow in spring (65–70°F.).	* 3–4" stem cuttings in summer (60–65°F.). When rooted give weak feed till winter, then keep fairly dry. Pot in early spring.	60–70°F. (winter 50°F.) (min 40°F.). Partial sun. Keep moist in summer, nearly dry in winter. Maintain humidity. 8" pot.	Extraordinary flowers thought to represent the Passion of Christ. *P. edulis* has more attractive leaves and delicious fruits like pale green eggs. Fast-growing climbers. Prune hard in early spring, cut side shoots to 2–3". If frosted, plant will often send up new shoots from base. Look out for spider mites.
Philodendron *Araceae* *Philodendron*	Nonclimbing varieties can be propagated by seed. Sown in April (75°F.).	3–6" cuttings in June or October 70°F. Some species can be divided.	55–65°F. (min 50°F.). Good indirect light. Add extra peat to soil. 10–12" pot.	Keep soil and atmosphere moist, especially in summer. Most need staking; damp moss on stake will encourage aerial roots.

Pinks
See Carnations and under Annuals

* Preferred method of propagation

Plant Name	Propagation by Seed	Vegetative Propagation	Growing Conditions	Comments
Poinsettia *Euphorbia* *Pulcherrima*		Take 3–6" cuttings in spring; dip in powdered charcoal (60–65°F.). Keep fairly dry until well-rooted, then water young plants freely.	Winter 55–60°F., rest of year 60–75°F. Full sun in winter, partial sun in summer. Allow soil to dry between waterings, then water well.	Not really worth keeping for a second year, but if you want to try, keep just moist in winter; gradually dry off after flowering. Cut back to 2" from base. Start watering again in April. Keep humid atmosphere when growing. Can be put outdoors in summer. Needs long nights to flower. Provide 2 hours extra darkness from October on to produce flowers by Christmas. Commercial growers use dwarfing hormones to keep plants short.
Primulas See under Annuals				
Salvias *Lamiaceae* *Salvia argentea* *S. fulgens* *S. patens* *S. rutilans*	Sow seeds in March (65°F.).	3" cuttings April or September (55–60°F.).	50–60°F. (min 35°F.). Water well in summer; keep nearly dry in winter. 6–8" pots.	Brilliantly colored red or blue flowers. Can be made to bloom indoors in winter, or grown for summer garden. Pinch. Prune to 4–6" in February. Look out for spider mites.
Schefflera *Araliaceae* *Schefflera actinophylla,* syn. *Brassaia* *actinophylla*	Sow fresh seed with bottom heat (70–75°F.).	Air layer.	60–70°F. (min 55°F.). Good indirect light. Water moderately; keep nearly dry in winter. Maintain humidity. 8–10" pots.	Shiny leaves and attractive structure. Keep leaves clean. Can grow to 6 feet. Difficult to propagate, easiest to buy small plants.
Snapdragon See under Bedding Plants				
Solanums and Capsicums *Solanaceae* *S. capsicastrum* (winter cherry) *S. pseudocapsicum* (Jerusalem cherry) *C. frutescens* (ornamental pepper)	Sow shallowly in March (60–65°F.). Pinch.		70–80°F. (55–60°F. in winter)(min 50°F.). Full sun. Water well. Maintain humidity. 4–6" pots.	Ornamental fruits in winter. Will fruit again if pruned hard, potted, and put outside for the summer. Keep fairly dry to rest in spring. Mist plants while flowering to encourage fruit set. Look out for spider mites and whitefly.

* Preferred method of propagation

Plant Name	Propagation by Seed	Vegetative Propagation	Growing Conditions	Comments
Wandering Jew *Commelinaceae* *Callisia* *Setcreasea* *Tradescantia* *Zebrina Purpusii*		Take 3" cuttings in summer. Root in peat-sand mix or just water (60–65°F.). Three in a pot will quickly produce a bushy plant.	60–75°F. (min 50°F.). 4–6" pots.	Hard to keep for more than a few years, but easy to propagate. Pinch young plants to promote bushiness. Remove any nonvariegated shoots. Water freely in summer, less in winter.
Wax Plant *Asclepiadaceae* *Hoya carnosa* *H. bella* (miniature)		Take 3–4" cuttings of mature stems in summer. Root in peat-sand mix (60–65°F.). Layer shoots in spring.	60–70°F. (winter 55–65°F.) (min 45°F.). Full sun in winter, partial shade in summer. Maintain humidity. 6–10" pots	Fragrant flowers drip sweet nectar. Pinch back young plants, but do not prune older ones. Keep moist in summer, cooler and drier in fall and winter. Dislikes root disturbance.

Annuals & Bedding Plants

Plant Name	Growing Temperature	Sowing Conditions	Date to Sow for Blooming Season
Ageratum *Asteraceae*	45–60°F.	65–75°F. in light	August for spring, February-March for summer
Alyssum *Brassicaceae*	45–60°F. TPS	65–75°F. in light	August for winter, March for summer
Aster *Asteraceae*	60–70°F.	65–75°F.	August for winter, December for spring, February for summer
Baby's-breath *Caryophyllaceae* *Gypsophila elegans*	60–70°F.	70–75°F.	September for November
Begonia See under Tender Perennials			
Black-eyed Susan *Acanthaceae, Thunbergia alata*	65–70°F.	70–75°F.	March for summer
Browallia *Solanaceae*	55–70°F.	70°F. in light	February for summer July for winter
Calendula *Asteraceae*	40–55°F.	65–75°F. in dark	January for spring March for summer August for winter

TPS = tolerates partial shade

Plant Name	Growing Temperature	Sowing Conditions	Date to Sow for Blooming Season
Candytuft *Brassicaceae, Iberis*	45–60°F.	60–65°F.	December-February for summer Fall for spring
Cosmos *Asteraceae*	55–65°F.	60–70°F. (max 70°F.)	March for summer October for spring
Dusty Miller *Asteraceae, Artemisia,* *Stelleriana*	50–70°F.	60–70°F. in dark	February-March for spring
Forget-me-not *Boraginaceae, Myosotis*	40–60°F. TPS	70–75°F.	Use early flowering variety Takes 4 months to bloom August for winter
Heliotrope *Boraginaceae*	45–65°F.	60–65°F.	February for summer July for winter Cuttings bloom in 4–6 months
Lobelia *Campanulaceae*	50–60°F. TPS	60–75°F.	February for summer September for winter December for spring
Marigold *Asteraceae, Tagetes*	50–65°F. (min 45°F.)	65–70°F.	February for spring April for summer August-September for winter
Nasturtium *Tropaeolaceae*	45–60°F.	55–65°F. Hard to transplant, use peat pots.	August-September for winter February for summer
Nemesia *Scrophulariaceae*	50–65°F.	60–65°F. in dark	July for winter March for summer January for spring
Pansy *Violaceae*	45–60°F.	60–70°F. in dark	December for spring March for summer July for winter
Petunia *Solanaceae*	45–60°F. TPS	0–70°F. on surface	November for spring March for summer
Phlox *Polemoniaceae*	50–60°F.	55–65°F. in dark	March for summer September for spring
Pinks, and Sweet William *Caryophyllaceae, Dianthus*	50–60°F.	65–75°F.	March for summer
Portulaca (moss-rose) *Portulaceae*	50–70°F.	65–70°F. in dark	March for summer
Primula *Primulaceae, P. kewensis,* *P. malacoides, P. obconica,* *P. vulgaris*	45–60°F. TPS Add extra peat *P. vulgaris* will stand frost.	60–70°F. in light	March for winter

TPS = tolerates partial shade

Plant Name	Growing Temperature	Sowing Conditions	Date to Sow for Blooming Season
Salpiglossis *Solanaceae*	55–65°F. (min 50°F.) TPS	65–70°F. in dark, on surface	February for summer September for winter December for spring
Salvia *Lamiaceae*	55–60°F.	70–80°F.	March for summer
Pincushion flower *Dipsacaceae, Scabiosa*	50–60°F.	65–75°F.	March for summer
Schizanthus *Scrophulariaceae*	45–60°F.	in dark	August for spring June for winter; pinch often
Snapdragon *Scrophulariaceae* *Antirrhinum majus*	45–65°F. TPS	70–75°F. in light	Sow anytime for flowers in 3–4 months (up to 6 months in winter)
Stock *Brassicaceae* *Matthiola*	50–55°F. (min 45°F., max 65°F.)	70–75°F.	January for summer August for winter
Sweet Pea *Fabaceae* *Lathyrus odoratus*	45–55°F.	55–60°F. in dark	January for spring June for fall August for winter
Sweet William, See Pinks			
Tobacco Plant *Solanaceae, Nicotiana*	45–60°F. TPS	65–70°F. in light	March for summer August for spring
Zinnia *Asteraceae*	60–75°F.	65–75°F.	April for summer August for winter

Bulbs

Plant Name	Planting Time	Planting Depth	Growing Conditions	Propagation	Comments
Amaryllis *Amaryllidaceae* *Hippeastrum*	September-October for February-March (treated bulbs for January).	Half bulb depth	60–70°F. (min 55°F.). Full sun. Feed after flowering.	Detach 1½" offsets as growth begins. Grow on, will flower when 3–3½". Sow seed in March (60–65°F.), takes 2–8 years to bloom.	Keep fairly dry after leaves yellow, very dry if below 55°F. Water sparingly when new growth appears, usually early winter. Water more after bud appears.
Anemone *Ranunculaceae* *Anemone*	September-October for January-March.	2"	50°F. (60°F. when in flower). Full sun.	Sow seed in late summer; takes several years to bloom.	Needs good drainage. Water sparingly until growing well. Reduce water in winter.

Plant Name	Planting Time	Planting Depth	Growing Conditions	Propagation	Comments
Crocus *Iridaceae* *Crocus*	September-October for December-February (8–10 weeks in dark plus 2–4 in light).	Just cover corm	35–45°F. in darkness until well rooted. Then 50°F. in full sun.	Offsets will bloom the following year. Sow seed in summer, takes 2–4 years to bloom.	Winter-flowering varieties will be ready first. Species crocus have smaller but more plentiful flowers than hybrids. Do not try to mix colors as they are likely to bloom at different times.
Cyclamen *Primulaceae* *Cyclamen*	August for winter.	Leave half of corm showing	Day, 55–65°F. Night, 50–55°F. Good, indirect light or partial sun. Use ordinary potting mix. Maintain humidity.	Sow seed in August or September (60°F.). Takes up to 2 months to sprout, 15–18 months to bloom. Can take leaf cuttings with a bit of corm attached.	Keep moist but provide good drainage and avoid wetting corm. Keep fairly dry and allow to rest after blooming. In August, as new leaves appear, repot if necessary and begin watering to restart growth.
Freesia *Iridaceae* *Freesia*	August-November for December-April.	1"	Day 65°F., night 50°F. (min 45°F.). Full sun.	Sow seed in spring (60°F.). Do not transplant. Takes 9–12 months to bloom.	Water sparingly until buds appear. Best discarded after blooming. Support leaves and flowers with canes.
Gloxinia, Achimenes *Gesneriaceae* *Sinningia speciosa* *Achimenes*	January-April for summer.	Gloxinia crown level with surface. Achimenes 3–4 rhizomes per 4" pot. Lay horizontally ½" below surface.	Day 65–75°F. Night 65°F. (min 60°F., max 70°F.). Partial shade or good indirect light. Water well. Maintain humidity. 5" pot.	Divide tubers or rhizomes in March. Root 2–4" stem cuttings in June with sliver of tuber attached. Sow gloxinia seed in fall or winter (70°F.) in light. Takes 6–9 months.	Needs humid warm atmosphere, but avoid wetting leaves. Gradually dry off when leaves yellow, then store at 50–60°F. in darkness. Repot and begin watering sparingly in early spring.
Iris *Iridaceae* *Iris reticulata* and others	November-January for February-April.	Leave tip of bulb showing.	40–50°F. until buds color, then 60–65°F.	Divide tubers after leaves die back. Offsets will bloom in 1–3 years.	Buy specially treated bulbs for forcing. Not as easy to grow as hyacinths and narcissi.
Narcissus *Amaryllidaceae* *Narcissus*	September-November for December-March. (Tazettas 5–8 weeks after planting; others 8–10 weeks in dark, plus 3–4 weeks in light).	Leave tip of bulb showing.	35–45°F. in darkness (except for Tazettas, which can be placed immediately) until well rooted, then 50–55°F. in full sun till bloom, then 60°F.	Offsets will bloom in 1–2 years. Sow seed in summer when ripe; takes 3–7 years to bloom; usually poor quality.	Buy specially prepared bulbs for very early flowers. Tazetta narcissi (with several flowers on one stalk, e.g., Paper white or Soleil d'Or) will bloom sooner than others. Plant in sand, gravel, bulb fiber, or soil. Keep some in dark longer for succession of blooms.
Tulip *Liliaceae* *Tulipa*	September-October for January-February (8–12 weeks in dark, plus 3–5 weeks in light).	Leave tip of bulb showing. Put flat side of bulb toward outside of pot.	35–45°F. in darkness until well rooted, usually 8–10 weeks; then 50–60°F. in full sun.	Some produce offsets that will bloom in 2–3 years. Sow seed in summer to bloom in 5–7 years; usually poor quality.	Single and double earlies will bloom soonest and are easiest to force.

LAWNS AND LANDSCAPES

Planning is a very important step in landscaping your own garden. Some people think that because they aren't experts or master gardeners, they can't design a home landscape — but this isn't true. Anyone can do it. Keep in mind that a plan is essential if you are to achieve two important goals: a yard that is both good-looking and convenient to use.

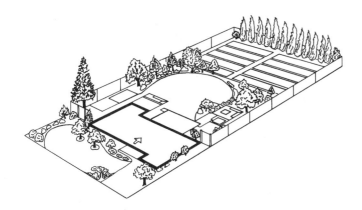

PLANNING YOUR LANDSCAPE

Survey: What Have I Got?

The first step is to determine and record what you already have. Observe the land in the yard — is it level or bumpy? Are there steep slopes, and if so, in what direction? What kinds of trees and shrubs do you have? How large are they? Have they been fertilized and pruned over the years, or are they a mass of tangled branches? Are there "weed" trees

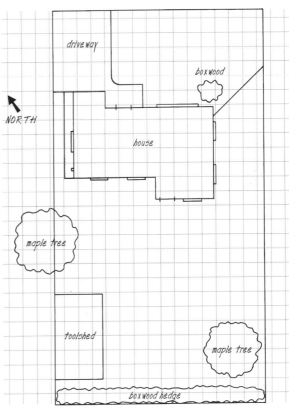

A scale drawing translates your rough sketch into an exact plan of your property.

and shrubs sprouting here and there? Are gardens already established? What is growing in them? Do you have undesirable views, or a lack of privacy? Are there fences, walls, paths, or driveways?

Now make an accurate "map" of your lot. Begin by taking some graph paper (the grid lines makes it easy to draw to scale), a tape measure, a pencil, a ruler, and, of course, an eraser to clear up mistakes. Measure and mark down the property line on the graph paper. Next, draw in the house with its existing driveway, entrance doors, deck, porch, patio, or other architectural features. Finally, indicate on your map any large trees that may be on the property. Don't add anything else: just draw the large plants and objects that are there.

Next, find out what the climate is like. If you are new to the area, consult your local extension agent for weather records, and check them out at garden centers and with your neighbors.

Finally, walk around the neighborhood, observe other front yards, and find out if there are any unspoken rules about certain plantings on your street. For example, does every front yard have to have a purple-leaved plum to give uniformity to the neighborhood and thus make the whole street beautiful? If all the other yards are open and unfenced right out to the sidewalk, you won't want to put up a fence or a hedge around yours and spoil the overall pattern. On the other hand, every yard on the street may be quite different. The important thing for you is to take a look. By observing your neighbors' gardens you can also learn what successes and mistakes have been made. Best of all, you may see plants with shapes and textures that you like and want to use in your own garden.

Dreaming: What Do I Want?

The second stage of planning is to sit down with your family and write down everyone's needs, wants, and expectations for the new garden. Consider which things are really necessities and which are perhaps just "wants." The important thing is that the garden should fit your family's life-style and reflect its personality.

Now, before going any further, think of your

LANDSCAPE WISH LIST

✔ Front yard should reflect the friendliness and warmth of our home, inviting our friends and neighbors to come in and join us.

✔ Area on right side of house should be screened in some way to eliminate eyesores in the service area, where we have tool storage and trash cans: would shrubs be better than a fence?

✔ Left side should be an open expanse of lawn.

✔ Shrubs (or beds of annual flowers?) will serve to suggest a division of the left side lawn from the rear area.

✔ Backyard should be an extension of our life inside the house: a place for entertaining and for evening family meals: a playing area for the children and their friends, including a sandbox now and perhaps a pool when we can afford it: space for frisbee playing and volleyball: flower and vegetable gardens--- fit in as many activities as possible without having the area look crowded or allowing activities to encroach upon each other.

whole property as being broken into three distinctly separate sections: the front yard, the backyard, and the side yard. All of them are adjacent to your house, but each serves a very different purpose. You must be clear in your own mind how you will use each of these sections before you decide how to plan and plant them.

The front yard is often referred to as a public area because it is between your front door and the street. It is not only for you to enjoy, but also for your neighbors and others who walk by. Even though some of the plants in your front yard may match those in your backyard, the overall design should be simpler and should provide harmony and unity between the garden and the house. A rule of thumb in landscaping a front yard is to keep it simple and low maintenance, yet pretty and colorful. It should complement the neighborhood's landscaping style, yet have its own personality so that it not only welcomes the members of the family home every day, but also invites friends and visitors to the house. Remember, too, that the planting you do in the front of the house is to be fairly long-term.

Consider carefully the growth habits and height of trees you wish to use. A common mistake in landscaping a front garden is choosing the wrong trees and planting them in the wrong place. Oversized trees often occupy the whole front yard, where their roots ruin the lawn and sometimes extend into and crack the foundation of the house or sidewalk.

Another common mistake is to choose a kind of shrub that grows too fast, overshadowing the windows, cutting out the natural light, and blocking the view. Sometimes too many things are placed without any design or plan at all, or plantings are clumped together and end up looking like a jungle. Some people cover their yards with bark mulch or wood chips and plant two evergreen shrubs in the middle, while others put a small fence in front or plant a tall hedge along the property line. Either of these plans blocks the openness and gives a feeling of confinement. Yet a whole front yard with nothing but lawn looks very boring.

Depending on the size and layout of your property, the functions of side and back yards may vary, but both are a very different story from the front yard. In general, the back yard, is for the family's private life — for relaxation and entertaining, almost a roofless extension of your living room or den. It can be a bit more complicated than the front, because it serves more functions as a garden and private outdoor living area, with a place for the children and pets to play, as well as areas for flowers, vegetables, and fruit. A rough way to decide how to allot space in a small yard for all these different functions is to set aside about one third for the lawn and shrubbery, one third for the vegetable garden, and one third for a deck or open area.

The side yards might be used for utility/work areas, with places for your garbage, tools, mower, perhaps a storage shed, and possibly a hard surface to work on. In other words, here is a place where you can be messy, unseen from the front yard or the back.

Planning the Design

Once you have your survey and wish list, it is time to get out the graph paper plan of your property as it now exists. Fit a piece of tracing paper over the original and trace over the lines. On this tracing paper, you will start your new design, including all the new ideas you would like to incorporate into your yard: fence, patio or deck, children's playhouse, lawn, flower beds, and trees.

Design for Low Maintenance

You can make things easier for yourself right from

Common Landscaping Mistakes:
An oversized deciduous tree blocks the entrance, while the roots of both it and the large evergreen on the corner will inevitably spread into the foundation of the house; the shorter evergreens along the other side of the house have been allowed to grow over and hide the windows.

LANDSCAPING TIPS

Choose plants that are native to your area

This includes the lush wild things that you can transplant from roadsides and wooded lots (do be careful about collecting protected species or collecting from private or restricted lands). Many improved hybrids are relatives of your native plants.

In the Southern United States, the high humidity and heavy rainfall support magnolias, palms, and pine trees. Improvements on these native plants have produced more attractive varieties that still tolerate the clay soil and summer heat of that region.

Plant your local nursery's version of these native plants and you'll already have Mother Nature on your side. There's no need to apologize for your soil or climate when the plants you choose already have their ancestral roots buried in your dirt.

The same idea works in the arid Southwest. Heat-loving wildflowers like yucca spring up even in the desert. Why fuss with watering worries for thirsty plants when you can have drought-resistant wildflowers instead? Any plant that survives in the desert will do just as well when ignored in your unwatered garden.

Make the most of what you've got

Is there a low wet spot in your yard that rots the roots of every plant? Plant a bog garden with moisture-loving lilies, wild irises, and pretty astilbe.

Is the soil dry and rocky out front? Put in a rock garden with gravel-loving alpine plants and sedums.

Too much shade? Plant a woodland garden of ferns and bleeding-heart or a more formal display of begonias, lobelia, and hosta.

Does a steep slope or hillside make gardening a terror for you? Turn the terror into terracing and display roses, grapes, or a garden of blooming vines on the site.

Work with what you've been given, and Mother Nature may reward you with less maintenance and more original landscape design.

Repeat your successes

Most homeowners plant too many different kinds of plants and end up with a confused collection. It makes good design sense to repeat the same trees or shrubs, especially in a formal front-yard design.

- If a plant survives happily in your yard, reward it by inviting its relatives to move in, too.

- If your lilac bush blooms beautifully each spring, don't just brag about it — put in a lilac hedge.

If pine trees survive your cold winter winds when everything else is blown to bits, use pines to form a screening hedge.

If you've discovered irises blooming in an overgrown or neglected corner of the yard, then get more irises, or peonies, or whatever it is that blooms in that spot without making any demands on your precious time.

Whatever grows well, plant more of it. You don't need a lot of different kinds of plants as long as the plants you have look great.

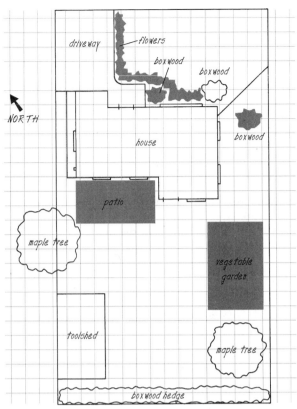

Sketch plants into your home landscape plan.

the very beginning if you choose only plants that will be relatively easy to grow. For instance, plant perennials that do not need to be supported with stakes and ties. Check with your local extension agent or nursery to be sure, *before* you plant, that you are choosing varieties that will do well in your climate zone; this will prevent disappointment as well as the unnecessary loss of plants and consequent work of replanting.

A time-consuming gardening chore is watering. The best way to get around this is to design your landscape with native plants that will thrive on average local rainfall. If your climate is dry, plant drought-resistant species, which are likely to be more successful anyway. Otherwise, if you simply must grow exotics or have a putting-green lawn in the desert, you can install sprinkler and drip irrigation systems. Drip systems are available in most garden centers or from mail-order catalogs. Designed to deliver measured amounts of water either underground or on the surface, these systems are usually as easy to install as a garden hose. Underground sprinklers can also be easily installed to help carry out watering jobs efficiently and with a minimum of effort. Plant most of your annual flowers close to the edge of the lawn where they can share the ample watering of your lawn sprinkler. If your garden is large, install a watering system right in your shrub and flower bed. Use a soaker hose, or drip system, to carry out vegetable and rose garden watering. Most plants stay healthier when water is directed toward the roots rather than the leaves, and less water is wasted than with aerial sprinklers.

If the landscape permits, try to keep the grade of your garden level overall. It is true that terraces and small hills make a landscape more interesting, but they are more labor-intensive and harder to maintain. Carefully select plant material so that as plants develop, their varying sizes and shapes will simulate different dimensions and levels.

Other elements you may want to consider in your landscape design are shade and ornamental trees, stonework, ponds or water courses, fences, steps and walkways, a gazebo or swing chair, terraced gardens (if your yard is on a slope), vegetable gardens, fruit tree orchards, and flower beds or border gardens.

Remember, you won't achieve a beautiful new landscape around your house overnight, especially if you do it yourself. Do it step by step. Take your time and enjoy the all-important planning stage. It might take a few years to complete, but it won't exhaust you, and it won't exhaust your pocketbook either. Everything takes time. The plants will take time to grow. But by doing it yourself, it will be *your* perfect garden, custom-built for *your* family's pleasure.

ESTABLISHING AND GROWING A HEALTHY LAWN

Step-by-step landscaping requires you to mark out the lawn first on your plan. Then the shrubs, trees, flowers, pools, and other focal points will easily fit into place around and within it.

A healthy lawn in your backyard gives the feeling of a big green carpet that is an extension of your living area. It helps to keep down dust and constantly freshens the air with oxygen. In a home garden, flowers, flowering trees and shrubs, and spring bulbs will give you seasonal splashes of bright color; but the lawn will give you an all-season treat (at least in many parts of the country) with its soft green, eye-pleasing color always a focal point in your garden, highlighting everything around it.

A lawn in the front yard, no matter how big or small, is not only a visual delight, but also the best solution to cover the area between your door and the street. In most residential areas, an open front yard with a green lawn is the most popular design. It links homes within neighborhoods together, making the street look wider and neater. In extremely dry, cold, shaded, or other conditions where grass won't grow well, you can get a similar effect by planting a groundcover that's better suited to the area.

Installing a New Lawn

The best times to sow a new lawn are spring and fall. In the fall, however, do not leave it until too late as it will need a week or more to germinate and six weeks or more to grow to maturity. Timing will depend on your local area, so check with your local extension agent about what you can expect from the weather.

The actual installation is not a very difficult chore nowadays, because you can usually rent the equipment you need when you purchase lawn seed and fertilizer from your garden center.

Prepare the Soil. Careful soil preparation is essential in building a fine lawn. Whatever preparation you put into your soil will show in years to come. Loosening up the soil is a hard chore, and this is where a rototiller is useful. Set the blades to cut into the soil 6 inches deep. Till the area in a criss-cross pattern, as this really does chop up the soil better than going in the same direction all the time.

When the soil has been tilled, remove all the roots, stones, and other debris. Next, give the area a good raking and continue to remove debris that

The area to be seeded for a new lawn should be tilled first in one direction and then at right angles to the first.

appears.

After raking, give the whole area a fine grading. The easiest way to do this is with an old tire attached to a rope. Letting the tire lie flat on its side, draw it over the whole seedbed several times to level the hills and bumps. The excess soil from high spots will collect in the center of the tire and lawn on a gentle grade and build a dry creek bed into your landscape plan at the lowest end so the excess water can drain away.

When the grading is finished, give the whole area a good watering. Sprinkle it thoroughly once a day for at least a week or two. The water will help settle the freshly tilled soil and encourage the weed seeds that are hiding in the soil to germinate.

Three weeks after the first tilling, repeat the tilling, raking, and grading procedure once more. This second tilling and grading not only loosens up the soil better, but also kills all the young weed seeds that have germinated as well. I would not use an herbicide to help clear the soil of weeds. Not only will it affect the germination rate of the grass seed, but traces of it will remain in the soil for a year or more and kill some of the new grass seedlings as well as the weeds. After the second tilling you may consider adding some new topsoil, either to raise the ground level, if needed, or to add some better soil to the area if yours is particularly poor. A layer of topsoil is also an easy way to hide the installation of an underground sprinkler system.

Now is also the best time to test the pH, or acidity, of the soil. This you can easily do by purchasing an inexpensive soil-testing kit at your garden center. Soil that tests below 7 pH is acid; if the pH value goes below 5, the soil will not sustain a luxurious lawn. You can decrease its acidity by adding lime. Lime has other benefits as well; it alters the mineral structure of the soil so some kinds of minerals are more readily available as food for plants; it makes some harmful soil elements powerless; it improves soil texture by helping to break down clay and compact sand; and it helps soil bacteria convert valuable nitrogen into plant-food form.

A rule of thumb is to spread between 50 and 80 pounds of lime per 1,000 square feet of lawn to decrease the soil's acidity. You may wish to experiment by applying lime in a limited area and retesting the soil after a period of time to determine the effect.

In addition to correcting the soil's acidity, you may have to improve its texture. If you have an extremely heavy, claylike soil with poor drainage, instead of putting in an expensive arrangement of drain tiles, you can try to amend the soil with some manure, compost, coarse sand, or even very well-rotted sawdust — peat and vermiculite are far too expensive — or compost, which will also improve the nutrient composition of the soil. Or, you can add a new topsoil mulch, 2 inches deep over the whole area.

All of this may seem like an awful lot of time and energy spent in preparation, but it is much easier to build up the soil and level the ground *before* the grass is established, and the more care you put into the preparation, the less maintenance you will have in the long run.

Choosing the Seed. There are two major groups of lawn grasses. The cool season grasses are sold for the northern two thirds of the United States. The majority of the grass mixes used in the Northwest are fine fescue, rye, and bluegrass. The grasses used in Hawaii and the lower third of the United States are warm-season varieties, such as Bermudagrass, zoysia, and St. Augustine. These grasses flourish from March through August; in the fall they turn brown and go dormant.

Cool-season grasses, because of their very nature, grow best and more rapidly in the spring and fall — March through June and September through November. They are dormant in the winter months, and then in the hot summer they become almost dormant again. They should be fed regularly in the cool seasons during the periods of their most rapid growth, but not so much in the summer. Likewise, warm-season grasses need to be fed during their period of growth, March through August.

Local garden centers sell only lawn grass mixtures that are appropriate for the conditions in their particular planting zone of the country. The available mixtures or blends are almost always mixed by a commercial wholesaler who chooses the varieties of seeds that assure continuous growth for particular climatic needs. Don't try to mix your own blend; leave it to the experts.

Before buying seed, you should answer the following questions. First, is the lawn in full sun or partly shaded? Second, do you want a lawn with a fine texture and soft green color, or do you want a deeper green, coarser mixture that is probably more rugged for family use? Third, how much grass seed do you need? Always purchase a little more than seems necessary. When you buy the lawn seed, read the label carefully and make sure you understand what type it is. The more expensive grass seed is always the better buy because it is almost totally free of weed seeds as well as seeds of undesirable coarse grasses.

Fertilize Before Planting. At the same time that you are buying the seed, you may want to purchase some fertilizer. Commercial preparations of 12-4-8 or 10-5-5 contains a good amount of phosphate for lawn seed. (The numbers indicate percentages of nitrogen-phosphorus-potash.) Phosphate promotes germination and encourages the formation and development of healthier, stronger roots. Use a fertilizer spreader to distribute the fertilizer evenly all over the seedbed area before you actually sow the seed. The amount you should use will be written on the side of the bag. Be careful and don't overdo it. Too much fertilizer will only burn young seedlings, and the excess may leach out and contaminate groundwater.

Sowing the Seed. After the fertilizer has been applied, broadcast the lawn seed evenly over the whole area. For a regular-sized home lawn, the best tool for broadcasting lawn seed is a hand-cranked spreader. This is a spinning disk that throws the seed out in an arc about 5 to 6 feet in diameter. Control the cranking at a steady speed and walk at a steady pace, which will ensure that the seed is evenly spread. Touch up the edge with a bit of hand sowing after you have finished with the spreader. Do your best to prevent the seed from going beyond the staked-out edge of your new lawn or it will create a big weed problem in your flower or vegetable area later.

After the seed is sown, walk backward over the seeded area using a garden rake to rake in and evenly spread the fertilizer and seed as you go. You walk backward in order to work yourself out of the area and to avoid making footprints in the seedbed. Rake gently and lightly, in a row-by-row pattern, making sure you don't overlap where you have already raked. Go over the area only once — that's enough. This gives the seeds better contact with the soil around them so that germination will be more uniform and the new grass will appear in a fine, overall pattern.

After Planting. Use a thin layer of mulch to protect the newly sown seed and to keep the soil moist. The best mulching materials are seedless hay (especially where heavy rain or runoff may wash away the loose soil) or moist peat moss. Be sure to keep peat moss moist as you spread it, so that it will not dry out and form a crust. It is hard to spread peat moss evenly by hand, so use a special drum-style roller, which you can rent from your local garden center, to spread the peat moss thinly and evenly over the whole area. The surface of the drum is covered with a metal fabric, the mesh of which is just large enough to sift the peat moss through. Fill the drum and spread the peat moss by pulling the drum behind you in a row-by-row fashion that eliminates your footprints in the seeded area. The roller makes this hard chore a cinch.

It's important to keep the soil moist until the seed germinates. Under average conditions, you'll probably need to sprinkle the whole lawn with a

An old tire pulled over the freshly tilled area does the job of leveling out the hills and hollows. Go over the entire seed bed several times.

fine spray of water for about half an hour twice a day. Do this for a week, cutting down to once a day for another week. Be sure to keep track of the time, and move the sprinkler from location to location to give the whole lawn an even watering. Later, you can cut back even more, depending on weather and local conditions.

With such good care, your new lawn will germinate evenly within as little as seven days.

Taking Care of a New Lawn

The newly germinated grass seedlings are so tender and delicate that they can be easily crushed by people, pets, and equipment running on them. So, to protect the newly emerging blades, it is wise to fence the new lawn temporarily with sticks and string. Keeping the soil moist is very important also. Too little water will create bare spots, and too much or uneven watering will also damage the new lawn, especially in the first months after the seeds have germinated.

Check your new lawn daily. Never let it get too dry. Weeds will show up in the lawn from the very beginning, but don't panic. If you try to pull them out too early, you will also pull up many good grass plants with the weeds. Later on, the mowing will kill many of the weeds or, after the grass is established, you can start on weed control.

Mowing. Six weeks after you sow seeds, the lawn grass will grow to be more than 3 inches tall. By then, too, it should have developed a healthy root system, and it is at this stage that you start the mow-

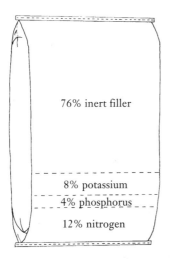

76% inert filler

8% potassium
4% phosphorus
12% nitrogen

A bag of 12-4-8 fertilizer.

ing. Every mowing will encourage the secondary growth of lawn grass, so it will grow thicker after each time. Use a hand mower for the first few mowings. It is lighter and easier to control than a power mower and less likely to damage the new blades of grass and the soft ground. Once you feel the ground has settled down enough, you can use a power mower. In either case be sure the lawn mower blades are sharp; dull blades may actually tear up young plants. Continue to mow the new lawn weekly. This will encourage the rhizomes and stolons to develop and make your lawn grow into a thick, lush green cover.

Fertilizing. New lawns require more feeding than established lawns. Apply a special lightweight, slow-releasing, non-burning, high-nitrogen fertilizer as soon as the first mowing is finished. Keep feeding

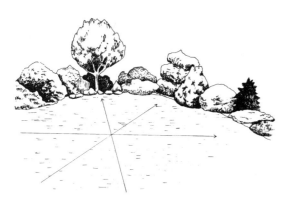

To avoid "stripes" in your lawn, alternate the direction in which you mow week by week.

monthly for three to four months; the amount you feed each time should be half or even less than half of the amount recommended on the label. No matter how hard you worked on the soil preparation, you may find that some areas show up uneven in color. Each time you fertilize, give the lighter spots a little bit more; this way you will help to provide a more even growth overall.

RENOVATING AN OLD LAWN

Improving a poorly growing lawn is not as difficult as you might think. Generally speaking, the cause of the problem is simply neglect. If the lawn is really bad, you may need to aerate the soil or de-thatch it, or, in some really poor spots, reseed. All of these are major renovations.

Weeds

Before you assemble an arsenal of herbicides or spend hours of back-breaking labor pulling individual plants, there are a few things you should know about weeds. First, since nature tries to cover every inch of soil with something green, unwanted plants will fill in where grass isn't growing. Second, just because a plant isn't the species of grass you originally intended doesn't immediately mean you have to get rid of it. There's no crime in leaving a few weeds scattered over the lawn (they're still green). Third, the conditions in which grass thrives aren't always hospitable to more opportunistic plants, so a naturally healthy lawn is less susceptible to hostile weed takeovers. And finally, if your lawn isn't healthy, the type of weed growing there is often a good indicator of what the problem is. Fortunately, most of the growing conditions for a healthy lawn aren't so inviting to weeds.

Know Your Enemies. The first step in getting rid of weeds is identifying them. Weeds tend to fall into a few basic categories: *Narrow-leaf weeds* look like grass, but not the kind you want in your lawn. *Broad-leaf weeds* are easily identifiable; among the most common ones are dandelions and plantain. *Annual weeds* grow one season and die, leav-

SPOT-SEEDING A LAWN

Prepare the Spot

Spot-seed when you need to re-establish small areas of lawn, such as thin or tire-damaged sections. The simplest way to spot-seed is first to pull out the weeds, and then to scratch up the soil with a heavy metal dirt rake or cultivating tool. If there is already some good grass growing, carefully work around it.

Next, mix 1 part sphagnum peat moss with 2 parts good garden soil to get it light and spongy. Add 1½ cups of balanced organic fertilizer per bushel of soil, making sure that whatever fertilizer you use has plenty of phosphorus to stimulate root growth. "Starter fertilizers" are meant to be used with seed or sod, and are high in phosphorus, so use one of these if you can. Spread this mixture over the bare spot until it is slightly higher than the soil level of the surrounding grass. If possible, gently mix it into the scratched-up original soil. This way there won't be extremely good soil sitting on top of bad soil.

Plant the Seeds

Now sprinkle on your seed. Use a seed type similar to the existing grass, unless it was the wrong grass to begin with. Don't skimp: 15 to 20 seeds per square inch is right. Bury the seed ⅛ to ¼ inch into the soil. Dragging a spring rake with the tines inverted is a good way to work the seeds deeper without pulling them away. Now gently tamp the soil until it's level with the surrounding soil. Don't tramp hard enough to compact the soil, because you want water to soak in easily. Throw some extra seed just to the outside of the spot-seeded area. This helps the new grass blend in better when it grows.

Bigger Problems

To repair deeper damage, such as tire ruts, tamp the soil mix more firmly before adding the last inch or two of soil. This way you won't sink into the ground when you walk on it later. If the ruts are quite deep and you want to conserve your mix, fill the bottom of the ruts with good soil and put the mix on top.

ing seeds to germinate the following year. *Perennial weeds* may drop seeds every year, but they spread primarily by underground roots that live through dormant seasons even when the tops die back.

If you don't recognize a particular weed, you might find it in a field guide or dig one up and take it to a local nursery, lawn-care professional, or agricultural extension service for identification and preferred growing conditions. In general, southern grasses prefer hot, drier weather and turn brown in winter. Certain broad-leaf perennials grow from seed in bare, infertile, sandy, or acidic soils. Broad-leaf annuals tend to thrive in cool, moist, shady areas with slightly acid soil.

Treat the Problem. The best way to combat weeds is to maintain a thick and healthy stand of grass. If your weeds thrive in acid soil, add some lime to neutralize the acidity. If they like it dry, water the lawn more. Annuals can sometimes be halted by regular mowing before they have a chance to produce seeds.

For a few scattered weeds, hand pulling or digging is usually the best solution. It may be difficult to get rid of deep-rooted perennial weeds that are apt to grow back from tiny root pieces left in the soil. A good trick here is to dig out as much of the root as you can, then pour boiling water in the hole to kill off the rest of it.

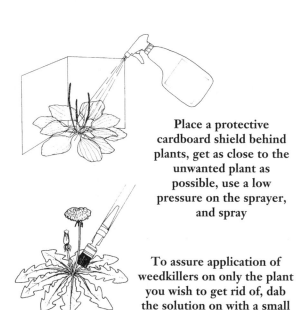

Place a protective cardboard shield behind plants, get as close to the unwanted plant as possible, use a low pressure on the sprayer, and spray

To assure application of weedkillers on only the plant you wish to get rid of, dab the solution on with a small brush.

Herbicides. For many years, lawn-care professionals have relied on chemicals to kill weeds. While many commercial products claim to be safe and biodegradable when used correctly, there is always a danger of toxic reactions and environmental contamination. To date, there are no natural products that can be spread over the whole lawn and kill only the weeds without harming the grass.

If you must use an herbicide, proceed with caution. Spot killing individual plants tends to be saf-er, easier, cheaper, and more effective than covering the whole lawn.

Choose products carefully, use them wisely, and then try to improve the lawn conditions so you won't need them again. There are several kinds of herbicides.

Pre-emergent herbicides are spread on the lawn to create a film that kills annual weeds before seeds sprout.

Post-emergent herbicides come in two forms and are applied directly on weeds, mostly broad-leaved kinds, that are up and growing. *Systemic* formulas are absorbed into the system of the plant and kill the whole thing. *Contact* formulas smother the leafy tops of the plants, but are not effective on plants that may grow back from thick root systems. Although post-emergent formulas are suppose to be safe for lawn grass, if the grass is already stressed and unhealthy, the herbicide may destroy the lawn.

Non-selective herbicides will kill any vegetation they are applied to, including lawn grass. Newer products on the market claim to be environmentally safe and break down in the soil to permit reseeding within a few days.

Thatch

Thatch is a layer of dead plant material on the surface of the soil. When it is allowed to build up more than ¾ inch deep, it slows or even stops the penetration of water, air, and fertilizer into the soil. The lawn then begins to show dry, dead patches; when you walk on the lawn, the ground feels springy.

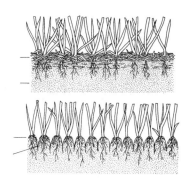

The turf above has thatch, that below is free of thatch

Dethatching should be done every three to four years. You can rent a dethatching machine, which is about the size of a lawn mower and is quite easy to operate. It has 8 to 12 blades that cut through the thatch and bring it to the surface. After all the thatch is removed, apply fertilizer, and water the lawn daily. It takes about six weeks for the lawn to recover completely, but this simple process will make your whole lawn look and feel brand new.

Aerating and Improving the Soil

Aerate by renting an aerator-spiker from the garden center. This tool takes out little cores of soil about ½ inch in diameter and 2 to 3 inches long. Next, to benefit the roots, add a top dressing of sand and peat, plus some good topsoil mixed with some processed organic manure, such as steer or chicken manure; this will fill in the holes made when you aerated. For a home garden, use mature, well-processed manure purchased from a garden center, rather than raw manure from a farm. Raw manure may contain weed seeds and other debris or, if very new, may burn plants. Processed manure mixes well with the peat/sand/topsoil blend and is easy to spread by hand. Broadcast the mixture by hand over the whole area and then brush or rake it in. This also helps to fill in dips and hollows in the lawn and generally to level it off.

GROUND COVERS FOR PROBLEM AREAS

Sometimes it is just about impossible to coax a desirable lawn grass to grow. Perhaps the growing area is too dry, too wet, or too shady. The best shade grasses you can find won't survive under an old tree, and the tree's roots stick up into the lawn to make your job even more difficult. Bare soil is an eyesore on your property, and kids constantly track it into the house. If you can't easily change the conditions that are preventing grass from growing, or if you don't want grass at all, a simple solution is a ground cover, a mulch, or both.

What is a Ground Cover?

A ground cover is a bed of low-growing, spreading, or multiplying plants. These plants fill in areas rapidly and will grow under conditions that make grassy lawns impossible. They also require very little maintenance. Ground covers are not used solely for difficult lawn areas. They are often included in landscape designs as part of bed or foundation plantings. Oftentimes they provide erosion protection.

Most ground covers will grow rapidly to fill open spaces.

Any plant that tends to spread and isn't too high can be used as a ground cover. You can be very imaginative with your choice as long as it will grow under its planting conditions. Lilies, ferns, herbs, flowers, vines, bulbs, and even special grasses can function as ground covers. Small shrubs such as low-growing junipers or euonymus will spread over a slope or bed with or without rerooting along the way, and can still function as ground covers.

Planting Procedures

If you want ground cover you'll have to get rid of whatever grass you have in the planting area. This shouldn't be too difficult — sometimes a quick scraping with a hoe is all you need. Other times the grass must be dug out, tilled under, or covered over.

To encourage a ground cover to grow well, you'll need to prepare a bed 6 to 8 inches deep. If you're competing with tree roots, add soil and organic matter to build up the bed. In other situations you can turn over or till up the soil. Whenever you are making a new bed, mix in at least 2 inches of organic matter. Use aged leaves, clippings, sawdust, compost, manures, and peat moss. If some of the materials aren't aged enough (not

COMMON GROUND COVER PLANTS

Bugleweed (*Ajuga*). Ajuga is found in all but the hottest climates. It is a 6-inch plant which spreads quickly by its roots and produces dark blue flowers. It tolerates both sunny and shady conditions.

Candytuft (*Iberis sempervirens*). This 8-inch evergreen is popular because of its clusters of white flowers in May and June. It spreads

Candytuft

slowly by above-ground runners, grows in the sun or shade, and will grow in most of the United States.

Common violet (*Viola papilionaceae*). This 5-inch to 8-inch plant grows in sun or shade. Although it can be a nuisance in a lawn, it makes an excellent ground cover — spread rather fast by dropping seeds — and produces pretty flowers. Quite hardy.

Violet

Creeping lilyturf (*Liriope spicata*). This beautiful evergreen grows in the mid-Atlantic and southern climates. It has lavender, bell-shaped flowers on spikes up to 15 inches tall. Liriope tolerates sun or shade, heat, salt, drought, and poor soil. Some people actually use it as a grass because it has similar foliage.

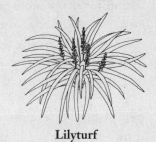

Lilyturf

English ivy (*Hedera helix*) or **Baltic ivy** (*Hedera helix* cv. 'Baltica'). A creeping ground cover that can also be a climbing vine, English ivy forms a thick (9-inch), fast-spreading ever-

English ivy

green mat that turns slightly purple in the winter. Ivy roots quickly as it spreads, so it is very useful on slopes.

Japanese spurge. (*Pachysandra terminalis*). An 8-inch evergreen with dark, glossy leaves, pachysandra will grow in shade or sun in all but the extremely hot or cold sections of North America. It prefers a moist, loose soil and spreads slowly with underground roots and stems to form new plants. Occasional cutting back will accelerate spreading. The white flower spikes are barely noticeable.

Japanese Spurge

Lily-of-the-valley (*Convallaria majalis*). You need well-drained soil for this very fast-spreading, 6-inch-tall plant. It spreads by underground stems and dies back each fall. Each May or June it produces wonderfully scented white, bell-shaped flowers. It grows in sun or shade.

Lily-of-the-valley

MORE COMMON GROUND COVER PLANTS

Myrtle or periwinkle *(Vinca minor)*. This is a 4-inch to 9-inch evergreen with oval leaves along a wiry stem. Its light, violet-blue flowers bloom in late spring and early summer. *V. minor* spreads both by roots and above-ground runners. It will prevent erosion once established, and it can grow in sun or shade in a slightly moist soil. It will survive as far south as the Gulf Coast.

Myrtle

Stonecrop or Live-forever *(Sedum)*. There are many varieties of sedum, noted for their fleshy, swollen leaves indicative of many plants that have to survive in sunny, dry conditions. They take the full sun. Some varieties have colorful flowers, and a few are evergreens.

Stonecrop

even partially decomposed), add a high nitrogen fertilizer to speed up decomposition. Let it work a couple of weeks before planting.

Most ground covers need a good soil to help compensate for the poor conditions that caused you to plant them to begin with. The better soil will help the ground cover establish itself quickly, and will facilitate spreading and multiplying. You should build up a bed higher than the lawn so it will drain easily, and for aesthetic purposes as well.

The smaller the plant, the closer the spacing in the bed. Keep the plants from drying out. A 1-inch to 2-inch layer of shredded wood mulch will conserve moisture and discourage weed growth.

Ground cover plants are not as durable as a thick lawn. They should not be walked on much, if at all. If you need a path through a section of ground cover, install stepping stones.

SHRUBS FOR YEAR-ROUND APPEAL

Shrubs are among the most versatile of garden plants. They can fill the landscape with color, shape, and texture all year long — flowers in the spring, lovely foliage in the summer, berries and bright leaves in the autumn, and distinctive shapes and evergreen leaves in the winter.

Lilac and azalea blossoms

Shrubs have an added virtue of fast growth, sometimes maturing in as little as five years and lasting for many more years, with relatively little care. Some, in fact, require no care at all!

A shrub is usually defined as a plant that has multiple trunks or stems and does not grow to a height of more than 20 feet. Of course, nature sometimes doesn't choose to go along with such well-planned categories. But we can safely say that shrubs are woody and perennial, or will live for more than two years.

Shrubs include both evergreen and deciduous plants, those that drop their leaves in the fall. But when we speak of flowering shrubs, we usually mean deciduous shrubs. Shrubs can grow in all parts of the United States and Canada, although most shrubs will fail if the temperature drops to 40 or 50°F. below zero. Some shrubs are native plants, such as bayberry, sumac, and witch hazel, but many of the familiar shrubs, such as lilac and forsythia, come from China and Japan.

Designing with Shrubs

When you have a list of shrubs you like, remember to consider both the nature of the plant and the function you want it to perform in the landscape. Some flowering shrubs are so lovely they can stand alone as a specimen plant, but many shrubs can serve more than one purpose. They may also provide a protective screen from a neighbor, act as a wind-break, or provide berries to feed hungry birds. Shrubs can hide things such as compost piles or garbage cans. They can even define areas and give you instant outdoor "rooms" with the right planting.

Size and Shape. Consider the plant's ultimate height and shape before planting. Some plants that grow in neat compact shapes give a more formal look, while those that run rampant in their growth habits will give a more informal feel to a landscape. A line of boxwood will look very different from a hedge made of lilacs, though each is lovely in its own right.

When combining shrubs in your garden, be careful to not mix too many different shapes together. One rule landscapers go by, at least for an informal planting, is that you can combine two shapes in a single planting but almost never three. For example, planting low spreading shrubs with tall pyramid shapes would work well. But if you introduce a third shape, such as a formal mounded shape or a weeping type of shrub, the design could easily lose its focus. If you are planning a formal planting of clipped yews, then it is easier to mix different styles and shapes because they are pruned to keep the lines you want to achieve.

Informal plantings tend to work best with the design of most homes, and maintenance is kept to

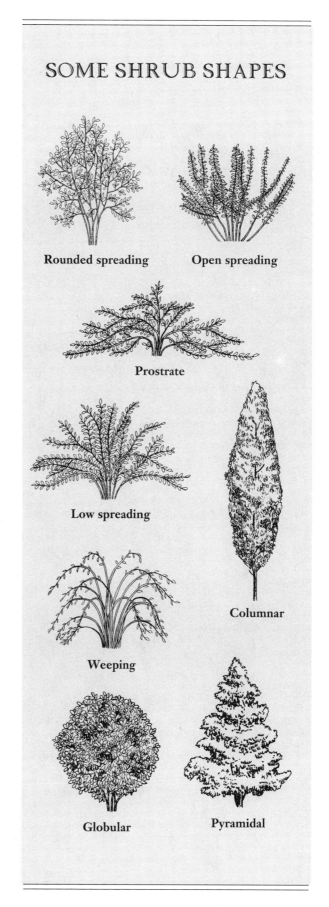

SOME SHRUB SHAPES

Rounded spreading   Open spreading

Prostrate

Low spreading

Columnar

Weeping

Globular   Pyramidal

FAVORITE FLOWERING SHRUBS

Bush cinquefoil *(Potentilla)*. There is nothing as easy to grow as the *Potentilla*. These are 2-foot-high to 4-foot-high shrubs that traditionally have bright yellow flowers, but are now available in white and red shades also.

They do best in full sun but can tolerate some shade. Ordinary garden soil with good drainage is all these plants need. They do not need pruning or spraying and will keep their blossoms nearly all summer long.

Butterfly bush *(Buddleia)*. Called butterfly bush because it attracts so many butterflies when in bloom. A prolific, late-blooming plant that is not always hardy in the North and needs winter protection. If they do suffer winter-kill, cut them back to the ground, and the roots will usually survive.

Butterfly bushes like full sun and well-drained soil that is rich in loam.

Daphne. Daphnes are known for their fragrant blossoms. The shrubs are slow growing, but after five years or so will be about 3 feet high. For this reason they are good to plant near the house. Daphnes will grow in any good soil but prefer a loose sandy soil that is neutral or even slightly alkaline. They also like full sun and cool roots; be sure to put mulch around the base of the plant.

D. burkwoodii (Burkwood daphne), is covered in the spring with star-shaped pinkish white flowers. In warmer areas, the plant might be called an evergreen, but it needs protection farther north with a mulch in the winter. Plant near the front of the border, by your doorway, or by a terrace to catch the lovely scent.

D. mezereum (February daphne), has very fragrant pink blossoms that open early. Red berries follow the flowers. Plant in a protected spot if you live in the North.

Plant daphnes in the spring so they will have time to adjust before winter arrives. Stay clear of bare-rooted plants. Look for those grown in containers or the balled and burlapped varieties to ease the transplanting shock. All varieties require little pruning.

Dogwood *(Cornus)*. The ever-popular dogwoods are a large and important group of shrubs and trees grown for their flowers, fruits, and brightly colored twigs.

The red-osier dogwood, *C. sericea*, has bright red branches that bear 2-inch clumps of small white flowers in late spring. Later in the summer small white berries appear and the leaves later turn red. It doesn't mind growing in wet conditions, where you will often find it growing in the wild.

Cornelian-cherry dogwood

Another variety, *C. sericea flaviramea*, has bright yellow stems. Both the red and yellow stemmed dogwoods are great additions for the winter landscape. Hardy to zone 3.

C. mas, or Cornelian-cherry, is a shrub that is hardy to zone 4 and covered with small clusters of yellow flowers in the spring. You can cut these branches in the middle of winter and force them to bloom indoors. In late summer, the shrub is covered with a cherry-like fruit. This shrub is good for growing in the city.

Prune the osier dogwood in early spring to bring on an abundance of new colored shoots. Prune Cornelian-cherry after the flowers have formed, if at all. These are all easy to grow in any good soil.

Flowering quince *(Chaenomeles)*. All of the members of the Chaenomeles family are popular shrubs: *C. japonica*, Japanese quince, and the common flowering quince, *C. speciosa*, are two of the most popular.

Flowering quince

These shrubs are hardy to zone 4 and bear 1-inch to 2-inch flowers in shades of pink, red, and white. In the fall, they bear yellow fruit that is often made into jelly. Many quinces tolerate city growing conditions well; also they make good hedges and border plants.

The Japanese quince usually grows to 3 feet high and bears bright red flowers. The flowering quinces get taller, sometimes up to 6 feet, and come in many different varieties of color and height. Both quinces do best in full sun and any good soil. This is a good one to plant in the fall since it starts growing so early in the spring. Prune after flowering in late spring.

Hydrangea. Hydrangeas are good to have in the garden because they bloom in the summer and the blossoms last a long time. Most have white flowers and some turn a light green with age. Others turn pink, or rose as they grow. Some of the more tender hydrangeas have blue, deep pink, or purple flowers depending on the acidity of the soil.

Hydrangeas prefer full sun or light shade and do well in a moist well-drained soil. Add peat moss, compost, or leaf mold.

H. paniculata 'Grandiflora,' also known as peegee hydrangea, is probably the most common hydrangea and the hardiest. This plant has conical flower clusters that can be 15 inches long and 12 inches across. The flowers are creamy white turning to pale pink and can be dried for lasting bouquets. If you see a hydrangea that has been trained to grow as a tree, it is probably this variety. Prune these in early spring before new growth starts.

The oakleaf hydrangea, *H. quercifolia*, is another excellent choice though it is not as hardy as the peegee. The foliage looks like that of an oak tree and is dark green on top, silver underneath, and turns a lovely red in the autumn. This plant will do well in deep shade, and its flowers are especially attractive in midsummer.

Lilac *(Syringa)*. Lilacs can be purple, white, pink, and even yellow and can bloom all summer long. Some are miniature shrubs and others have heavenly scents. All are easy to grow.

Lilacs like full sun but can tolerate partial shade. They like a neutral soil or one that has had some peat moss or leaf mold added to it. It is important to cut the flower heads off

Chinese lilac

FAVORITE FLOWERING SHRUBS (*continued*)

each year to encourage blossoms the following spring; cut them off as soon as they fade. Prune the bushes at this time as well, cutting off all dead stems or old ones that aren't blossoming well. You can cut old lilacs down to within 4 inches of the ground and they will send up new growth and in a few years be healthy shrubs again.

Rhododendron. There is little to compare with this family of plants for their evergreen foliage and incredible blossoms. Both rhododendrons and azaleas are members of the same genus, *Rhododendron*. Many rhododendrons are not hardy in the North, but gardeners in warmer areas can have incredible arrays of color with these beauties. All rhododendrons are alike in their need for a moist, acid soil (pH 4.5 to 5.5) and most prefer light shade.

If you want to try growing these plants, either near the house or in a mixed border of other shrubs, it is best to purchase them locally from a reliable grower who can assure you of the plant's hardiness for your growing area. Protect the evergreen varieties from winter sun and winds.

Spirea. Spireas thrive in almost any garden soil; they are easy to move around, have no pests, and do not mind a little shade. You can also take an old spirea that is on your property and revitalize it fairly easily by cutting it back to the ground.

Ask your nursery owner about the spireas hardy in your area. Some of the traditional ones include the bridalwreath spirea (*S. prunifolia*) and the Vanhoutte spirea (*S. vanhouttei*).

Viburnum. There is a large variety of viburnums from which to choose. All are easy to grow and tolerant of most soils. Many have lovely flowers and fruits and do not mind a little shade. Their blooming time varies as well. You can have viburnums growing in early spring up until late summer, and then still be amazed by the fall fruits and foliage.

Arrowwood viburnum

a minimum. In these plantings, all shrubs are allowed to keep their natural shapes. Of course, they may be pruned for health reasons, or to keep them in some kind of form.

Foundation Plantings

You can plant shrubs next to the house to hide exposed concrete, to accent the terrace or steps, or to help the house blend into its site. These plantings are called foundation plantings. Foundation plantings need to have interest throughout the year and should be slow growing. You do not want a shrub that will quickly grow to 30 feet, and you do not want to have to keep pruning plants to keep them in shape.

Shrubs planted near the house should complement the house and not be ungainly. Many flowering shrubs do not exceed 3 feet in height. Think about the viburnums, brooms, cotoneasters, poten-

Shrubs make good foundation plants.

tillas, spireas, and barberries. In addition to these plants, other shrubs have varieties that stay small, or grow very slowly, making them good choices for foundation plantings.

Hedges

Shrubs are often used in hedges, which can be a screen for your yard or can be used to define different areas of the yard, keeping children out of some areas or marking spaces for sitting and gardens.

A formal clipped evergreen hedge will need countless hours of pruning and clipping to keep it neat. But hedges can also be informal and unsheared. Shrubs can still be planted together in the form of a hedge, yet can be allowed to grow in their natural state. Of course, this type of hedge will need more room to grow than the narrower, clipped hedge.

If you want to plant just a single line of shrubs, it is better to plant one kind of shrub rather than mixing a variety of plants. Remember that the shrubs will grow wider as well as taller, so plant accordingly. Fill half the space you want to eventually fill to allow for this growth.

Shrub Borders

A border is any grouping of plants designed to please the eye. The primary purpose of any border in the garden is to be decorative. Shrub borders have the added advantage of also being able to act as wind breaks, barriers, and screens. For your border to be successful and one you enjoy for many years, consider it an intricate garden made up of many varieties of plants.

Get out the graph paper again before you design the border. Sketch the length and width of the border you are planning and then fill in with the approximate sizes of the plants at maturity. The border may look sparse for a few years, but you can fill in those spaces with annuals or simply leave it sparse. Before long you will be amazed at how quickly everything has grown in and filled the void.

It is usually easier to start planning the border from the back — starting with those shrubs that grow tallest. Think of the ultimate height you want these plants to be. A good choice is 8 to 10 feet. If plants are much higher than this, they can be a good screen, but they can also block out breezes and light to the yard. The shrubs at the back of the border should be planted closer together than those in the front. That way they are an effective backdrop for smaller plants and also provide the screening effect you may be looking for in the garden.

Group the various types of shrubs and colors of blossoms rather than place them spottily around the garden. The most interesting garden of shrubs, like those of other plants, are not straight edged but curved and left with spaces where other low-growing plants can fill in between the groupings. Cluster the shrubs in groupings of different bloom color and bloom time and you will have waves of color throughout the season. While the garden is filling in, you can plant masses of spring-flowering bulbs or perennials to further enhance the beauty of the background colors and textures.

Choosing Shrubs

Remember that most shrubs can grow in both sun and shade to varying degrees. Flowering shrubs tend to need some sun in order to bloom. But some shrubs, such as *Pieris japonica*, grow best in almost constant shade.

Be sure to look at the amount of light available to the shrubs you are planning to plant. Is the sunlight direct or is it filtered through neighboring trees? Is it morning sun or late afternoon sun? If there is no shade, will the plants be in bright sunlight for most of the day? All of these are consider-

POPULAR ORNAMENTAL TREES

Common Name	Latin Name	Bloom Season	Description	Height	Soil Type	Hardiness
Bartlett pear	*Pyrus communis*	March, before foliage	Pyramidal tree with leathery, glossy, bright green leaves; profuse, beautiful white flowers develop into very sweet, thin-skinned, tender fruit	30'; can be kept smaller	Rich, well-drained soil	Zone 1–9 Origin: Europe
Chinese pear	*Pyrus serotina* 'Chojuro'	March, before foliage	An Asian tree similar to the Bartlett, with larger foliage and greenish-brown, apple-shaped, very sweet, crunchy fruit	30'; can be kept smaller	Fertile, well-drained soil	Zone 1–9 Origin: China
Camellia	*Camellia japonica*	Winter and spring	Dark green, shiny, 4-inch leaves; red, pink, white, or mixed, 5-inch, single or double flowers	6–12'	Partial shade; well-drained, rich, slightly acid soil	Zone 5–9 Origin: China, Japan
Golden Hinoki cypress	*Chamaecyparis obtusa* 'Aurea'		Flattened, dark green foliage; only young growth is golden; can be kept small as tree is slow growing	30'	Any normal soil	Zone 5–9 Origin: Japan
Golden thread cypress	*Chamaecyparis pisifera* 'Filifera aurea'		Slow-growing, shrublike tree with weeping yellowish green foliage and branches; prune to keep in bounds	Up to 8'	Any normal soil	Zone 5–9 Origin: Japan
Japanese black pine	*Pinus thunbergiana*		Broad, conical tree with spreading branches; 4-inch, paired, sharp-pointed, bright green needles; good bonsai tree	100'; can be kept smaller	Any normal soil	Zone 1–9 Origin: Japan
Japanese laceleaf maple	*Acer palmatum* 'Dissectum Viridis'		A grafted garden form, more like a small shrub; drooping branches with pale green foliage that turns orange and gold in fall	5–10'	Any normal soil with good drainage	Zone 7–9 Origin: Japan
Japanese flowering cherry	*Prunus serrulata*	Early May, before foliage	Deciduous flowering tree with strong horizontal branches; pink buds develop into white, double and bell-shaped flower clusters	20'	Fertile, well-drained soil	Zone 5–8 Origin: Japan, Korea, China

Common Name	Latin Name	Bloom Season	Description	Height	Soil Type	Hardiness
Japanese Maple	*Acer palmatum*		Early spring foliage is red, turning soft green in summer and scarlet-orange in fall	15'	Any normal soil	Zone 1–9 Origin: Japan, Korea
Japanese umbrella pine	*Sciadopitys verticillata*		Very slow-growing evergreen with symmetrical, dense branches; dark, glossy, flattened needles cluster at branch ends and radiate out like umbrella spokes	30'	Rich, well-drained, slightly acid soil	Zone 5–9 Origin: Japan
Jeffrey pine	*Pinus jeffreyi*		Bluish-green, 8-inch long needles in clusters of 3; straight trunk; open, pyramidal form	60'	Any normal soil	Zone 1–9 Origin: Oregon to California
Mugo pine	*Pinus mugo*		Shrubby, symmetrical little pine with short, dark green needles growing in crowded clusters	6'	Any normal soil	Zone 1–9 Origin: Europe
Peach plum	*Prunus persica* x *Prunus cerasifera*	Spring, before foliage	Large, brownish red fruit with small stone and sweet flavor; midseason	25'; can be kept smaller	Rich, well-drained soil	Zone 6–9 Origin: China
Pink flowering dogwood	*Cornus florida* 'Rubra'	May	Long-time favorite for its pink flower bracts	20'; can be kept smaller	Any normal soil; better in partial shade	Zone 1–9 Native to eastern United States
Saucer magnolia	*Magnolia soulangiana*	Early spring, before foliage	Flowering deciduous tree with 6-inch leaves; white to pink or purplish-red flowers vary in size and forms	25'; can be kept smaller	Moist, fertile soil	Zone 1–9
Shiro plum	*Prunus salicina*	Early spring, before foliage	Fruit large, golden yellow, thin-skinned, and juicy; midseason	25'; can be kept smaller	Rich, well-drained soil	Zone 6–9 Origin: China
Star magnolia	*Magnolia stellata*	March	Starlike white flowers bloom profusely in late winter and early spring; a shrubby, slow-growing tree; yellow foliage in fall	10'; can be kept smaller	Well-drained, fertile soil	Zone 1–9 Quite hardy, though flowers may be nipped by late frosts
Twentieth-century pear	*Pyrus serotina* 'Nijuseiki'	March, before foliage	White blossoms; yellow-skinned, apple-shaped, sweet, juicy fruit, tenderer than Chojuro	30'; can be kept smaller	Fertile, well-drained soil	Zone 1–9 Origin: Japan
White flowering dogwood	*Cornus florida* 'Cherokee Princess'	May	Shorter trunk than other varieties of dogwood; small white flower clusters cover the tree before leaves expand; 6-inch long, 2-inch wide oval leaves turn scarlet in fall	20'; can be kept smaller	Any normal soil; does better in partial shade	Zone 1–9 Native to eastern United States

ations before choosing your shrub. Keep them in mind when you go to the nursery.

Nursery owners recommend that you buy young plants at about half the size of what they will be at maturity. That means if you are buying a plant that will grow to be 6 feet tall, then purchase one that is about 3 feet tall now. The plant you buy should look healthy — no brown in the leaves, no dead stems. Plants should look as if they are well watered. Do not buy one that is wilted or very dry looking. It may not make it.

How Shrubs are Sold. Shrubs are sold in three ways: bare-rooted, balled and burlapped, and container grown.

Bare-rooted plants are usually the least expensive, but if you see them for sale they are probably the ones to avoid. If the roots have been exposed to the air and sun and have not been kept moist, they are worthless. Mail-order houses, however, often ship bare-rooted plants wrapped in sphagnum moss and wrapped well in plastic to keep the moisture in the roots.

Balled-and-burlapped shrubs are dug out of their growing medium so that a ball of soil surrounds the roots. This is then wrapped in burlap and tied. These plants are found in nurseries where they are grown because they are not shipped as easily as plants grown in containers.

Container grown plants are often not as satisfactory as those that are balled and burlapped. Often plants that have been placed in containers will later die when planted in the garden because of root damage at the time they are dug. What you want with a container plant is one that has been grown in the container and not simply dug from the field and placed in the container.

Planting Shrubs

Soil pH. Many flowering shrubs grow well in soil that is mildly acid, registering between 6.0 and 7.0 on the pH scale.

Many of the more popular flowering shrubs, such as rhododendrons and azaleas, blueberries, and bayberries, require very acidic soil, with a pH of 4.5 to 5.5. Leaves of these plants will turn yellow in a neutral or alkaline soil because they cannot get enough iron. If the pH is lowered, the iron is freed in the soil and the plants are able to absorb it. See chapter 2 for more information on soil amendments and adjusting your soil pH.

When to Plant. Fall is the best time to plant most shrubs. Some tender shrubs and shrubs of questionable hardiness for your area should be planted in the spring, but others can wait until fall. Container grown plants, if properly cared for, can be planted any time the soil can be worked. In the North, it is best to give the plants an early start so they are somewhat established before the ground freezes, so plant early in the fall. In the South, where the soil seldom freezes, planting can extend throughout the winter. Fall planted shrubs will probably bloom the following season, while spring planted ones may not flower the first season.

How to Plant. Plant your shrub within a few hours of purchase. If you can't plant immediately, place the shrub in the shade and keep it moist. Wet the ball or water the container.

If the shrub is bare-rooted, never let the roots dry out. Fill a bucket with water and add some soil. Dip the roots in this mixture so all are coated. If you can't plant right away, leave the shrub in the bucket until you are ready to plant. If you cannot plant for more than a few days, then make a trench in the garden and lay the roots in the trench, cover with soil, and shade the top of the plant from the sun. Water well.

Be sure planting hole is larger than the width of the shrub's roots.

Since you will only plant the shrub once, it is worth doing a good job the first time. The hole you dig should be bigger then the width of the roots when they are spread out in their natural position. The extra room in the hole can be used for an additional amount of loose soil and humus to be added around the roots of the shrub. When you dig, take out the topsoil, the first 5 to 7 inches of soil, and place it on a tarp beside the hole. Then take out the rest of the soil, the paler soil that lies beneath the topsoil, and take it to the compost pile. Add some organic matter and fertilizer to the topsoil you saved. If you are planting an acid-loving plant, such as an azalea, now is the time to mix something like cottonseed meal with the topsoil. Mix well and begin filling the hole.

If your shrub is bare rooted, prune the roots and some of the top growth. Remove any weak or broken branches.

When you plant a bare-rooted shrub, place it in the hole and spread out the roots with your hands so they reach out toward the sides of the hole. Then place a small amount of soil in the hole and cover the roots using your hands to tap the soil carefully. When the roots are covered and the hole is nearly filled, firm the soil with your foot. Do not plant the shrub deeper or shallower than it was planted before you purchased it.

Now water the shrub, being sure to saturate the soil around the shrub. When the water has drained away, fill in the hole using the remaining topsoil mixture. Make a rim with the soil to hold the water in around the shrub and water thoroughly again.

If the shrub is balled and burlapped, follow the same procedure and leave the burlap in place. Cut any ropes that are tying the ball together and pull the burlap down from the neck of the plant. Do not leave any burlap exposed above the soil as it will tend to act as a wick and take water away from the plant's roots. Make sure the material covering the ball is burlap and not a plastic material that will not break down in the soil.

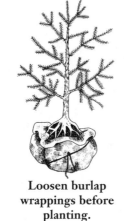

Loosen burlap wrappings before planting.

Container-grown plants need just as much, if not more, attention when being planted. Some-times they are grown in a soilless mix and need as much organic matter as you can work into the soil to make their transition a painless one. Slide the shrub out of the container, or, if necessary, cut the container off. If the roots are tightly bound, make cuts in them with a knife to stimulate new growth. Try to loosen the rootball and spread roots out in the hole as you plant the shrub. This will encourage the plant to send out new roots. If you prune the roots, be sure to prune the top growth of the plant also.

Try not to disturb the roots when removing plants from containers.

Shrubs you have just planted need extra care. They are very susceptible to water loss and need to be watered often. Once the plants are established they can endure dry periods.

Caring for Shrubs

Watering. Newly planted shrubs do need water if they are to flourish. When there hasn't been a good soaking rain for a week, give the shrubs a thorough watering.

When the shrubs are planted in the fall, you need to water until the winter snows or rains arrive. Shrubs set out in the spring need weekly watering until late fall. After the plants have been in the garden for a season, they need little watering, except during dry periods, or if you have very sandy soil.

Fertilizing. If you have taken care when planting your shrubs, they will need little fertilizing. Too much fertilizer with newly planted shrubs can cause root burning, which will weaken or even kill the plants. However, if you have planted your shrub carefully, and if after a few months, it fails to grow any new stems or its leaves turn yellow, you may want to apply fertilizer.

The type of fertilizer you use will depend on the shrubs. For those that do not require acid soil conditions, a common garden fertilizer is fine. A typical mix for feeding shrubs is 5-10-5. Usually just ¼ to ½ cup of this mix is sufficient for an average-sized shrub. Fertilize in the early spring. Fall fertilizing may encourage new growth which can be damaged by winter frosts.

Mulching. A mulch will help the soil around your shrubs stay moist and cool throughout the year. Good choices for mulch are leaves (crumbled or shredded), wood chips, hay, grass clippings, pine needles, or coarse peat moss. Apply right after planting in a layer about 2 inches deep. Do not get the mulch too near the stem of the shrub, and do not pile it too thickly as it can cut off air that roots need. Water before applying any mulch.

Pruning. All shrubs need a certain amount of pruning if only to remove the dead or damaged branches. Lower branches in shrubs that do not get much light tend to die and are the first to become diseased. So once a year it is a good idea to remove these. Early spring is a good time to do this cleaning routine before the leaves appear and hide some of the damage. Cut off the dead wood as close to the stem as possible. Next, cut the branches that are broken and take off any branch that rubs on another or crosses over it in any way.

Make pruning cuts just above a bud or side shoot.

Rejuvenation is a natural part of annual pruning. Many shrubs that send up new shoots (spirea, mock-orange, and deutzia) will benefit if you take a few of the older stems off at ground level each year.

When a shrub gets out of hand, it needs severe

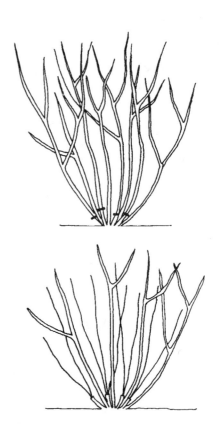

(Top) With a small saw, cut the largest stems down at ground level; (bottom) new growth will spring from the pruned branches to create a fuller shrub.

pruning. But do not cut every branch back the first year. Cut some back to the first main side shoot, then next year cut the remaining branches. Afterward, shape as needed. Many shrubs that grow in a pendulous form need to have their old wood cut out at ground level (forsythia, weigela).

Pruning to Increase Bloom. Flowering shrubs can be divided into two groups according to how they produce flowers. The groups are determined by the time the buds form, not when the flowers bloom. Some shrubs blossom from the buds that are formed on stems that grew during the previous summer. Some of these include forsythia, lilac, and quince. These shrubs should be pruned soon after they have flowered on the previous year's growth and before new buds start to form on the new growth.

Other shrubs blossom from the buds formed on the current season's growth. These shrubs need to be pruned early in the spring before the new

PRUNING GUIDE

Shrubs	When	How
Barberry	Early spring	Little pruning required except to remove a few old branches occasionally to encourage new growth. Head back as necessary to keep plant in shape.
Butterfly Bush	Early spring	Cut out all dead wood. Remove some old branches and head-in as necessary to keep plant properly shaped.
Clematis	Spring	Cut out weak growth but save as much old wood as possible.
Crab	Early spring	Prune moderately. Cut out dead and broken branches and suckers.
Deutzia	After flowering	Remove a few older branches and all dead wood. Do not let growth get too dense.
Dogwood, Flowering	After flowering	Remove dead wood only.
Dogwood, Other	Spring	Varieties grown for colored twigs should have the old growth removed to encourage brightly colored new shoots.
Elderberry	After fruiting	Prune severely. Remove one-half of the season's growth.
Forsythia	After flowering	Remove a few older branches at the ground each year and head back new growth as necessary.
Honeysuckle, Bush	After fruiting	Cut out some old branches. Keep bush open.
Hydrangea	Early spring	Hills of Snow variety: cut back to ground. Others: remove dead and weak growth, cut old flowering stems back to two buds.
Laurel, Mountain	After flowering	Prune very little. Remove a few old branches at the ground from weak, leggy plants to induce growth from the roots.
Lilac	After flowering	Remove diseased and scaly growth, cut off old flower heads, and cut out surplus sucker growth.
Mock-Orange	After flowering	Cut out dead wood and a few old branches to thin out plant.
Rhododendron	After flowering	Treat same as Laurel, Mountain.
Roses, Climbing	After flowering	Cut out about one-half of old growth at the ground and retain the vigorous new shoots from the root for next year's flowers. Head back as necessary.

PRUNING GUIDE (*continued*)

Shrubs	When	How
Roses: Tea, Hybrid, Perpetual	Spring after frosts	Cut away all dead and weak growth and shorten all remaining branches or canes to four buds for weak growers and five buds for vigorous varieties.
Rose-of-Sharon	When buds start	Cut out all winter-killed growth back to live wood.
Snowberry	Early spring	Thin out some old branches and cut back last season's growth of that part remaining to three buds.
Trumpet Vine	Early spring	Prune side branches severely to the main stem.
Weigela	After flowering	Prune lightly. Remove all dead, weak growth and head in as necessary. Cut out a few old branches at the ground to induce new growth.
Wisteria	Spring	Cut back the new growth to the spurs at the axils of the leaves. This can be repeated in midsummer.
Viburnum	Early spring	Prune lightly. Remove all dead, weak, and a few of the old branches.
Virginia Creeper	Spring	Clip young plants freely. Older plants require little pruning except to remove dead growth and some thinning.

growth starts; or just as the buds that will produce new stems begin to swell. Examples of these shrubs are the crape myrtle and the Rose-of-Sharon. You do not have to be afraid of early spring pruning. Hard pruning can result in fewer flowers but the flowers will be bigger in size.

Shrubs that flower on wood of the current season's growth include *Abelia grandiflora, Berberis, Clethra, Hydrangea arborescens* and *H. paniculata, Kerria, Ligustrum, Lonicera, Rhus, Rosa, Spirea, Stephanandra,* and *Tamarix.*

Sometimes hedges need to be pruned to make them denser. The theory is that more than one shoot will grow in the place from which one shoot is pruned. So if you prune, more shoots will grow and you will get a denser hedge. Remember to prune a hedge so that it is broader at the base and tapers towards the top. Then air and sun can reach the lower branches.

Some shrubs die back. They have roots that are winter hardy but tops that are not. The tops should be pruned as early in the spring as possible. They include *Abalia grandiflora, Buddeleia caryopteris, Ceanotnus, Tamarix,* and *Vitex.*

Rejuvenating Old Shrubs. Sometimes you will find that you will have to do a major job of rejuvenation. If you move into a house and find shrubs that are very overgrown, you can work wonders with pruning. Cut every stem all the way back to the ground in early spring. It will not kill the shrub and will force numerous canes to grow from the stumps. These will not bloom for a few years but when they do the blossoms will be plentiful. If you feel you need to do a drastic pruning job, do not be timid. Get out the pruning saw and cut stems back until they are 2 to 5 inches high.

Forcing Blooms on Flowering Shrubs

Flowering shrubs can provide blooms not only in the spring and summer but in the season when you need color the most — the winter. By forcing bloom, you can encourage flowers to blossom indoors in the middle of winter or early spring. Some shrubs that work best are forsythia, pussy willow, flowering quince, winter honeysuckle, Japanese barberry, and several of the hazels and spireas.

Most of the shrubs are early bloomers and the closer to the normal outdoor blooming season the shrub is cut, the sooner you will see blossoms. Some shrubs refuse to be forced into bloom. But experiment. If you see any swelling of buds, give it a try.

The best time to cut branches for forcing is when you have a relatively mild winter's day with the temperature above freezing. Then the transition is not as difficult for the branches when they come inside. First give the branches lots of water. Then lie the branches in a tub of tepid water. (You can use the bathtub.) Let them soak overnight so they can absorb plenty of moisture. If you cannot do this, place the branches in a tall vase or bucket and give them a shower.

After they have soaked, the branches still need lots of water. First peel the stems back with a sharp knife from the bottom, or, if the stems are thick, slice them down the center to help with the water uptake. Change the water in the vases daily, and wrap newspaper or clear plastic wrap around the branches for a few days to help them hold in the moisture. Also be sure you have the branches in the coolest part of the house, out of direct sunlight.

Check the branches daily to see if the buds show any color. When they do, remove the wrapping and place in a cool, brightly lit room. Soon the branches will be filled with blossoms and your winter doldrums will seem a bit less serious.

Cutting Flowers from Shrubs

Cutting the stems of flowering shrubs is like cutting any flower: It is best to cut the branches late in the day. Choose stems whose flowers are just beginning to open as these will last longer indoors.

When cutting flowers, remove all leaves from the stem that will be below the waterline in your vase. If the stem is woody, it is best to crush it with a hammer or make cuts in it with a sharp knife to help it draw water. Place the stems immediately in warm water and let them sit overnight before you arrange them in a permanent spot.

Remember, that as you cut your blossoms to bring indoors, you are also pruning the plant, so pay attention to where it will be best to cut.

Remember, too, that it is best to remove flowers from a shrub once they have faded, except on those plants whose flowers are followed by fruit. Simply remove the blossom with garden hand shears at its place of origin. This will keep the plants clean looking and increase bloom the following season.

Propagating Shrubs

Propagating most shrubs is not all that difficult. Several methods work depending on the type of shrub you want to propagate. A few of the simplest ways to multiply plants are division, cuttings, and layering. These work well with most of the common shrubs.

Division works well on lilacs, oakleaf hydrangeas, kerria, deutzias, many spireas, deciduous azaleas, Siberian dogwood, and other shrubs that send out underground branches. The stems grow out of the ground near the plant. These can be dug up in early spring and planted elsewhere.

Look for a sucker that has grown at least 12 inches above the ground. Cut a circle around the sucker so it will be severed from the main plant. Dig this small plant carefully and be sure to bring up all its deep roots. Replant at the original depth and water well.

Softwood cuttings. Many shrubs can be easily propagated by means of softwood cuttings. These are pieces of the stems taken in late spring from new growth. Cut 4-inch to 6-inch pieces at an angle from the ends of healthy branches. Dip these pieces in a rooting hormone and place them in a suitable rooting medium.

Coarse sand, peat moss, or a mix of the two are good rooting mixes to use for cuttings. Perlite or vermiculite can also be used. Any container that has good drainage will work as long as it is deep enough to hold about 4 inches of the rooting medium.

Cover the cuttings with a clear plastic bag or a big glass jar. Place in bright light but not direct sunlight. The cuttings will take about a month or two to root. Remember to water them often. You can also place the cuttings outside in the shade but remember to keep them watered.

When new leaves appear, it is a signal of root growth. The stems can be transplanted to a good potting soil mix but should wait in a cold frame until the following spring to be planted in the garden.

Shrubs that propagate from softwood cuttings include: mock-orange, boxwood, quince, evergreen azalea, *Clethra, Potentilla, Deutzia, Euonymous, Tamarix*.

Hardwood Cuttings. Hardwood cuttings are a bit more complicated than the softwood. These are 5-inch to 12-inch cuttings taken from a plant when the wood is mature in late fall or even midwinter. Take cuttings that have at least three to four nodes and cut at a slant (A). Then slice an inch or so off the bottom bark away from the stem to make it easier for roots to grow. Dust this cut area with rooting hormone (B). Tie the cuttings in bunches and bury the bundles in a can of vermiculite, cold frame, or in the garden over the winter (C).

In early spring, dig up the cuttings and place in a cold frame or narrow trench in the garden. Bury them so that only the top bud is above the ground

(D). A covered cold frame will help retain moisture. You should soon see leaves sprouting above the ground (E). Leave in the cold frame for an entire season until transplanting time.

Shrubs that propagate from hardwood cuttings include: *Buddleia davidii, Erica, Hibiscus, Rhododendron, Salix, Spiraea, Weigela*.

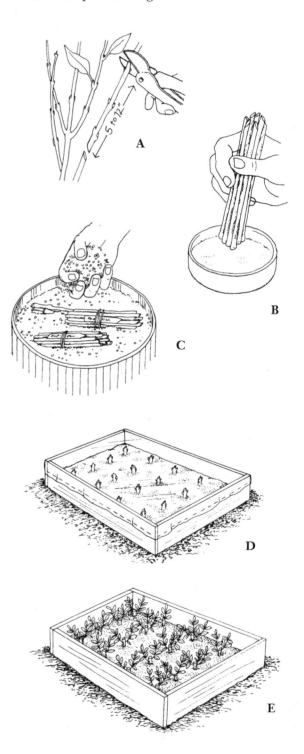

SPECIALTY GARDENS

Do you have an open hillside you'd like to convert into a garden? Or a shady spot that would benefit from some well-chosen foliage plants. Not every garden can be laid out on level, well-drained soil in full sun. For gardeners whose sites offer special challenges, there are special gardens to turn problem areas into places of beauty.

And for those gardeners who seek out challenges, regardless of their sites, there are special theme gardens — gardens that offer more than fragrance, color, and visual appeal. In this chapter we explore shade gardens, wetland gardens, wildflower meadows, rock gardens, and special gardens for bird lovers, butterfly lovers, and flower arrangers.

SHADE GARDENS

The term "shade" encompasses so many different light conditions that it's hard to describe gardening techniques that will fit every situation. Shade can range from the dense darkness of a pine forest where only plants such as Indian pipe will grow, to the light-dappled shade under birch trees which allows a great deal of sunlight to filter through. It may also connote an area that gets strong skylight but no sun, such as the north side of a building.

If you are not already familiar with light conditions in your prospective garden spot, it will be helpful to observe that area for one entire growing season to determine the quality of shade at various times of the day and year. If deciduous trees are the source, note whether the shade is dappled when they are in full leaf, as it is under a poplar tree, or very dense, as under an oak or maple. If the shade seems too heavy for the proper growth of most plants, cutting off a few lower limbs from the offending trees will sometimes allow more light to enter from the sides.

Under trees is a good shade garden spot.

The amount of moisture a shady spot receives may affect what you can grow there as much as the amount of light. The soil under pine trees is usually dry because the tree acts as an umbrella and falling rain seldom reaches there. It is just as likely, however, for a shaded spot to be excessively moist. If you hope to grow any plants when the soil is soggy for most of the summer, you must either drain it, build it up by adding topsoil, or choose only those specimens that do well in both bog and shade.

Where the soil is thin and tree roots completely fill the area, even strong plants may not survive such competition. If you run into roots when you dig, either add a thick layer of topsoil or plant only shallow-rooted ground covers such as English ivy, myrtle, *Pachysandra*, and other woodland plants that normally grow under such conditions.

Choosing Plants for Shade

Choose varieties appropriate to the type of shade you have. Most plants need at least a few hours of direct sun and filtered light or full skylight (known as light shade) for the rest of the day. There is a long list of perennials that will grow in places which get little or no sunshine, but have an abundance of filtered light (medium shade). Only a few plants can thrive in the darkness of an evergreen forest (dense shade), although *Pachysandra*, English ivy, myrtle, the Canada mayflower *(Maianthemum)*, and moneywort *(Lysimachia nummularia)* are worth a try in the slightly open areas where small amounts of light filter through to ground level.

In light shade it is possible to have continuous bloom beginning with a carpet of spring bulbs such as snowdrops, *Scilla, Muscari*, and daffodils, and continuing into the spring with lily-of-the-valley, violets, and similar species. Plants such as *Dicentra eximia* (fernleaf bleeding-heart) that blossom throughout the growing season, and different varieties of hosta and *Hemerocallis*, will provide bloom for a long period.

Ferns are especially useful plants for shady areas, not only because they thrive there, but because they are so beautiful. They're ideal as border plants along a shady path, clumped in sunless garden corners, or on the north side of a building or high fence where even grass doesn't grow well. Most prefer the dappled shade created by deciduous trees to that of an evergreen forest, and most also like a woodsy, acidic soil, and benefit from a mulch of rotting leaves or needles.

Ferns can be transplanted from the wild in very early spring or late fall, but you will undoubtedly establish a more successful fern bower if you buy mature potted plants from a nursery or garden center.

Designing a Shade Garden

If your perennial bed gets mostly light shade, simply choose the proper plants for that area by using the list on page 295, and coordinate their colors and heights the same as you would in any other bed.

The design of a medium-shade planting is more challenging. To grow a conventional perennial garden in an area partially shaded by trees, or on the north side of a house, is well-nigh impossible. But a woodland garden is ideal for such a spot. (Although the name suggests a forest area, a woodland garden can flourish even in the shadow of tall city buildings, if the right soil and moisture conditions exist.) Foliage plants are especially attractive, the different colors of which can be combined to add interest and unusual textures. The large hosta leaves contrast pleasantly with the delicate, lacy green of ferns, for example.

The colors of a shaded garden may in actuality appear quite different from those you had carefully planned on paper, since our perception of color differs according to the quality of the light that falls on it. In general, white and pastel blooms provide a bright, glowing quality in a sunless garden. More vivid colors may appear dim or, in certain shade situations, shine brilliantly and clash so much that they must be shifted from one spot to another.

In a shady planting, as in a rock garden, running water, old stumps, stones, and pools add greatly to the atmosphere. If there are no natural features in the area, you may be able to design substitutes and add such welcoming features as benches or other garden seats.

PERENNIALS FOR SHADY SPOTS

SP = Spring blooming
ES = Early summer blooms
SU = Summer blooming
L = Late summer or fall blooms

NO * = full sun to light shade
* = light to medium shade
** = medium shade to dense shade
*** = dense shade

*Aconitum, monkshood, SU
Aegopodium, bishop's weed or goutweed, SU
*Ajuga, bugleweed, SU
Alchemilla, lady's mantle, SU
Anaphalis, pearly everlasting, SU
Anemone, wood anemone, SU
Aquilegia, columbine, ES
**Arenaria, sandwort, ES
Aruncus, goat's beard, SU
**Asperula, sweet woodruff, SP
Aster, L
Astilbe, perennial spirea, SU
Aubrieta, purple rockcress, ES
Baptisia, wild blue indigo, ES
*Bergenia, SP
*Brunnera, ES
Campanula, bellflower, SU
*Cimicifuga, bugbane, snakeroot, SU
Clematis, SU
**Convallaria, lily-of-the-valley, ES
*Corydalis, SU
*Dicentra eximia, fernleaf bleeding-heart, SP, ES,
SU, L
Dictamnus, gas plant, SU
*Digitalis, foxglove, SU
*Doronicum, leopard's bane, SP
*Epimedium, SP
Euphorbia, spurge, SU
*Gentiana, gentian, L
Geranium, crane's bill, SU
*Helleborus, Christmas rose, L
Hemerocallis, daylily, SU, L
*Hesperis, sweet rocket, SU

Heuchera, coral-bells, SP, ES, SU, L
Hibiscus, L
**Hosta, plantain lily, SU
Iberis, candytuft, ES
*Iris cristata, crested iris, ES
I. foetidissima, Gladwin iris, ES
Lamium, dead nettle, ES
Ligularia, golden-ray, SU
*Lilium, lily including L. canadense, L. martagon, L.
aurelian, and Oriental hybrids, SU
**Liriope, lily-turf, SU
*Lobelia, cardinal flower, SU
**Lysimachia, loosestrife, SU
Lythrum, purple loosestrife, SU
**Mertensia virginica, Virginia bluebells, SP
*Monarda, bee balm, SU
*Myosotis, forget-me-not, SP
Omphalodes, navelwort, SP
**Pachysandra, spurge, SP
*Phlox divaricata, wild blue phlox, ES
P. subulata, moss pink, SP
*Polemonium reptans, Jacob's-ladder, ES
*Polygonataum, Solomon's-seal, SP
*Polygonum affine, fleeceflower, SU, L
**Primula, primrose, ES
*Pulmonaria, lungwort, SP
**Rodgersia, Rodger's flower, ES
Stachys byzantina, lamb's-ears, SU
*Thalictrum, meadow rue, SU
*Tiarella, foamflower, ES
**Trillium, SP
Trollius, globeflower, ES

FERNS

Because ferns are so popular for shady gardens, we list here some of the most suitable.

Bladder Fern *(Cystopteris bulbifera)*. Grows from 12 to 24 inches tall and produces small bulbs along the stem at the base of the leaves. Likes moist soil, is not particular about acidity, and grows into a dainty attractive plant.

Fern fronds

Common Polypody *(Polypodium virginianum)*. Small evergreen fern, 6 to 12 inches tall. Grows in sun or shade, acid or sweet soils. Good for rock gardens where it will develop into a thick mass.

Cup Fern *(Dennstaedtia)*. These evergreen ferns grow in full sunlight, although some kinds do well in shade. So vigorous it can become weedy and cover entire pastures of worn-out soil. Does especially well in a less acid soil, but this is not imperative.

Flowering Fern *(Osmunda)*. **Cinnamon fern** *(O. cinnamomea)* grows about 3 feet tall with spores borne on cinnamonlike sticks in the center of the fronds. Likes moist places, sun, or shade. **Interrupted fern** *(O. claytoniana)*, another impressive specimen, is happy in moist spots, grows in sun, but seems to be at its massive best in light shade. It grows up to 36 inches tall, with spores growing about midway in the middle of its large fronds.

Glade Fern, Lady Fern *(Athyrium)*. This is another large group of ferns, *A. filix-femina* (the lady fern) being the best known. It, too, is not fussy about soil pH, grows in sun or shade, but needs adequate moisture or the leaves become brown. Grows to a height of 30 to 36 inches.

Hartford Fern *(Lygodium palmatum)*. A climbing plant that grows to about 4 feet. Prefers moist, acid soils and a shady location.

Holly Fern *(Polystichum)*. One of the best is *P. acrostichoides*, Christmas fern, a beautiful evergreen resembling the Boston fern. It likes the shade of deciduous woods, but can be grown in the sun if kept well watered. It grows 1 to 3 feet tall.

Holly fern

Christmas fern *(P. acrostichoides)*, a beautiful evergreen resembling the Boston fern. It likes the shade of deciduous woods, but can be grown in the sun if kept well watered; 1 to 3 feet tall.

Maidenhair *(Adiantum)*. These lacy ferns are among the most beautiful of all and are not difficult to grow. They like an area that gets only a little morning sun and a large amount of skylight during the day. An acid soil is not required. The native *A. pedatum*, the most recommended, grows to a height of about 20 inches.

Maidenhair fern

Ostrich Fern *(Matteuccia)*. This massive plant grows up to 6 feet tall, likes moist soil, shade, and should not be planted too deeply.

Rattlesnake Fern *(Botrychium)*. There are several common varieties of this species, growing from 5 to 24 inches tall. It likes moderately acid soil and sun, and is unique because it produces seeds in small clusters on the fronds.

Sensitive Fern *(Onoclea sensibilis)*. Grows fast enough to become weedy, especially in moist locations. Grows in sun or light shade, is very tender to fall frosts, and reaches a height of 30 inches. Produces interesting fruits that are widely used in dried flower arrangements.

Walking Fern *(Camptosorus rhizophyllus)*. A creeping fern, less common than many of the others, it is found growing near rocks where the soil is moist and relatively sweet. Useful in rock gardens if enough moisture is present.

Wood Fern *(Dryopteris)*. There are over a thousand varieties in this genus, many of which are especially attractive. They like shade and are not particular about soils. *D. spinulosa*, often called fancy fern or toothed fern, is semi-evergreen, very attractive, and often collected by florists because it is so long lasting. It is also outstanding in the landscape.

Woodsia Fern *(Woodsia, W. obtusa)*. A small fern, up to 12 inches, that likes dry, shady places. Since these ferns thrive in difficult spots where there is little soil, they are useful in the shady parts of a rock garden.

Planting and Caring for a Shade Garden

Planting a garden in the shade is not much different from planting an ordinary border in the sun. Soil acidity may be more of a problem, however, so test the soil before planting. Add lime only if the pH is below 5.5, and only in spots where you plan to grow perennials rather than acid-loving wildflowers and ferns. Allow more space for each plant in the shade than you would in full sun — the foliage will then have room to spread out and absorb all the available light.

Plants in woodland locations must compete with trees for nutrients, so fertilize them more heavily than you would those in a conventional garden. A thick mulch of organic material helps to create the woodland conditions they like. Check plants growing under trees each spring to see if fallen leaves or needles need to be cleaned away — such debris could smother the plants. In addition, make sure that plants under a canopy of trees, or sheltered from wind-driven rains by buildings, walls, or tight fences, are getting the moisture they need.

CREATING A WILDFLOWER MEADOW

Wildflowers can be established with modest investments of time in planning, preparation, properly selected seeds, and patience. In addition to providing low-maintenance landscaping, wildflowers are extremely versatile. If portions of your yard are too dry or too wet for the usual lawn grasses, certain wildflowers mixed with native grasses may be a beautiful solution to the problem. Many species (such as black-eyed Susan, butterfly weed, and purple coneflower) will attract butterflies to your garden. Scarlet sage and standing cypress, with their bright red flowers, are pollinated by hummingbirds. These species and others (such as gayfeather, blanketflower, and wild bergamot) make excellent cut flowers as well.

How to Obtain Wildflowers

Wildflowers should never be dug from the wild except as part of a rescue operation to save plants that would otherwise be destroyed. Wildflowers are usually propagated either by making cuttings and divisions or by planting seeds. There are a growing number of reputable wildflower propagators who grow their own stock rather than digging plants from the wild. Many of these suppliers will take phone and mail order requests for wildflowers. However, live plants are quite expensive, perhaps prohibitively so if you intend to plant a large area.

By far the least expensive means of growing wildflowers is from seed. The quickest way to obtain wildflower seeds is to purchase them from a reputable supplier. Seeds are generally available year-round and can easily be sent through the mail. If you are planning to plant large areas, you should inquire about wholesale prices for wildflower and native grass seeds.

Use caution before using prepared wildflower seed mixtures. Although some suppliers will carefully formulate mixes especially for your region using high-quality native species, others simply add the cheapest, most readily available seeds regardless of their desirability. If you are going to spend your money on wildflower seeds, you might as well purchase species that will survive well in your region and not *pay* for roadside weedy wildflowers that you wouldn't want in your backyard. So find out what is in the mixture of wildflower seed before you buy.

By far the most pleasant way to obtain wildflower seeds is to collect them from the wild. If you collect seeds, remember to follow common sense conservation guidelines. Collect a few seeds or fruits from each of many plants and *only from common species that are locally abundant*. Be careful not to trample nearby plants while you are collecting. Do not collect fruits and seeds from plants growing in public places, and be sure to obtain permission from property owners before you collect on private property.

One of the most satisfactory ways to collect small seeds from wildflowers is to make a small bag out of nylon stocking. When the flowers start to wilt, gently place a section of stocking over the developing fruits, and tie both ends using twist-ties, being careful not to crush the stem. When the fruits are fully ripe and dry, simply snip the stem and place the nylon bag into a paper sack.

It is best to separate the seeds from the dried remains of the fruit. Place the collected material on sheets of heavy white paper and gently crush the dried fruits. Blow gently across the paper to remove most of the unwanted husks and fruit residues, being careful not to blow the seeds away. A kitchen sieve is quite useful for cleaning small seeds. Put the seeds in small coin envelopes or zip-closure bags and store them in a cool, dry place.

Selecting Grasses

Natural meadows and grasslands are a combination of wildflowers and grasses. The grasses provide support and the ideal amount of competition for the wildflowers to grow straight and tall. Without the grasses some of these wildflowers might become scraggly or "leggy." In northern regions, the dead remains of the grasses provide additional insulation, protecting the overwintering roots of the wildflowers.

Not all grasses are the same; different species grow in different ways. Some grasses form "sod," which is ideal for lawns, tennis courts, and putting greens, where a continuous, tight cover is required, but is not much of an environment for wildflowers. Other grasses form distinct clumps or "bunches" when they grow, allowing space for wildflowers to coexist. When establishing your wildflower meadow, the grasses you interplant with the wildflowers should be bunch grasses. Avoid planting ryegrasses or bluegrasses, which would form sod turfs and crowd out the wildflowers. Native wildflower seeds should be combined with a mixture of native grasses suited to your region.

Grasses should comprise about 60 to 90 percent of the seed mixture. The wildflower and grass seed mixture should be sown at a rate of 5 to 20

WILDFLOWERS BY REGION

Common Name	Scientific Name	NE	MW	SE	GP	RM	SW	NW
Annual phlox	Phlox drummondii	X	X	X	X	X	X	X
Baby-blue-eyes	Nemophila menziesii	X	X	X	X	X	X	X
*Black-eyed Susan	Rudbeckia hirta	X	X	X	X	X	X	X
Blanketflower	Gaillardia aristata	X	X	X	X	X	X	X
Blue flax	Linum lewisii	X	X	X	X	X	X	X
Blue-eyed grass	Sisyrinchium bellum						X	X
Butterfly weed	Asclepias tuberosa	X	X	X	X	X	X	X
California poppy	Eschscholzia californica	X	X	X	X	X	X	X
Chinese-houses	Collinsia heterophylla		X	X		X	X	X
Colorado columbine	Aquilegia caerulea	X				X	X	X
Cosmos	Cosmos bipinnatus	X	X	X	X	X	X	X
*Eastern columbine	Aquilegia canadensis		X	X	X	X		X
Farewell-to-spring	Clarkia amoena	X		X		X	X	X
*Gayfeather	Liatris pycnostachya	X	X	X	X	X	X	
Lance-leaved coreopsis	Coreopsis lanceolata		X	X	X	X	X	X
Linanthus	Linanthus grandiflorus					X	X	X
Mexican-hat	Ratibida calumnifera	X	X	X	X	X	X	
*New England aster	Aster novae-angliae	X	X	X	X	X		X
Pasqueflower	Anemone patens	X	X		X	X		X
*Purple coneflower	Echinacea purpurea		X	X	X	X		X
Scarlet sage	Salvia coccinea	X		X	X		X	X
Spiderwort	Tradescantia virginiana	X	X	X		X		X
Standing cypress	Ipomopsis rubra			X	X		X	X
Tidy-tips	Layia platyglossa	X				X	X	X
Wild bergamot	Monarda fistulosa		X	X	X	X		
Wind poppy	Stylomecon heterophylla						X	X

*Requires cold treatment for germination of seeds

NW = Northwest	SW = Southwest
RM = Rocky Mountain	GP = Great Plains
MW = Mid-West	NE = Northeast
SE = Southeast	

pounds of live seeds per acre, depending on the species composition. If species with small seeds (such as switch-grass and California poppy) make up the bulk of the mixture, the seeding rate should be lower than when the mixture is composed mainly of species with large, heavy seeds (such as northern dropseed and wild bergamot). If you purchase wildflower and grass seed in bulk, the supplier can make specific seeding-rate recommendations, but typically 6 to 7 pounds of wildflower seeds are mixed with enough grass seeds to sow an acre.

When to Plant

Wildflower seeds germinate in response to ample moisture and warm temperatures. Ideally you should plan to plant the wildflower and grass seeds to take advantage of the natural precipitation and temperature patterns of your region. Here are a few suggestions for the various wildflower growing regions.

In the United States, the Northeast (NE) has ample rainfall throughout the year, with cold winters and mild summers. The best time to plant is in the autumn (October to early November) and the next-best time is in mid-spring (late April to mid-May). The best time to plant most western wildflowers in the Northeast, however, is in the spring.

The Southeast (SE) region also has precipitation that is ample and evenly distributed throughout the year. Summers are hot and humid, and winters are generally mild, though frosts may occur anywhere except on the south coasts of Florida and Texas. The autumn (October and November) is the best time to plant, and in the spring after frost danger has passed is the second choice.

Midwest (MW) has cold winters and hot summers. There is increasing tendency for periodic summer droughts toward the West, where there is generally less precipitation than in the East. The optimum planting time is in the early spring as soon as the ground can be worked (mid-March to late April). Mid-autumn (October and November) is the next-best time to plant.

The Great Plains (GP) stretch from Canada to Texas and have a range in winter temperatures from very frigid to cold. Summer temperatures are generally hot. There tends to be less precipitation here than in the Midwest or Southeast since the Great Plains lie in the rain shadow of the Rocky Mountains. Soil moisture is more plentiful in the spring than in other seasons, so it is best to plant in the late fall, before the ground freezes, to allow the wildflowers and grasses to take full advantage of the natural moisture.

The Rocky Mountains (RM) region typically has cold winters and warm summers with low humidity. Most of the precipitation accumulates in the form of snow during the winter and is released in the spring when most of the wildflowers bloom. The best planting in this region is during the autumn.

The Southwest (SW) is an area of scanty rainfall. In southern coastal California, most of this rain comes during the winter. Summer thunderstorms occur more frequently inland. The summer and early autumn temperatures are frequently in the 90 to 100°F. range. Winter temperatures range from cold in the North to balmy in the southern portions of California and Arizona. The best time to plant is in the late autumn just before the winter rains start.

The Northwest (NW) has cool winters and mild summers with considerable amounts of rainfall throughout the year, especially during the winter. Whether to plant in the spring or fall depends upon the species of wildflowers and grasses being planted. Spring-flowering wildflowers should generally be planted in the early fall, and autumn-flowering wildflowers should be planted in the spring.

Preparing Bare Ground

The easiest time to create a wildflower meadow is when the land is bare and you do not have to deal with established, competing grasses, weeds, herbaceous plants, or woody seedlings. If you are planting a large area of bare ground it may be easiest to hire a landscaper to disk and then rake the soil surface with tractor-drawn equipment. Smaller areas can be raked by hand. Most wildflower and grass species benefit from additions of rotted manure, compost, or other appropriate seed-free organic matter along with ground limestone at the time the soil is being prepared.

If time permits, have the ground raked again about three weeks later. The second raking will help kill any weeds that sprouted from seeds brought to the surface by the initial soil preparation. Then plant the wildflower and grass seed mixture. If you cannot plant your meadow until the following planting season, sow a cover crop of buckwheat, oats, or annual rye on the area in the fall, and plow it under as a green manure before sowing the wildflower and grass seeds.

How to Plant Seeds

It is best to sow the wildflower and grass seeds on a windless day, broadcasting them by hand or using a whirlwind seeder. Try to apply the seeds as uniformly as possible over the ground surface. If large areas are to be planted it may be worthwhile hiring a landscaping contractor to use a seed drill to plant them. Hopefully, your planting has been timed to take advantage of natural rainfall; but if the rains should fail, keep the soil moist, but not wet, until the seeds have germinated and seedlings start to become established. A light covering of seed-free straw will help conserve moisture and reduce erosion until the meadow is established. Do not use baled field hay, which is likely to contain the seeds of exotic grasses, species you want to prevent from invading your meadow.

Cold Treatments. Some wildflower seeds require exposure to cold temperatures in order to germinate. Typically these are wildflowers from regions with cold winters and have evolved this protection to prevent their seeds from germinating in the autumn only to have the tender seedlings killed by frost. However, most of these wildflowers can be grown successfully even in regions with mild winters if the seeds are first given an artificial cold treatment. Once established, these wildflowers will produce flowers and seeds, but the new seeds will not germinate unless they also receive cold treatments.

If you live in a region with cold winters, it is best to plant the seeds of these wildflowers outdoors in the autumn. If you live in a region with mild winters and want to give these species a try, or if you want to plant the seeds in the spring rather than in the autumn, give them an artificial cold treatment before planting them. Sprinkle the seeds on a moistened paper towel or damp peat moss, place them in a zip-closure bag (labeled in waterproof ink with the name of the species), and put them in the refrigerator for two to three months. This treatment will enable the seeds to germinate quickly in the spring. If some of the seeds sprout during the cold treatment, just plant them in the spring, being careful not to disturb their fragile root systems.

Transforming an Existing Field

Instead of bare ground, you are more likely to be confronted with an existing lawn or field that you want to convert to a wildflower meadow. *Resist any impulses to use herbicides or fumigants to kill the existing vegetation.* Herbicides are more likely to create problems for the wildflower enthusiast than solve them. They cause damage to the environment and are not likely to save you any time in establishing a wildflower meadow.

The least effective way to try to create a wildflower meadow is to simply scatter seeds into an existing lawn or meadow. Most of the seeds won't make it through the existing grass but will be consumed by insects or small mammals. Few of the seeds will germinate and become established. The best way to turn an existing field into a wildflower meadow is to start on a small scale and not tackle the entire back forty at once.

Two strategies can be deployed in your battle against existing sod: spot seeding and transplanting live plants that you have raised. In either approach you need to carefully prepare the site before planting. It is best to start a year in advance, or at least start in the previous spring for fall planting or in the late summer for spring planting.

As soon as the soil can be worked at the beginning of the growing season, dig up patches of the field, turning them over with a sharp spade or rototiller. The patches should be 3 to 8 feet in diameter and dug in a random pattern, to create a more natural effect than would result from placing them in straight rows. Remove as many of the existing grass roots as possible, and water the soil to encourage the germination of weed seeds that have been stirred up in the process. Then cover the patch with heavy-gauge black plastic sheet mulch, pieces of discarded carpet, or even thick sections of newspaper. If you do not care for the sight of such coverings, you can spread a layer of bark mulch or soil on top of them. If the covering is thick enough, it will eventually shade out and kill off any remaining grass and the newly germinated weed seedlings. Enough rain will soak through or get under the coverings to keep the ground below moist.

Leave the coverings on the patches throughout the growing season, then remove them at planting time. (If black plastic mulch or carpet sections have been used, it may be possible to use them again to create the next year's patches). Rake the ground surface, and plant the grass and wildflower seeds, gently raking them below the soil surface. Alternatively, the seeds can be mixed with an equal volume of soil and the mixture broadcast in the bare patches.

Instead of planting wildflower seeds in the patches you may wish to transplant live plants. These may be raised in your own nursery beds or in plastic trays with small conical depressions, producing "plugs" of wildflowers. Grass seed can also be planted in small pots to make plugs. If you plant seeds in containers, use a mixture of sand and peat moss as a starter soil. Whether you sow the seeds in beds, flats, or trays, do it at the beginning of the growing season. By the time the patches are prepared, the plants will be ready for transplanting.

Plant the plugs in the patch, spacing the grass clumps 12 to 15 inches apart, and placing the wildflowers in between them. Alternatively, wildflower plants can be transplanted into the patches, and the grass seed sown around them. In either method, the meadow will benefit from an initial watering and a light mulch of seed-free straw.

If your meadow already has bunch grasses, and you do not care to introduce new grass species, live wildflowers can be planted directly into the field. Clear a small patch about a foot in diameter with a cultivator and pick out the grass roots. Set the wildflowers so the bases of their shoots are at ground level. Press them down firmly so the roots are in good contact with the soil beneath, and water well.

Repeat the steps each year until you are satisfied with your wildflower and native grass meadow. It may be a slow process, but even in nature, a beautiful wildflower meadow, resplendent with a great diversity of desirable plants, is rarely produced in a single year.

Wildflower Meadow Maintenance

Once the wildflower meadow is established, it is relatively easy to maintain. Mow the meadow once a year with a rotary mower, after the growing season is over and the seeds have set; otherwise the natural process of succession may eventually turn your field into a forest. Woody plants will be clipped off and eventually eliminated by mowing, but grasses and wildflowers will be relatively unaffected.

Meadows, grasslands, and prairies can also be maintained by periodic burning, which kills invading shrub and tree seedlings. Do not burn a meadow until after the second season, but then you can burn it every several years. Meadows are best burned in the dormant season on windless days, when the grass is dry but the soil is still wet and the humidity is sufficiently high to minimize any fire danger to surrounding areas. If the meadow grass is too thin to support the fire, dry straw can be scattered about and ignited. Be careful to observe local, state, and federal regulations concerning outdoor burning, in addition to the usual safety practices. Check with your local fire department about obtaining an outdoor burning permit.

ROCK GARDENS

If your property has a slope dotted with interesting or weathered rock formations, it may be an ideal spot for a rock garden or rockery, as it is sometimes called. But any garden that features rocks

A rock garden of wildflowers.

prominently can be called a rock garden. It is not even necessary to have a slope — one can be created on a flat location with just a few loads of top soil and a pile of rocks.

Some purists feel that a rock garden should contain only those plants which grow naturally on rocky slopes in poor soil, but most rock gardeners use a wide variety of low-growing perennials, annuals, bulbs, and shrubbery. The term "rock plants," however, usually refers to species that grow in temperate areas rather than subtropical desert spots, and it is those species that are described here.

If you want the overall effect to be beautiful, a rock garden must be carefully designed rather than aimlessly constructed. Yet even though it may have been weeks in the planning, it should look as if it evolved naturally.

Because rockeries must be planted and cared for by hand, it is best to start with a small area unless you have lots of time, interest, and skill. If you have the perfect spot, you may not need to do more than choose plants, locate paths, and create level outcroppings as kneeling places. But if you must bring in rocks and soil you'll have more planning and work ahead. Choose rocks that are compatible with the landscape, if they are available, rather than those that are quarried, highly colored, or polished. If excavating is necessary, dump the topsoil in piles close by while the work is being done, so that you can replace it later. Set the rocks in the lowest, front part of the garden first and work upward, burying more than half of each rock firmly so it will be well anchored. After the rocks are in place, let the soil settle around them for a few days before planting. Check your construction frequently at the early stages by viewing it from a distance as well as close

up, to be sure the positioning is aesthetically pleasing.

Most rock garden plants need full or nearly full sun, and although they do not require extremely fertile soil, it should be at least 8 inches deep and have excellent drainage so that water pockets will not form. To accomplish this, spread a layer of crushed rock between the rocks before putting back the topsoil. If the soil is heavy mix in some sand and peat moss to lighten it. If any of the plants you are using need more fertility than ordinary rock plants, mix a little compost, leaf mold, or manure into the soil where these will be planted.

Choosing Plants

There is a wide variety of plants to choose from, which makes it a challenge to find the perfect species for your site and combine them aesthetically. The best plants are compact, low-growing perennials. To achieve pleasing combinations, consider not only plant color and mature height, but also form: are they rounded (crane's-bill), spiky (iris), or prostrate and spreading (thyme or ground phlox)?

The size of the plants should be on the same scale as the garden itself. Tiny plants look best in a small space; taller perennials, dwarf evergreens, and low-growing shrubs, such as potentilla or spreading cotoneaster, are more appropriate to a long wide hillside. And because so many of the plants best suited to a rock garden bloom only in the spring, you may want to consider strategic placement of summer-blooming heaths, heathers, and perhaps some annuals to add more color during the rest of the growing season.

Select those plants that are best for your climate and exposure — whether it is a cool, north-facing hillside or a dry, sunny slope. If you live where winters are long and the growing season short, you may be able to establish a true alpine garden of plants that are native to the European mountain ranges, Rockies, White Mountains, or other high elevations. Most of these are small or compact with rugged root systems that enable them to live in poor soil and under severe weather con-

TRADITIONAL ROCK GARDEN PLANTS

The following perennials are well suited to rock gardens.

Achillea tomentosa (wooly yarrow). Yellow, flowering dwarf plant about 12 inches tall.

Adonis amurensis plena (amur adonis). Early blooming, with yellow-green flowers 6 inches tall.

Aethionema cordifolium (Lebanon stonecress). Dwarf plant, seldom over 3 inches tall, with blue foliage and soft pink blossoms.

Ajuga (bugleweed). Fast-growing, dwarf ground cover. *A. reptans rubra* has purplish-red flowers and purple foliage. A. *reptans alba* has dark green foliage and 6-inch white spikes for blooms.

Alchemilla (lady's-mantle). Good ground cover that spreads rapidly from seed. Grows 8 to 12 inches tall.

Alyssum saxatile (basket-of-gold). Excellent for edging perennial borders and rock gardens. The varieties *A.s.* 'Citrina' (pale yellow), *A.s.* 'Compacta' (dwarf with bright yellow blooms), and *A. flora plenum* (yellow double blooms) are all better than the common variety.

Anchusa (summer forget-me-not, bugloss). *A. myosotidiflora* is a dwarf variety suitable for rock planting.

Anemone pulsatilla (pasque flower). Grows 8 to 12 inches tall with finely cut grayish leaves and purple flowers. Needs acid soil; blooms in spring. *A.p. alba* is a white-blooming form; *A. magellanica* also has white blooms and is recommended where winters are too severe for *A. pulsatilla* varieties.

Aquilegia (columbine). Native wild varieties are best for rock gardens. Has red, white, blue, or yellow flowers, sometimes in combinations. Grows about 15 inches tall.

Arabis (rockcress). *A. caucasica* is the common form, but *A. alpina* blooms better; both have white flowers. 'Flor-pleno' has double-white blossoms, and 'Rosabella' has rose-pink ones.

Arenaria (sandwort). *A. montana*, or mountain sandwort, grows to a height of 4 inches and is one of the best of this genus for rock gardens.

Artemisia. Usually planted for its silvery-gray foliage rather than its bloom. *A. schmidtiana* (silvermound) is one of the best for rock gardens.

Asarum (wild ginger). Low-growing plant with fragrant rootstocks and attractive foliage. Likes woodsy soil filled with leaf mold.

Aster. Many dwarf kinds are suitable for rock gardens.

Aubrieta deltoidea (purple rockcress). Grows well in the poor dry soils characteristic of rock gardens. Many hybrids, some of pink, red, and lavender.

Bellis perennis (English daisy). Low-growing, free-flowering dwarf plants with daisylike blooms. Spreads rapidly both by division and by seed.

Bergenia cordifolia (heartleaf bergenia). Thick, rosettelike leaves with pink flowers on

12-inch stems. They prefer afternoon shade and sandy soil combined with lime.

Cactus. The hardy cacti, *Opuntia*, are good rock garden plants. They need light soil with lots of leaf mold, loam, sand, and enough lime so that it's not at all acidic. Extra water is required during the summer.

Campanula (bellflower). Dwarf bellflowers make good rock garden plants. Among the best are *C. carpatica*, *C. garbanica* with star-shaped blooms, *C. glomerata*, *C. portenschlagiana*, and *C. rotundifolia*. They do best when mulched over the winter and should be divided at least every three years.

Catananche caerulea (cupid's-dart). Attractive blue or white flowers, excellent for drying, and easily grown.

Cerastium tomentosum (snow-in-summer). A low-growing plant with pure white flowers, that looks like a snowy carpet.

Ceratostigma plumbaginoides (leadwort, plumbago). Valuable for its blue flowers that appear over a long season, and also for its glossy-green foliage. Needs winter protection in cold regions.

Corydalis lutea. These small plants (up to 12 inches high) are ideal for the rock garden. They grow well in light, dry soils and can tolerate both sun and shade.

Dianthus (garden pinks). Many species of *Dianthus* are appropriate for a rock garden. Their free-flowering habits add color when little else is in bloom. Among the best are sweet William, the grass pink, and maiden pink, although there are many more. They need a well-drained soil to ensure a long growing period and must be divided often. Sweet William should be treated as a biennial and planted each year, even though it may live longer.

Dicentra eximia (fernleaf bleeding-heart). This neat little plant blooms for most of the summer. It has attractive foliage, does best in light shade, and should be divided often.

Dracocephalum ruyschiana (Siberian dragonhead). Purple flowers in spikes that grow about 12 inches tall. Easy to grow from seed.

Epimedium (bishop's-hat). Twelve inches tall with a variety of blossom colors. Likes moist, sandy loam and light shade; must not be allowed to dry out.

Euphorbia (spurge). There are over a thousand species of this one plant, many of which are suitable for rock gardens. Most like sandy, dry soils; some have brightly colored blossoms.

Ferns. Although most ferns like moist soil, a few thrive on dry, rocky land. Four of the most useful in a rockery are common polypody, hayscented fern, sensitive fern, and rusty woodsia.

Festuca glauca (blue fescue). A silvery-blue, tufted grass that grows to a height of 10 inches.

Filipendula (meadowsweet). *F. hexapetala* 'Flora Pleno' grows to 18 inches, has double blooms, and attractive foliage.

Gaillardia (blanketflower). One of the best varieties is known as 'Goblin'; it grows only 12 inches tall and has red and yellow blooms from July until frost. This genus likes warm, sandy soils and full sun; should be divided annually.

Galium boreale (northern bedstraw). Feathery leaves and tiny flowers resembling wild baby's-breath. Grows easily, but is too tall for many places.

Galium odoratum (sweet woodruff). Good ground cover. Grows well in the tiny crevices between rocks, but can become weedy. Sometimes listed as *Asperula odorata*.

Geranium sanguineum (crane's-bill). There are many varieties of this low-growing plant; they like moist, cool places and are easily grown from seed.

Geum (avens). Double and single flowers of good size on 12-inch plants. They grow best in sun or light shade in nearly any kind of soil, but should not be in a wet place over the winter.

Gypsophila repens (baby's-breath). The dwarf varieties *G. alba* and *G. rosea* are both excellent for the rock garden. Plant in full sun and water frequently.

Helianthemum (sunrose). Shrubby plant, good for hot, dry places and a limestone soil. Needs winter protection in the North.

Hemerocallis (daylily). The dwarf kinds add summer bloom when the flowering season of many rock plants is over.

Heuchera sanguinea (coral-bells). These small and dainty flowers bloom all summer in pink, red, and white.

Hosta. Miniature varieties such as 'Pinwheel' are recommended.

Iberis (candytuft). Low-growing, evergreen, shrubby with white blossoms. Likes full sun, plenty of moisture, and once established should not be disturbed.

Iris. Dwarf iris are ideal for rock gardens — they like sun and need little care. 'Sea Jewell' and 'Aqua Star' are outstanding new introductions.

Leontopodium alpinum (edelweiss). One of the best known and beloved of all alpine plants, it is easily grown in the rock garden. Likes rich, somewhat sandy soil with a little lime, and enjoys growing among rocks.

Limonium (sea lavender). Grows well nearly everywhere if the soil is not too heavy.

Linaria alpina (alpine toadflax). One of the best *Linaria* for the rock garden.

Linum (flax). These blue-flowering perennials make ideal rock plants.

Lychnis (campion). Many of these are ideal for the rock garden.

Mertensia virginica (Virginia bluebells). Early pink and blue blooms.

Myosotis (forget-me-not). Allow them to go to seed, which will keep new plants coming.

Phlox. Dwarf, creeping kinds are best as rock garden plants; they need full sun. *P. subulata* comes in several bright colors.

Polemonium (Jacob's-ladder). Does best in rich soil and light shade.

Primula (primrose). These prefer heavy, rich, slightly acidic soil, and plenty of moisture.

Ranunculus (buttercup). Easy to grow, but may not overwinter well in the North.

Saponaria (soapwort). Fast-spreading, creeping plant with pink flowers; blossoms in early spring.

Saxifraga (saxifrage). These come in many forms, which are ideal for the rock garden because they grow easily in tough places.

Sedum. Old reliables of the rock garden. They grow fast, and some kinds can quickly take over an entire slope. Plant in sandy soil and full sun for best results.

Sempervivum. The hen-and-chickens and houseleek varieties are ideal.

Silene schafta (moss campion). Summer-blossoming dwarf plant with pink blooms.

Stachys lanata (betony). Lavender flowers that appear in summer.

Thymus (thyme). Some of the thymes make thick mats that are ideal for the rock garden. An added attraction is their heavy bloom of pink and lavender flowers.

Tunica saxifraga (tunic flower). Makes a thick mat with pale pink blooms that last throughout the summer. Also called *Petrorhagia*.

Veronica (speedwell). The low-growing kinds are best for rock gardens. They like sun, moist soil, and occasional feeding.

Viola (violet). An easy-to-grow perennial. Choose varieties carefully — some like sun, others do best in shade.

---

ditions. They need cool weather — especially cool summers — and perfect drainage to do well.

Certain nurseries specialize entirely in alpine and rock garden species and their catalogs are good sources of planting ideas. The American Rock Garden Society and other horticultural associations can be invaluable resources, too. The members often swap seeds, plants, and ideas. A few of the most popular alpine plants are listed in box (right).

Rock Garden Care

Your rock garden could be compared to a collection of potted plants, and they will grow best if you tend them accordingly. Be sure each "pot" is well drained so that water will not collect there and drown the plant. Loosen the soil in each pocket occasionally with a small garden fork. Although most rock plants do well in poor soil, add dry manure or liquid fertilizer if the plants seem weak.

Housekeeping chores include cutting back any leggy plants after flowering, clipping off dead portions, and dividing any plant that becomes rootbound or too large for its space. Check for insects

COMMON ALPINE PLANTS

Anemone alpina, alpine anemone
Aquilegia alpina, alpine columbine
Arabis alpina, alpine rockcress
Aster alpinus, alpine aster
Dianthus alpinus, alpine pink
Hymenosys grandiflora, alpine sunflower
Lenotopodium alpinum, edelweiss
Myosotis alpestris, alpine forget-me-not
Papaver alpinum, alpine poppy
Satureja spp., savory
Silene quadrifida, alpine catchfly

and diseases as in any other bed; slugs may be especially pesky because they enjoy the shelter found among rocks. Never let weeds grow in the nooks and crannies, not only for appearance's sake, but more importantly, because they will quickly crowd out the other plants.

Winter weather can be hard on tender plant varieties because they are more exposed to cold winds and dehydration in a rock garden than when growing in level beds. Alpines on their native mountaintops have become toughened, but are also accustomed to a heavy snow cover. If you don't get much snow, a mulch will help to protect both hearty and more tender plants. In particularly exposed regions of this continent it is a good idea to cover the entire bed with evergreen branches or straw as well just after the ground starts to freeze.

THE BIRD WATCHER'S GARDEN

Gardeners may rate plants for their visual appeal, but birds are more interested in cuisine. If you provide a yard that offers a lush menu of fruit, seeds, nectar, insects, and perhaps a feeder or two, it will get a five-star rating from the winged world! Fortunately, it is easy to develop such a landscape because a great many of the most colorful and popular flowers, shrubs, and trees are ideal habitats for a variety of birds.

Create a Hummingbird Haven

No matter where you live, some kind of hummingbird may find you. East of the Mississippi, it will be the ruby-throated, but several others, including the rufous, broad-tailed, and black-chinned are found in the West. All are attracted to flowers by sight rather than scent. Their favorite colors are red, pink, and orange because flowers with those hues are most likely to provide nectar, especially those with tubular shapes, such as the fuchsia. Color triggers such an automatic response in these birds that they will curiously inspect even a red umbrella, orange shirt, or red-handled hoe! In a shady spot, bright orange shades appeal most to them; in dry,

desert locations where flowers, leaves, and grass are scarce, they are attracted to green flowers.

Obviously, the perennials in a hummingbird garden should feature their favorite colors. Plant plenty of them, because the birds need a great deal of nectar to satisfy their voracious appetites. Try to choose species with blossoming seasons that overlap, to provide a constant food supply. Red-hued annuals, such as petunias, salvia, geraniums, cosmos, scarlet runner beans, and snapdragons can be interspersed to provide nectar throughout the summer when there are gaps in the perennial blossoms. Many flowering shrubs are also attractive to hummingbirds.

Hummingbird garden

The return of the hummingbirds from their winter home is timed to coincide with the blooming of nectar-producing flowers in the spring, but some years blossoms are delayed by cool, wet weather. You can help to ensure the survival of the birds by providing artificial nectar. Place a solution of one part sugar to four parts water, that has been brought to a boil, in a hummingbird feeder, and the birds will quickly find it. Do not use honey, because it can quickly develop bacteria in warm weather. The sweet syrup provides energy, but not much nourishment — for that they'll need nectar from your flowers, as well as aphids, tiny spiders, and other small insects. Avoid using insecticides or other chemicals that might diminish their food supply or poison them.

HUMMINGBIRD FAVORITES

Perennials

Red-hued varieties of the following perennials attract hummingbirds and supply nectar as well.

Althaea, hollyhock
Aquilegia, columbine
Asclepias, butterfly weed
Campanula, bellflower
Delphinium, larkspur
Dianthus, pinks, carnation, sweet William
Digitalis, foxglove
Echinops, globe thistle
Hemerocallis, daylily
Heuchera, coral bells
Iris, bearded kinds
Lilium, lily
Lupinus, lupine
Lychnis, campion
Lythrum, loosestrife
Monarda, bee balm
Nepeta, catmint
Papaver, poppy
Penstemon, beardtongue
Phlox paniculata, garden phlox
Salvia, sage
Saponaria, bouncing bet
Stachys, betony

Shrubs & Vines

Red-flowering varieties of the following shrubs and vines are also attractive to the hummers and may be used to complement the perennials.

Buddleia, butterfly bush
Caragana, pea shrub
Chaenomeles, flowering quince
Cotoneaster
Kolkwitzia, beauty bush
Lonicera, honeysuckle
Rhododendron, azalea
Ribes, flowering currant
Syringa, lilac
Weigela

BUTTERFLY GARDEN

Few sights are more delightful than that of a butterfly dancing on the breeze. But sadly enough, butterflies have become all too rare in our rapidly expanding world. The sheer beauty of butterflies has, in the past, prompted the collection and sale of these insects. Twenty years ago this could have been blamed for their disappearance, but it is unusual in this day and age for a collector to capture and kill a butterfly. Most modern day collectors capture their beautiful specimens on film.

So where have the butterflies gone?

The disappearance of butterflies must largely be blamed on ourselves. Condominiums and shopping malls have taken over the fields and grassy meadows that served as the breeding grounds for many of our butterflies, and the misuse of backyard pesticides has left them with no alternative environment in which to live and multiply.

By growing a few chosen plants in your yard, you will be making a major contribution toward the preservation of these fragile insects, supplying them with a haven in which to live and breed.

You don't need a large area to have a successful butterfly garden teeming with winged color. A butterfly garden can be grown in a window box, from hanging pots on a terrace or balcony, or from a patch of yard. All it takes is a little planning.

You will, however, need to plant your butterfly garden in a sunny spot, as butterflies are notorious sun-worshipers. But most butterfly flowers are easy to grow and require little care, which affords you plenty of time to sit back and enjoy the view of color, not just on the ground, but in the air as well.

How a Butterfly Garden Works

Although butterflies need a shady spot to find respite from the sun during those days we consider scorchers, for the most part they spend their time in the sunshine. This is due to a butterfly's need to raise its body temperature in order to fly. Butterflies perch on flowers and shrubs to bask in the sun and absorb the solar benefits until their bodies reach a temperature of 86 to 104°F. So it should come as no surprise that most butterfly flowers are those of the sun-loving variety.

BUTTERFLY FAVORITES

Perennials

Asclepais tuberosa, butterfly weed
Buddleia, butterfly bush
Centaurea macrocephala, globe centaurea
Dianthus, pinks, sweet William
Digitalis, foxglove
Echinops, globe thistle
Eupatorium colestinum, mistflower
Hesperis, rocket
Liatris, gayfeather
Lilium, lily
Lupinus, lupine
Monarda, bee balm
Rudbeckia, gloriosa daisy, golden-glow

Annuals

Antirrhinum majus, snapdragon
Cassia, cassia
Cosmos bipinnatus, cosmos
Helianthus annus, sunflower
Heliotropium, heliotrope
Ipomoea, morning-glory
Lunaria annua, honesty
Tagetes, marigold
Tropaeolum majus, nasturtium
Viola, pansy
Zinnia, zinnia

The colors in a butterfly garden also play a major role in their attraction. Scientists now know that butterflies have the ability to identify colors. Purple, pink, yellow, and white are the colors most often preferred by butterflies, so when planning your garden you'll want to keep these colors in mind.

A true butterfly garden contains plants that provide food for the larvae caterpillars, as well as nectar for the butterfly. In general, the wildflowers that are part of their natural environment are the best choices for planting in a butterfly garden. The Monarchs, for example, choose milkweed as the spot to lay their eggs, and they can often be found in the fall on goldenrod.

Pest Control in the Butterfly Garden

Obviously, pesticides are out of the question in a butterfly garden, so what can you do when pests invade?

First of all, invasions themselves can often be avoided. Many common garden pests can be stopped if their presence is detected early on. A daily inspection of your butterfly garden is helpful.

Keeping the perimeter of the garden free of weeds is often a good idea, as many pests, such as aphids, first hide among the weeds. But don't forget that weeds are often the plants that butterflies are most attracted to.

If you do detect the onset of aphids in your butterfly garden, a fine spray of the garden hose should get rid of them. The same goes for many beetles. Beetles are large enough to be picked off by hand, however; aphids are more difficult to see.

THE FLOWER ARRANGER'S GARDEN

The flower arranger is an artist whose materials are those things that grow around him or her. Choosing and growing your own materials can be as creative an experience as making the finished arrangement.

Growing your own plant material for flower

arrangements allows you to plan ahead. With some forethought, you can grow certain flowers for a special event such as a wedding or a flower show, have enough foliage for large arrangements, and decorate your home year-round with bouquets of homegrown flowers.

A flower arranger's garden does not, however, have to be large. A garden can be created on a small scale that will give you flowers and foliage throughout the year. Trees, shrubs, edging plants, and even herb and vegetable gardens can be planted with a flower arrangement in mind. Chive flowers dry beautifully and work well in small bouquets. A few leaves of a red lettuce can be tucked into a bowl of green Envy zinnias for a striking, and maybe ribbon-winning, arrangement.

Choosing Flowers for Cutting

Before planting something you should consider not only how it will look in the garden but also how it will do when cut and brought into the house. In addition, there are other questions to consider when choosing a plant:

- Does it flower?

- When will it bloom?

- What is its lasting quality when cut?

- Is it fragrant?

- Is it available during the barren seasons?

- Does it have a good form or color when viewed up close?

- Does it have interesting branches or foliage?

- Can it be dried or preserved for continuous use?

- Will its color work in the home and with the other plants already in the garden?

Not all of the plants you grow will be suitable for cutting. Some flowers won't take up water and will quickly wilt when placed in a vase of water.

In planning your garden, you may first want to consider what already grows around your home. If there are evergreens planted near the house, you may have enough foliage for winter arrangements. Perhaps you have lilacs for May bloom and need color in July and August. Or, you have only yellow flowers in a perennial border and yellow is the one color that does not work in your peach living room. Make a list of the kind of plant material you already have and another list of what you would like to have. Then, think about where you could plant this.

Trees and Shrubs for Floral Arrangements

Trees and shrubs are the backbone of every garden and can provide excellent foliage for flower arrangements. They are also very useful in the autumn, winter, and early spring when there isn't much else in the garden. Since they will probably be the biggest plants in your garden, it is wise to consider them first.

If your garden is small you will have to be careful of the eventual size of the plants you choose. The small yew purchased at the nursery today might take over the garden in five years and have to be pulled out. In addition to size, check the plant's hardiness, freedom from disease, and ease of growth. And — something that is often overlooked — what does the plant look like in each season? Is a lack of flowers more than offset by brilliant red foliage in the fall? Does it have berries that last all winter long? Is it deciduous? Is the foliage variegated or plain? Is the bark interesting? Do the branches grow in a curving pattern?

There are many excellent specimen trees that do well in arrangements. The flowering cherries, crabapples, dogwoods, magnolias, hollies, and birches (with their wonderful bark), are dramatic accents in a garden as well as later in a mixed arrangement. The miniature red-leafed Japanese maple has foliage that is worthwhile, and is small enough so that it can easily be placed into many different garden plots.

Trees

Maple (*Acer* species). There are many forms of this deciduous tree that do well in most parts of the country. The smaller varieties are good for the arranger, as the leaves in autumn, and in some varieties all year round, can provide excellent color in arrangements. All varieties need good soil to grow; some will retain the red or yellow color of the foliage throughout the year. A popular variety is the threadleaf Japanese maple (*A. palmatum dissectum*). This has finely cut, blood red leaves and graceful branches. Its leaves, mixed with a few pale pink peonies, are delightful.

Dogwood (*Cornus* species). An excellent choice for flower arrangements if you don't live too far north, though some cultivars can withstand cold temperatures and brisk winds. Dogwoods prefer a rich soil in either sun or shade. The variety *C. alba* 'Sibirica' has brilliant red stems which can be used in striking winter flower arrangements.

Cherry (*Prunus* species). Those in the *Prunus serrulata* group grow to 25 feet, with single or double, pink or white flowers that bloom early, before the leaves appear. Check for hardiness for your area. *P. yedoensis* grows to about 48 feet and is a very attractive tree with graceful branches and slightly fragrant white to pink flowers.

Shrubs

Shrubs are good choices since they can be used as the framework of many floral arrangements. In the fall or winter, a few branches of a dark green yew or a lighter juniper in a vase with one or two pur-chased flowers will easily lift your spirits, and won't be too hard on your budget since the basis of the arrangement is already in the garden.

There is a wide selection of shrubs for a mixed garden border. Some can go almost unnoticed in a garden but are handsome additions to a flower arrangement. These include cotoneaster, spirea, potentilla and the dwarf hollies. Other shrubs are more dramatic and won't recede into the background. These include many of the azaleas, the viburnums, *Enkianthus campanulatus* (with its autumn foliage), the many forms of euonymus, pyracantha (with its orange-red berries), and many of the dark green yews and silver-gray junipers. Underneath shrubs is a good location for ground covers such as pachysandra, vinca, and ivy, which are essential. A bowl filled with pachysandra can be a long-lasting base for many future flower arrangements.

Hedges are something else to think about. You can grow such delights as forsythia, bush honeysuckle (*Lonicera* species), the old-fashioned mock orange, the *rugosa* roses (which have large hips in the late summer and fall), and many species of *Syringa*, including the common lilac.

There are numerous shrubs that work well in a garden and are excellent for the flower arrangement. The choice depends on your needs, which may be for foliage, early spring bloom, winter berries, or perhaps all of these.

Butterfly Bush (*Buddleia*). Very fragrant blossoms and naturally curving stems which provide needed line in flower arrangements. *B. alternifolia* is a hardy variety with small, lavender flowers. *B. davidii magnifica*, the oxeye butterfly bush, is commonly grown. Its flowers are dark blue with orange eyes.

Box or Boxwood (*Buxus*). A wonderful shrub for both the garden and the arrangement, provided it will grow in your area. The English box (*B. sempervirens*) and its many varieties are not considered hardy north of Zone 6. Look for locally grown plants that will be hardy in the area where you live. Box foliage is extremely long-lasting in a flower arrangement and attractive for background filler.

Cypress (*Chamaecyparis*). An evergreen with flat branches and small cones. Many of the cultivars have excellent spraylike foliage that can be used all year-long for background and to hide mechanics in a flower arrangement. It grows well in rich, moist soils and does not like dry or windy areas of the garden. It may not be hardy in some northern areas. Cultivars of *C. lawsoniana* (hardy to Zone 5) are good to look for.

Broom *(Cytisus)*. A must, not only for its myriad blossoms in different colors, but for its stems, which can be curved and dried into pleasing shapes for arrangements. The only problem with broom is that it is rarely hardy north of Boston. Some varieties will survive in the North with protection or in locations near the coast. The branches may be picked in the winter and look lovely alone or mixed with other flowers for an elegant line arrangement. *C. scoparius* (Scotch broom) is a native to Great Britain and has become naturalized in many parts of this country. It has masses of yellow flowers in the early summer and its many hybrids have flowers in different colors. *C. praecox* (Warminster broom) is a bit hardier than *C. scoparius*, and has yellow flowers and evergreen branches.

Eucalyptus *(Eucalyptus)*. Provides gray foliage to those lucky enough to live in warm climates. Its leaves absorb glycerine easily, keep their color well, and look fine with fresh flowers even when dried.

Euonymus *(Euonymus)*. Another must. It comes in many varieties and can be grown as a shrub, tree, or rapidly growing ground cover or vine. Its foliage is long lasting when cut and is great filler or base material for many arrangements. It comes in all-green or variegated forms. *E. fortunei* is very hardy with leathery, glossy green leaves. It has many cultivars with different colored leaves and growth habits. *E. japonica* is not as hardy but has many popular variegated varieties, such as *E. japonica albomarginata*, whose leaves have a thin rim of white around the edge.

Forsythia *(Forsythia)*. Can grow to absurd heights of over 12 feet and can get just as wide, but its really yellow blossoms are easy to force indoors and are such a welcome sign of spring that most gardeners find a spot for it. Forsythias do well in most any soil but they do prefer the sun for early flowering.

Witch Hazel *(Hamamelis)*. Has feathery flowers on its stems and makes a simple arrangement with little else added. *H. virginiana* blooms late in the fall, which is a plus. Others bloom very early in the year, sometimes in February or March, before the leaves appear. For this reason alone, it is a useful plant. *H. mollis* is a popular witch hazel with yellow flowers from winter to spring and yellow leaves in the fall.

Holly *(Ilex)*. Where it is hardy, holly is an excellent choice for a border. It is traditional for winter arrangements. It is very long lasting once picked and placed in water and looks well with most flowers. *Ilex aquifolium* is the common holly and the parent of many useful cultivars.

Mock Orange *(Philadelphus)*. Is very hardy and has fragrant blooms in midsummer. There are many varieties of *Philadelphus* that work well in a garden and in an arrangement.

Rhododendrons and Azaleas *(Rhododendron)*. Come in many varieties and colors. Some azaleas will not be hardy in the North, and they like lime-free soils. If you can grow them you will be rewarded with fine materials for flower arranging.

Lilac *(Syringa)*. Comes in many varieties in addition to the common lilac, *S. vulgaris*. There is a wide range of colors available, from deep purple to pale pink and clear white. A few lilac blooms mixed with their own dark green leaves and set in a white pitcher always looks good almost anywhere in the house.

Viburnum *(Viburnum)*. One of the best shrubs for a flower arranger because it has flowers, winter berries, and distinctive foliage. Among the many varieties to choose from are *V. plicatum* (Japanese snowball), *V. prunifolium*, with flat clusters of white flowers and black fruits, and *V. carlesii* (fragrant viburnum), with a delightful scent.

Flowers

Once trees and shrubs are selected for your yard, you will want to add the annuals, perennials, and bulbs for the variety that only flowers can give. One of the most important parts of your plan is to ensure continuous bloom throughout the season, beginning as early as you can, with spring tulips and daffodils, and continuing through the fall, with chrysanthemums and late bloomers, such as *Helenium*.

Seed catalogs are a good place to start when planning a cutting garden. Look for plants that are labeled "good for cutting." This usually means that the flower will hold up well after it has been cut. Flowers with long, firm stems are good, though weaker stems can be strengthened later by the addition of a thin florist's wire. Avoid flowers that fade quickly or fall apart soon after cutting. Sometimes you won't know this until you've tried them out one year.

Annuals

Annuals have a long period of bloom and bloom more abundantly the more they are cut, features which make them the mainstay of a good cutting garden. They are also easy to grow, fairly free of disease, and come in a wide variety of shapes and colors. Annuals can be tucked in between perennials, shrubs, or even vegetables. Or, they can have their own space, a bed apart from the rest. They're most adaptable.

Some seedlings can be started directly in the garden. Others have to be started indoors and then moved to the garden after danger of frost has passed. Proper spacing (depending on the size of the grown plant) is required, and weeding is necessary as the plant grows. Cut off any spent blooms to encourage further flowering. Annuals may need some liquid fertilizer during the growing season but most don't need to be fed frequently.

The list of annuals is long. Try anything that appeals to you. One to start from seed is salpiglossis or velvet flower. Its trumpet-shaped blossoms give a certain elegant touch to an otherwise simple arrangement. Others are asters, nasturtiums (with sunny leaves and bright blooms), petunias, cleome, and the daisy-type flowers, such as *Helianthus*. Others, not quite annuals, but grown as such, include

the gladioli and the dahlias. Here are some other annuals to try in your arranging garden.

Snapdragon (*Antirrhinum*). These tall, pointed flower stalks are excellent in flower arrangements, giving good form and line to many styles. They come in a wide variety of colors and are easily grown in light, rather rich soils in full sun. Start these seeds indoors, and place the plants in the garden at least 15 inches apart. They will flower all season.

Calendula (*Calendula officinalis*). This hardy annual is easy to grow. It comes in shades of orange, yellow, and cream, and holds up well in flower arrangements. Its rough texture makes it ideal for casual arrangements such as might be made in baskets or pottery bowls.

Calliopsis, or Annual Coreopsis (*Coreopsis*). These small, long-lasting flowers come in shades of yellow, orange, deep mahogany, and crimson. They look good even after all the petals have fallen off! Their brown stigmas and feathery foliage are delightful. They are easy to grow from seed.

Cosmos (*Cosmos*). The different forms of cosmos are attractive and long lasting when cut. Some of the tall-growing varieties need plenty of room to grow but the smaller ones can fit in most anywhere. If kept cut, they will bloom all summer long. Good single color varieties include the clear white 'Sensation' cosmos or the brilliant red *C. sulphureus* 'Diablo.' A dainty newer variety is *C. bipinnatus* 'Candy Stripe,' with white flowers edged in crimson. Cosmos starts easily from seed and likes a poor soil. If the soil is too rich you are likely to get lush foliage and small flowers. Sow seed indoors in the spring or directly in the garden.

Flowering Tobacco (*Nicotiana*). These tube-shaped, starlike flowers come in a number of colors, including a lime green that is effective in flower arrangements. Nicotiana can be used in both formal and informal flower arrangements. Seeds should be started indoors and plants may be grown in full sun or part shade, spaced about 12 inches apart.

Marigold (*Tagetes*). Some people don't grow marigolds for arrangements, saying they are too common and don't add anything to a floral display. But marigolds, if chosen for color and style, can add long-lasting, colorful blooms to many casual bouquets. Some forms are large chrysanthemum types, while others are small and airier. They are all easy to grow and are best started indoors and moved to the garden. When cut, they need a lot of water.

Zinnia (*Zinnia*). These in all their varieties are fundamental for an arranger's garden. The single-color varieties rather than the mixed will enable you to grow the specific colors you want. The distinctive apple green color of the Envy zinnia always looks good when picked and added to a bouquet. Cut-and-come-again zinnias are good because they do just as their name indicates. Zinnias like full sun and rich soil to which compost or manure has been added. They start easily from seed sown directly in the garden or earlier indoors.

Perennials

There are so many perennials, it's difficult to choose. Yarrow, astilbe, and heliopsis are favorites for their constant bloom. Other musts include irises, delphiniums for their grandeur, and all the veronicas and salvias. Extras would be the perennial asters, *Helenium* for the early fall, feverfew, the alliums, monkshood, baby's breath and all the lilies. Biennials to include would be foxglove and sweet William. Lavender makes a good edging plant and its silvery leaves and purple, spiked flowers are excellent in a small arrangement. All the silvery artemisias are good additions. Their foliage holds up well and mixes nicely with many flowers. Hosta is a good choice for a shady spot. Although it is difficult to choose from the many varieties that are excellent for arrangements, here are a few to get started with.

Artemisia (*Artemisia*). Grown for its silver-gray foliage, which looks pretty arranged with pink or blue flowers. *A. ludoviciana* 'Silver Queen' is good for the border and easy to grow in well-drained soil, in full sun, or partial shade.

Astilbe (*Astilbe*). Has feathery, plumed spikes that grow above its ferny foliage. It likes fertile, moist soil with quite a bit of organic matter in it. Both flowers and leaves are excellent in arrangements, and very long lasting. The flowers also air dry well. Varieties to try include *A. x arendsii* 'Avalanche' (white flowers), *A. x arendsii* 'Ostrich Plume' (salmon-pink flowers), and *A. taquetii* 'Superba' (good-sized, bright pink plumes).

Baby's-breath (*Gypsophila paniculata*). Used a great deal, fresh and dried, in arrangements. Its starlike, small flowers add a light, airy touch to many arrangements and are good filler for those holes in masses of flowers. White is the usual color, though a pale pink is also useful. It prefers a well-drained, rich soil and does not like to be moved once established. It needs to be staked to keep it from sprawling in the garden.

Bee Balm (*Monarda didyma*). A showy flower that looks best in informal arrangements. 'Cambridge Scarlet' has brilliant red blooms and 'Croftway Pink' has light salmon-pink flowers. They are easy to grow but are invasive.

Bellflower (*Campanula*). Blends well with other garden flowers in mass arrangements. Choose varieties with long stems, such as *C. persicifolia* 'Grandiflora Alba' with white flowers on 2-foot stalks, and *C. persicifolia* 'Telham Beauty,' with blue flowers. They do well in sun, in a fertile soil with a dressing of lime, if needed.

Chrysanthemums (*Chrysanthemum*). Make excellent cut flowers and are invaluable for autumn arrangements. There are numerous varieties to choose from. Look for those in colors that will work well in your home. *C. maximum* is the favorite Shasta daisy which works well in so many arrangements and looks lovely in a garden border.

C. coccineum (pyrethrum) has daisylike flowers of bright pink or red. The flowers are very useful and work well in informal arrangements or used as a filler. They are easy to grow in sandy or loamy soil and like full sun.

Columbine (*Aquilegia*). Makes excellent cut flowers and lovely border plants, blooming for four to six weeks beginning in early June. The color range of the flowers covers pink, blue, yellow, red, and white. The hybrids to try include *A.* 'Langdon's Rainbow Hybrids,' *A. chrysantha* 'Crimson Star' (with long crimson spurs) and *A. chrysantha* 'Silver Queen' (pure white). Columbines are easy to grow from seed and prefer a cool, well-drained spot in partial shade or sun.

Coral-bells *(Heuchera sanguinea)*. Lovely, long-lasting cut flowers. Used to establish height in arrangements, the stems are slender but strong, and can be gently curved. The foliage is also useful in small arrangements. Coral bells is low growing and works well as an edging plant. It is easy to grow and will do well in sun or partial shade. *H. sanguinea* has crimson-red flowers that bloom from June to September. *H. sanguinea* 'White Cloud' is the white form.

Coreopsis *(Coreopsis)*. The lovely daisylike yellow of flowers of *C. grandiflora* have long, sturdy stems and make excellent, long-lasting cut flowers. Coreopsis likes a sunny location and will do well in any well-drained soil.

Delphinium *(Delphinium)*. An ideal outline material for very large arrangements. They are somewhat difficult to grow and require fertile soil, winter protection, and staking. There are many varieties; among the best is the Blackmore and Langdon strain, with large flowers and strong spikes. Though delphiniums are known best for their blue and purple shades, there are lovely pinks and whites to choose from as well.

Doronicum *(Doronicum cordatum)*. Blooms in early spring with yellow daisylike flowers. It is worth including in the garden for it looks lovely in a bouquet with red tulips and yellow narcissus. It goes dormant in the summer but is easy to grow in moist soil in either full or partial sun.

Gaillardia *(Gaillardia)*. A useful cutting flower, with bright blooms on sturdy stems. The daisylike flowers prefer a rich soil in full sun and will bloom all summer long if kept cut. Varieties to try include *G.* x *grandiflora* 'Burgundy' and 'Monarch Strain.'

Hosta *(Hosta)*. Grown for both its leaves and flowers. The flowers are long lasting and work well in masses of pastels, and the leaves can be used all summer long in all types of arrangements. There are many forms and sizes of hostas, some with pale green, solid-color leaves, others with variegated leaves. Hosta is easy to grow in ordinary soil but it prefers shady sites.

Iris *(Iris)*. An excellent flower for early spring arrangements. There are many types of iris, from the large bearded varieties to the simple Siberian and Japanese irises.

Lady's-mantle *(Alchemilla)*. Has clusters of unusual greenish or yellowish flowers that stand above the leaves and last a long time in water. The leaves also work well in arrangements. A good variety is *A. vulgaris*, with large, roundish leaves. It does well in sun or partial shade and ordinary garden soil.

Lily *(Lilium)*. One beautiful lily used by itself with a stalk of broom can be enough for an arrangement. Look for long-stemmed lilies in colors that go with the rest of your color scheme. They prefer filtered light and good air circulation, and can be planted in the fall or early spring. When you cut them, remove the stamens to prevent the inner surface of the flower from being marked by pollen.

Monkshood *(Aconitum)*. A beautiful flower for arrangements where blue is needed. Monkshood is a poisonous plant, however, so wash your hands after handling it. *A. napellus* 'Bressingham Spire' has violet-blue flowers on 3-foot spikes. *A. napellus* 'Album' has white flowers. They grow best in damp shade, but will grow in sun if kept moist.

Peony *(Paeonia)*. If you have room for just one peony be sure to plant it, for the foliage is long lasting and can be used as a base for arrangements all summer long. The back of a peony leaf, with its silver-gray cast, can be used as often as the darker green side. The flowers are elegant and rich looking, and the effect of a few massed in a bowl or just one floating in a dish of water are reason enough for this long-living plant. They like rich soil in full sun and a lot of space, as they become quite bushy when fully grown.

Phlox (*Phlox*). Old-fashioned flowers that look best in mixed summer bouquets. They like rich soil, and planting a few different varieties will help ensure blooms all summer long. Choose colors you like in the light pink or white range. Don't let them go to seed in the garden, as their seedlings tend to be a magenta color of little use.

Pincushion Flower (*Scabiosa*). Comes in shades of blue that are most useful to a flower arranger. The long stems make them good choices and they look good growing in the garden. They prefer a well-drained, light soil in full sun. *S. caucasica* grows to about 24 inches and blooms all summer.

Sage (*Salvia*). Comes in many forms and its chief value is the long life of the cut flowers. The taller varieties provide an arrangement with excellent outline. *S. haematodes* is a tall plant with lavender-blue flowers, and *S. x superba* has branching spikes of violet-blue flowers, and tends to be shorter.

Veronica (*Veronica*). Valuable for its many spiked flowers which last all summer and dry well. Some of the deepest blues come in this flower, and other colors range from white to pinks and purples. *V. latifolia* 'Crater Lake Blue' is 12 to 18 inches tall with true blue flowers. *V. spicata* has many cultivars worthy of cutting, including 'Red Fox,' with rosy flowers, and 'Blue Peter,' with deep blue blooms. Veronica is easy to grow in any well-drained soil, in either sun or partial shade.

Yarrow (*Achillea*). Yarrow is easy to grow and prefers a sunny spot in the garden. Its feathery foliage has a pungent odor and the plants flower throughout the summer and into the fall. Yarrow is available with yellow, white, and red flowers. All dry well and can be used in dried as well as fresh arrangements. Some varieties to grow include *A. filipendulina* 'Coronation Gold,' with lemon yellow flowers, and *A. millefolium* 'Red Beauty,' whose rosy flowers fade to pink and white as they grow.

Cutting and Conditioning Flowers

Success in flower arranging depends on knowing the best ways to condition and maintain plant material to keep them looking fresh.

Conditioning is the plant's process of taking on more water than it gives off, so as to put it into a prime state of freshness. It is all-important for creating flower arrangements that will last for more than a day. It is silly to spend all the time it takes to make a lovely arrangement only to have it begin wilting after a few hours because the material wasn't properly conditioned.

The general rules for conditioning most flowers are the same but there are specific things to do for various blooms. One rule is certain, however: it is best to cut plant material in the evening, because sugar has been stored in the plant tissue all day. The next best time to cut is early morning, and the poorest time is in the middle of the day.

Flowers should be cut with a sharp knife or a good pair of garden clippers. Cut the stem from the plant and remove all unnecessary foliage. As soon as the flower is cut, place the stem up to its neck in a bucket of warm water and place the flowers in a cool room for at least six hours, or overnight. A darkened room will slow the development of the blooms. Any that you want to open should be placed close to an indirect light source.

Special Treatment. Brittle stems (such as on chrysanthemums) should be broken to expose a greater surface for water intake. Woody stems (such as lilac) should be peeled back and split an inch or so. Milky stems (such as poppies) must be sealed with a match or other flame, or by dipping the end momentarily into boiling water. Milky stems need to be resealed each time they are cut, so they are not suitable for needlepoint holders, which pierce the stem.

Foliage plants should be cut when they are mature. Tender new growth usually should be removed. Most foliage can be immersed completely and some must be. Wilted plant material is not necessarily dead; it may be just thirsty. Recut the stems and place in hot water and most will revive. After conditioning, place the plant material in cool water in a cool room.

Preservatives. Some commercial chemical preparations added to the water in which plants are con-

CONDITIONING CUT FLOWERS

Flower	When to Cut	Treatment for Conditioning
Anemone	½ to fully open	Scrape stems
Aster	¾ to fully open	Scrape stems
Azalea	Bud to fully open	Scrape and crush stems
Bachelor's-button	½ to fully open	Scrape stems
Bleeding-heart	4 or 5 florets open	Scrape stems
Calendula	Fully open	Scrape stems
Carnation	Fully open; snap or break from plant	Scrape stems
Chrysanthemum	Fully open; break off	Scrape or crush stems
Daffodil	As color shows in bud	Cut foliage sparingly and scrape stems
Dahlia	Fully open	Sear stems in flame
Daisy	½ to fully open	Scrape stems or sear in flame
Delphinium	¾ to fully open	Scrape stems, break off top buds
Gladiolus	As second floret opens	Scrape stems
Iris	As first bud opens	Leave foliage, scrape stems
Lilac	½ to fully open	Scrape and crush stems; put wilted branches in very hot water for 1 hour
Lily	As first bud opens	Cut no more than ⅓ of stem
Marigold	Fully open	Scrape stems
Peony	Bud in color or fully open	Scrape or split stems
Poppy	Night before opening	Sear stems; a drop of wax in heart of flower keeps it open
Rose	As second petal unfurls; cut stem just above a 5-petal leaf	Scrape stems; cut stems again while holding under water
Tulip	Bud to ½ open	Cut foliage sparingly, scrape stems, stand in deep water overnight
Zinnia	Fully open	Sear stems in flame

ditioned have value in that they check maturing, nourish plants, sweeten the water, and help slow decay. Other tips to keep in mind are remove the pollen from self-pollinating flowers, cut the stems under water to keep air bubbles from entering (important with roses), put water in the container before you start the arrangement, and cut the stems straight across for needlepoint holders, and on an angle for deep vases.

WATER GARDENING

Water gardening is a fascinating and unique hobby. Although it may include growing plants around a fountain or pool, a bona fide water garden contains aquatic plants, such as waterlilies that are grown entirely in water, and semi-aquatic plants (moisture-loving shrubs and perennials such as pitcher plants) that grow well in natural bogs or swamps.

One of the nice things about gardening with water is that minimal work is required after the initial construction and planting has been completed. As long as the ecological balance of the area is maintained, there is no hoeing or cultivating, little weeding, and of course, no watering!

You may not need to construct a pool to grow waterlilies if you already have a shallow pond or slow-moving stream. Those with a naturally wet area, can scoop out part of it to create a pond about 2 feet deep. In these kinds of ponds the waterlilies can be planted directly in the muddy soil at the bottom, provided the water isn't more than 2 feet in depth. Most farm and fish ponds are much too deep and many are too cold for successful waterlily culture. If you raise water plants in your pond, don't try to keep ducks or geese there because they'll rapidly wreck the plantings.

Aquatic Plants

The term "aquatic" usually refers to all plants that live in water, whether they are free-floating or rooted in soil, with submerged or floating leaves. Those most cultivated are members of the Nymphaeceae family which includes waterlilies, lotuses, and similar plants. The *Nuphar* and *Nymphaea* genera are the common pond lilies in this country. The *Nymphaea*, both hardy and tropical, have been widely hybridized. Waterlilies range in size from the *Victoria* genus, one of the largest, with flowers that are 15 inches in width, to tiny pygmy varieties that are only 1½ to 2 inches across. Of the fifty or so cultivars and species of waterlilies available today, the Marliac hybrids are among the best for home growers.

The Pool

Waterlilies need at least five hours of full sunlight each day, so select a spot for your pool that will provide it, and make sure the location is away from trees that might drop leaves or needles into the

Waterlily

water and contaminate it. The pool should be from 2 to 2½ feet deep for best results. At one time, most pools were built of reinforced concrete, but now fiberglass or heavy polyvinyl plastic are most often used because they are easier to install and less likely to crack in freezing temperatures. Nurseries that sell water plants frequently stock preformed pools and liners in many sizes.

Although a pool does not need fresh water running through it all the time, plumbing should be installed so that additional water can be added whenever evaporation makes it necessary. Since it needs cleaning occasionally, a drain and plug at the lowest end of the pool will save you the trouble of pumping out the water.

Planting

You will want the water in your garden pool to remain somewhat clear, so set your plants in containers rather than in soil at the bottom. The size of the container should correspond to plant size. A

WETLAND PLANTS

Below are some of the plants you may want to grow in ground that is always saturated or under water.

Acorus calamus, sweet flag
Arundo, giant reed
Iris pseudacorus, yellow flag
Iris versicolor, blue flag
Marsilea, water clover
Nelumbo lutea, lotus
Nuphar, cow lily
Orontium, golden club
Osmunda regalis, royal fern
Peltandra virginica, arrow arum
Pontederia cordata, pickerelweed
Sagittaria, arrowhead
S. sagittifolia 'Flore Pleno,' swamp potato
Sarracenia purpurea, pitcher plant
Typha angustifolia, narrow-leaved cattail

Plants for Alternately Moist/Dry Places

You may own land that is not only moist for much of the year, but fluctuates occasionally between being covered with water during prolonged rains and drying out during hot or arid spells. These areas are difficult to plant because most common garden perennials and wildflowers won't tolerate these conditions. The following plants, however, can stand considerable moisture as well as dryness for short periods.

Aletris farinosa, star grass
Asclepias incarnata, swamp milkweed
Aster novae-angliae, New England aster
Boltonia asteroides, starwort
Caltha palustris, marsh marigold
Eupatorium perfoliatum, boneset
E. purpureum and *maculatum,* Joe Pye-weed
Ferns, cinnamon, royal, and sensitive varieties
Gentiana andrewsii, closed gentian
Hibiscus moscheutos, rose mallow or swamp mallow
Hosta, plantainlily
Iris sibirica, Siberian iris
Lobelia cardinalis, cardinal flower
L. siphilitica, blue lobelia
Lychnis flos-cuculi, ragged robin

Lysimachia terrestris, swamp candles
Lythrum salicaria, purple loosestrife
Mertensia, Virginia bluebells
Miscanthus, zebra grass
Monarda didyma, bee balm
Myosotis, forget-me-not
Phlox maculata, summer phlox
Pontederia cordata, pickerelweed
Ranunculus, swamp buttercup
Rhexia, deer grass, meadow beauties
Sagittaria latifolia, duck potato
Solidago graminifolia, lance-leafed goldenrod
Typha latifolia, cattail
Veronicastrum virginianum, culver's root
Viola cucullata, blue bog violet

10-inch pot is suitable for the small pygmy water-lilies, but the huge tropical varieties will need at least a bushel-size tub.

Place only one plant in each container. Water plants are heavy feeders — the soil mix should contain at least one part well-rotted manure to four parts fertile garden soil. Mix in a small amount of commercial fertilizer, such as 5-10-10, too. Waterlilies grow from rhizomes, which should be placed in the container so that the crown is barely exposed. Cover the top of the soil with coarse sand to keep it from clouding the water. Then water the pot thoroughly before submerging it; otherwise it may float back to the surface.

For best results, place the containers so that the rims are 4 to 8 inches under the surface of the water. Adjust the height, if necessary, by placing rocks, bricks, or concrete blocks under the containers. Space them according to the size of the mature plants, from 3 to 5 feet apart. Most waterlilies need at least 10 square feet of water surface when mature, except for the pygmy size, which take up only about 4 square feet. Plant hardy waterlilies in early spring, but tropical varieties should not be put outside until the water temperature is a minimum of 70°F. Don't be alarmed if the leaves stay submerged for the first few days before they rise and float to the surface.

The fragrant flowers of the hardy waterlilies and certain tropical varieties do not stay open round-the-clock, but usually unfurl on a summer day at about 8 a.m. and close about 6 p.m. The length of the daily bloom depends on the amount of light and the temperature (some of the tropical types are night bloomers). One of the fascinating things about these unusual plants is the slow, hour-long unfolding — one by one — of the petals each day. When they close, the same process repeats itself in reverse. You'll also notice that the color of certain varieties will change considerably from day to day.

Hardy varieties will survive even a northern winter as long as their roots remain below ice level. If your pool is likely to freeze almost or completely solid, remove the containers and store them in a cool root cellar or basement until spring. Trop-ical varieties require a completely frost-free environment — they *must* be taken inside except in those regions where no frost is likely. Never let the stored plants dry out during the winter.

Water gardening in earthen ponds is most successful when everything is ecologically balanced among the plants and other living organisms. To achieve an ecological balance in an earthern water garden, a good formula for each square yard of water surface includes:

- 1 large waterlily (for beauty, and also because the lily pads prevent loss of pond oxygen)

- 2 bunches oxygenating grasses (they replace oxygen and prevent algae formation)

- 2 fish (goldfish or koi, about 5 inches long to eat flies, mosquito larvae, algae)

- 12 snails (they consume algae)

Within two to three months a balance will become established in the pond and the organisms will support each other.

Caring for the Pool

Although a water garden requires less care than one planted in soil, it cannot be completely neglected. Remove any unsightly yellowed foliage and seed pods as they appear, and if the plants are not thriving, place soluble fertilizer tablets around their roots every two weeks. (Select fertilizers carefully, as they may harm your fish and snails). Waterlilies grown in the soil bottom of a shallow pond can be left undisturbed, but those in containers should be divided every two to five years. If the plants get too large, the flowers will become fewer and smaller, but if they are given proper care the plants may live for 50 years or more.

Like their soil counterparts, aquatic plants are affected by pests. The waterlily aphid (*Ropalosiphum nymphaeae*) is the most common insect. It can be controlled by spraying; when the flowers are closed, use a solution of one part kerosene emulsion to 15 parts water. (You may want to take your fish and snails out of harm's way before applying any chemicals.) The Japanese beetle, the leaf-eating beetle, and caterpillars of the *Noctuid* or *Hydrocamp propalis* moths may also feed on the plants, but can be controlled by pyrethrum or rotenone. Move fish, frogs, and snails out of the pond before spraying any insecticides; even botanicals will kill fish and beneficial insects. Never use chlorinated hydrocarbon insecticides as pest control in ponds, especially if you have fish or frogs there. In hot, humid weather a fungus disease sometimes develops on the leaves of waterlilies if conditions in the pond are crowded. It can be controlled by a careful, limited application of a fungicide, but be careful not to spill any into the water.

Bog or Swamp Possibilities

Few people choose to deliberately create a swamp or boggy area in their backyard, but if you already have one somewhere on your property, it can be made into a spot that is more interesting than annoying. The aquatic and semi-aquatic plant life that grows in such places is unique and endlessly fascinating.

You may want to investigate the possibility of scooping out a portion of your swamp to make a small, year-round pond. If it is dug to a depth of 1½ to 2 feet, with a greater depth in the middle, you will be able to raise *Nymphaea* as well as those that grow upright, with their roots submerged in water. Part of the earth moved from the bottom can be used to build small low islands or hummocks where water ferns, mosses, pitcher plants, and other bog plants can be grown. Such plants need little care or fertilizer, and because most like an acid environment, lime or wood ashes shouldn't be used on them.

15

GARDEN TOOLS AND HARDWARE

If you're just starting a garden, chances are you'll need to do some tool shopping. Hardware stores, garden centers, department stores, and mail-order garden suppliers offer endless supplies of hand and power tools, tillers, composting systems, coldframes, and miscellaneous gadgets that might easily overwhelm the casual gardener. The average home gardener doesn't need to go broke buying everything in the catalog. You can get started with a few essentials, and you may even be able to build some larger pieces, like composters and potting benches, yourself.

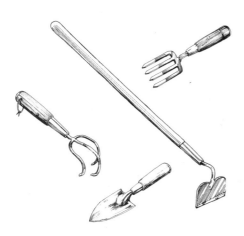

TOOLS

The choice between hand and power tools is a matter of personal preference. For most home gardening, you probably won't need the heavy-duty, expensive tools that commercial farmers and orchardists prefer, but flimsy, cheaply made ones are no bargain if you have to replace them every year.

When you're looking for equipment, get advice from more experienced gardening friends (who aren't trying to sell you anything). Try tools out to see how they feel in your hands before buying.

Using the right tools properly will make the job easier and probably save you a lot of aches and pains. And proper care will make any tool last longer.

Buying Tools

The size and scope of your garden will determine most of your tool needs. Obviously you won't need a tractor for a small flower bed, and you probably won't want to prepare a half-acre vegetable garden with just a shovel. The important thing is to have the right tool for the job. After the few fundamental tools such as a shovel, digging fork, hoe, and rake have been bought, others may be added as needed or desired.

It is always advisable to buy tools prior to the opening of the season, when suppliers have the best selection and more time to give advice or answer questions about the pros and cons of various equipment. Extra clerks hired during the spring rush are usually less informed. In choosing any equipment, especially lawn mowers or hand-power machines like garden rollers, avoid getting a size too large for the person who is to operate it.

Shopping List

Before you go shopping, make a list. Consider what chores you have to do and what you'll need to complete them. The following list probably won't suit your garden exactly, but should give you some ideas.

Cultivator — hand-cultivator or rototiller for digging, turning and loosening the soil.

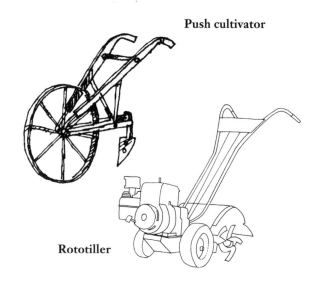

Push cultivator

Rototiller

Shovel — D-handle or long handle for digging, turning soil, spreading manure or compost and many other uses. Because you will use it so much, it is especially important to get one that's durable and easy to handle.

Spade — D-handle or long handle, generally a sharper more pointed blade than a shovel, useful for digging in packed soil.

Lawn edger — for cutting a neat line along borders between the lawn and garden beds or walkways.

Containers — seed flats and pots for starting seeds and larger pots and planters for container gardening.

Spading fork — for breaking clods of soil. Hay forks or spading forks are also useful for dividing clumps of plants and for spreading compost or manure in the garden.

Hoe — for cultivating soil and preparing planting rows. There are several kinds for various purposes.

Hose — for watering. You may want one with a nozzle and reel. Attachments are also available for spreading liquid fertilizer.

Rake — basic kinds are: bamboo or metal leaf rakes and steel garden rakes for smoothing soil, covering seeds, or weeding.

Knife — various kinds are useful for small pruning jobs, harvesting, cutting open peat pots, and dividing root clumps.

Labels — for garden rows, seed flats, pots, and trees.

Lawn mower — in addition to the lawn, this can be useful for leveling the garden at the end of the season before tilling and planting winter cover crops.

Leaf rake

Garden rake

Pruners — several kinds are available, including loppers, shears, hand clippers, and saws or snippers mounted on long poles.

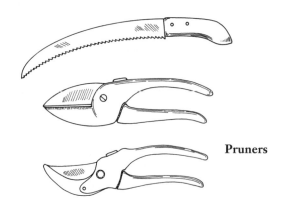

Pruners

Trowel — for digging planting holes. Many kinds are available, and cheap ones don't last long.

Watering can — for small-scale watering needs. Screw-on rose head attachments provide a shower for smaller plants that might be knocked down by a heavy stream. However, most plants do better if you can wet the soil without watering the leaves.

Weeders — many hand and hoe types available for scraping annual seedlings off the soil surface or reaching into the soil to get at deep-rooted perennials.

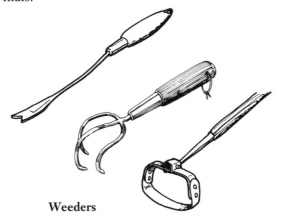

Weeders

Wheelbarrow or garden cart — for moving topsoil, fertilizer, manure, and other heavy loads. Also, this can be a useful container for mixing soil amendments.

Scythe or sickle — for cutting hay or other tall crops (also useful for cutting down cornstalks at the end of the growing season).

Irrigation equipment — drip hose or sprinkler for watering larger areas like lawns and large gardens.

Dibble — for planting bulbs. Other specialized tools are available for this purpose, or you may get along with a pointed stick for small bulbs and a trowel for larger ones.

Step ladder — for overhead harvesting in the orchard and for pruning jobs where a long-handled saws aren't appropriate.

Sprayer or duster — for spreading insecticides and fungicides. Be especially careful in choosing this equipment.

Plant supports — tomato cages; trellises; bamboo, metal, or wooden stakes; pea fences; even cut branches can be used, depending on the needs and habits of your plants.

Tying material — for holding plants to supports. Choose carefully. Wires to hold trees should be covered so they won't cut into the bark. In the garden, natural materials will break down in the soil more readily if you lose or discard them at the end of the season.

Basket — for collecting your harvest.

Care of Tools

Proper storage and maintenance will keep tools in good condition for years.

Storage. Exposure to weather or the dampness of a wet cellar or basement soon destroys the edge of cutting tools, spades, rakes, and hoes and rusts other parts. The tool shed or other quarters should always be dry to prevent rusting, and lighted to make tools easy to find or put away.

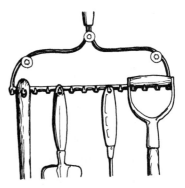

An old garden rake with the handle removed makes a handy tool rack.

Every tool should have its own place. An excellent way to store tools with long handles such as rakes and hoes, is upright in racks with holes bored for the handles in the lower horizontal member or hung on hooks or nails in the wall. Larger equipment, such as lawn mowers and wheelbarrows should be placed against the wall with their wheels held in place by cleats on the floor and their handles kept upright by hooks attached to the wall. Small tools such as saws, trowels, shears, and hand weeders are best stored in well-ventilated cupboards hung on hooks screwed into the door and on inside surfaces.

Another good trick is to paint the wooden part of all hand tools some bright color so that if one is left lying around in the garden it is conspicuous against the earth or foliage. Extending this idea, the positions of tools stored on or against a wall may be outlined in paint so that the absence of any item will be obvious.

Cleaning. It is important to clean every tool promptly after it has been used. Moist soil is easily cleaned from metal parts by scraping with a flat-ended stick, but after it has dried, it is difficult to remove if it contains much clay. The longer soil is allowed to adhere to a tool, the more rust is likely to develop. When all the loose soil has been removed with a stick or old broom, a rag or carpet scrap should be used to clean off any remaining traces.

Rust must be fought constantly, not only because it makes work more difficult, but because it shortens the life of tools. At the close of the season, they should be thoroughly cleaned with kerosene to remove grease, caked oil, and dirt. Finally, all metal parts should be swabbed with oil (a good use for automobile waste oil) before they are put away for the winter. One convenient way to oil such tools as spades and rakes is to put clean sand in a long narrow box, saturate it with oil, and work tools back and forth in it a few times before hanging them up. Otherwise use an oily rag.

Seasonal Maintenance. At the close of each season, all tools should be examined and all machines overhauled. Worn and broken parts should be replaced and every implement repaired, sharpened, oiled, repainted, or otherwise renovated to put it in proper condition. Oiling all bearing parts (especially of lawn mowers during the season and at the season's end) is one of the most important but most commonly neglected of all tool care essentials. Lack of lubrication is one of the chief reasons that machines wear out. If you're not sure how to tune up your lawn mower, rototiller, or other garden machines take them to a professional. In addition to bad performance, poorly maintained machines can be dangerous!

Sharpening. Care of tools also includes maintaining an edge on spades, hoes, sickles, scythes, weed-ers, and the like, because sharp blades increase efficiency and lighten the labor of using them. In ordinary cases a file or whetstone will serve, but if a tool is allowed to become very dull, it will be necessary to develop a new edge. There is a certain art to maintaining a good sharp edge, and it's easy for a beginner to cut some fingers (or worse) in the process. If you're not experienced at sharpening tools, get some help from an expert or take them to a professional.

BUILD A PLANT STAND

You can buy a plant stand for starting seedlings — or you can invest an hour on a stand that's fine for starting tomatoes and all the rest.

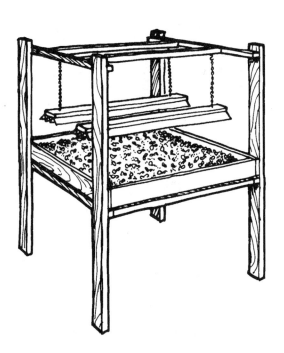

Plant Stand Materials

four 2" x 4" x 72" uprights
nine 2" x 2" x 28" horizontal pieces
four 1" x 6" x 48" sides of plant area
one 48" x 48" particle-board or plywood
    shelf
one 60" x 60" plastic sheet, for shelf
    covering

two 48" two-tube fluorescent units, with hooks and chains

Optional:

one 2" x 2" x 96" to be cut into four supports

Construction Details

Use wood screws throughout. Construct shelf frame and end units, then place shelf at a height comfortable for you. Screw the two top bars into position. Mount steel hooks into the underside of the top bars so that light units suspended from them will be centered. Attach shelf to frame and add 1" x 6" side pieces. Place the plastic sheet inside the shelf unit and fill it with peat moss. Keep the peat moss damp to increase humidity around the plants.

Buying 48-inch-long shop lights is a lot cheaper than buying fancy plant lights from a garden shop. Replace one fluorescent tube in each fixture with a grow-light. Keep a distance of 5 to 6 inches from plant foliage to the reflector and give plants 14 to 15 hours of light each day.

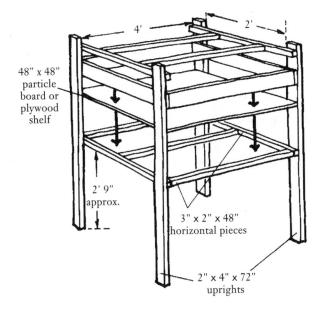

48" x 48" particle board or plywood shelf

4'

2'

2' 9" approx.

3" x 2" x 48" horizontal pieces

2" x 4" x 72" uprights

BUILD YOUR OWN COLD FRAME

Cold frames can be built as grand or as humbly as you desire. The plans given here are for a durable, low-budget model.

This is a portable structure which can be easily collapsed for storage in an area of about 3 feet by 6 feet by 1 foot.

The work should be a weekend project for anyone who has access to a basic collection of hand tools and the skill to use them.

The primary component of the cold frame is wood. Select decay resistant such as cedar, cypress, or redwood.

Cold Frame Materials

one 1" x 1" x 10' (cut into four pieces of 7"; four pieces of 10"; three pieces of 11")

one 2" x 2" x 8' (cut into two pieces of 18"; two pieces of 20")

one 1" x 8" x 12' (cut into one piece of 69"; two pieces of 35¾")

one 1" x 4" x 3' (cut to 35¾")

one 1" x 6" x 12' (cut into two pieces of 69")

¼ lb. 6d common nails

thirty-six 1¼" slotted wood screws

one ⅛" x ½" x 12' weatherstripping

1 set 4" T hinges. These usually are sold with screws included. If not, buy a dozen 1" slot head wood screws as well.

one 36" x 72" storm window

1 qt. wood preservative (not creosote)

Tools Needed

measuring tape square
hammer
hatchet
saw
screwdriver
pencil
bar of soap
    (handy for easing the driving of screws)
putty knife
    (if you plan to use an old storm window)
glazier points

chisel (if you build your own window)
safety glasses and ear protection

Construction Details

1. Prepare the Old Storm Window. Assuming you have chosen to use an old storm window, scrape away all cracked and loose paint, and the putty if it is cracked and dry (A). Saturate the cleaned areas with wood preservative and allow ample drying time.

Check the recessed joint where wood meets glass. When the window is tilted in position atop the cold frame, these areas will tend to collect rainwater. Thus they deserve special attention now.

Look where the putty was for small, triangular pieces of metal which hold the glass in position. Each pane of glass should have at least two of these glazier points along each of its four sides. If more are needed, insert them into the wooden part of the window with firm pressure from the tip of a screwdriver.

Once the glass is secured, ready some glazing compound. Knead a small wad of compound until it is soft and pliable. Using a putty knife, work small dabs of the compound into the recess where glass meets wood until a uniform depth has been applied around the perimeter of the glass.

Starting at a corner of the pane, hold the putty knife at such an angle as to form a triangle of glazing compound that is flush to the top of the surface of the wood and extends about ¼ inch out onto the glass. Steadily and evenly, draw the knife down the joint until a corner is reached. Reposition the

knife and continue to the next corner, repeating until all the putty is new.

Next paint the window with a good grade of exterior enamel trim paint to provide a long-lasting and attractive finish.

2. Building the Frame. Saw the 2" x 2" piece into four lengths, two at 18 inches and two at 20 inches. On each of these measure up 8 inches from an end. With the hatchet, hew down this 8-inch section to a point. These are the posts that will anchor the cold frame in the ground.

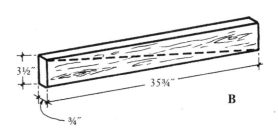

Take the board 1" x 4" x 35¾" and lay a straightedge from the lower right corner to the upper left corner (B). Mark that line and saw along it to form two identical triangles. Try to hold the saw perpendicular to the surface of the board.

Next, saw the 1" x 1" piece into cleats. Four of these will be 7 inches long, four 10 inches and three 11 inches.

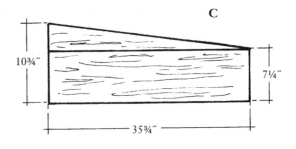

Coat all the lumber with preservative. The sawed ends and edges will be especially absorbent.

The two triangular pieces that were cut from the 1" x 4" x 35¾" board will form the tops of the east and west walls of the cold frame. The bases of these end walls are the pieces 1" x 8" x 35¾", which should now be laid edge to edge with the triangular boards. When placed together the end wall components should appear as shown (C).

3. Partially Assembling the End Walls. Apply the 1" x 1" cleats, which will serve both to hold the end wall boards together and to fix in place the north and south walls of the cold frame. Start at the wide end of one of the end walls. Lay a 10-inch piece of the 1" x 1" stock flush with the ends of the boards and centered vertically. Mark locations for two screw holes, taking care to avoid knots, splits, or other defects.

Remove the cleat and drive a nail in at the marks, then extract it to leave pilot holes for 1¼-inch screws. If you have a drill, use a bit one size smaller than the screws for the pilot holes. Push the screws into a bar of soap to coat the ends. Lay the cleat back on the wide end of the board and screw it into place.

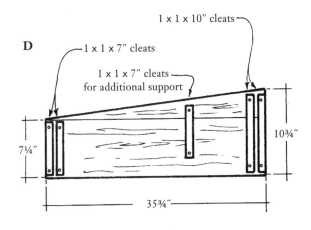

After the first cleat is fixed, lay a second piece of 1" x 1" x 10" alongside it and draw a pencil line along the edge of the second cleat toward the center of the end wall. Move the second cleat over and flush to this pencil line, leaving a gap of slightly more than ¾ inch between the two cleats. Mark the second cleat for screw holes, make pilot holes, reposition the cleat and screw it down (D).

Using 7-inch cleats at the narrow end of the boards, repeat this procedure by putting one cleat flush to the edge, marking a ¾-inch gap and applying the second cleat of 7 inches to the inside of the mark (E).

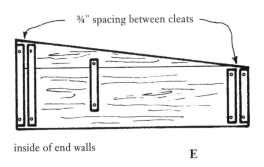

The other pairs of cleats are applied in similar fashion to the opposite end wall. From the remaining 1" x 1" stock, you may want to cut two additional 7-inch strips to be screwed 12–14 inches in from the wide end. These cleats will further strengthen the connection between the two boards.

Now turn over the end walls end for end so that the cleated sides are down. From each end measure in 8 inches. At the narrow end, lay one of the posts of 2" x 2" x 18" stock so that it lies between the lines but is flush against the 8-inch mark. The top of this post should protrude about an inch above the edge of the triangular upper board. The sharpened end of the post should extend beyond the base of the 1" x 8" about 8 inches. Nail this in place with 6d nails. Be sure that at least one nail fastens the post to the base board and another to the triangular piece.

Use a 2" x 2" x 20" at the wide end of the end walls. Lay it to the inside of the 8" mark. Again, the square end of the stick should be about 1" above the triangular piece and the sharp end about eight inches below the base. Nail it.

Duplicate this pattern on the other end wall.

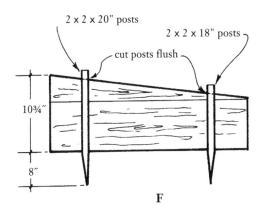

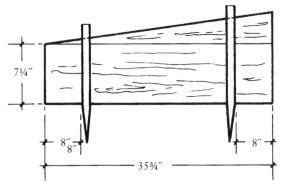

End wall with posts

4. Installing the Posts on the End Walls. Using a handsaw, cut off the tops of the posts flush with the tops of the end walls (F). These components are now completed. Now lay the two boards 1" x 6" x 69" edge to edge lengthwise. Measure in from each end two inches. Lay in position two of the 1" x 1" x 11" cleats. Mark them for screw holes, make pilots, and install them, using four screws in each cleat. The remaining cleat should be centered and screwed into place.

5. Construction. The cold frame is now ready to go up.

Move the wooden components to your selected site, taking along pencil, hammer, screwdriver, nails, measuring tape, hatchet, hinges and screws, weatherstripping, and a scrap of sturdy lumber.

Position one of the side walls so that its high point is to the north and the cleats are toward the area you wish to enclose.

Lay the scrap of heavy lumber atop one of the posts and start driving it in with the hatchet. When the post is halfway home, drive the other post until it too is about halfway down. Tip the top of the wall so that it leans slightly toward the area to be enclosed, and finish driving the posts.

Slip the end of the 1" x 8" x 69" board into the groove between the cleats at the narrow end. At the wide end, slip the cleated 1" x 6" x 69" boards into the gap between the cleats.

Make a mark in the soil along the ends of these boards. Remove the boards. The cleated side of the second end wall should line up with these marks. Align the second end wall so that these marks fit

into the gaps between the cleats.

Drive each post halfway, tilt the end wall inward slightly, and complete the driving of the posts.

The slight cants of the end walls should make for secure placement of the north and south walls of the cold frame. Slip the ends of the 1" x 8" x 69" board into the grooves between the cleats at the narrow ends of the end walls. Tap it into place until its top aligns with the end walls.

The cleated pair of 1" x 6" x 69" boards will fit similarly into the grooves at the high ends of the end walls, completing the framework. Tap it until it aligns with the end wall.

If the north and south walls are not snug within their channels, drive nails through the end walls and into the ends of the long walls. Leave the nail heads exposed about ¼" for ease of disassembly in the future.

6. Installing the Window. Position the window on top of the walls so that the ends of the window extend about ½" beyond the edges of the end walls and the north edge of the window is flush to the outside top of the north wall.

With the window so located, mark in eight inches from each end of the northern edge of the window. Position a hinge to the inside of one of these marks with the rectangular leg of the hinge flush to the upper edge of the window, and the triangular leg hanging down the north wall of the cold frame.

With the hinge so placed, mark the six screw holes. Position the second hinge as was the first and mark those six holes.

Remove the window. Using a nail as a center punch, make shallow pilot holes at the centers of the pencil marks along the edge of the window. Attach the rectangular legs of the hinges to the window using 1" screws.

Replace the sash on top of the cold frame walls and line up the triangular straps over the pencil marks. Make six more shallow pilot holes and drive in the remaining screws.

Trace a pencil line along the outside of the east, south, and west walls of the cold frame onto the underside of the window. Prop open the window and apply to the inside of this pencil mark the piece

Completed cold frame

WOOD AND WIRE STATIONARY THREE-BIN COMPOSTING SYSTEM

With three bins, you have a complete composting system. Completed compost, ready for the garden, will be in one bin; raw materials in the process of composting will be in the second bin; while the third bin can be filled with raw materials as they are generated.

Composter Materials

two 2" x 4" x 18', treated
four 2" x 4" x 12' or eight 2" x 4" x 6",
    treated
one 2" x 2" x 9'
two 2" x 2" x 6'
one 2" x 6" x 16', cedar
nine 1" x 6" x 6', cedar
twenty-two feet ½" hardware cloth, 36" wide
twelve ½" carriage bolts, 4" long
12 washers and 12 nuts for bolts
3 lbs. 16d galvanized nails
½ lb. 8d galvanized casement nails
250 poultry wire staples or power stapler with
    1" staples
one 12-foot and one 8-foot sheet 4 oz. clear
    corrugated fiberglass
three 8-foot lengths of wiggle molding

of self-sticking weatherstripping.

No weatherstripping should be applied to the underside of the window along the hinged edge. It would act as a shim to prevent proper closure of the window.

A simple handle attached to the southern edge of the window will prove useful, as will a notched stick to use as an adjustable prop for the window. An inexpensive thermometer located as high as possible on the inside north wall is handy as well.

Bank the outside walls of the cold frame with two or three inches of dirt and the structure is done.

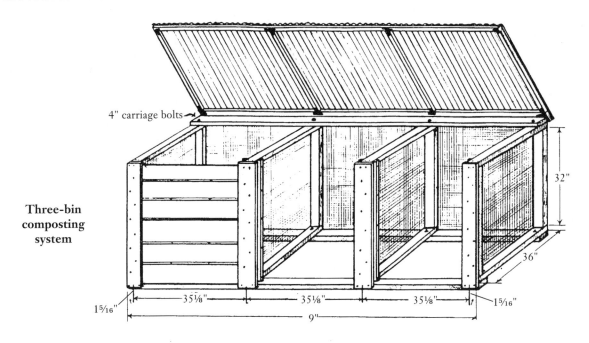

Three-bin composting system

4" carriage bolts

32"

36"

1⁵⁄₁₆"   35⅛"   35⅛"   35⅛"   1⁵⁄₁₆"

9"

40 gasketed aluminum nails for corrugated
    fiberglass roofing
two 3" zinc-plated hinges for lid
eight flat 4" corner braces with screws
four flat 3" T-braces with screws

Tools Needed

hand saw or circular power saw
drill with ½" and ⅛" bits
screwdriver
hammer
tin snips
tape measure
pencil
¾" socket or open-ended wrench
carpenter's square
safety glasses and ear protection
(optional — power stapler with 1" long
    galvanized staples)

Construction Details

1. Build Dividers. Cut two 31½" and two 36"
pieces from each 12-foot 2x4. Butt end nail the
four pieces into a 35" x 36" square. Repeat for other
three sections. Cut four 37" long sections of hardware cloth, bend back edges 1". Stretch hardware
cloth across each frame, check for squareness of the
frame and staple screen tightly into place every 4"
around edge.

2. Set Up Dividers. Set up dividers parallel to
each other 3 feet apart. Measure and mark centers
for the two inside dividers. Cut four 9-foot pieces
out of the two 18-foot 2x4 boards. Place two 9-

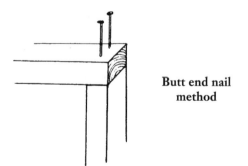

Butt end nail
method

foot base boards on top of dividers and measure
the positions for the two inside dividers. Mark a
center line for each divider on the 9-foot 2x4. With
each divider, line up the center lines and make the
base board flush against the outer edge of the divider. Drill a ½" hole through each junction centered 1" in from the inside edge. Secure base boards
with carriage bolts, but do not tighten yet. Turn
the unit right side up and repeat the process for the
top 9-foot board. Using the carpenter's square or
measuring tape between opposing corners, make
sure the bin is square, and tighten all bolts securely. Fasten a 9-foot-long piece of hardware cloth
securely to the back side of the bin with staples every 4" around the frame.

3. Front Slats and Runners. Cut four 36" long
2x6s for front slat runners. Rip-cut two of these
boards to 4¾" wide and nail them securely to the
front of the outside dividers and baseboard, making them flush on top and outside edges. Save the
remainder of rip-cut boards for use as back runners. Center the remaining full width boards on
the front of the inside dividers flush with the top
edge, and nail securely. To create back runners,
cut the remaining 2x6 into a 34" long piece and
then rip cut into four equal pieces, 1¼" x 2". Nail
back runner parallel to front runners on side of divider leaving a 1" gap for slats. Cut all the 1x6
cedar boards into slats 31¼" long.

4. Fiberglass Lid. Use the last 9-foot 2x4 for
the back of the lid. Cut four 32½ inch 2x2s and
one 9-foot 2x2. Lay out into position on ground
and check for squareness. Screw in corner braces
and T-braces on bottom side of the frame. Center
lid frame, brace side down on bin structure and attach with hinges. Cut wiggle board to fit the front
and back 9-foot sections of the lid frame. Predrill
wiggle board with ⅛" drill bit and nail with 8d casement nails. Cut fiberglass to fit flush with front
and back edges. Overlay pieces at least one chan-
nel wide. Predrill fiberglass and wiggle board for
each nail hole. Nail on top of every third hump
with gasketed nails.

SUPPLIERS

SEED, BULB, AND PLANT SUPPLIERS

The following suppliers distribute by mailorder or retail distribution.
Write for catalogs, which may cost a nominal fee.

W. Atlee Burpee Co.
Mail Order Catalog Division
Warminster, PA 18974
Plants, Seeds, bulbs, books, tools,
and related garden equipment.

Comstock, Ferre & Co.
263 Main Street
P.O. Box 125
Wethersfield, CT 06109
Seeds, specializing in disease-
resistant vegetables, annuals, and
perennials.

Henry Field Seed & Nursery
1723 Oak Street
Shenandoah, IA 51602
Plants, seeds, tools, and growing
supplies for vegetables, fruits,
nuts, and flowers.

Gurney Seed and Nursery Co.
Page Street
Yankton, SD 57079
Plants and seeds for ornamentals,
fruits, and vegetables; also tools
and canning supplies.

Inter-State Nurseries
Catalog Division
Louisiana, MO 63353
Plants and bulbs, specializing in
hybrid roses and perennials.

Jackson & Perkins Co.
2518 South Pacific Highway
P.O. Box 1028
Medford, OR 97501
Planting stock, specializing in
roses, fruits, vegetables, and bulbs.

Johnny's Selected Seeds
Albion, ME 04910
Vegetables, herbs, flowers, and
grains for commercial crops; also
growing supplies and books.

J.W. Jung Seed Co.
Box 340
335 South High Street
Randolph, WI 53957
Plants, seeds, bulbs, and supplies
for growing fruits, roses, perenni-
als, and various ornamentals.

Kelly Nurseries
Catalog Division
Louisiana, MO 63353
Nursery stock, including fruit and
ornamental trees, shrubs, vines,
and ground covers.

Lilypons Water Gardens
P.O. Box 10
6885 Lilypons Road
Lilypons, MD 21717-0010
Plants, books, and supplies for
water gardens.

Earl May Seed & Nursery
208 North Elm
Shenandoah, IA 51603
Plants, seeds, bulbs, tools, and
other gardening supplies.

Mellinger's, Inc.
2310 West South Range Road
North Lima, OH 44452-9731
Plants, seeds, bulbs, tools, and
other gardening supplies.

Sources are listed in this directory for the convenience of our readers
and in no way constitute an endorsement by the publisher.

J.E. Miller Nurseries
1524 West Lake Road
Canandaigua, NY 14424
Plants and supplies, specializing in fruit, nut, and ornamental trees, shrubs, and vines.

George W. Park Seed Co.
P.O. Box 46
Cokesbury Road
Greenwood, SC 29648
Plants, seeds, bulbs, tools, and other gardening supplies.

Clyde Robin Seed Co.
3670 Enterprise Avenue
Haywood, CA 94545
Seeds and books, specializing in wildflowers.

R.H. Shumway
628 Cedar Street
P.O. Box 777
Rockford, IL 61105
Seeds for vegetables, flowers, green manure crops, and fruit plants.

Spring Hill Nurseries Co.
6523 Galena Road
Peoria, IL 61632
Plants and bulbs, specializing in garden flowers, shrubs, ground covers, and houseplants.

Stark Brothers Nurseries
Highway 54
Louisiana, MO 63353
Plants and supplies, specializing in fruit or ornamental trees, shrubs, and roses.

Stokes Seeds, Inc.
737 Main Street
P.O. Box 548
Louisiana, MO 63353
Vegetable and flower seeds and supplies, primarily for commercial farmers, but also packaged for home gardens.

Thompson & Morgan
Dept 13-0
P.O. Box 1308
Jackson, NJ 08527-0308
Seeds of all types.

K. Van Bourgondien & Sons, Inc.
P.O. Box A
245 Farmingdale Road
Babylon, NY 11702
Plants and bulbs, specializing in spring or summer bulbs and perennials.

Vermont Wildflower Farm
Route 2
Charlotte, VT 05445
Specializing in wildflower seeds.

White Flower Farm
Route 63
Litchfield, CT 06759-0050
Shrubs, perennials, bulbs, books, and supplies.

For information on other suppliers, contact:

The Mailorder Association of Nurseries
Dept. SCI
8683 Doves Fly Way
Laurel, MD 20723
(301) 490-9143

BIOLOGICAL AND ORGANIC GARDENING SUPPLIES

The following companies produce and/or distribute supplies for organic pest control, composting, and soil enhancement. Also, consult agricultural extension services for local suppliers.

Association of Applied Insect Ecologists
100 North Winchester Blvd.
Suite 260
Santa Cruz, CA 95050
Beneficial insects.

Bio-Control Co.
P.O. Box 337
57A Zink Road
Berry Creek, CA 95916
Beneficial insects.

Bio-Resources
P.O. Box 902
1210 Birch Street
Santa Paula, CA 93060
Beneficial insects.

Dyna-Prep, Inc.
2215 Broadway
Yankton, SD 57078
Diatomaceous earth.

Fairfax Biological Lab, Inc.
Clinton Corners, NY 12514
Milky spore powder.

The Fertrell Co.
P.O. Box 265
Bainbridge, PA 17502
Fertilizers and soil amendments.

Green Earth Organics
9422 144th Street East
Pulyallup, CA 98373-6686
Natural lawn care products.

Green Pro Services
380 South Franklin Street
Hempstead, NY 11550
Natural gardening products.

Growing Naturally
P.O. Box 54
149 Pine Lane
Pineville, PA 18946
Natural gardening products.

Mellinger's
2310 West South Range Road
Lima, OH 44452-9731
Fertilizers, soil conditioners, and soil amendments.

Natural Gardening
Research Center
Highway 48
P.O. Box 149
Sunman, IN 47041
Beneficial insects and supplies for organic gardening.

Nitron Industries
4605 Johnson Road
P.O. Box 1447
Fayetteville, AR 72702
Organic gardening supplies, including natural fertilizers and soil enhancers.

Ohio Earth Food, Inc.
13737 DuQuette Avenue, NE
Hartville, OH 44632
Natural gardening materials, specializing in sea products.

Reuter Labs, Inc.
8540 Natural Way
Manassas Park, VA 22111
Natural pest controls.

Ringer Corporation
9959 Valley View Road
Eden Prairie, MN 55344
Organic soil amendments, beneficial insects, garden tools, and irrigation equipment.

Safer, Inc.
60 William Street
Wellesley, MA 02181
Pest controls, natural soaps, and natural herbicides.

Zook & Ranck, Inc.
RD 2, Box 243
Gap, PA 17527
Fertilizer and soil amendments.

TOOLS AND HARDWARE

The following companies manufacture or distribute gardening equipment.
Write for catalogs and information regarding local dealers.

Country Home Products
Ferry Road
P.O. Box 89
Charlotte, VT 05445
Mowers, trimmers, clippers, and various garden tools.

Garden Way, Inc.
102nd Street & 9th Avenue
Troy, NY 12179-0009
Mowers, rotary tillers, garden carts, and various garden tools.

Gardener's Supply Co.
128 Intervale Road
Burlington, VT 05401
Greenhouse kits and garden tools.

Kemp Company
160 Koser Road
Lititz, PA 17543
Shredders, chippers, compost tumblers, and other gardening supplies.

Mantis Manufacturing Co.
1458 County Line Road
Huntingdon Valley, PA 19006
Lawn and garden equipment, including tillers, chippers, and mowers.

The Plow & Hearth
301 Madison Road
P.O. Box 830
Orange, VA 22960
General gardening tools and accessories.

Smith & Hawken
25 Corte Madera
Mill Valley, CA 94941
Tools, ornaments, and planting stock.

GARDENING ASSOCIATIONS

American Community
Gardening Association
c/o University of California
Cooperative Extension Service
2615 South Grand Avenue,
#400
Los Angeles, CA 90007

American Society of
Horticultural Science
701 North Saint Aspaph Street
Alexandria, VA 22314

Garden Club of America
598 Madison Avenue
New York, NY 10022

Herb Society of America
9019 Kirtland Chardon Road
Mentor, OH 44060

Men's Garden Clubs of
America
5560 Merle Hay Road
P.O. Box 241
Johnston, IA 50131

National Association of
Women in Horticulture
1311 Butterfield, Suite 310
Downers Grove, IL 60515

National Council of State
Garden Clubs
4401 Magnolia Avenue
St. Louis, MO 63110

National Gardening
Association
180 Flynn Avenue
South Burlington, VT 05401

National Junior Horticultural
Association
441 East Pine Street
Freemont, MI 49412

North American Horticultural
Society
7931 East Boulevard Drive
Alexandria, VA 22309

Seed Savers Exchange
RR 3, Box 239
Decorah, IA 52101

INDEX

Page numbers in **boldface** represent tables.

strawberries, 165
wide rows, 3–4
Heath, spring, 214
Heating cables, 46
Heat requirement for seed germination, 46. *See also* Temperature requirements
Hedeoma pulegoides. See Pennyroyal
Hedera. See Ivy
Hedges, 283, 312. *See also* Shrubs
Helenium. See Sneezeweed
Helianthemum. See Sunrose
Helianthus. See Sunflower
Heliopsis. See Sunflower, false
Heliotrope, **262**, 310
Heliotropium. See Heliotrope
Helix. See Ivy
Helleborus. See Christmas rose
Hemerocallis. See Daylily
Henbit, **8**
Herb(s), **7**, **8**, 64, 121, 151–160, 200, 203. *See also* specific herbs
Herbicides, 275
Heritage rose, 234
Heron's-bill, 215
Hesperis. See Rocket
Heuchera. See Coral-bells
Hibiscus, **219**, **258**, 292
Hibiscus moscheutos. See Mallow
Highbush blueberries. *See* Blueberries
Hill system for strawberries, 163–164
Hippeastrum. See Amaryllis
Hoe, 324
Holly, 313
Hollyhock, 215, 309
Honesty, 310
Honeysuckle, 14, 15, **289**, 309
Hops, 156
Horehound, 156
Hornworms, 79, 100
Horseradish, **8**, **12**, **75**, 150, 156
Horticultural fabrics, 76–78
Hose, 324
Hosta, 306, 316
Hosta. See Hosta; Plantainlily
Hot beds, 10–11
Hot caps, 11
Hoya. See Wax plant
Humidity requirements for seed germination, 46
Hummingbirds, 297–298, 308–309
Humulus lupulus. See Hops
Humus, 21, 241
Husk tomatoes, 19
Hyacinth, **233**
Hybrid tea rose, 234, **238**
Hydrangea, 281, **289**
Hydrated lime, 26
Hymenosys grandiflora. See Sunflower, alpine
Hyssop, **7**, **8**, **75**, 156
Hyssopus officinalis. See Hyssop

Iberis. *See* Candytuft
Ilex. See Holly
Impatiens, **219**, **220**, **258**
Imported cabbage worms, 95–97

Informal garden design, 229, 279–282
Inoculated seed, 28, 47
Inorganic fertilizer, 68
Inorganic mulches, 62
Insect(s), 87–112, **201**, 204–206. *See also* specific fruits and vegetables
attracting hummingbirds and, 309
beneficial, 200
control, 87–112, 204–206
butterflies and, 310
companion planting, 4, 6–9, **75**, 76, 81
insecticides (*see* Insecticides)
integrated pest management (IPM), 74
natural, 200–204
plant covers, 76–78
prevention, 73–78
soil sterilization, 77
timed plantings, 76
traps, 200–204
identification, 81–82, 87–112, 200
life cycle, 81–82
wide rows and, 4
Insecticides, 78–81
Bacillus thuringiensis (Bt), 79
botanical, 80, 202–203
bug juice, 79
diatomaceous earth, 81
dormant oil spray, 79, 203
dusts, 78–81, 202
plant juice, 79
soap sprays, 78–79, 203
sprays, 78–81, 166, 173, 203, 208, 250
Installing new lawn, 270–272
Integrated pest management (IPM), 74
Intercropping, 64, 120, 188
Invasive herbs, 152
Ipomoea. See Morning-glory
Ipomopsis rubra. See Cypress, standing
Iris, **264**, 306, 309, 316, **318**
bearded, 215, 223
Crimean, 214
Dutch, **233**
netted, 214
Siberian, 320, 320
Iris pseudacorus. See Flag
Iris versicolor. See Flag
Iron, **25**
Irrigation, 25, 66, 176–177, 269, 325
Ivy, 15, **258**, 277

Jacob's-ladder, 306
Jade tree, **256**
Japanese beetle, **8**, **75**, 91–92, 203, 322
Jasmine, **258**
Jasminum. See Jasmine
Jerusalem-artichoke, 47, 150
Joe Pye-weed, 320
Jonquil, 214

Kalanchoe, **258**
Kale, **12**, 19–20, **244**
ornamental, 19, **51**, **56**, **219**
Kiwis, hardy, supports for, 15
Kniffen pruning system, 183–184
Kniphofia uvaria. See Torch lily

Kochia, **219**
Kohlrabi, **12**, **56**
Kolkwitzia. See Beauty bush

Labels, 324
Ladybells, 215
Lady's-mantle, 304, 316
Landscaping, 265–292
edible, 18–20
Lantana, **219**, **258**
Larkspur, 215, 309
Late blight, 115, 145
Lathyrus. See Flowering pea
Laurel, 154, 155, **289**
Laurus nobilis. See Laurel
Lavatera, **219**
Lavender, 81, 156
Lavendula. See Lavender
Lawn edger, 324
Lawn mower, 324
Lawns, 269–273
Layering, 153
Layia platyglossa. See Tidy-tips
Leadwort, 305
Leaf curl, 172
Leafhoppers, 80, 103–104, 179
Leafminers, 104–105
Leaf mold, 35
Leaf roller, red-banded, 179
Leaf spot, 115, 145
Leeks, 19, 70–71, 131
Legumes, 28, 47. *See also* Beans
Lemon balm, 156
Lemon verbena, 156
Lenotopodium alpinum. See Edelweiss
Leopard's-bane, 215
Lettuce, 2, **7**, 19, 47, **48**, **56**, 65, **244**
planting times for, 2, **12**, 41, **51**
Levisticum officinale. See Lovage
Liatris. See Gayfeather
Life cycle of insects, 81–82
Light requirements
annuals, **218–220**, **261–263**
aquatic plants, 319
bulbs, 229, **263–264**
grapes, 181
perennials, 221, 248, **252–261**
rock gardens, 303
roses, 234
seedlings, 46–49
shade plants, 294
shrubs, 283, 286
for starting seeds indoors, 43, 46–48
vegetables in containers, **244–245**
Lilac, 281–282, **289**, 309, 313, **318**
Lily, **233**, 309, 310, 316, **318**, 320
Lily-of-the-valley, 215, 277
Lilyturf, creeping, 277
Lima beans, 41–42, 47, **51**. *See also* Beans
Limestone, 26, 121, 241
Limonium. See Sea lavender
Linanthus, **299**
Linaria alpina. See Toadflax, alpine
Linum. See Flax
Lippia citriodora. See Lemon verbena

Liquid chemical fertilizers, 32
Liriope spicata. See Lilyturf, creeping
Live-forever. *See* Stonecrop
Loam soil, 23
Lobelia, **219**, **262**, 320
Lobelia. See Cardinal flower
Locusts, 102–103
Lonicera. See Honeysuckle
Loopers, 79, 95–97
Loosestrife, 215, 309, 320
Lotus, 320
Lovage, 156–157
Lunaria annua. See Honesty
Lupine, 215, 309, 310
Lupinus. See Lupine
Lychnis. See Campion
Lychnis chalcedonica. See Maltese cross
Lychnis flos–cuculi. See Ragged robin
Lygodium palmatum. See Fern(s), Hartford
Lygus bugs, sabadilla and, 80
Lysimachia terrestris. See Swamp candles
Lythrum. See Loosestrife

Macleaya cordata. *See* Poppy, plume
Magnesium, **25**, 65, 121, 133
Magnolia, **285**
Maintenance
    of garden, 57–71
    landscape, 267–269
    requirements, annuals, **218–220**
Majorana hortensis. See Marjoram
Malabar spinach, 15, 47
Mallow, 215, 320
Maltese cross, 215
Malva moschata. See Mallow
Manganese, **25**
Manure, 10, 31–32, 37, **63**, 241
    green, 27–30
Maple, 311, **284**, **285**
Marigold, **7**, **8**, **75**, 81, **262**, 310, 314–315, **318**
    African, **219**
    French, **219**
    marsh, 214, 320
Marjoram, 153–154, 157
Marrubium vulgare. See Horehound
Marsilea. See Clover
Mass plantings, 212
Matted row for strawberries, 163
Matteuccia. See Fern(s), ostrich
Matthiola. See Stock
Meadow beauties, 320
Meadowrue, 214
Meadows for wildflowers, 297–302
Meadowsweet, 215, 305
Mealybugs, 78, 79, 80–81
Melissa officinalis. See Lemon balm
Melon(s), **7**, 9, 41–42, 70, 78–79, **245**. *See also*
    specific melons
    supports for, 14, 15
    winter, 19
Mentha. See Mint
Mentha pulegium. See Pennyroyal
Mertensia virginica. See Bluebells, Virginia
Mexican bean beetle, **8**, **75**, 79, 92–93
Mexican-hat, **299**

Mice, **8**, **75**, 85
Michili, 125. *See also* Chinese cabbage
Microclimate, 173
Mid-west gardening, wildflowers, **299**, 300
Milkweed, 320
Miniature rose, 234, 238
Mint, **7**, **8**, **75**, 81, 153–154, 157
Miscanthus. See Grass, zebra
Mistflower, 216, 310
Mites, 79, 80–81, 105, **201**, 206
    cyclamen, 166
    spider, **8**, 78, 105
Mock-orange, **289**, 292, 313
Modified leader, 196–197
Moisture
    meters, 65
    requirements, 46, **218–220**
    shade garden and, 294
    in soil, 65, 67
Mole plant, **8**, **75**
Moles, **8**, 22, **75**, 85
Molybdenum, **25**
Monarda. See Bee balm
Monarda fistulosa. See Bergamot, wild
Monkey flower, **219**
Monkshood, 215, 216, 316
Monochromatic color harmony, 213
Montbretia, **233**
Morning-glory, 15, 310
Mosaic, 115–116, 172
Mosquitoes, **8**, **75**, 79
Moss pink, 214
Moth crystals, 84, 85
Moths
    cabbage, **8**, **75**
    coddling, 79, **201**, 203, 205
    grape berry, 184
    oriental fruit, **201**, 206
Mound planting, 55–56, 146–147
Mountain bluet, 214
Moving, perennials, 225
Mowing lawns, 272–273
Mugwort, 216
Mulch, 30–31, 62, **63**, 85. *See also* Mulching
Mulching, 3, 55, 56, 61–64, 82. *See also* Mulch
    annuals, 217
    blueberries, 176, 177
    bramble berries, 170
    bulbs, 230, 231, 232
    fruit trees, 190
    ground covers, 278
    herbs, 154, 154
    new lawns, 272
    roses, 235, 237, 238
    seedlings, 54
    shrubs, 288
    strawberries, 165
Mummyberry, 178–179
Muscari. See Grape-hyacinth
Musk mallow, 215
Muskmelon, **12**, **48**, **51**, **56**. *See also* Melon(s)
Mustard, **12**. *See also* Cabbage family
Myosotis. See Forget-me-not
Myrtle, 278

Narcissus, 214, **264**
Narcissus. See Daffodil
Narrow-leaf weeds, 273
Nasturtium, **7**, **8**, 19, **75**, 81, **219**, **262**, 310
Nasturtium officinale. See Watercress
Native plants, 268, 279
Neck rot, 116
Nectarine trees, **188**, **201**. *See also* Fruit trees
Neem oil, 80–81
Nelumbo lutea. See Lotus
Nematodes, **8**, 22, **59**, **75**, 77, 105–107
Nemesia, **262**
Nemophila menziesii. See Baby-blue-eyes
Nepeta cataria. See Catnip
Nettle, dead, **8**, **75**
Newspaper, for mulch, **63**
New Zealand spinach, 41, 47, **51**, 128
Nicotiana, **220**. *See also* Flowering tobacco
Nicotine, 80
Nitrogen, 24, 37
Northern gardening, 286, **299**, 300
Nuphar. See Lily, cow
Nutgrass, 60, 61
Nutrients, **24**, **25**, 62
Nut trees, 79, 187

Ocimum basilicum. *See* Basil
Okra, **12**, 71, 19
Onion(s), **48**, **56**, 71, 121, 129–131, **245**
    companion planting and, **7**, **8**, 9, **75**
    giant, **233**
    planting times for, **12**, 41, **51**
Onion maggots, 107
Onion thrips, 108
Onoclea sensibilis. See Fern, sensitive
Open center, 196, 197
Opentia. See Cactus
Orange rust, 172
Orchard. *See also* Fruit trees; specific fruits
    care of, 194
    design, 188–189
    diseases, 206–209
    insect pests, 204–206
    planning, 185–186
    sprays for, 199, 208
Orchid, **259**
Oregano, 19, 153–154, 157
Organic disease controls, 202–203
Organic fertilizers, 67
Organic gardening supplies, suppliers of, 334–
    335
Organic matter in soil, 21, 35–38
Organic pest controls, 202–203
Organisms in soil, 21–23
Oriental fruit moth, **201**, 206
Origanum majorana. See Marjoram
Origanum vulgare. See Oregano
Orontium. See Golden club
Osmunda. See Fern(s)
Overwatering, 65
Overwintering, 2

Pachysandra terminalis. *See* Spurge, Japanese
Paeonia. See Peony
Pansy, 214, 215, **220**, **262**, 310

Tomato fruitworm. *See* Corn earworm
Tomato hornworm, 100
Tomato worm, **8, 75**
Tools, 323–326
    for planting bulbs, 230
    sharpening, 326
    for soil preparation, 38
    suppliers of, 335–336
    for turning under crop residues, 57
    for weed control, 58, 325
Top-dressing, 69
Top working, 191
Torch lily, 214
Tradescantia. See Wandering Jew
    virginiana. See Spiderwort
Transplanting, 49–55, 223
    cabbage family, 122
    herbs, 154
    wildflowers, 302
Transplant(s), 52–53, 68–69
    shock, 217
Trap crops, 9, 76
Traps
    for animals, 84–85
    for insects, 202
Tree(s)
    bulbs and, 229–230
    for cut flowers, 311–314
    fruit, 79, 185–210. *See also* specific trees
    nut, 79, 187
    ornamental, 267, **284–285**
    roses and, 235
Trellises, 13–18, **144**, 147, 182
Trollius. See Globeflower
Tropaeolum majus. See Nasturtium
Trowel, 325
Trumpet vine, 14, 15, **290**
Tulipa. See Tulips
Tulips, **233, 264, 318**
Tunica saxifraga. See Tunic flower
Tunic flower, 307
Turning under green manures, 29
Turnips, **7, 12, 51, 56**, 141–142
Turtlehead, 216
Two-spotted spider mites, 105
Typha. See Cattail
Tying materials, 325

Variegated cutworm, 98
Varieties, 76
    blackberry, 167
    blueberry, 174
    fruit tree, 187, 188
    grape, 181
    nut tree, 187
    rose, 234

strawberry, 162
vegetables in containers, **244–245**
Vegetable(s), 119–150. *See also* specific
        vegetables
    container-grown, 243–246, **244–245**
    extending the season for, 2, 9–13
    families of, 119
    fertilizing, 68
    garden design, 119–120
    in greenhouse, 251
    perennials, 148–150
    planting times, **12**
    space requirements, **56**
    started indoors, 43
    for transplanting to garden, **48**
    for vertical growing, 15
Vegetable weevils, 110
Verbena, **220**
Vermiculite, 241
Veronica, 214, 316
Veroniscastrum virginianum. See Culver's root
Vertical growing, 13–18, 120. *See also* specific
        plants
Verticillium wilt, 114–15, 172–173, 209
Viburnum, 282, **290**, 313
Vigor of tree, pruning and, 197–198
Vinca, **220**
Vinca minor. See Myrtle; Periwinkle
Vine(s), 15
    crops, 146–147
    ornamental, 309
Viola. See Pansy; Violet
Violet, 214, 215, **257, 277**, 307, 320
Viral disease(s), 82
    of blueberries, 179
    of bramble berries, 172
    mosaic, 80, 115–116
    of strawberries, 166
Virgina bluebells, 214, 215
Virginia creeper, pruning, **290**
Volunteer annuals, 217

Walnut trees, **186**
Wandering Jew, **261**
Warm-season grass, 271
Wasps, 109–110
Water, in soil, 22
Watercress, 160
Water gardens, 319–322
Watering, 10, 22, 55, 64, 65–67, 73–74, 269
    annuals, 217
    blueberries, 176–177
    bramble berries, 170
    bulbs, 231, 232
    container-grown plants, 242–243
    fruit trees, 190
    lawns, 270, 272

perennials, 225
roses, 235–236
seedbeds, 29, 46
seedlings, 43–44, 49
shrubs, 286, 287
Watering can, 325
Watermelon, **12, 48, 51, 56**. *See also* Melon(s)
Water sprouts, 198
Wax plant, **260**
Web worms, 180, 203, 206
Weed(s)
    annual, 58–60, 217–218
    control, 5, 57–61, 62, 162–163, 164, 177,
            217–218, 270, 272, 273–274, 275, 325
    identification, 273–274
    perennial, 58
    soil solarization and, 77
Weeders, 58, 325
Weevils, 110–111, 166, 179
Weigela, **290**, 292, 309
Wheelbarrow, 325
Whiteflies, 111–112, 203
White flowers, 213
White grubs, 22, 162, 166
Wide-rows, 1–4, 60
Wildflower meadow, 297–302, **299**
Wilt, **201**, 209
Windbreaks, 9
Windflower, **233**
Winter
    mulch, 62
    protection, 165, 208, 237–238
    pruning, 199
Winter aconite, 214
Wintering over lettuce, 2
Wireworms, 112
Wishbone flower, **220**
Wisteria, 15, **290**
Witches broom, 179
Witch hazel, 313
Wood ashes, 36, 37, 202
Woodchucks, 84
Woodsia. See Fern(s), woodsia
Woolly apple aphid, 87
Wormwood, **8, 75**, 160

Yarrow, **8**, 215, 304, 316
Yellow jackets, 109–110
Yellow raspberries, 167. *See also* Raspberries
Yellows (aster), 117
Yields, 2, 175–176, 183, **188**

Zebrina purpusii. *See* Wandering Jew
Zinc, **25**
Zinnia, **219, 220, 263**, 310, 315, **318**
Zucchini, 71, **56**, 245. *See also* Squash, summer